WOOSTER
OF THE MIDDLE WEST

Volume Two / 1911–1944

WOOSTER

OF THE MIDDLE WEST

LUCY LILIAN NOTESTEIN

Volume Two / 1911–1944

The Kent State University Press

To my father

J. O. NOTESTEIN

whose love of the classics, appreciation of beauty,
zeal for the exact statement, and "habit of mastery"
he passed on to many generations of Wooster students

Contents

Preface

I hesitated a long time before agreeing to undertake this second volume of the college history. But finally I decided that there was virtue in continuity, and besides, since I am a Wayne Countian who has grown up with the college practically in my blood, it seemed as if I was as well fitted to carry on as anybody else. There was, I'm sure, some question in the minds of various persons whether I could handle with an objective mind the controversial chapters of Wooster's history, the fraternity row, the summer school, and the dean-of-women contentions. Many years had passed since those days; besides I was not present at that time and the bitterness of the period, though I had heard about it, had not entered into my soul as it had for some others. I think I have handled these controversies objectively.

In the process of preparation I have read almost everything I could lay my hands on that pertained to the college during the period covered: *Minutes* of the faculty and the trustees, the Annual Reports of the Board to the Synod, *The Voice*, the Wooster *Alumni Bulletin* in its successive incarnations, the recollections of President Wishart and President Holden and of others as published in *The Wooster Daily Record*. I have read innumerable files in the Treasure Room of the college library, programs, campaign literature, athletic programs, (*The Gridder*), random letters included there, pamphlets, inaugural addresses, sermons and addresses, biographical data, and tributes to individuals. I have read *The Wooster Quarterly*, the college catalogues, many of them page by page, as I searched for changes in the curriculum, *News from Wooster's Campus*, *Wing Span*, many of the *Indexes*, the college *Bulletins*, the sheet sent out during the Second World War, *On Land, at Sea, and In the Air*, *The Standard Bearer*, and a great many things down in the vault, some of which might better have been burned long ago. And I have dipped into books written by the Wooster faculty just to get the feel of their personalities. I have bothered many persons for their recollections, not so many as I wish I could have bothered, and I have had letters from some Wooster alumni. I am not recording the names of these persons, for it seems wiser not to involve others in responsibility for this tale. I promised them anonymity and I abide by that promise.

Yet I must acknowledge the help of a few persons: that of John D. McKee through the pages primarily of the Wooster *Alumni Bulletin,* and occasional articles in *The Wooster Daily Record;* of Mrs. Estella King, more recently editor of the *Alumni Bulletin,* of Curt Taylor, for many years secretary of the college, as well as private secretary of two presidents, and of Daniel Funk, college attorney, for random bits of information; of those in the college library, who have so meticulously kept and filed the items in the Treasure Room, particularly Sarah Painter and Norine Flack; of the treasurer, Kermit Yoder, for digging out random facts and figures and verifying others from his office records, of Mrs. Marion Strater, now keeper of the official college archives, of Rodney Williams, secretary of the college; of President Howard Lowry for several bits of random information and for reading and commenting on the first seven chapters when they were in the rough; of William Taeusch for reading and criticizing the manuscript chapter by chapter; of Mrs. Jean Stophlet Flattery (daughter of Laura Gailey and Samuel W. Stophlet, '88 and '78), who was most helpful toward the end in checking for me many details and quotations; of Mrs. Orcelia Angert (Mrs. Paul) who typed the manuscript from my roughly-typed pages, full of interlarded changes, marginal notes, deletions, and insertions; of my family, who have been more or less patient with me over many months.

A few other things perhaps I should explain. This time I have stopped at the end of Mr. Wishart's administration. Mr. Lowry's administration would be better handled by someone who is a more skillful ball player than I; besides, Mr. Lowry did not wish me to write of his administration, it was too much a part of the current scene. I have used throw-backs, notably in the first chapter, to introduce stories that never were incorporated in volume one and to provide an easy transition to this second volume, which also treats a part of President Holden's administration. I had expected to include, as I did in the earlier volume, much more detail concerning student and community life, the little stories that individuals cherish and talk about as they get older. But my appeals to alumni, faculty, and trustees, published in the *Bulletin,* brought little response. To get answers I had to write personalized letters; these took time and there was not the time to do an adequate job of this kind. When I did write such letters, I drew answers, and some of these were very helpful. Yet in the end I decided that it was just as well that I had not pursued this lead further, for as the college grew it presented so many new facets; it was not the simple place it once had been; one had to confine oneself to important personalities, events, changes in the curriculum, "the firsts" as they came along, and to try to put these in their proper background; one could not go into every little detail without making a book too long for anyone to publish or to read. I have gone perhaps slightly out of my way to bring many of the faculty into the story, for the memories of an alumnus of a college are likely to concentrate not so much around events as around two or three personalities in the college, those who have opened for him doors to hitherto unknown worlds. It has seemed worth while, so far as one can in a paragraph or two, to try to bring these varying personalities back into focus even if for a moment. Those persons whose major activity fell in Mr. Lowry's administration I have scarcely mentioned if at all. I leave to a later historian the challenging task of outlining their contributions to the life of Wooster.

I am still entitling this second volume, *Wooster of the Middle West*. This is a legitimate part of the educational history of the Middle West in our generation. We were half-way through the Second World War before we really found out that we were a part of the great world outside.

LUCY LILIAN NOTESTEIN

October, 1969

WOOSTER

The blood of the Middle West is in your veins,
The lusty, ardent blood of the pioneers;
Their urgent whispers beat on sensitive ears
Where, tower on tower, you gaze down on the plains.
These were the breed of men who scorned kings' chains,
And more the chains of superstitious fears;
Your ivory walls are debtor to their years
And every brick is mortised with their pains.

Tread softly then, Novitiate, speak low;
No ordinary heritage is here!
Truth taps you on the shoulder as you go
From door to door. Let not your compass veer
From that North Star your fathers worshiped so,
Nor noble purpose seem to you less dear.

EARL MEADOW DUNBAR

From *Earl Meadow Dunbar, February 25, 1899–August 31, 1939.*
Privately printed, 1939. Quoted by permission.

I

Spreading the Net

I T had been a golden afternoon that July day when Louis Edward Holden with John Cook McClaran first climbed to the high tower of Old Main and looked for twenty miles around to woods and hills and fields green with corn. Then, almost in the words of James Reed, of whom he had never heard, he exclaimed, "What a site for a college!"

He had surprised himself in being here at all. His coming had really been but a courteous gesture to a group of insistent men. Back in June out of the blue he had had one day a telegram from A. A. E. Taylor, President of the Wooster Board of Trustees.[1] Would he be interested in considering the presidency of that university? "No," had been his emphatic rejoinder, "nor that of any other institution." He had not bothered to tell even President Eaton of Beloit, with whom for ten years he had been working, seeking money for that college. After all he was happy at Beloit in his association with its president and in his teaching of oratory. Almost immediately, however, he had had a letter from Mr. Taylor. Evidently, it had said, Holden was not familiar with Wooster. The "committee of five distinguished men" (Taylor often had his tongue in his cheek) craved the chance of telling him about the university and of showing it to him. Would he come to Wooster to meet the committee? Again he would not. This time he mentioned the letter to President Eaton, who commended him for the wisdom and firmness of his decision. There came a second letter. If Holden would not come to Wooster, would he let the committee come to Beloit to talk with him? This was too much, and yet he was probably feeling a sneaking respect for the tenacity of this man. President Eaton advised a compromise—he might offer to meet them in Chicago; that might quell this mosquito technique. The meeting was so arranged, then because of unforeseen circumstances changed to Columbus, Ohio, Taylor's home town.

When Holden arrived at the hotel in Columbus, the committee was waiting. The five distinguished men were Taylor—with his long and well-tended white beard and his glinting eyes he did have an air of distinction [2]—Judge John McClaran of Wooster, the Rev. Mr. O.

A. Hills, small and dapper and very sober, pastor of the First Presbyterian Church of Wooster, the Rev. Mr. David Meese of Mansfield, Ohio, and the Rev. Mr. William C. Stinson of Chillicothe, Ohio, one of Holden's classmates in theological seminary.—Mr. Stinson had suggested Holden in the first place.

The talk, warm and friendly, lasted till midnight. Taylor outlined something of the history of the college, the thought, and prayers, and struggles that had accompanied its beginnings and early years, that had continued indeed until this day, the quality of its faculty and students, its world-wide influence through the many missionaries it had sent out. It was well on its way, if properly supported, to being the outstanding Presbyterian college not only of the Middle West but of the nation. What it needed now was a young man of Holden's vigor, and personality, and experience, as president. They had looked seriously into his qualifications, knew his background,[3] his own struggles to get an education, his sympathy with youth, even why he had been suspended as a boy from his home academy in Utica, New York.[4]

Then the talk became more general. They discussed with him the current problems of the university, eager to get his slant on them. How could the apparent apathy of Ohio Presbyterians, moneywise toward the college, be broken? The more they talked together, the more they liked him. Here was a sound young man, alert to the values of Christian education and the needs of a small but growing college. In an interval of the conversation McClaran asked a pointed question, did Holden use tobacco? The answer was forthright: "Yes, sir, I don't know of anyone in the world who enjoys a pure Havana cigar more than I do . . . I would not accept the best job in America if it limited my liberty of enjoying a good cigar when my day's work was done." McClaran held his peace. Hills expressed regret. Taylor abruptly left the room. In a moment he was back, clutching a fistful of Havana cigars. Soon four of those cigars were glowing, though the day's work was not yet done. Hills and Stinson had abstained. In years ahead often on a summer evening Holden could be seen smoking away on his back porch.

Before they finally parted for the night, the committee suggested that Holden should go back to Beloit via Wooster. It would be "just as easy"; the main line of the Pennsylvania Railroad from Pittsburgh to Chicago ran through Wooster. Hills would have Holden to lunch the next day at his fine new home on College Avenue, then McClaran, who had a farm northwest of town and a stable of fine horses, would take him for a drive to let him see the community and the college.

So it was arranged. Though there is no record to say as much in the *Minutes* of the Board or in President Holden's own account, written fifty years later, Mr. Taylor couldn't have slept much that night; he was too busy sending telegrams to his Board of Trustees summoning them to Wooster for a meeting the next evening. Now that they thought they had found their man, the committee was spreading a net for him.

Nor is there any available account of that drive the next day except that we know it lasted three hours or more. It is surely safe, however, to assume that when McClaran appeared at the Hills' door to pick up his guest, the phaeton was freshly polished, the horse sleek and restless to be off. McClaran, however, was in no such hurry; he would be spending the afternoon driving up one tree-lined street and down another, reminiscing as he went. Wooster was a small town, as Beloit was, yet it had something of an air. The houses looked comfortable, many of them set far back on wide lawns, some of them with porte-cocheres which suggested an easy graciousness, where frequent guests came and went. On that memorable afternoon he saw undoubtedly many of the houses of townspeople. There was, for instance, that of Robert Larwill at the top of Spruce Street, a fine red-brick mansion, filled with exquisite antique furniture. It had been an inn for many years, even before Wooster as a town was founded. There was the Martin Welker home where former President Rutherford B. Hayes had once been a guest. Martin Welker himself had been one of those deeply interested in bringing the university to Wooster.[5] The then conservatory of music, with its tower and mansard roof, had been until a year before the home of John H. Kauke, one of the founding fathers of the college, a trustee, contributor, and a deeply interested friend even now in his old age. Just to the east Carey Kauke, his son, lived in a house built in 1817 by General Reasin Beall.[6]

Up near the university was Col. C. V. Hard's residence,[7] and down farther that of James Mullins, who had large coal holdings and was the owner of the local Minglewood Coal and Ice Company. His son, Walter Mullins, who was also a son-in-law of President Scovel, had been the first man in Wooster to have an automobile. One day, he with Mrs. Mullins had driven the Scovels to Chippewa Lake, fifteen miles to the north, to a church picnic.—It had taken them two hours to get there.

Down on North Market Street lived other warm friends of the college. William Annat was one; he had the large stone store on the Public Square. He was a fine man, of great integrity, a Presbyterian, too, and like the Scotsman that he was, loved fine linens and made rather a specialty of them in his store so that people from neighboring towns, Mansfield and Canton, came to purchase from him. It was always a pleasure to have him show his linens; he all but fondled them, loving to draw them through his fingers. Mrs. Annat was a graduate of the college and active on the Women's Advisory Board. The old brick house with the stone trim, on the east side of the street belonged to John McSweeney of the class of 1875. He was an Episcopalian, but a good friend of the college and very generous. He collected books, especially old books with fine leather bindings, and those having to do with the classics. Except for a window to the front, a small one to the north, and a fireplace on one wall, the shelves in his library reached all the way around and to the ceiling. The house, too, was full of paintings. Nearly across the street was the residence of Walter D. Foss, manufacturer of Wooster brushes, which were known across the nation. He imported the bristles from China. Next to him lived his brother-in-law George Schwartz, one of the most hospitable of persons and the kindest. Again across the street to the east was the Frank Miller home. Miller headed a farm machinery company in Canton and every day commuted by train to his office. A son, Will, would be registering at the college in the fall.[8] Close below in the yard bordered by the ornate iron fence stood the residence of the I. N. Kinneys. Their three children were still too young for college, but the house itself was notable for its graceful Queen Anne architecture and for the fact that it had been built in 1850 by a one-time treasurer of the United States, John Sloan, as a wedding present for his niece. And there was the almost monumental home of Captain J. B. Taylor,[9] one of Wooster's lawyers, who as a young man had fought at the Siege of Vicksburg. Two of his children had attended the college. With its tower in front, its large parlors on either side of its wide entrance, it asked for the gay parties that were always taking place there. All these people were often opening their homes for students. The most cordial relations existed between them and the college.

There were others of course. McClaran would not have failed to point out, as he drove by, the one-time home of Leander Firestone, one of the founding fathers of the college, who had been a trustee from 1866 until his death in 1888. He had been a distinguished physician in these parts, a professor at Charity Hospital College in Cleveland who continued to teach there, and later to serve as dean, after it had been absorbed as a department of the University of Wooster. In its day this Greek Revival Firestone house at the corner of North and North Market Streets had seen many a hoop skirt come swirling down its long curving stairway and out to a waiting carriage.

Nearly every street had some home of special interest; one could not see them all in three hours. Perhaps McClaran only mentioned another home with a history just to the north of town, that of General Aquila Wiley, who walked with a wooden leg. He had been severely wounded at the battle of Shiloh, and later his horse had been shot from under him and his knee crushed as he led a charge at Missionary Ridge. He lived far back among the trees in a commodious red brick house; behind it was a spring and over this a two-storey springhouse. There and in the attic of the house were a great box and a barrel of old letters stored away. Occasionally he had let one or two boys of the neighborhood go digging for stamps in that cache, which was for them a kind of pot at the end of a rainbow, for they found there not only stamps but letters that had been posted before the day of stamps—envelopes inscribed in the right-hand upper corner with the signature of the postmaster and the amount paid.

All in all Wooster was a pleasant place in which to live. No doubt McClaran showed him also the two hotels on Liberty Street. The older and the larger had been built by Andrew Parrish and named for his son Archer who had died. He would have pointed out also the many churches, the Lutheran, the Methodist, the Baptist, and Episcopal, almost side by side and only a block away the English Reformed, and the Church of Christ. There were others, of course, notably the First Presbyterian on West North Street, the United Presbyterian on

Bever, and of course the college church, Westminster, which met in the college chapel.

At length McClaran hitched his horse to a post and he and Holden walked to the entrance of Old Main. To the west like a turtle squatted the gymnasium, to the east lay the domed observatory, and to the northeast Hoover Cottage. So this was the university. Together they climbed the long flights of stairs to the tower and there looked out over the roofs of the town below, beyond to the Ohio Agricultural Experiment Station, and all around. What a site indeed for a college! Fifty years later, writing his memoirs for *The Wooster Daily Record,* Holden said that at the moment of looking at this scene there had been born in him the feeling, though unexpressed, that maybe he would like to have some part in building this university.

Of course at some point in this trip Holden was shown the president's house, that he would occupy should he come to Wooster. It was near the college, even then a venerable structure of red brick with front windows reaching to the floor. It had been built by Lucas Flattery,[10] vice-president of the University's Board of Trustees. Lucas Flattery's widow, and son and daughter still lived in Wooster in a house that he had built later on College Avenue, shaded by a wide-spreading oak. Holden saw without doubt the homes, too, of some of Wooster's faculty, the Seelyes, the Bennetts, the Mateers, probably that of T. K. Davis, the librarian, who as fiscal secretary for the university while the building itself was still a dream, had ridden horseback all over Wayne and neighboring counties in search of funds to make the dream come true. Probably, too, he saw the beautiful Samuel Kirkwood home.[11] It was worthy of one who delighted to measure corners accurately and to look at the stars. He was one of Wooster's first professors of mathematics and astronomy, and was still teaching. There was poetry in his soul. He was always quoting bits from the *Divine Comedy;* once even giving a course in Dante. Across from the Kirkwood house he would almost certainly see the "Inky" (incubator), once the home of Orange N. Stoddard[12] of Wooster's first faculty, and since owned and operated by the Presbyterian Board of Foreign Missions as a home for the sons of missionaries, and farther down the street the similar residence hall for the daughters of missionaries, formerly the home of A. A. E. Taylor while he was president of the university. And of course he had been shown the house of Elias Compton, who at this time was camping in the woods in Michigan. He and his family had been going there every summer, gathering strength for the college year ahead. There they lived an outdoor life, fishing, swimming, walking, picking berries in the woods. Mrs. Compton indeed often brought back crates of blueberries, raspberries, even blackberries which she had canned for winter use.

Finally, at 7:30 they drew up in front of the First Presbyterian Church. The lights were on as if for a meeting. "Let's go in," said McClaran. Inside they found the university Board of Trustees in session. Taylor came forward and reaching out his hand introduced Louis Edward Holden as president-elect of Wooster University. He was stunned, and at once disclaimed having given the committee any encouragement. He as yet knew too little of Wooster, and Wooster knew too little of him. Moreover he had promised Mrs. Holden and President Eaton that he would come to no decision without talking it over with each of them. "However," he went on, "I will promise you that after studying the matter and presenting it to them, I will give you my answer within two weeks." [13]

No salary was mentioned immediately. The Board did not wish to bid against Beloit. They wished him to base his decision on other grounds. They would, however, make the salary "satisfactory" to him (that turned out to be $3000).

There was one question on his mind that he asked before he left. Had Wooster "any way" to Andrew Carnegie or to Henry Clay Frick? To Carnegie, "No," Taylor told him. But Henry Clay Frick's father lay in Wooster cemetery. His two sisters, Mrs. J. S. R. Overholt and Mrs. W. A. Lott, still lived in Wooster. Moreover, his uncle, Jacob Frick, was president of the Wayne County National Bank, and a warm friend of the college.

With that Holden bade them all goodbye. In Beloit he had much to consider. Wooster, he confessed to himself, had an appeal. It was beautiful. He longed to meet Frick and Carnegie. He had read their rags-to-riches stories, and admired their industry, their courage, their audacity, their never-say-die attitude. Even the nearly successful assassination of Frick during the Homestead strike of 1891 had not stopped the man. He had had the imagination to see possibilities where others failed to see them, and then had the personality to see them through. If Holden were to go to Wooster, he might have the chance to interest Frick in Christian education and so do a service not only to Wooster but to Beloit and other small Christian colleges of the country. So, as he thought, "the whole problem began to solve itself." President Eaton did not stand in his way. In two weeks the Board of Trustees had their answer. Holden would come to Wooster, would be there in September. Having made his decision, he, too, took off for the north woods, to Port Arthur, Ontario, on the north shore of Lake Superior.

There, as soon as he got the news, Professor Compton sought him out; president and dean should know each other before they met officially. There they could fish and talk. A few days later Compton returned to Wooster. He liked this young man; in his calm, judicious way he was enthusiastic about Wooster's president-to-be. Soon others were to be equally so.

Two weeks after he came to Wooster Holden called on Jacob Frick at the bank, and asked for a letter to his nephew. Frick gave it willingly, warning him the while that though the letter would surely get him into his nephew's office, he could promise nothing further; Henry Clay Frick's interests were not in Christian education. Holden took the challenge. The next morning he boarded the train to Pittsburgh. He went straight to Frick's office, sent in his letter, and was shown in. Frick looked up.

"What did you wish to see me about?"

"I wanted to have the privilege of a few moments conversation with you in reference to Christian education as carried on at the University of Wooster."

"Well, sir," said he, "it would do you no good. It would take your time and mine, too. It is a subject I am not interested in."

I looked him in the eye and said, "I think you are greatly mistaken, Mr. Frick. I listened to President Eaton at Beloit College for half an hour defending your stand with labor as a business man and manufacturer, just after you were stabbed at Homestead. Can it be that the colleges of this country can command their students to listen to their presidents set forth your interests as business men when you are not interested in them? You wouldn't want me to go out of this office and announce to the Associated Press that you were not interested in Christian education, would you?"

I never saw in all my life, a man change so quickly, and become a friend instead of a foe. . . . He looked up. . . .

"You have said just the right thing to me. I withdraw my statement. I am interested in Christian education and I haven't known it. Tell me, what can I do for you?"

"Mr. Frick, I did not come this morning to get your money. I came to get you. I have been a long time coming, for I thought that some day I might have the opportunity of telling you what the Christian colleges of this country mean to the country at large."

"Well, sir," he said, "you have got me now. What have you in mind that I shall do? You must have something in mind for me to do for Wooster."

"Someday," I replied, "I am coming to talk to you about building a memorial to your father and mother in the form of a library building for Wooster. May I?"

He took his pencil and a slip of paper and wrote, "I owe the University of Wooster a library building. Honor Dr. Holden's drafts upon me $10,000.00 at a time until the library building is paid for."

He showed me his memorandum and put it on his spindle, arose, shook hands with me, and thanked me for coming. "Select your own architect. Have it built to suit yourself! Draw on me for the cash!"

. . . I returned to Wooster greatly encouraged and prepared for my inauguration.

Not until that time did Holden make any announcement of Henry Clay Frick's gift.

Twelve Years Later

NEARLY twelve years had passed since then, years wherein dreams had taken solid shape.[1] A new college stood on the hill. Its ideals had not changed, yet it now faced forward with hope and expectation. As the sun set on that winter world of December 31, 1910, for a second time within the last four years a major campaign had been brought to a successful conclusion.[2] In early spring ground would be broken for the men's dormitory to the north and west, just beyond the oak grove; and, when plans were complete, for the new gymnasium, too. But better even than these buildings was the addition of $400,000 to the endowment. Was it really true? Those older professors who had scraped the bins these many years to feed their families did not dare to think what this might mean, yet it was good, very good.

When President and Mrs. Holden entertained the faculty at a reception on the night of January 3, 1911, they were all still pinching themselves. It was a gay party. The president was in a most affable mood. No wonder. Everyone grasped his hand with more than the usual warmth. At their meeting last June when he had told his trustees that he had been asked by the College Board of New York to become an associate secretary, they had pulled long faces, then passed a resolution: "It is the sense of the Board that the services of President Holden for the present and for years to come are indispensable to the progress and development of the University of Wooster, and that it would therefore be a calamity at this time to substract from it his forceful personality." Tonight he knew that he had a loyal faculty behind him. Indeed they had been so all along; as yet no really sharp differences had arisen. Now, with the self-assurance which had always been his, he could go ahead with modifying in some ways and enlarging in others the internal structure of the university. The heroic era might have passed. But President Holden was still a romantic figure.

The college had been growing. The freshman class, matriculated on December 4, had numbered 161; there would be 81 in 1911's graduating class, the largest in all Wooster's years. The summer school last year under the administration of Mr. Dickason had reached 1002.—Mr. Holden had some reservations about this summer school.—For several years an instructor on a temporary and part-time basis had been teaching pedagogy; now the time had come to institute a chair in this field. So many of Wooster's graduates taught for a while at least, especially the women. Through the years Wooster's professors had been overloaded, for time to time offering all sorts of courses not in their specific fields. History, for instance, needed a full-time professor. The instructor in history had to teach economics, political science, and even sociology. Even so the young Mr. Caldwell had this year added an elective in American constitutional history. Next year he would be transferred to the Hoge Professorship of Political Science and Economics and a new man would be brought in for history. Come September, there would be other changes. The faculty were already anticipating 200 freshmen. It would be best in the required freshman and sophomore work that classes be limited to twenty-five. This would allow an instructor to give individual attention, to know his students, to measure their several abilities, to encourage their growing interests, disciplining when necessary, yet always striving to bring out the best in each individual, while stressing the necessity for accuracy, and inspiring in them an eagerness for truth and beauty wherever found. In this was the joy of teaching. This was what Wooster believed in.

For good teaching of course the faculty needed books, then more books, books of many sorts. They would be eternally grateful to President Holden for seeing the need for a library building and for seeing it so soon, grateful to him and to Henry Clay Frick. It was what a library should be, clean, simple, classical in its lines, a worthy place for those who would be scholars. Inside as one stood in its lobby looking from end to end of the reading rooms, one was made aware of the long tradition of learning, for there on the frieze in letters a foot high were inscribed these names:

HOMER SOCRATES PLATO PHIDIAS MOSES DARWIN COPERNICUS RAPHAEL ANGELO CALVIN LAVOISIER MILTON ST. PAUL BEETHOVEN HANDEL SHAKE-SPEARE CICERO NEWTON KANT DEMOSTHENES

The whole world was encompassed there: science, literature, art, music, oratory, sculpture, philosophy, religion. With those names ever before it Wooster would surely never forget its heritage in the classics or its zeal for science. Here Moses and Darwin appeared side by side. Was this by design or accident? Yet it was in Wooster's own tradition, for had not Mr. Lord in his inaugural as first president of Wooster, declared:

Real knowledge, of whatever kind, and true religion, are in ultimate and perfect harmony. This is my summary logic: All knowledge leads to truth; all truth to God; as the effect to its cause; as a rill to the fountain; as a ray of light to the sun. . . . Honored, indeed, in these halls, be the great names of every clime, and of every creed, who have added to the sum of human thought and knowledge, and so have contributed to the elevation and enfranchisement of the race. Honored be the poets, the orators, the philosophers, the men of letters and science of all ages, according to the quality of their powers, and the value of their deeds.

They all belong to the glorious fellowship of benefactors. Bring hither the volumes in which are embalmed the achievements of their learning and genius. Let them have fitting place, not only upon our walls, but in our minds and hearts.

Yet if one went through the gates of the reading room to the stacks behind, one soon found gaps that were painful to any good professor or student. Little by little, Mr. Notestein, still chairman of the library committee, had been trying to fill these in, adding missing numbers to the files of standard periodicals, interesting here and there some friend in sponsoring an alcove for some department. He had been greatly heartened last year when Solon Severance, brother of the generous L. H. Severance, had unexpectedly sent down $500 for this purpose. When the more-or-less usual budget for books for the library had been $200 or $300, this was a windfall. Just a year and a half ago it had taken a special action of the Board to have allocated $100 for books in the library for the English department. What they needed now was an endowment of $100,000 for the library alone. This year, however, as a result of the campaign there would be $2,000 for books and binding. With this they would first of all get a new *Encyclopaedia Britannica* and the *Dictionary of National Biography,* working tools.

The president was concerned in other respects for his faculty. Some few of them had been in the harness for many years. What would happen if any of them were to be seriously disabled? What would happen to the widow and children if one of them should die? He had tried and failed to have the charter of the university changed so that Wooster could qualify under the Carnegie Pension Fund. He had carried the proposal through the Board itself yet with some strong opposition, but the Synod had turned it down "overwhelmingly." Even some of the faculty had seriously questioned any such change, though it would have been greatly to their interest. They did not wish at any cost to lose Wooster's close tie with the church that had founded it. Of course the Synod could raise the $200,000 necessary if they would. Yet the Synod and its presbyteries were made up of ministers most of whom perhaps would look with envy on Wooster's top salaries of $1500. No, the Presbyterians of Ohio were still apathetic: they wished to control the college, but they did not wish to pay for it. Holden was realistic; he would have to look for large givers to provide Wooster's pension plan. At present he did not know where to turn.

There must, however, be something immediate done, however little. On February 14 and 15 of 1911, Holden made to his trustees his recommendation, and in June they took first action: that any professor retiring because of disability, and with the approval of the Board, would receive a retiring allowance equal to one-fortieth of his last annual salary for each year of his service up to thirty years. They extended this provision to include the voluntary retirement (with the consent and approval of the Board) of "any person having served this University as its President for fifteen (15) years; or any person having served as professor, or as an assistant professor, . . . for twenty-five (25) years or any such person who shall have attained the age of sixty-five." Apparently also previous service in another institution counted toward the twenty-five years. This provision, they added, shall include all teachers in all departments of the university, also the librarian, treasurer, and registrar. On the death of such pensioned professor the widow was to receive "during her widowhood one-eightieth of her husband's last annual salary for each year she has been his wife up to thirty years." There was a further provision that "upon the death of the surviving widow, his surviving minor child or minor children may annually be paid said amount at the pleasure of the Board of Trustees." This of course was far better than nothing, provided the college could really pay it. It was all that Wooster could do. It might be disastrous to the college if too many persons became eligible for retirement or disability pensions at the same time. But there was that saving phrase, "with the approval of the Board of Trustees." The faculty were grateful, but they knew that individually they must continue to dream up ways of accumulating something toward the future.

President Holden knew this, too. He remembered their loyalty, how they had stood by him at the time of the fire, how they had contributed their share and more than their share in every campaign. In one crisis they had freely offered one tenth of their salaries. At that time the Board had entered in its *Minutes* a note of appreciation. With growing families to feed and clothe all this could not have been easy. There must have been many times when in moments of deep discouragement they had said to themselves:

> Does the road wind uphill all the way?
> Yes, to the very end.

But they were a dedicated group. They lived by faith. So also their wives.

Yet Holden and his trustees had done something quite special for them when in 1906 they had instituted the sabbatical year program. Of course it was not really a program, for the leave of a year was rather the opportunity of a lifetime, not of every seventh year. This year of 1910–1911 the Bennetts were just back, full of enthusiasm for the delights and benefits of travel. They had spent much time in Berlin. This past summer John G. Black had gone to Switzerland on a geological walking trip, rucksack on back. The rest of the year he was spending on geological investigations in the United States. Next year it would be Dr. Mateer's turn.

Holden believed in sabbaticals. He was glad to have his faculty thus refresh themselves; they were better teachers for the chance. Summers he liked to go away himself. Travel indeed opened one's eyes and allowed one to build up a wealth of illustrations for the many speeches a president had to make. It gave him, moreover, a certain aplomb, to be able to talk easily about Oxford and Cambridge, about the Louvre and other art galleries and some of the great cathedrals. H. C. Frick, poor boy though he had been, had early set himself to collecting works of art. Carnegie owned Skibo Castle in Scotland. There, by invitation, he and Mrs. Holden had visited him. Even in the Wooster faculty there were those with degrees from German universities. Holden craved for himself and his faculty this larger knowledge of the world. Seelye as a young man had been to Greece, and partly because of that fact, had been able to make vivid his recent lectures on archaeology.

He was proud of his faculty, of the older men whom he had found at Wooster, of the younger ones whom he had himself appointed.— At Wooster it was still the province of the president to make all appointments.—He had made only a few mistakes. Harvey Carson Grumbine admittedly had his crotchets.[4] Every Sunday, according to the girls of Holden Hall, who made a point of watching the Grumbines on their way to morning services, he was always ten to twenty feet ahead of her. Often he would glance back slyly to see that she was following dutifully. If she seemed to be gaining on him he would quicken his pace. At the chapel some of them saw the end of this singular procession. Reaching the steps of the chapel he mounted them, then turning, with his most sardonic grin, waited for her. One winter morning everything was glazed with ice. As she came to the foot of the steps a student, "Shock" Palmer, happened along. He took her arm, helped her up the five or six steps, then tipping his hat gallantly said to Mr. Grumbine, "Mrs. Grumbine, I believe." But Mr. Grumbine added spice to the community. Besides, he had quite won the president's heart in presenting the portrait of Louis Severance. Mrs. Grumbine was the artist. Anyhow Holden could always count on Grumbine, always knew where he would stand.

James Milton Vance was a success, as had been his brother before him. He was thorough, made his students toe the mark. Mrs. Vance, too, was an asset to the college. She had a lovely voice and had taken over the Girls' Glee Club as her responsibility. Under her tutelage they were giving very acceptable concerts in town and occasionally out of town. How well Chalmers Martin had fitted! The one golf-playing member of the faculty, he had done much for town and gown relations, had been active in the organization of the Country Club. He was much called upon as a toastmaster, for he could turn a phrase. He entered into many activities, was a regular member of the oratorio chorus. One loved to watch him there, especially in *The Messiah*—"Hallelujah! Hallelujah!" As he sang with his head thrown back, there was such delight, such enthusiasm in his every movement and facial expression. Besides, there was always a twinkle in his eye as he spoke to one.

Mr. Hutchins, too, whose field was vocal music, had recently given one of his recitals. "He introduced," said *The Voice* at the time, "a somewhat novel feature by singing a few of the songs in the expressionless manner of the ordinary performer, then with the thoughtful expressive interpretation of the finished artist." J. Lawrence Erb, head of the conservatory, was another; he was an easterner through and through, yet, bald and genial, he had taken captive this mid-western community.

As for Delbert G. Lean everyone was enthusiastic. Never had interest in debate and oratory been greater. Teams chosen by preliminary tryouts from some forty applicants had debated the income tax with Allegheny and Pittsburgh. They had lost one round and won the other. Even the "preps" had caught the fever, had debated Orrville high school and were about to meet the team from Oberlin's preparatory department. For two successive years Kuo of the present senior class had won the intercollegiate oratorical contest of the Chinese Students Alliance of North America and had thereby been entitled to hold the cup given by the Chinese ambassador. Mr. Lean gave almost unlimited attention to his students, in class and out. Some years later he was to put a light at his back door as a signal to his students; if the light was on they could come in; if it wasn't on, he was not to be disturbed. He helped debaters analyze the issues, and then to follow through. The inexperienced freshman he got up on his feet. One of them wrote years later: "He led me through the immortal words of Shakespeare, patiently insisting that I repeat over and over one simple line, 'The king comes here tonight.' until I found the proper cadence." [5] Lean had won his place in the community as well. At nearly every party he was called upon for "O'Grady's Goat." Now for the third successive year, ever since he had come to Wooster, he had read Dickens' *Christmas Carol* in Memorial Chapel on an evening just before the holidays. It was his Christmas gift to the students and the community, as it would continue to be for fifty years. In June of 1910 shortly after commencement he had married a delightful young woman, pretty, vivacious, petite. Soon she, too, had endeared herself to both students and faculty.

All fall and winter and spring there had been the usual rash of student parties: rushing parties, initiation parties ending with a banquet usually in the fraternity chapter houses,[6] sometimes at a hotel downtown, where more of the visiting alumni could be accommodated. There were the sophomore-senior and freshman-junior banquets, more formal than class "socials." At one of these, three well-roasted porkers were featured and the toasts carried out the theme: a "Welcome to the Pig" and an "Answering Squeal." Dean Compton, a special guest, responded to "What's in a Name," and Wayne Putnam reaffirmed that "Pigs is Pigs," and so to the inevitable end on that fragrant May night. The tables, reported *The Voice,* "were decorated with delicate peach blossoms," probably filched from the faculty orchard.[7] The Hoover girls entertained the faculty, the trustees, and their wives and put on a burlesque opera. Some of the literary societies held open houses. Quadrangle was entertained by John McSweeney; the Dramatic Club held initiation at the Seelyes. There were fudge parties and taffy pulls. And the formal annual dinners given by the national fraternities and sororities and those locals now petitioning for national charters were occasions. There would be grapefruit for a first course—grapefruit had but recently reached Wooster; it was a special treat. If it was a sorority dinner, the girls would have worked in shifts for hours arranging candles, favors, flowers. For coming and going there was Ira Droz and his equipage at their sleekest. With her evening dress, her long gloves, her slippers, a flower perhaps caught in her hair, each girl that night as she came tripping down the long stairway felt herself for a moment a queen.

Besides there were concerts and lectures to be attended, and the annual plays given by Willard and Castalian. The oratorio chorus in March of 1911 presented Stainer's *Daughter of Jairus* and Liszt's *Psalm XIII.* Downtown the Board of Trade gave two band concerts at the Opera House. Several girls went in a group to Canton to hear Mme. Schumann Heink. Whitney Brothers Male Quartet had appeared at the Opera House. Hamilton Holt had lectured.

No dates were allowed on Sundays until three in the afternoon. This restriction gave rise to the impromptu musicals in Holden Hall after the noon dinner. All the girls gathered in the parlors. Someone went to the piano, then one or another of the girls would sing, or some girl would bring down her violin and would play for them. This happy custom lasted for some years.

Of course on spring nights there were serenades in front of the dormitories, coasting on Beall Avenue in the winter. That was great fun, yet as the big sled gathered speed everyone wondered whether the boy who was steering would ever be able to stop it when they came to Liberty Street. Then there were those spur-of-the-moment drives when they sent for "Nigger Smith"—as he called himself in those days—and his battered cab drawn by a broken-down, sway-backed horse, either Christmas or Easter. Smith named his horses for holidays. Then one day Christmas died and a different horse appeared. Smith didn't know quite what to name him; Fourth of July didn't seem really appropriate; the horse didn't have enough "git-up" for that. The students were not baffled for a moment. They had just been experiencing the annual campus holiday, Day of Prayer for Colleges. He should be named that, and he was.

Of course there had been games with all the usual fanfare before and afterwards, pep meetings and bonfires, though there had been very little occasion for bonfires during the football season; the team had scarcely scored. In basketball, however, Wooster had won eleven out of fourteen games, in baseball the team picked up toward the end, defeating Otterbein and Kenyon and tying Case. Thirty men had gone out for track, but Reserve had walked off with the laurels. Much interest had been shown in intramural sports. The fastest runner in the college had made 100 yards in 9¾ seconds. All the classes had basketball teams. The Holden and Hoover girls on Thanksgiving morning had put on two hare and hound races, one to Reddick's Dam, the other to Highland Park, but never a hound caught up with a hare. In the fall, too, the "Hilltop Terrors" (Betas) and the "Human Catapults" (Phi Gams) had put on a benefit game for the "Stibbs Boulevard" football championship. Admittance was fifteen cents, and the proceeds went toward buying sweaters for the Varsity team.

One Saturday morning Mr. Notestein rounded up a dozen or so boys from the class of 1911 and as many shovels and they all took off for the woods northwest of town. There under his direction they dug twenty or more young dogwoods, brought them back and planted them on a knoll to the west of Hoover. As the boys finished, he said to them, "Come back some spring ten years from now and you will see a beauty spot." They did come back, some of them, ten, twenty and fifty years later, and it was still a beauty spot. *Haec olim meminisse juvabit.*

Spring brought other interesting events: hobble skirts appeared on the campus, and on March 8 ground was broken for a men's dormitory, which they—the elusive they—said would last for hundreds of years. It was to be ready for occupancy in September and was to be called Kenarden Lodge, the name of Mrs. John Stewart Kennedy's (the donor) summer home at Bar Harbor, Maine. It sounded very sophisticated. Her lodge presumably stood on a headland looking out to sea. For its namesake there would be no such view, only woods and rolling hills and the plumes of smoke from the old brick works in the valley beyond the ridge. No salt air here, no lobster boats. Yet often through the years, as students have met there in combat, the corridors of that Lodge have been drenched and deluged in water.

Then on Friday, May the twelfth, in that languorous season when even bumblebees go lurching from flower to flower as if half-drunk, came Color Day on the quadrangle once again. There were the usual stunts, the winding of the Maypole at eleven, and as focus for all this, the crowning of Wooster's first Queen of the May. She was the radiant Helen Harrington (Compton), of the class of 1912.

So the spring wore on. It had been a good year free from major tensions save for the last fateful days of the campaign in December. Then came commencement. In his Baccalaureate address President Holden gave an urgent plea to "stir up the gift of God, which is in thee . . ." (Timothy 1:6). There were the usual occasions: the 1875 Junior Oratorical Contest won by Z. T. Ing, on China's Appeal for Justice; the 1911 play, *The Ulster,* Willard-Castalian Public, and the oratorio chorus. The latter presented Coleridge-Taylor's *Song of Hiawatha.* For it they had the assistance of an orchestra from Cleveland and out-of-town soloists. One of these was Bechtel Alcock, tenor, of New York, formerly a home-town boy.

Many, however, in town and college were sad that this would be Mr. Seelye's last commencement. He had been granted leave of absence, to be sure, but he was planning to go to Auburn Theological

Seminary to prepare himself for the ministry. His daughter Katharine was being graduated this year, with honors and was, indeed, one of the speakers on commencement day. Last year she had been a graduate in music. The Seelyes had been here twenty years. Everyone had thought of them as fixtures. Their home near the campus had been a rallying place for many persons or organizations. It was sophisticated in the best sense. They would be truly missed in church and college and town.

The Board of Trustees was as usual meeting this commencement season. They always came prepared to stay a while, possibly from Monday through Thursday, with day as well as evening sessions. They did not always follow that rigorous program, however, for they would now and then take a recess to attend, perhaps the Junior Oratorical or possibly a cantata; even Willard Public once attracted them. Nor were they going to be mired down by their environment, for sometimes they met in the Trustee Room, sometimes in the library, rather often in the Council Chamber of the City Hall (maybe they could smoke there) and, as we have already seen, occasionally in the lecture room of the First Presbyterian Church.

It was customary at these meetings to hear a report from the "Ladies' Advisory Board." [9] It was their responsibility to study the conditions surrounding the young women of the college and to make recommendations. In June of a year ago (1910) a committee representing them, Mrs. Butcher, Mrs. Taylor, Mrs. Platter, had come to make their report and to recommend that hereafter Hoover Cottage be used for freshman and preparatory girls only. The Board listened, discussed, and then adopted the recommendation. The plan had worked out well. This year they had another recommendation; that a dean of women be appointed as soon as a suitable person could be found. Wooster this past year had had over 400 students. The time had come. Again the trustees agreed.

At this meeting also the budget for the coming year came up for review. Anyhow, in the *Minutes* there were listed the salaries to be paid and several other items of probable expense: Postage—$350; telephone—$150; campus expense—$500; traveling expenses—$1200; library expense—$2000—evidently the item for books and binding passed in February. Salaries had gone up all along the line, some of them as much as $500. The older professors could now draw a deep breath, the younger ones could look forward to probable advancement in time. Most of the new young instructors would be getting more than some of the full professors a year ago. There appear here no separate columns for income and expenditures, no balancing, no estimate of how much the university would be in the black or red when all these items had been paid. Probably Jesse McClellan, the treasurer, had them on a separate sheet of paper or just possibly in his head and could come up with the figures when questions were asked. He, by the way, as of last February's meeting, had been given an assistant, James McLaughlin. He and his assistant arrived every morning at the office at seven o'clock. It was the custom. College classes began at 7:30. Breakfast in Hoover Cottage was at 6:15.

There were other items of some interest at that meeting, among them the approval of the opening of the library during the coming year for two evenings a week, Thursday and Saturday night from seven to nine. Then came the real problem of this session: the summer school. It was growing out of bounds; it used the facilities of the college, yet it had no corporate relation to the college. At the February meeting they had voted a resolution that after the summer of 1911 the summer school was to be under the full supervision and control of the Board and coordinated with the university. The question now was exactly how they were to implement this resolution. They asked therefore that Dickason, Notestein, and Dean Compton be invited to the meeting in the afternoon. At that time Dickason outlined his plans and methods and expressed his belief that he could not conduct the summer school successfully as a department under the control of the university. Notestein then suggested the plan of a separate summer school affiliated with the university, the faculty and trustees to have final approval of the teachers for those students desiring university credits. Dean Compton "spoke along the same lines and reviewed the advantages of a properly conducted summer school." After considerable discussion, a plan was formulated as follows:

Be it resolved that the University of Wooster recognize the Wooster Summer School as a separate but affiliated institution. That so long as the Summer School have its habitat on the Campus of the University of

Wooster all teachers therein shall be nominated by the Principal of the Summer School, shall be recommended by the Faculty of the University of Wooster, and shall be confirmed by the Board of Trustees of the University of Wooster. Emergency appointments may be made by the Principal; . . . their temporary validity shall hold only until passed upon by said Faculty and Board of Trustees.

That the extension of work for the Masters [*sic*] degree to the Summer School be made under regulation for teachers, courses, and theses adopted by the Faculty and confirmed by the Board of Trustees of the University of Wooster.

McClaran then proposed an addition: That Dickason spend a portion of the time during the college year in a canvass "of the State . . . for Students for the University in its several departments, and that for this service he be allowed the sum of $500 in addition to the salary of $2000 heretofore granted him."

Dickason agreed that the arrangement as stated would be satisfactory to him. Holden moved its adoption, and it was passed, one trustee, McClure, abstaining. Mr. Severance, president of the Board, emphasized the happy conclusion they had reached. One more hurdle seemed to have been crossed.

A few days later the announcement was made that the attendance at the summer school had reached an all-time high: 1100 students.

Treading Lightly

DURING the summer Kenarden Lodge had been completed and made ready for occupancy. It was a half quadrangle facing into the campus, its back door on Bever Street. Not built on the usual dormitory plan, it had no long corridors for roughhousing; instead there were seven completely separate sections, of suites and single rooms. Each section was of three storeys with its own entrance. It was fireproof with concrete floors and stairways, and looked altogether indestructible—though the boys would soon enough do their best to test that point. Its face was of vitrified white brick [1] to match the other buildings. The steep roof was broken by many single sharply gabled dormer windows of brick, and, between these, hooded dormers of wood. At the top of those of brick was the Kennedy family [2] escutcheon, a shield against which blazed a torch. Perhaps this would prove to be a symbol of a new sophistication that the president was dreaming of for Wooster.

In the fall of 1910 Mrs. John Stewart Kennedy, the donor, had made a visit to Wooster, at President Holden's invitation. He thought it would be pleasant for her to see the place where she was investing so much money in the comfort of college boys. Anyhow it might interest her to attend the A. F. Schauffler lectures on the Bible being given at the college by her brother-in-law. She would indeed be happy to come but refused to stay at any private home; she would go to a hotel. When he found there was no changing her mind, the president was staggered, but only for a moment. Wooster was no Bar Harbor. At their very best the hotel accommodations were dreary. He hurried down to Liberty Street, picked out the lightest and airiest room he could find, ordered everything out of it, and that it be scrubbed and polished. Then he took off to see what he could find. He sent in a decorator to freshen up the walls, hunted curtains, draperies, and carpets, and the best furniture that the town could offer. When he had fitted it all out, it was the most luxurious hotel room in the Wooster of its day. Whether Mrs. Kennedy ever discovered the plight for which she had been the unsuspecting occasion the story does not tell, though she may well have guessed. Before she left she arranged a "Thanksgiving banquet" for the boys and girls of Westminster and Livingstone Homes. This may well have been her way of saying thank you. A college president's life, Holden had long since found out, was in no way drab. There was a new and different crisis almost every day. Even though the dean relieved him of the more routine chores, he must have often felt himself a lone manager of a traveling circus.

When the college convened in September, 1911, the president had the sad task of announcing the death in late August of George D. Gable, the much loved and esteemed professor of mathematics and astronomy. Mr. Gable had been ill for several weeks with typhoid fever, yet he was in early middle life and apparently vigorous; everyone had assumed that he would pull through. He had been four years at Wooster, had built a house on College Avenue, and settled in as if he meant to stay. He was a genial soul, with an irresistible quality of gaiety, yet he was serious too, and had an understanding of young people that had made him invaluable on the discipline committee.[3] He left a wife, and a daughter almost ready for college. The president had had to scurry around to find a replacement before the opening of the college year. Professor Benjamin F. Yanney, who had been teaching in Mt. Union for twenty-five years, was on hand for the first convocation. Though he had no doctor's degree, he had had a year of graduate study at the University of Michigan and another at the University of Chicago and he had a reputation of being able in the classroom.

The other major appointment this year was in the chair of Greek language and literature, an important post, for Wooster had many students looking toward the ministry. He was John B. Kelso, a man whom Wooster valued from the first for his scholarly approach, his wide interests, and sane judgment, and was to count on more and more with each passing year. Tall and handsome, he looked every inch the gentleman and scholar that he was. In every sense he had background. Born of missionary parents in India, he was deeply sympathetic with Wooster's ideals of Christian service. He had traveled widely in Europe, knew Greece and Italy well, had taken his Ph.D. in Leipzig, Germany. He had done further graduate study at Yale and at the Western Theological Seminary, where he had also taught for a year. He came to Wooster from a professorship of Greek at Grove City College in western Pennsylvania.

Never had there been so many young men on the faculty, instructors fresh from their graduate work. There was Clarence Gould in history ("Tubby" the students were to nickname him) and Gentry Cash in chemistry, both of them with Ph.D.'s from Johns Hopkins, the red-haired Walter J. Gifford in education, who after two years at Columbia had just received his M.A. from Teacher's College. He was an A.B. of Oberlin, and had spent the past summer teaching in the normal department of Butler College, Indianapolis. Ross Thomas,[4] who was to instruct in both physics and mathematics and to give an elective in mechanical drawing, was fresh from Case. This year there were 209 freshmen and eight divisions of mathematics. It had been desirable, consequently, to add another instructor, Lyman C. Knight,[5] who had been teaching in the preparatory department ever since his graduation from Wooster in 1904. Rutherford B. Hunter had been a professor of physics in small Cornell College in Iowa for four years. He came to Wooster as instructor in physics though with the prospect that if he proved his value he would be advanced to the professorship, which was vacant. There was also a new instructor in French and German, John W. Olthouse, who had both his Bachelor's and Master's degrees from the University of Michigan. He was a thorough, thoughtful, young man, of Dutch extraction,[6] who soon fitted himself into the local community, became a member of the German Evangelical Church in town, and was to spend, save for several periods of advanced study, the rest of his life in Wooster. He would be giving an elective in scientific German. A new director of athletics was also on the ground, Harry Lloyd, and Richard Douglas, '10, was brought in to read themes and hold conferences as assistant to Mr. Dunn.

This was the galaxy of young men that had come to Wooster in the fall of 1911. Four of them had found places in one of the sections in Kenarden Lodge and were boarding there as well.[7] The president was happy over the fresh air that they were bringing to the institution, happy to feel that they were young men of promise, most of them anyhow with advanced degrees, and almost without exception, also with the experience, if not of European universities, at least of large universities in this country, and also that of living in cities, Baltimore, New York, Cleveland. They had been around a bit; they would add tone, he felt, to the college.

Soon after his inauguration President Holden had written an open letter to Wooster's alumni (December 15, 1899). In this he had said in part:

I have been deeply touched by the cordial welcome extended by the Alumni of Wooster University to me, the new President of their Alma Mater. . . . My soul was stirred within me, on inauguration day, as I witnessed the enthusiasm of the Alumni for their Alma Mater. It seemed to me that I could discover in the faces of the Alumni present the thought that here at Wooster they have gotten their ideals, and in some way or other it had been their Jerusalem, where they had tarried through their College days, that they might be endued with power. . . .

. . . . .

I wish to assure you that as I take the place assigned me in your College home, I shall step lightly, not as a vandal to whom nothing is sacred, but as a member of your family circle, interested in all that interests you, rejoicing in your successes and mourning with you in your afflictions. Your College home shall be my College home, and your God my God. I have already caught your vision for your Alma Mater, and my own horizon has been enlarged by it. I long to see her multiply her noble influences of the past and go forward in every good line and work, increasing in power and numbers in the years to come. That this may be accomplished, I must have your hearty cooperation. Without it I shall fail. You are an important part, I had almost said the most important part, of this institution, and the success of my administration lies largely with you. I want you to claim your birthright in your Alma Mater, and have weight in her counsels, and be seen at her commencements, and be enthusiastic for her extension and expansion along all right lines.

It was a letter almost pathetic in its expectancy.

He had gone slowly in these intervening years in making drastic changes. And even in the last few years the president had done his best still to step lightly. He had built up indeed a great reserve of good will as faculty and alumni watched with pride the new Wooster rise upon its hill. One could see its white buildings [8] from afar, spread out among the trees, as one topped the rise and came down into town from the west or east or south. At commencement the alumni as they came back sang the "Wooster Love Song" fervently.[9] They had not yet become so sophisticated as to be ashamed of its sentimentality.

It had not been the accidental brainstorm of an architect that Kenarden had been planned in sections. It had been well thought out.[10] If congenial boys could be housed together in groups there would cease to be much reason for fraternities. It was a prophetic move, though probably no one except the president had thought much about it. Mr. Severance had come down for the opening of college. He and President Holden had had dinner at Kenarden on the first night of its opening. Thus they had given it their official blessing. Soon thereafter Dean Compton had gone over and talked to the boys of a plan for self-government. Later they set up a parliament, one member from each section.

All through the year of 1911–1912 there was an air of peace and well-being on the hill. Work had been started on the new gymnasium out in the grove behind Kauke Hall. It was announced that the Friday after Thanksgiving would be a holiday; many students would be able to go home. The faculty were having fun; they were holding monthly parties, the first a corn roast at the Hutchins' home in Bloomington, and after supper they had all played drop-the-handkerchief. The Dean and Mrs. Compton entertained the bachelor members of the faculty for dinner. Several of the college girls had gone to Cleveland to see Maude Adams. Miss Winona Hughes, an alumna, who had visited the college several times in the last year or two, had been appointed a new fiscal secretary for the institution. Miss M. Bine Holly who taught German so successfully in the academy had had a textbook, *German Epics Retold,* published by the American Book Company. (Dear Bine! Who does not remember her with affection, seemingly as stiff and formal as that tightly bodiced green dress that she was always wearing, and yet how gentle!)

There were several interesting events. The freshmen won the annual tug-of-war against the sophomores, twenty on each side. In late October a new bronze tablet in memory of the Rev. John Robinson, first president of the Board of Trustees, had been unveiled by Mrs. Holden in the trustee room of Kauke Hall. It had been given by Mr. Robinson's son, of Cleveland, to replace that lost in the burning of Old Main.[11] Mr. George Schwartz of North Market Street had given to the college two prizes for extemporaneous speaking, one for $35 and one for $15. Two months before the contest a list of subjects would be given out, among them the one finally chosen and announced an hour before the contest. The contestants would be called up one by one in no predetermined order, without having heard any previous speaker. Thiry-five dollars or even fifteen were worth working for. Then as December began, the wonder of wonders occurred. The students petitioned for a postponement of the Christmas vacation, that it not begin until noon of December 22 and that the college open again on January 8, 1912. The occasion was the local option election in Wooster on December 22. If the college were to close on the date originally set, some sixty students would either have to stay over or lose their votes. The election was likely to be close. Wayne County had been dry since 1908. The students did not wish to see a return of saloons to the town nor did they wish to see sixty of their friends deprived of a part of their legitimate vacation. The petition was of course granted.

During the season, however, there had been one bit of distressing news. Gentry Cash, who had been proving himself a brilliant teacher of chemistry, was leaving at the end of the semester to take a position with the Standard Oil Company of Indiana. Already Wooster was beginning to feel the pinch of industry in the field of science. Mr. Holden was fortunate in finding a replacement at once, Samuel Morris from Washington State College. The midwinter season had been comparatively dull. The weather was so bad that work on the new gymnasium was delayed. However, the mood of the students suffered no set-back; they had a winning basketball team. They had defeated Wittenberg, Reserve, Case—twice—Ohio Wesleyan, Kenyon, Marietta, and Oberlin. A. A. Blaser, Walter Corry, Worth Collins, Ralph Fulton were heroes. This season was as good as the football season just past had been bad. There had been also the sixth biennial minstrel show, the highlight of which was a farce entitled "Prexy's Dream." In this Prexy, several of the faculty, and even Gus Eberly, the overall janitor, had been burlesqued. The second act with the usual student Dantesque imagination took place in Hades. There had also been the celebration of the Dickens centenary. Walter Bradley Tripp had read from *David Copperfield* one night at the chapel, and two of the faculty, Lean and Dunn, with two of the senior girls had presented on another occasion a different Dickens evening.[12]

Then presently it was spring again. The sun was warm on one's back. The skunk cabbages poked their blunt noses through the swampy ground all up and down Clear Creek valley, and the doves mourned in the trees. For some weeks now the white walls of the new gymnasium had been rising higher every day. The roof would soon be on and the windows in place. Both the dedication and Color Day had been set for May 17. Meanwhile much else was going on. The Boston Symphony had come to Canton on a spring tour and thirty persons from the college had gone over. The boys who played tennis were out working on their courts—the responsibility to maintain them had been put on the student players by the college. Tournaments were scheduled with Illinois State University, Michigan State, and Pittsburgh. Every fair afternoon the men and the coach were out on the baseball practice field. Perhaps this year they would have a winning team. They had, they knew, in Blaser a "superb pitcher." Mr. Lean, too, was busy coaching Jesse Baird, a senior and a transfer this year from Grove City College. Baird had won every oratorical contest he had gone out for so far. On May fifteenth he would be in Northfield, Minnesota, Ohio's representative—and Wooster's—in the interstate, intercollegiate, oratorical contest.

All spring the president had been watching nervously the progress on the new gymnasium. Almost every day he was over there. Finally he announced that only a stairway was lacking and he had been promised that that, too, would be in place before the day of dedication. That glorious morning saw the chapel packed well before the hour set. On the tick of 8:30 Mr. Erb at the organ began Wagner's *Pilgrims' Chorus.* It was a simple service lasting only half an hour. After the invocation, the president of the Student Senate, Hurd Miller, '12, chairman for the day, introduced President Holden to give the dedicatory address. Speaking of the donor's generosity and high aims for the university, he explained that when Mr. Severance had discovered that his original gift of $100,000 would not cover the expense of building and equipment, he had immediately offered whatever more might be necessary to complete it and equip it according to the high standards he insisted upon. It would be, said President Holden, "the finest college gymnasium in Ohio." "He [Mr. Severance] desired," the president continued,

that the whole structure should be suggestive of health and strength, vigor for mind and body. This building . . . is emblematic of the purpose of the donor, that all who may enter here may become strong, pure-minded and more manly in their daily living. . . . Therefore, as we receive the gift of our new gymnasium, let us not mistake the purpose of the gift. It is not that the sons of Wooster may win victories in athletic contests, but that they may have vigorous and healthy bodies, pure hearts, clean minds, a necessary equipment for those who dedicate themselves to the service of mankind. His greatest desire for us is that our lives may be strong and triumphant in the faith of our fathers.

Others spoke, Chalmers Martin, representative of the faculty, read a long original poem in honor of the occasion. The coach, Harry Lloyd, referred to this as the "greatest day in Wooster's history for the coach." "Hap" Maurer, captain of the football team, expressed the gratitude of all the boys to both President Holden and Mr. Severance. Then Mr. Erb struck up the swelling Largo of Handel's *Xerxes*. At the end as they rose to go out, they waited a moment and then as if to affirm once more their loyalty sang the "Wooster Love Song." It was over. During the latter part of the service souvenir programs had been distributed. They showed pictures of the new building, inside and out, and the familiar portrait of Louis H. Severance under which were inscribed the lines from Mark Antony's funeral oration for Julius Caesar:

> Moreover he hath left you all his walks,
> His private arbours, and new-planted orchards,
> On this side Tiber; he hath left them you,
> And to your heirs forever.
> (Act III, Sc. 2)

The moment had come for inspecting the building. Here they found offices, examination rooms, reading and resting rooms connected with the lobby, private rooms for visiting teams, a great floor for basketball furnished as well for all sorts of exercise, a running track, a turf-floor baseball court 50 by 60 feet and 25 feet in height, a swimming pool 50 by 25 feet, 4 feet deep at one end and 8 at the other, shower baths, locker rooms, lavatories upstairs and down. There was a special locker room for the faculty with a private stairway to their own Turkish bath department in the basement. Everything everywhere was finished in white tile, or white enamel brick, Alberine stone, Tennessee marble. "Magnificent" was the word on everybody's lips. How sad they were that Mr. Severance could not have been here this day himself. He had been detained by business.

There was much else that day of sunshine and rain. They had never had so good a Color Day. Even in the evening after supper the May queen, Marian Howell, '12, led a march from Holden Hall down Beall Avenue past the Wilson Club and the president's home, where they stopped to give him the Chautauqua salute, past some of the fraternity houses, then across to College Avenue and up again to the campus, to and around the library. All along, others had joined the march till at the end it was a great broad twisting serpent. Under the trees on the quadrangle the Volunteer Band had set up an ice cream stand. And in the chapel as night came on J. Lawrence Erb sat down at the organ and played.

The college year was almost at an end—a few days of classes, examinations, the festivities and solemnities of the 42nd commencement, then until the opening of summer school there would be silence under the elms. The faculty would soon be taking off in every direction. Compton and Lean would go to their respective summer places on lakes in Michigan and Wisconsin. President and Mrs. Holden were bound for the North Cape to see the midnight sun, and then to the Austrian Tyrol. Kelso and Vance also would be on their way to Europe. Olthouse would be studying this summer in Paris. Behoteguy would be leaving for his sabbatical year in France, but first he would go to Cleveland to marry Miss Claribel Durstine, art teacher at the college and long his next-door neighbor in Wooster. The spring and early summer indeed were bringing a rash of marriages among the faculty. In March Walter Gifford had gone to Berea and brought home a bride. Now Samuel Morris was bound to New York to meet a steamer from which his fiancée was landing. She had been studying music in Vienna. They would be married and come to Wooster later in the summer. Lester Wolfe, the registrar, was marrying, and so a few months hence was L. C. Knight. Because of all this the president's reception to the seniors and faculty was merrier perhaps than usual. No punch bowls were in evidence, but in the dining room, where Mrs. Erb and Miss Riggs were officiating, there were plates of fresh strawberries and ice cream with cake and coffee in addition. Many of the seniors, however, were beginning to feel that their sky was tumbling. Already one early morning around a symbolic fire on the old athletic field their "braves" had met those of their ancient enemy, 1913, to smoke the traditional Pipe of Peace. When all was set, the chief of 1912 had advanced across the circle to place upon the shoulders of the chief of 1913 his own gown, symbol of the responsibility he was passing on. Then one by one all the others crossed the circle to greet their opposites. There were a few brief speeches and the ceremonial puffing at the pipe, and then they were gone to other duties.

This year some of the alumni had been advocating another custom that was later to become traditional, the procession of the classes to the alumni banquet. Alumni were becoming conscious of themselves as an influence and an entity. Class gifts, too, were becoming more and more important. As 1910 had given the handsome grandfather clock to the library "guaranteed to last 100 years," and 1911 had given the clock on the tower of Kauke in memory of Professor George D. Gable, so 1912 was to give four lamps for the quadrangle, on standards each thirteen feet high.

As one walked about the campus, there was other news in the air. The trustees had just added 20 more acres to the campus toward the northeast, for future expansion. In all, the college now owned 33 acres to the west of Beall, and 40 to the east. A new student monthly magazine was making its appearance this June, *The Wooster Literary Messenger,* the purpose of which was "to foster and develop the literary spirit of the University of Wooster." Mr. Dunn, of course, had been behind it and was shaping its development. The name was derived from that of *The Southern Literary Messenger,* of which for a while Edgar Allan Poe had been the editor. It would contain the best of Wooster's literary output, essays, short stories, sketches, critical articles, poems, book reviews, and would have also a contributors' club. It had a student editor, but manuscripts were solicited not only from students but from alumni and faculty. The other news was that Oscar F. Wisner, professor of Missions, had resigned and would be going to North Carolina to oversee "a survey of rural life."

When in 1911 the Ladies' Advisory Board had recommended to the trustees that a dean of women be appointed, they had added significantly, "as soon as a suitable person can be found." Wooster was beginning to grow up. These women saw that it would take time to find the right person. They saw that the college girls should have not only a woman resident who could see that a dormitory was properly run, that the girls had the care that they needed, especially in sickness, but also a woman of maturity and academic stature to guide them and direct them as they were coming of age intellectually, spiritually, and socially, taking on responsibility as members of society. The matron, as the head resident of a dormitory was then called, had been hostess, housekeeper, dietician, chaperone, policewoman and foster mother. Wooster had been fortunate in some of her matrons, who had been women of more than casual background, but this was not all that was needed. They must have in this deanship someone who could hold her own with the best men on the faculty, and who was their intellectual peer. Such a woman, they realized, would not be just some woman with social graces and a warm heart, however essential these were, but a person who could meet situations with firmness and with tact, not one who wondered what should be done after an unhappy situation had arisen but one who had anticipated the situation and so planned that it never happened. That took brains of high quality, and know-how in dealing with both men and women; it meant real leadership. For if she did not command the respect of men, she would soon lose that of the women. President Holden had indeed been taking his time in finding this person. For a year he had been watching a likely candidate as she went around the state as a fiscal secretary.

Now at the opening chapel service in the fall of 1912 she was sitting on the platform, Wooster's first dean of women, Winona Alice Hughes, '91. She had been known, of course, as a student to the older faculty, Notestein, Bennett, Compton, Black, Mateer. She had shown unusual interest in chemistry and had later done two years and more of graduate work in that field at the University of Chicago, with additional summer study at Cornell, at Harvard, and Woods Hole. For a year she had been a Fellow at Bryn Mawr, and for the five years of 1906–1911 a highly regarded instructor in chemistry at Mt. Holyoke. Before that time she had taught science for a number of years in high schools in Ohio and Iowa. In the year she had just completed as fiscal secretary for the college she had had a chance to familiarize herself with Wooster's clientele within the state. She was herself originally an Ohio woman, her home in Marion. Only a month or so after the opening of college she had already started to make changes, according to a student writer in *The Voice,* she was

by no means as ferocious and tyrannical as some believe. Miss Hughes has imposed no new restrictions in the government of the dormitories, but on the contrary she has been instrumental in securing the repeal of several rules which she regarded as unfair to the young women. . . . Contrary to the custom of former years there is [now] no regular 'calling night.' Instead, visitors are permitted at the Hall and the Cottage any night of the week. When asking for a young lady, men are requested to give their own names also. . . . Another new provision . . . permits Sunday evening church dates. [She gives credit to Dean Compton for this]. . . .

Against one thing our new Dean does seriously object . . . extended nocturnal promenading. . . .

[She says] 'I want the young people of the University to have anything they desire that is good and right and fair.'

The writer adds, "She especially desires to become acquainted with the young men of the college and their interests." By February *The Voice* had reported that she was "already famed for her abilities as a hostess."

Another new appointment was that of Emery A. Bauer as director of physical education for men. He came from Ohio State University with a B.P.E. degree as well as a B.S. Two credits of physical education were now required for graduation. Although as yet there had been no provision for the use of the new gymnasium by women, and would not be until the following February when the trustees finally took action giving the girls exclusive use of the gymnasium on Thursdays, a director of physical education for women had also been appointed. She was Miss Berenice F. Wikoff with a B.S. (domestic science) from Ohio State University. She had spent the summer of 1912 studying at Harvard. Before the college year was out both the men's and the women's departments had given Wooster's first annual gymnastic exhibitions. They were by invitation only, a month apart, and consisted for the most part of rather routine drills, exercises in elementary and advanced apparatus, games, a barn dance and for the men, at the end, the "dance of the Jumping Jacks." The women's exhibition in April was similar except that they had added more dances, some folk dances, and one representing autumn leaves. At the end they formed a U and sang the "Wooster Love Song." They had obviously made good use of the large recreation room in the basement of Holden Hall for their drills.

A major appointment in the year 1912–1913 was that of Clinton Tyler Wood,[13] brother of Mrs. J. M. Vance, to the professorship of missions. He was a graduate of Princeton and had had a unique experience in Cape Province, South Africa. There for fifteen years he had been a minister and a professor in the missionary training school of the Dutch church at Wellington. He was to remain at Wooster until January, 1926. A man of strong religious faith, exuberant cheerfulness, with a genuine interest in his students, he was a welcome addition to the faculty.

The fall of 1912 saw also the coming of a new pastor to Westminster Church, the Reverend Mr. William F. Weir, for the eight preceding years at Ashtabula, Ohio. He was to remain only four years and then to go on as director of men's work for the Presbyterian Church, U.S.A.—he continued to live in Wooster, however, until 1921 and remained a member of Wooster's Board of Trustees until 1944. He had a somber mien as if the clouds around hung low. Yet he was a sincere and devout man, an acceptable preacher, and with some exceptions, of course, was well liked by his congregation and the community. When in November of his first year he led the Y.M.C.A. Week of Prayer, the men came to the services in crowds, and in 1913 *The Index* was dedicated to him. It was during his pastorate that an affiliated membership in Westminster was extended to students who chose to accept it.

The exact relationship of college and church had often been up for discussion. In June, 1909, the University Board of Trustees thought to clarify it by passing the following resolution:

The Board of Trustees would emphasize the college pulpit as a vital part of Wooster's influence upon her students. For years past by arrangement with Westminster Church the college and the church have each filled the pulpit for half the time. In order to unify the work it has seemed best to unite college and church in the support of one pastor; the college requests the privilege of supplying the pulpit at such times as it deems wise not exceeding half the Sundays of the collegiate year. . . .

But as they gained a pastor they were presently to lose their organist and choir director. The news that broke in December, 1912, was a blow. J. Lawrence Erb had fitted into the college so well. Students loved him; so did many of the faculty. He had been initiated into the Phi Gamma Delta fraternity, had become a member of the student Dramatic Club. *The Index* of 1912 had been dedicated to him. His department of music had been growing steadily. More than one hundred students were now enrolled, and through his teaching and his performance he was developing in the community a love of music. Everyone looked forward to his occasional Sunday afternoon vespers, and his recitals were sheer delight. Two years before, John Timothy Stone of Chicago—who would some years later become chairman of Wooster's Board of Trustees—had preached at Westminster, had been attracted to Mr. Erb and had made his acquaintance. Now he was enticing him away to become organist and choir director for the Fourth Presbyterian Church of Chicago. This would be truly a loss to Wooster. Mr. Erb was not only a musician and a teacher but as a person was both warm and gay.

In the fall of 1912 Wooster lost another old friend, one whom very few in the community knew, but one on whom the president for some years had been calling at intervals, and from whom he had rarely if ever come away emptyhanded. Michael O. Fisher and his brother William lived near East Liverpool on adjoining farms. They had never gone to any college; it is doubtful whether they had ever seen Wooster. They were, however, devoted Presbyterians and skillful farmers, and over the years they had accumulated some money with which it gave them pleasure to be generous. They had always supported the church of which they were members, had contributed liberally to the Presbyterian Boards, and eventually had become interested in Christian education. They were true inheritors of the dream of such men as had founded Wooster in the first place. William had given, also, to Omaha Theological Seminary. Michael O. had taken out an annuity in favor of Wooster University, and had built it up to $20,000,[14] enough to endow a professorship of history at the college when he and his wife would no longer be living. The two brothers, only two years apart in age, who had lived almost side by side, died within a week of one another. Both were in their eighties. Their wives survived them. Michael's wife was to live three more years. Then the chair of history at Wooster became officially the Michael O. Fisher professorship named for the farmer who looking across his fields had seen there not just corn and wheat and pasture lands but a procession of young people and the patterns of world history.

The Gang's All Here

WOOSTER had now more than 1700 alumni and hundreds of others, former students, who, though they had not continued till graduation, still held dear the experiences and friendships of college days. By and large, Wooster's graduates had gone and were still going into the professions, into the ministry, into teaching, into medicine, and law. In this, Wooster was not unlike many another small, middle western liberal arts college where not only was service to humanity stressed but where the enthusiasm for learning of perhaps two or more professors had inflamed with like enthusiasm young and eager men and women. One had but to scan the rolls of faculties in the universities and ivy-league colleges to discover how many on their teaching staffs had come originally from such small colleges. Wooster, like these other denominational institutions, drew its students from small towns and villages and farms. Wooster's came from Ohio and western Pennsylvania, a Presbyterian stronghold, with a sprinkling from farther west, from Montana and Utah especially.

But unlike most, it had come to have over the years something of a cosmopolitan flavor.[1] To and from its memorial furlough homes [2] missionaries from everywhere came and went, changing every year. Sunday after Sunday the pulpit of Westminster might be filled by someone from the Far or Middle East, from Africa, South or Central America, even Alaska. Yet it got still more a continuing sense of the great world beyond the U.S.A. from the sons and daughters of these missionaries left behind for their education to live here in Livingstone ("The Inky") and Westminster Homes. Years later, in 1935, in a book about Tibet, one of these boys, Gordon Enders, *ex* '18, described the life in these homes:

Nowhere else in America could such a strangely assorted group be found. Not a single one of the fifty had less than two languages; some of them spoke a half-dozen strange tongues and dialects. All of them had lived in far-off lands where strange adventures were commonplace. I was immediately thrown into fast growing friendships with youths from China, Korea, Persia, Japan, Syria, Siam, Indo-China and Manchuria. My Asiatic background, hitherto confined almost entirely to Northern India and Tibet, began to fill in with a detailed picture of the peoples and problems of all other parts of that vast continent.

For five years at Wooster College I met this group constantly, at meals, study and recreation. . . . We all had parents or relatives in Asia, and the daily mail . . . consisted largely of letters with foreign stamps and postmarks, supplemented by superscriptions in Arabic, Hindi and Chinese hieroglyphics. The letters brought news to be exchanged and discussed: somebody's father had shot a tiger, somebody's brother had been marooned by a flood, there was an epidemic of bubonic in somebody's home city or famine in another, there was war in Kansu or insurrection in Laos.

We had our individual loyalties . . . I insisted that the Indian method of eating with fingers was far superior to the Chinese use of chopsticks. I stuck up for the Indian sport of fighting partridges as against the Siamese duels between paradise fish or the cricket fights of Kwangtung. The magic shows of the Indian jugglers seemed to me better theater than the acrobatics of the Chinese strolling players or the long-winded singsong of the Arabian professional storytellers. I defended the art of India—the squirrel-brush paintings on ivory as against the conventionalized Chinese line drawings on silk and the half-Europeanized art of Japan. . . .

We discussed the politics of Asia, endlessly: the rape of Korea, the bedlam of China, the supremacy of the bandits in Manchuria, the thwarting of Russia, the future of Mongolia, the rise of Japan; and into all these discussions I stanchly thrust my unwavering belief in the benevolent imperialism of Britain and the inevitable importance of Tibet in the Asiatic picture.

We exchanged information on the various religions of our countries: I was the acknowledged authority on Lamaism, and had an opportunity to compare it in detail with the doctrines of Confucius, with pure Buddhism as known in China and Japan, with the animism of Tao, the modified Hinduism of Siam, the Moslem faith of Arabia and many other creeds, from the ancient fire worship of Persia to the demonology of the hairy white Ainu of Northern Japan.

When we got into a really intense discussion of such matters, the English language frequently proved inadequate. There were many untranslatable words, and we naturally fell back on colloquialisms in a dozen tongues. Without conscious effort I came to have a smattering of Arabic, Chinese and Japanese, together with an auxiliary vocabulary of words and phrases from Siamese, Korean and Russian.

My roommate at Wooster was . . . a . . . chap from Chefoo. . . . He belonged to a group of fifteen boys from China. . . . After two years of association with them, I knew China almost as well as if I had lived there, and I understood enough Chinese to follow their conversation, which was always richly interlarded with native words.

Our evenings, in the downstairs drawing room, were filled with tales of travel and adventure. As I look back over that period, it seems to me to bear a notable resemblance to the "Thousand and One Nights" of Harun-al-Rashid. I contributed many tales of Tibet, drawn from the endless border stories that I remembered from my talks with Chanti, Jowar, Wu Ming-fu and others. My Wooster comrades had story reservoirs no less rich than mine.

Zenos Miller, notable for his flaring red hair and baritone voice, had escaped from Boxer killers by climbing over a fourteen-foot mud wall with his family, and had been four months in reaching safety.

Bill Eddy . . . had lived through so many Armenian massacres in Asia Minor that he was always getting them mixed up and spoke almost casually of mass deportation, starvation, and slaughter.

Paul Wright, our silver-voiced tenor, came from Persia and had lived through the siege of Tabriz; his stories were a strange combination of old and new—modern gunfire pitted against Oriental treason, deceit and double-dealing; famine in the midst of plenty; Eastern indifference to pestilence and suffering.

Jan Baird . . . came from Korea and was steeped in a naive and childlike legendry which has no counterpart anywhere else in Asia. He had watched the turbulent Japanese occupation of the peninsula, and was almost a maniac in his hatred of the invader.

My tales of the perils of mountain climbing in the Himalayas had their equal in Alan Chalfant's adventures on the flood-lashed plains of Shantung, or Sarah Campbell's encounters with wild animals in the jungles of Siam, or Edwin Wright's wanderings among the treacherous Kurds in the foothills of Mt. Ararat.

. . . . .

Sarah Campbell . . . knew Siam and Laos and the Shan States better than any foreigner I have ever met.

. . . .

At Wooster, the most abused book in the drawing-room library shelves was a big red atlas, in which we had marked the border between Tibet and China with red chalk. Whenever a story was told of friction somewhere on this 1,200 mile line, or whenever letters would come, reporting news of events or uprisings, we would get out the dog-eared map and make a penciled record of the spot. . . .

Tibet had no monopoly on the evening conversations. The maps of Persia, Japan, and Korea were in equal demand. . . . When the crowd around the fireplace was large, it would sometimes break up into several groups, each earnestly discussing a different country. Four or five stories might be running concurrently, and frequently the stories would get all mixed up, and in the end we all sounded like so much static. . . .

Geographical brain teasers were a favorite pastime. Someone would ask, with a pretense of innocence, "Which is farther south, Venice or Vladivostok?" and a chorus of wrong answers would ensue before recourse to the atlas proved that the Siberian city was the southernmost. Another catch question . . . was "Which is farther east, Shanghai or Harbin?" The usual answer, Shanghai, is wrong.

Many a thin dime changed hands in bets on distances between obscure cities in Asia, on the current political allegiance of small states, on the names of rulers and princelings.

It never occurred to us that there was anything unusual about our group or our conversation. Yet, for much of the time, we were as far removed from the ordinary atmosphere of the surrounding Ohio farm country as if we had been actually transplanted to Asia.[3]

Yet though as here described they were a group to themselves, as individuals they entered wholeheartedly into all the activities of student life. The tall Richmond Douglass of Shanghai, 6 feet 3.7 inches, could almost with a flick of his finger put a ball into its basket. The football and baseball teams could hardly have got along without the three Collins boys from Siam, and Harold Elterich broke his neck playing football and spent two years recovering. They were in the musical organizations, the big and little literary societies, in the Y.M. and Y.W.C.A. often as members of the cabinet, and they furnished a nucleus for the Volunteer Band, for many of them, when they finished their education, would inevitably find their way back as ministers, physicians, teachers, or wives to the lands they had loved as children and where there was still work to be done. They were nearly always popular and could be found in all the various fraternities and sororities. They brought the world to Wooster and as their friendships crossed all the usual artificial lines they were in a sense a democratic influence in college life.

Nearly all of them before entering college had had at least a year or two in the preparatory department or academy presided over by the benevolent John Howard Dickason ("Dicky") and the precise but equally benevolent Elizabeth Pendleton ("Aunty Pen"). Here could be found through the years also a succession of faculty children and those of an occasional local trustee, or of some old grad who preferred Wooster to all other places on the globe. Ministers or widows moving to town sent their children here, and once in a while, a local resident hoping that in the academy he would find superior teaching for his son or daughter. Besides, there were always boys and girls from farms or villages far removed from any reputable high school. And of course there were a few who came to college lacking a few credits. Many of these academy students, especially the faculty children, carried through their college life and beyond the friendships of this earlier day. No surface tensions engendered by the presence of fraternities or of rival literary societies disturbed these prior loyalties. These youngsters maintained a kind of happy independence, whatever fraternities, sororities, or literary societies claimed them as they entered college. In much the same way, I dare say, those who came up from the local high school kept their identity as a group.

In general, whether in the academy or in the college, Wooster was proud of its clientele. Many still worked their way in part at least, waiting on tables in the dormitories, living in homes in town where they tended furnaces and mowed lawns. Some, of course, had scholarships that helped. Probably a good many came from business or professional families that would be considered fairly well-to-do; very few had any money to throw around. Yet they were for the most part upper crust in the sense that they wanted, and their families wanted for them, an education. Yes, undoubtedly some girls came looking for husbands—and probably found them—yet very few at that time were coming to college just because "it was the thing to do."

Of course, once here, many students found themselves engulfed with extracurricular activities. There was no lack of these, musical groups or organizations, for instance. If a man had a good voice, he might try out for the Boys' Glee Club,[4] directed by Professor Harold Hutchins. It had been organized in 1907, and had sung first on Color Day of that year. It gave home concerts and later had been allowed to take a trip each year during a vacation period, sometimes for concerts in Ohio towns, sometimes also to western Pennsylvania or even farther east. Their programs were arranged for popular enjoyment rather than for classical taste. An accompanist went along. Among their soloists during these pre-war years were Carl Weygandt, '12, who was later to be Chief Justice of Ohio's Supreme Court and a member of the Singer's Club of Cleveland, and Clifford Cunard, *ex'*15, who later became a concert singer. For the men, too, there was an outlet for both dramatic and musical talent in the biennial minstrel shows. Though these made a point of satirizing college life, particularly the president and the faculty, there were always musical numbers, a cornet solo, perhaps a performance of the mandolin club, a vocal solo sung with exaggerated expression, "Because I Love You, Dear" or a popular duet, "You'll Do the Same Thing Over," or even a sextet, "Oh You Beautiful Doll." Informal groups of singers, too, from Kenarden, the Wilson Club, or the Suicide Club of the Inky could often be heard on moonlit nights, or on some special occasion, serenading the girls of Holden Hall or Hoover.

As for the girls they, too, had a glee club organized in February, 1908, under the direction of Mrs. J. M. Vance. They gave one or two home concerts a year, and by the spring of 1913 had won the privilege of an out-of-town trip into west central Ohio, during the spring vacation. Mrs. Vance sang most of the solos. Under the enthusiastic and expert leadership of Mr. Erb the conservatory in these years was gaining right along in numbers. Nearly everyone who enjoyed singing at all and who could spare the time was drawn sooner or later into either the choir of Westminster Church or into the oratorio chorus or both. For an hour on Wednesday and Friday afternoons the choir rehearsed the anthem they would sing on Sunday morning, and the oratorio chorus practiced for three months on Monday nights what they would sing in the December, March, and June concerts. Here they became familiar with Mendelssohn's *Elijah,* or Handel's *Messiah,* with Barnby's *Rebekah,* Gaul's *Holy City,* Wagner's *Pilgrims' Chorus*—which Mr. Erb had arranged for mixed voices—and with Dudley Buck's *Coming of the King.* Or in June it might be something with the feel of the outdoors, de Koven's *Robin Hood,* or *The Rose Maiden.* For all of these usually there were soloists from Cleveland, Pittsburgh, New York, and Canton and for a period of years also Louis Rich's twenty-piece orchestra from Cleveland. There was the memorable time in the spring of 1913 when the great flood laid Dayton waste, and even Killbuck had risen to such heights as to inundate the railroad tracks that led into Wooster. The soloists could not get here. With only a few hours notice, as Chalmers Martin wrote in *The Wooster Voice* (April 16, 1913), Mrs. Vance and Dessa Brown took over the contralto and soprano parts —"while Professor Erb added the role of baritone soloist to his task as conductor." With delight and something like anguish as the audience thought of all the persons known and unknown suffering and maybe dying throughout the state, they listened to the great arias, "Zion spreadeth her hands," "What have I to do with thee," and especially "Oh rest in the Lord," and "It is enough," sung with the depth and abandon generated by a crisis. The chorus, too, caught the feeling and was at its best. It was after all a wonderful evening. There were other wonderful evenings and wonderful days for these boys and girls who, light hearted and gay, were growing up, all unsuspecting—as indeed were also their elders—in these last years of an era.

They were serious, too, in their own way, these youngsters. On a Wednesday evening, known irreverently in Holden Hall as "ice-cream and no prayers," the girls went trooping off just after dinner to the Y.W.C.A. room in Kauke Hall. There they would have their own prayers, in anticipation of which the usual devotions in the dormitory had been skipped, and ice-cream at dinner substituted. Save on rare occasions when they asked Miss Gingrich or some other faculty member to talk to them, these meetings were in charge of the girls themselves: one would read the scriptures and another would speak on a theme assigned weeks before. The Y.M.C.A. meeting at the same time in its room in Scovel Hall, was more versatile. It rather often had faculty speakers, sometimes song services. Once in the spring of 1913, it is recorded, Mr. Kelso talked to them on Italy, giving the lecture in both Italian and English and illustrating it with stereopticon slides. Miss Giuseppina Bonazzi, also, had been brought in to sing Italian songs. To this occasion the Italian colony down beyond the railroad had been especially invited, and they came seventy-five strong, the Cicconettis, the Tomasettis, the Nolettis, no doubt led by the proud "Angelo" Santoro of Wooster's campus crew. It was he who for so many years would be greeting president and faculty and sometimes students with a strong "Buon giorno" and a welcoming smile as they passed him in the morning. Two weeks later they were to come back with their own band to take charge of a meeting for the Y.M.C.A. Occasionally the Y.M. and Y.W.C.A. would have a joint meeting. At one of these in 1913 Mr. Dunn spoke autobiographically on "Why I am a Christian." At another S. Hall Young, the mushing parson of Alaska, Wooster's own, who came back every few years and was always welcome, addressed both organizations and Westminster Church. There were special activities, however, beside the routine obligation of attendance at these meetings. Boys from the college were still going out northwest of town, a quarter mile or so beyond the Buchanan woods to hold meetings in the #9 schoolhouse, and in January, 1913, the Y.M.C.A. sent out two evangelistic teams, for four days each, to Condit in Delaware County and to Congress in Wayne County. The churches of these villages cooperated.

Morning chapel services in 1912 and 1913 were still devotional with occasional announcements as necessary. President Holden exhorted the students to greater zeal in their Christian life. So did Mr. Severance when he came to town. And the faculty made of the period a time of worship; they did not as now discuss from the chapel pulpit perhaps Moby Dick or Jane Austen or their own current research project. Once a year one day was set aside for the Day of Prayer for Colleges with a speaker from outside, and there was also still the Week of Prayer, for which leaders—often one for women, one for men—were brought in. There were special chapel services in the morning, meetings at night, and afterwards in the dormitories or elsewhere groups of girls and of boys came together for their own prayer circles. Perhaps the religious atmosphere in these days was not quite so stifling as it had been in President Scovel's day, yet it sometimes closed in almost like a fog. Sin and worldliness were words in common parlance among the "unco guid," yet the "unco guid," it is interesting to note, were not, except in special instances, the missionaries who had lived around the world and were but for the moment in Wooster, but those others whose lot had been cast for generations in the Middle West, who somehow found it harder to dwell on the beauty of holiness than on its grimmer aspects. Too much gaiety was somewhat suspect. Dancing and card-playing were still taboo at the college, though the theater and simple costuming were no longer frowned upon. Until President Scovel's administration dancing among Wooster's college students had been accepted.[5] He had come to Wooster from a pastorate in Pittsburgh, but his earlier life had been spent in southern Indiana. It may be that in this general period there had swept through much of the Middle West, as it had swept a little earlier through Britain, a kind of backlash of Wesleyanism, or of somber Calvinism, somewhat similar to the Clapham Sect or "coterie" in which Leslie Stephen had been reared and against which he ultimately revolted.

One must remember, however, that through this time Dr. Mateer had been teaching the new theory of evolution; indeed Wooster had been in the forefront of those Christian institutions that had done so. For Dr. Mateer the first chapter of Genesis was but a succinct statement of evolution or as *The Wooster Voice* put it: He "explained evolution in such a manner as to conform with the true idea of God as creator." To be sure, President Scovel did not fully approve but he had not forced Mateer to desist.

Nearly everyone belonged to a big or little literary society.[6] Willard and Castalian for the girls were still very much alive as were Athenaean and Irving for the men. Every Friday night around 6:30 there was a procession down the long west corridor of Kauke's second floor to their respective halls. Athenaean had been renovating its hall, buying a piano, and hanging on the walls photographs of many of its one-time members. In early days it had been a requirement of Irving members, and probably of those of Athenaean as well, that on graduation they should leave to the society their personal photographs. Later on they became satisfied with a group picture in *The Index*. The programs in all four societies were much as they had always been, declamations—the girls called them readings—essays, music sometimes, extemporaneous speaking on assigned topics, debates, orations, an occasional original short story or poem. The girls made more effort than the boys to build their program around a central theme, woman suffrage, for instance, a subject being then much discussed. At the end there was a critical estimate, by the judges, of each performer's work, on the content, on the delivery. These evaluations, though brief, often called for as much quick and careful thinking as may have gone into a performance. Yet sometimes the whole society by a sudden burst of laughter had made no comment necessary as when a green freshman impressed with his own importance announced the subject of his essay as "Intellectual Perspicuity," or "Social Conditions Past and Present, and The Outlook for the Future." Often, however, the literary society was a place where a boy who had never been far away from his own small home town could test his growing awareness of the world in a friendly atmosphere. There were fines for failure in attendance or in performance, and as late as 1912 Athenaean was summoning delinquent members to trial. To be sure, in an earlier day they had been liable to the judicial committee for other misdemeanors, for lounging on the chairs, for whispering, for making "irreverent allusions to the Scriptures," and for profanity. Irving had required that no one come into the hall without collar, tie, and coat. They had chaplains, too, who opened the meeting with scripture reading and prayer, and their constitution stated that a "continued use of a set form of prayer, e.g. the Lord's Prayer, shall not be countenanced." Whether in this Calvinistic institution nothing could be tolerated that savored of the ritualistic or whether this provision was an extension of their training in extemporaneous speaking to a new dimension, the record does not say. Aside from occasional open meetings the men did not parade their activities, though on Washington's Birthday they joined in preparing and presenting a suitable program in the chapel. The prowess in debate by their members (usually with Allegheny or Pittsburgh), the number of their orators who competed for the state, and interstate contests, for the Peace Prize, the Intercollegiate Civic contest, the 1875 Junior Prize Oratorical contest, the new Schwartz extemporaneous oratorical contest were well known. In fact the Forensic League in Wooster, made up of the members of Athenaean and Irving, had been organized "to secure a united effort in Wooster in oratory and debate." Athenaean, however, claimed that the college debaters and orators came very largely from their society.

For Castalian and Willard the high point of the year was the annual spring play given sometimes in the City Opera House, usually in the inadequate Taylor auditorium or the old gymnasium, transformed into a makeshift theater for the occasion. The two societies vied in the excellence of these presentations. Nearly every one of their members had a share in the work. Those who were not in the cast helped with properties or publicity or in ticket-selling. For a week beforehand the campus and town were plastered with placards.

The plays were ambitious: *Midsummer Night's Dream, School for Scandal, The Rivals,* for instance. Once Castalian presented *The Girls of '76* with elaborate colonial costumes. Once under Mr. Bennett's direction Willard gave Tennyson's *Foresters,* for which according to *The Voice,* Mr. Bennett had composed much of the music. He was never too busy or too tired to help with dramatics.

Already the college had grown too large to accommodate all the students in the four major literary societies. The four small ones, with membership limited by invitation, were coeducational. Stratford, organized originally under Mr. Bennett's sponsorship for a serious study of Shakespeare's works, was limited to eighteen. They met on alternate Wednesday evenings, and aimed to study three plays a year: in 1911–1912, for instance, *King Lear, Coriolanus,* and *Twelfth Night.* Ruskin, organized in 1903 for the study of painting, sculpture, architecture, sometimes digressed for a year to the study of Kipling, Thackeray, George Eliot, or Browning. Quadrangle, organized in 1904, sometimes studied poetry, sometimes history, or drama, or even the English philosophers, essayists, and novelists of the 18th or 19th centuries. It often brought in some member of the faculty to read or speak to them, Mr. Lean or Mr. Grumbine or Mr. Dunn. Franklin was founded in 1909, with Mr. Dunn as sponsor, for the study of American literature. It, too, varied its procedure, for though one year it might be studying Franklin and Howells and Longfellow, with one program perhaps on Sidney Lanier and another on O. Henry, the next year it might be concentrating on magazines or on differing religions. Though their purposes were serious in the beginning, gradually they were degenerating into social clubs with literary leanings. Ruskin would have a sleigh ride, Quadrangle would be entertained somewhere for dinner, Franklin would spend a pleasant evening at the Taggarts or have a party on St. Patrick's Day. They would go perhaps to Reddick's Dam for a picnic. All of these occasions offered a chance at least for a leisurely walk to and from the dormitories, and no opportunity was missed. There were other specialized clubs, the newly organized Dramatic Club, the Shakespeare Club, the Scientific Club. The last had as its aim the fostering of an interest in science for its own sake. Usually four of the faculty were invited to speak to them during the year. At one of its first meetings Dean Compton talked on telepathy, a subject in which he was much interested, as he was also in hypnosis. Mr. Black talked on the St. Lawrence River, and Mateer on evolution. They spent an evening on wireless telegraphy, and one evening Arthur Compton presented his theory of a way of detecting the direction and speed of the earth's rotation, and on another occasion Albert Good, back on furlough from the Cameroons, talked on African fauna. Mr. Bennett was the club's honorary member.

Of all these perhaps the most serious was the Congressional Club organized on December 16, 1908, by former President Scovel to make more real to some of the students the organization and procedures of Congress. It had a speaker, a clerk, a sergeant at arms, a chaplain, and a steering committee. Each of the sixteen members, at the beginning four from each class, chose a state to represent; it was his responsibility to become familiar with the political set-up and the continuing legislation of that state. Moreover, each member on being elected had to make a formal address before the organization. It was an honor to be asked into the Congressional Club.[7] Once a year they held a formal banquet to which their alumni members were invited.

With all these varying activities it was inevitable that someone would suggest an overall student governing board to keep a watchful eye on what went on, to correct evils and to do the more creative work of suggesting improvements and innovations. In 1908 Fred Eastman in his senior year had presented the idea of a Student Senate consisting of four members from the senior class, three from the juniors, two from the sophomores, and one freshman. The freshman had no vote. A senior was, of course, president. Its purpose allegedly was "to unify the student body in order to promote loyalty in spirit and honor in action among the students; furthermore to act as their representatives before the faculty." Also it was to "discourage by private reprimand" all unbecoming conduct on the part of students. The organization had limped along for three years doing little that was significant. To be sure, they had designed and won acceptance among the students for a Wooster recognition button. Yet they were still feeling their way, not knowing certainly where their responsibilities ended and those of the faculty began; happily they still believed that faculty and trustees did have a function.

Then in the fall of 1911 this Senate took over from the seniors the planning of the annual Color Day. It had been a day of fun, of a gay display of color on the campus and of many unrelated incidents: the Maypole dance, and a succession of rollicking stunts, most of them take-offs on college life. The whole needed pulling together, with a theme, a color scheme, and an order that made sense. They did not succeed, of course, in doing this all at once. Yet the Color Day of 1912, though still largely of class and faculty stunts, here and there showed a serious attempt at pageantry. The white throne was at the center of the quadrangle. For decorating it they had searched the woods for dogwood and honeysuckle. The queen, preceded by pillow bearer and flower girls, approached from the south to the music of the chapel organ. Her crown was of wild crabapple blossoms, and nothing could have been lovelier. And after the crowning and the Maypole dance, at noon came the grand march in which everyone took part. It was the senior stunt, however, that made the greatest impression, a pageant of education. They had drafted Mrs. William Annat from downtown to be Alma Mater. In a cream-colored satin gown with gold bands she, too, was seated on a white throne in the chapel, because it was raining outside. Her six attendants were in pastel colors. Behind them in procession bowing before Alma Mater came six girls dressed appropriately to represent Greek education, and six others singing a hymn in Latin, for Roman education. There followed a host of others, men and women, to suggest varying types and cultures: Moors and Hindus, dancers and warriors, shepherds and philosophers, jesters, troubadours, and crusaders, kings, and scholars. Of course the students couldn't resist introducing a comic element; and so Adam and Eve appeared with the serpent carrying a banner "Votes for Women," and the elephant and William Jennings Bryan trailed along side by side.

Soon, however, the Senate found itself involved in working out the plans for an honor system among the students. It had been suggested by the Y.M.C.A. cabinet worried by the obvious cheating on the part of many in examinations. The faculty had already this year suspended four students for such conduct, and the president berating the assembly in chapel one morning declared that at all costs "crookedness would be chased out of the University." The Senate had its go-ahead signal. The matter was fully discussed, passed by a majority vote of the students and approved by the faculty. The Senate drew up a constitution to be published in *The Voice* twice a year so that every incoming student would be aware of its provisions, and a judicial board was set up. This consisted of the president and one member of the Senate from each class. At the end of every examination the student signed his name to this statement: "I pledge on my honor that I have neither given nor received aid in this examination." The system was soon adjudged a success. It was not until the winter of 1913 that the Senate's judicial board, Clarence Bahler, president, was called to try four students under suspicion. One was found innocent; three were suspended for times varying from two weeks to a semester.

Before long the Senate turned its attention to correcting another grievance, that of politics in student elections. There had been for some years great complaint, and with justification, that the fraternities controlled the election of class and athletic association officers. After all, they could easily command votes whereas the non-fraternity group had no comparable organization. The Senate set up the rules. All nominations must be filed not later than Saturday at 6 P.M. of the second week of the college year and must be published in *The Voice* the following week. The Board of Elections consisted of one member each from the faculty, the seniors, the sophomores, and two members from the students at large. The first election under this system was held on October 5, 1912, and it was a success; in fact non-fraternity men and women won most of the offices. It is noteworthy that the president of the Student Senate during the time of these reforms was himself a fraternity man.

These were years when the students were becoming conscious of themselves as responsible individuals. Though they scandalized the community by occasional nightshirt parades and grieved the faculty by going to sneak dances downtown, though they sometimes yelled around a bonfire like so many wild Indians, and though they had all the fun the law allowed and often more, in their many activities around the campus they were training themselves for the days ahead, to be good citizens and good alumni: "Ever remembering, never forgetting."

Hurricane Alpha

AS attendance grew and organizations multiplied, the faculty which kept close surveillance over all student life and activities grew busier and busier. Not only did every change of course by a student require separate action of the faculty as a whole, but also every case of serious discipline, and sometimes ones not so serious. Even the minor organizations such as Franklin and Quadrangle, including the Congressional Club apparently had to seek reauthorization year by year; this was the faculty's way of seeing that they kept up at least a pretense of being study clubs. If a group of students hailing from west of the Mississippi wished to organize for occasional get-togethers to swap their own brand of tales, they, too, must make a formal request of the faculty. Of course every proposed public play must be sanctioned. No organization could have more than one formal party a year. Even on such occasions girls must be back in the dormitories with lights out by 10:30. Student behavior was indeed hedged in with rules. Several of these applied to athletics. No student taking fewer than twelve hours could play on a team, and no one under twenty-one, without written permission from his parents filed with the dean. A player who used profanity or was found indulging in intoxicating liquor at once lost his place. No games could be scheduled on Thanksgiving or Memorial Day without specific permission from the faculty and none at all that involved traveling on Sunday or required a student to be away from Wooster over Sunday. There was to be no card-playing, no dancing, no smoking on the campus, and no use of alcoholic beverages save as they might be prescribed by a physician. In the spring of 1912 the faculty felt it necessary to make a ruling that any student "is subject to indefinite suspension who at a minstrel show or on Color Day or any other public occasion ridicules or makes sport of the President."

At another time a freshman was called on the carpet by the dean for an innocent play on words, probably inspired by the boy's association with some of the Livingstone Lodge boys familiar with Moslem pious language. Anyhow, years later in writing of his Wooster experiences he said:

. . . It remains a mystery to me how a college president is selected. Presumably, his first qualification is that he be an intellectual giant. No sooner has he donned the robes of office than the trustees say, "Go out and raise money." He disappears from the campus for weeks at a time, hitting the road, trying to get his foot in the door of millionaires with angina. From one such money raising trip "Prexy" Holden returned home with a high temperature. For days he lingered on the edge of life, while the student body held its breath, since we had been indoctrinated to revere him as Enoch revered Cain. When the announcement was made in chapel, that he was out of danger, I was impelled by a naïve gratitude, to dash off one of the best bits of advertising copy I ever wrote. Larry and Ralph [his roommates at Kenarden] helped letter a huge sign which we tacked on the chapel door, feeling like Luther with his Ten Theses. The sign read "God is good. Prexy is better." Do you think Dean Compton appreciated that play on words? [1]

On another occasion a case of profanity came up to the faculty. They referred it to the president and dean for suitable action. In 1910 the Student Senate reported that three young women of Holden Hall had been found smoking cigarettes; they recommended punishment. The faculty referred the matter to the dean with power to act. The punishment having been determined and approved by the Student Senate, the girls were made to appear before all the occupants of Holden Hall and before the Student Senate to "express their sorrow" for the act, promise to do nothing so dastardly ever again in their college life and to throw their influence against smoking on the part of young women in the institution. There were of course more serious cases of discipline. Three boys from one of the fraternity houses, for instance, out on what they thought was a lark, hosed down one of the rooms in Holden Hall. This of course was unwarranted destruction of property. The ringleader was banished from the college, though the faculty, again by special act, admitted him the next fall. His aiders and abettors drew lighter sentences; one was "suspended from all college privileges, except attendance upon Sunday services," for six weeks, the other for eight weeks.

Fraternities, of course, were subject to special regulations. New members could not be pledged or initiated until they had completed satisfactorily at least a semester of college work at Wooster, which meant twelve credits, no failures, and an average of seventy-five in all studies, and then only with a certificate from the dean. This restriction was good from everyone's point of view, for the fraternities themselves were not wishing to enroll itinerant students. Rushing parties were limited to two; the adjustment to college work and college life was sufficiently hard for many students without their being bogged down with parties during their first few months. Anyhow it was better and less conspicuous if new friendships were made in a more leisurely and normal way. No sorority girl was allowed to accompany a rushee to a football game or to sit beside her in daily chapel unless the alphabet made such seating mandatory. Matriculation day might come in December but pledge day never until after all the grades were in and recorded in February. Because of all these restrictions, however, the two rushing parties were probably more elaborate than they might otherwise have been; they were usually not informal picnics but a luncheon somewhere, usually at the home of an alumna member or perhaps at an inn at Leroy or Smithville. For the privilege of going out of town they had to have a special act of the faculty. Once in the fall the Sigma Chi's had a rushing party at the county fair.

There had long been much criticism of the whole fraternity system by both students and faculty: it was undemocratic; its emphasis was on social rather than intellectual quality; it often led to a frittering away of time by young students not yet disciplined by life and unable to choose wisely among all the varied opportunities of college life; it added an expense which many students could not afford. For this reason the trustees had ruled that no initiation fee should be more than ten dollars; even that was prohibitive for some, especially when there would be annual dues, and assessments for parties. Many felt that fraternity loyalty tended to supersede college loyalty. The continued existence of the system had become more and more a moot question at Wooster.

When he came to the presidency, Mr. Holden, though he did not personally approve of the system, wisely decided to let well enough alone; it had evidently had the sanction of trustees and faculty since the early 1870's, and its abolition would have been freighted with dynamite for an incoming president. He had not, however, favored its extension. When one member of the faculty in the spring of 1908 had thrown the fat in the fire by introducing a resolution that no sorority be allowed to initiate further members, the whole question came up for discussion. Thereupon the alumni of the fraternities asked for a ruling from the trustees, for if they were going to build chapter houses for the active members, as they contemplated, they did not wish to get financially involved unless there was a reasonable expectation of the continued existence of the system.

Representatives of the Alumni Interfraternity Committee of the University headed by Karl Overholt, '97, John C. Hanna, '81, J. T. Miller, and Lee B. Durstine, '78, met in June, 1908, for an hour with the Board of Trustees discussing the whole question: (1) whether fraternities should be approved as "loyal in their general character and purpose to the highest ideals of the University and worthy of being utilized as proper instrumentalities for the advancement of the welfare of the students under their influence and of the University itself"; (2) the place of alumni cooperation and supervision of the active chapters; (3) the ownership and maintenance of chapter houses. This conversation they followed up with a letter in which among many other things they said:

. . . we further pledge without hesitancy on the part of ourselves, of the active chapters and of our general Fraternity, loyal and sympathetic cooperation with the Trustees and Faculty of the University in all acts and plans, as far as may be proper, for the advancement of the University, and especially for the maintenance of a high standard of character in the chapter life and the operation of the chapter houses.

. . . . .

They went on:

We suggest the adoption of a rule whereby no Freshman shall be initiated into any of our respective fraternity chapters until after the first semester examination, and further that no Freshman who loses his class standing by reason of his failure to pass such examinations shall be initiated.

In accordance with the suggestion of the President we will submit at an early date, if desired, a plan for the local supervision of the Fraternity chapter homes. . . .

Before adjourning in June the trustees had adopted a resolution setting up a trustee committee (chaired by Judge Frank Taggart) to work with a similar faculty committee to draft regulations governing the Greek letter fraternities in the university, and to investigate the whole question of the value of Chapter houses for such fraternities and the advisability of the establishment and maintenance of such Chapter houses in the University, and to report to the Board at the February [1909] meeting.

In the meantime the Interfraternity Committee of Alumni spent weeks working out their various suggestions and proposed an elaborate system of checks and balances and house rules for the governing of the active chapters. There would be a permanent alumni Interfraternity Advisory Committee, a faculty supervisory committee, and from each active chapter an elected governor and vice-governors, under oath, who were responsible for the internal conduct of the chapter. These officers were to work closely with the interfraternity committee and the faculty committee and to make monthly reports to the dean. In turn the dean was to furnish the governor at proper intervals a list of all members whose average had fallen below eighty. A member whose scholastic record was below standard could have no social engagements of any kind, including parties, concerts, lectures, calling dates, until he had regained this average. The minutest detail of house routine and individual behavior was here set down in black and white: there were to be specific and rigidly maintained study hours, no singing, no playing on instruments during these periods, no gambling, no profanity at any time, no smoking before noon, no entertaining of girls at the house except on the occasion of formal parties and then always with a chaperone. No boy might enter another's room without knocking and receiving permission to enter. "Ponies" were at all times discountenanced. In fact, it would seem that the governor had almost a full-time job.[2]

The trustee resolutions passed at the midwinter meeting in 1909 were much briefer. After a first Article governing eligibility for membership (as stated previously in this chapter) it dealt with:

Chapter Authorization and Initiation
  1. Permission to establish a new chapter or reorganize a withdrawn one must be obtained from the Board of Trustees of the University of Wooster.
  2. All initiation exercises shall be confined to the respective chapter halls or houses and shall not expose the candidate to personal injury or to situations inconsistent with the candidate's self respect.

Social Functions
1. Fraternity or sorority parties shall be limited to one a year for each chapter.
2. Fraternity parties shall be a privilege of the regular chapters and shall not be allowed to inter-fraternity organizations.

Chapter Houses
1. Chapters occupying special houses shall submit to the Dean the names of proposed matrons before making any agreement for their services.
2. Each chapter shall furnish the Dean with a list of all the initiated members. (Kept corrected to date.)
3. At stated intervals the Dean shall furnish to the authorized chapter officers names of those members who have fallen below 80 in any subject of study, specifying subjects.
4. Members who have failed to maintain eligibility requirements, or who have come under discipline shall be denied access to chapter houses until reinstated by the Dean.
5. Only students eligible to membership may room or board in chapter houses.
6. Chapter houses shall at all times be open to visitation by the University authorities.

The fraternities and sororities naturally enough interpreted this as a seal of approval, especially since at the June meeting of 1909 the Board further voted that "these fraternity houses shall be a component part of the men's dormitory group system, to be located by the Board of Trustees." Even President Holden had voted for this. As a consequence of these actions in 1908 and 1909, a third national sorority, Pi Beta Phi, had come into being at Wooster and a fraternity, Delta Tau Delta.

Despite all these resolutions and arrangements, early in 1910—as the reader of the first volume of this history may remember—Mr. Severance had written a letter to President Holden in which he stated in reference to the existence of fraternities at Wooster, "I am decidedly opposed to them," and had suggested that the fraternities and sororities disband and "turn their efforts and their energies" instead "toward the erection of two buildings, one for the young men and one for the young women," in which, he added, "could be housed the Y.M.C.A. and Y.W.C.A." In these buildings both men and women could each "have a social hall where all students could meet." If the students were so minded, he would be "glad to join them in the erection of these two buildings" and would "make a liberal donation toward the same." The offer might as well have been dropped into a well; yet it evidently had set up an undercurrent of conversation far beyond the fringes of the campus, for at the June, 1910, meeting of the Board, while Mr. Severance was still in Europe, President Holden took pains to read to his Board this signed statement:

The information has come to me from numerous sources that the impression prevails that the recent action of Mr. L. H. Severance in reference to Fraternities was inspired by myself. I can readily understand how this impression might naturally grow out of the intimate relations existing between Mr. Severance and myself. But in justice to both Mr. Severance and myself I wish to say with the utmost emphasis that the action of Mr. Severance came to me with as complete surprise as it did to you. I had no knowledge or the slightest intimation that Mr. Severance had any such action even under consideration. He is a man who does his own thinking, and likes to take his own time to do it. He has made this matter no exception to his habit of life.

This he asked to have recorded over his signature and read back to Mr. Severance for his confirmation when the latter was next present at a Board meeting. (This was done and Mr. Severance affirmed its accuracy.) At the same meeting there was written into the record also a telegram from alumni in Shanghai: "Alumni request continuance fraternities, two Fitches, Davises, Corbetts, Hayes, March, Henry." It was only a straw in a slowly rising wind. These men were some of the finest Wooster had graduated in their dedicated Christian service to humanity. It did not seem wise to the trustees to carry the discussion further at this meeting. Moreover, Mr. Severance had written to them that he wished no action taken on his offer now, for he felt that everyone was getting information that would be helpful "in reaching reasonable and wise conclusions." And so on Thursday after attending to other lesser matters they went out quietly into a campus already almost deserted. For the next six months all energies must be spent on winning the campaign. Perhaps in the meantime, some of them thought, the storm might take a different turning.

And for well on to two years it seemed indeed to have done so. In June of 1911 the alumni of the Phi Gamma Delta fraternity presented to the trustees a proposal to purchase from the university a lot upon which to build a chapter house. It was acknowledged and placed on file. Meanwhile the walls of Kenarden were rising.

In the fall of 1911 President Holden had been considering another campaign for a million dollars. He was in no mood to let grass grow under his feet. This time he planned to ask the General Education Board for a conditional offer of $200,000 toward a million. On November 13 he went to see Mr. Severance at his apartment in New York and told him of his purpose. Mr. Severance listened "very attentively," then said, "I wish to think through our problem before I do anything more." If Mr. Severance was not sure, Holden would certainly not go ahead to present any plea to the General Education Board. The matter could rest for the time being. Back at home everything was moving along satisfactorily. In fact, there seemed to be a general atmosphere of happiness and good feeling. Even one of the fraternities, Phi Gamma Delta, was having an open house for all college women. That was an unusual event. It was in November, harvest season. The dining room looked like a cornfield; the walls were lined with fodder and there were pumpkins lying all around. Punch and a light lunch were served. Each guest received a small favor.

Christmas came and New Year's. Then in February after examinations came pledge day, soon thereafter fraternity and sorority initiations, usually attended by town and some out-of-town alumni. Though hazing was strictly forbidden, often the boys amused themselves by making their pledges, as a preinitiation ordeal, do silly but harmless stunts. This time, however, one of the fraternities got rough with one pledge for his supposed insubordination in refusing to do chores for the fraternity at a time when he was due in classes. It was rumored that alumni were the major offenders. Anyhow the boy suffered acute pain, was unable to attend classes for a week, and a physician who examined him feared that there might have been damage to his sciatic nerve. If alumni, supposedly responsible grown men, could so behave, what could one expect of undergraduates? Control had broken down, and everyone who knew of the incident was outraged; even alumni of the guilty fraternity were reputed to have wept in distress. The faculty met in angry session. They would happily have banished the fraternity from the college but for the fact that such action was the prerogative of the trustees. The recent honeymoon of the fraternities had been short-lived. Yet even so on the sixteenth of March, 1912, Delta Delta Delta, a national sorority, was installed at Wooster.

In May of 1912 the dean circulated among the students a questionnaire "concerning all phases of student life." "The answers," said *The Voice* "will give the faculty a very thorough knowledge of conditions existing among the students of the University, socially, morally, spiritually, physically, as it includes questions that will give a complete knowledge of prevailing habits among students, mental and physical." On the first day of the June Board meeting a joint letter from the alumni of Sigma Chi and Phi Gamma Delta informed the trustees that they had taken an option on land adjoining the campus, the option to expire two days hence. With the permission of the trustees they were proposing to buy this land on which to build chapter houses for their respective fraternities. The lot, comprising two and one tenth acres, faced on Beall and Wayne Avenues. Karl Overholt of Pittsburgh, who held the option, would do the purchasing and hold the title in trust for the two fraternities. The request was granted. The petitioners had made a point that these houses would add to dormitory facilities, would "tend to bind a larger and more active body of alumni to the university," and would by their new proximity to the campus make for order, and college rather than exclusively fraternity spirit. They added that "the rapid growth of Wooster necessitates a larger social life." On the second day of their meeting the trustees voted to amend the rules governing fraternities so as to prohibit the initiation of any student into a fraternity or sorority before the beginning of the student's sophomore year. It was in the early days of this same June that the men who had so long been petitioning for a national fraternity, first for a renewal of Phi Delta Theta, later for Sigma Phi Epsilon, saw their hopes realized and a chapter installed.

At this long June meeting the trustees, however, had much more than the affairs of the fraternities to discuss. Mr. Severance was absent "because of serious illness," but President Holden read for their approval and suggestions his proposed letter to the General Education Board asking for another conditional gift for Wooster. He would not present this till later, in the fall, but he was getting ready, listing Wooster's urgent needs for buildings and for endowment, and its financial condition as of the present. Wooster, too, must look ahead to extending its campus. The Executive Committee was asked to consider an option on the adjoining Quinby land, and on the final day of their meeting they voted to buy from Albert Shupe for $6,000 sixteen acres of other land adjoining the campus. The records show that Mr. Severance paid for this for the college. Thus the college year of 1912 ended after all in quiet and in peace and in a spirit of optimism.

In the fall President Holden sent his carefully studied presentation of Wooster's needs to the General Education Board. He had of course gone over it with Mr. Severance and had had his approval. Mr. Wallace Buttrick, Secretary of the General Education Board, had given him an appointment in mid-November and had asked that Mr. Severance come along with him. In the meantime he would study the request. That November night Holden boarded the train for New York with high hopes—and anxiety. Even though his request was granted, and even though Mr. Severance once more matched it, there would be only $400,000 toward the million that he must have. The New Era Movement of the Presbyterian church had just collapsed. He had been counting on that, too, for a large gift. It was all a gambler's chance, but he had faith. What the General Education Board and Mr. Severance had done twice, they would probably do again. A business man did not build up a project just to let it drop. Wooster was deserving; that he knew. He had been gaining for it many friends. It would be a hard pull, to be sure, but he would win, God willing.

The next two days were momentous ones. But let him tell his own story in a letter written on November 14 from New York to Mr. Charles R. Compton, the dean's brother, and one of Wooster's financial secretaries. After a preliminary remark, on another subject, he said:

You are anxious to know how I have gotten on with the presentation of our appeal to the General Education Board, and I wish that I could sit down with you and tell you all that happened. Mr. Severance did not want to go down with me on the 12th, but after much urging he went on the 13th. On the way down he said to me that he had done a great deal of thinking during the past year concerning this new effort, and he had made up his mind to one thing and it was this,—that if he ever did anything more for Wooster, it must clear itself of what he considered to be its great peril, viz, fraternities. He said that he had discovered enough places to place his money that had no such tendencies, and that his mind was fully made up that he had done for Wooster all that he should ever do, if fraternities were continued there. I begged him not to say that, but he said "My interest in Wooster is its Christian aspect, and such a caste system is un-Christian and unwarranted in a Christian college. Now, what I do on this million dollar effort, if the General Education Board starts it, will be pledged only on condition that the fraternities surrender their charters at Wooster."

You can see what a serious predicament the college is in. He evidently feels keenly that no notice was taken of his offer to give to the college a clubhouse, if the fraternities would surrender their charters. It was a mistake on their part not to make some kind of reply, I think.

The question is what to do? Shall the college lose a friend such as **Mr.** Severance and all that it means to the college, or is there enough loyalty among the alumni of the fraternities to save the college from such a disaster and to do it with good spirit and friendliness. Surely, Wooster's growth stops for this generation without Mr. Severance, and I might as well conclude my administration at this point as to struggle along without his help.

It does seem to me that it would be nothing short of a calamity to have this cross of swords at the beginning of another campaign, and that it would take the heart out of us all for the struggle it involves. Do you think that there are wise heads enough, among the different fraternity alumni, to urge the undergraduates to surrender their charters before such a statement could get out?

With a heavy heart I continued the journey and we met Dr. Wallace Buttrick in his office, 17 Battery Place. We were there a little over one hour. Dr. Buttrick read our appeal aloud for $200,000.00 on a million. He commented on it paragraph by paragraph and turned finally to Mr. Severance, and said "You know we are interested in Wooster, Mr. Severance, because you are. You have set your heart on that institution and we believe you know it thoroughly. Do you think that Wooster needs another million to do its work most effectively?" He replied, "I do." "Well," said Dr. Buttrick, "this Board believes in you and is willing to help you realize your ambition to make Wooster the ideal Christian college. I will present this request to the Board at its next meeting, January 26th, and either Dr. Sage or myself will go to Wooster in the meantime to report to the Board in addition anything we may desire to know."

So there you have the facts as they are. If the General Education Board grants our petition of $200,000.00, and Mr. L. H. Severance should duplicate it on conditions above stated, there would be $400,000.00 which practically he would bring to us from his own purse and influence, conditioned as I have mentioned.

Shall we give up the effort or can it be accomplished and still have a loyal alumni?

In a memoir published in *The Wooster Record* [3] thirty-five years later President Holden added some details to the story. Briefly it appeared that an account of the hazing incident had somehow come to the ears of Mr. Severance. He, too, had been outraged but had said nothing until President Holden came to go with him to see Mr. Buttrick. He had made it his business, however, to investigate thoroughly the whole situation, calling in both fraternity and non-fraternity men and quizzing them.[4] He had for several years been gathering statistics on the subject of fraternities. As a result he had made up his mind that henceforth he would not give any money to an institution that tolerated them. To clinch this point he handed to President Holden to read on that memorable day a

deed of gift that he had dictated and had printed relative to a gift that he was about to give to Albany College [Oregon], in which he specified the following: "I understand that Albany College in soliciting this gift from me, has reported that it has no fraternities. If, at any later time, the Board of Trustees of Albany College sees fit to admit fraternities to that institution, this gift of mine shall revert to the College Board of the Presbyterian Church."

There is no doubting that President Holden, as he says, was greatly depressed on the way to Mr. Buttrick's office. He felt caught in the center of a storm. Right there, right then was a great peace, and the thought of a glorious future. Yet he could almost feel already the electrically charged atmosphere of the days ahead, and could see angry clouds rolling on the horizon. Mr. Buttrick had received the two of them most cordially, and had gone quickly to the point. As the conversation ended he had addressed Mr. Severance:

"Our committee has looked over his [Holden's] application, and we have determined that it is in order and a reasonable request, and as secretary of the Board I agree to report it at our next meeting as approved by our committee, provided I have a letter from you, stating that you will subscribe an equal amount toward this effort. May I have such a letter from you before the 17th of January?"

Mr. Severance replied in the following manner: "As President of the Board of Trustees, Dr. Buttrick, I wish to express to you our appreciation of your hearty cooperation with us in the matter of securing funds. I am perfectly willing to say to you at this time, that I expect to be able to write you such a letter as you request in a few days, but just at present there is a matter pending which I wish to have settled before I write this letter."

With that the interview had ended.

On the way back to the Waldorf, Mr. Severance recognizing President Holden's distress, had instructed him: "You go up to the hotel and dictate a letter to Dr. Elias Compton, dean, and to Charles R. Compton, your assistant in field work, and tell them word for word what I have said. Ask Dr. Compton to call a meeting of the faculty and read your letter to them. That's all you have to do. Don't say you are for or against Mr. Severance's proposition. Show them the dilemma in which you are placed and find out what the reaction of the faculty is." This he did.[5] Most of them favored immediate abolition of fraternities. Two were doubtful whether this would accomplish the purpose, whether it might stand in the way of any successful campaign; they could see a great storm in the making and the alienation of hundreds of now loyal alumni. There must be some better way of handling the whole matter.

When President Holden came back he spent three days interviewing every voting member of the faculty, detailing exactly what had happened in New York. When they met together they finally agreed unanimously on the following resolution:

First, that it is the judgment of the Faculty and instructors of the University of Wooster, that it is expedient at this time to request the Fraternities and Sororities to surrender their respective charters and to discontinue their organizations in the University of Wooster.

The following resolutions were also voted but laid on the table until called up by the president:

Second, that a copy of the above resolution be presented to the Trustees of the University.

That the details of the process necessary to carry the first resolution into effect should be left to the committee on fraternities to act in consultation with the president.

That those present at this meeting should refuse to discuss the matter with anyone until especially authorized by the committee on fraternities.

The committee on fraternities assigned to members of the faculty the task of presenting to the ten chapters this request—and the word request was emphasized—with the hope that if they would agree voluntarily to give up their special privileges for the good of the college, a major controversy might be averted. The faculty members were chosen with discrimination. Each one carried with him to read to the chapters three documents: Holden's letter to Charles R. Compton (already quoted), Holden's open letter to alumni in which he outlined the history of his attitude toward fraternities as one of "tolerant neutrality," and the story of his interview in New York with Mr. Severance. Mr. Severance's decision about fraternities had fallen on him, he said "like a bolt of lightning." He went on then to say:

I told him [Mr. Severance] that I had considered our fraternities at Wooster were made up of choice young women and choice young men, and that I had every reason to believe that they intended to maintain the good name and the high standard of the institution. He agreed that this was so. But he did not care to discuss the merits of the question for he had spent several years studying the matter from all sides and had come to his conclusion. He merely wished to drop out of the college life at this point, and wished as a friend, to let me know the reason. He did not even ask that we pay any attention to his feeling in the matter. He merely wants us to understand why he must withdraw as a supporter of The University of Wooster. He does not want the worry and friction that the whole subject has caused him.

It is my suggestion that should the fraternities desire to retain the friendship of Mr. Severance for their Alma Mater they might take action based on his generous offer to erect on the campus a Students' Union for the young men and one for the young women, as he has not withdrawn that offer with its conditions.

The third document was a copy of President Holden's presentation of Wooster's needs to the General Education Board. The college had closed the year 1911–1912 almost even with the world financially. This year of 1912–1913 had opened with a freshman class of 170; the total registration as of October 1 was 586. The summer school had enrolled 1194. Several new buildings were needed. The chemistry building erected ten years before to accommodate in its laboratories 88 students now was overcrowded. One hundred and eighty-eight students were taking chemistry. The college needed a chemistry building for 200, and the cost of this he estimated at $150,000. In the two women's dormitories every room was filled. Fifty-three girls had had to find rooms in town. Seventeen others were missionary daughters in Westminster Home, and fifty-four girls came from homes in town. For a new women's dormitory $150,000 would be required. Y.M.C.A. and Y.W.C.A. club houses were needed at a possible cost of $100,000. The observatory was small and inadequate; originally it had cost $3000 plus. To build and equip a suitable observatory now would require at least another $50,000. He listed as necessary endowment for the teaching staff $300,000 more and for pensions for the faculty an endowment of $200,000. Eight to ten persons must be employed in another year and these could not be had for less than $1500 to $2000 each. The library, which, in thirteen years had grown from 16,000 volumes to 35,000, should have an endowment of $100,000. At the present time there was still no fund for the purchase of books. He was therefore making application to the General Education Board for a conditional offer of $200,000 toward a total of one million dollars, $500,000 of this for buildings, $500,000 for endowment.

The result of this effort on the part of the faculty was that at once Delta Delta Delta, the newest of the sororities, agreed to turn in its charter. Kappa Alpha Theta also agreed to surrender its charter "at the end of the first semester, 1916, on condition that this surrender be not construed as an admission on our part that Kappa Alpha Theta is, has been, or will be a menace or deterrent to the Christian character of Wooster and second that this offer shall in no way be used to our disadvantage as compared with other fraternities." Kappa Kappa Gamma could not comply because of a lack of time for the active chapter to discuss all aspects of the question and to communicate with its alumnae. Pi Beta Phi and the six men's fraternities said that constitutionally they had no right to surrender their charters but they had forwarded the various letters to their national officers.

The Board of Trustees had been summoned to a special meeting on December 20. Mr. Severance begged off. He desired to be left out of the discussion, though he wished his general attitude toward fraternities to be made clear in advance. Seventeen members were present; the case was argued, a motion made but laid on the table until the regular February meeting. In the meantime a committee was to visit Mr. Severance "to get a more thorough understanding of the matters discussed." This was a severe blow to President Holden. He saw that his hopes for help from the General Education Board must be held over for another year, and that to do so allowed time for whatever storm was in the making to gain force and fury.

He must win the battle, if battle there had to be, in February. If he lost it—well, he had already written out his resignation to have ready —and so he wrote to Mr. Severance. Pending that meeting he and Mrs. Holden decided to take a brief vacation after New Year's, in Bermuda. He had been and was still under great strain; he was tired and disappointed. In New York they just missed the ship but soon found a freighter bound for the West Indies.

As the word went out, the college was deluged with letters. National officers of the various fraternities wished to know why. What were they to believe? Alumni both for and against fraternities wrote in. All fall *The Wooster Voice* had been carrying articles both pro and con and this argument continued. The general press got hold of the story and made the most of it—Wooster was selling out for a pot of gold. The place buzzed with excitement. To top it off there was a brief scarlet fever scare among the students; this happily turned out to be a mistaken diagnosis. In December faculty, local trustees, and Westminster Church had got together to celebrate the 75th birthday of the Reverend O. A. Hills, influential trustee and former pastor of the college church. No one would have guessed on that night that anyone in all the community had ever seen any storm signals; such was the apparent serenity of those present. Then came January, and spring seemed to have come. There was rain, sunshine, then thunder and lightning. The robins appeared, and twenty-five boys in Kenarden staged a nightshirt parade. Everything was normal.

The date of the Board meeting was February 13, 1913. This time Mr. Severance came and stated his position. He had been aware of the statements in the press. He denied that he had promised any gift to Wooster provided fraternities were ousted.[6] He had of course not written the letter to Mr. Buttrick; to do that he must wait for the *fait accompli.* He held that fraternities and a Christian college were not consonant. President Holden read a long statement, based on his experience as a student, as a professor at Beloit, and as president of Wooster. He condemned fraternities from almost every point of view. Dean Compton followed in kind. Dean Hughes was called in to say her piece against them. The resolution of the faculty was read and the result of the personal solicitation of the active chapters on the part of the faculty was reported. Nearly all day and far into the night arguments were bandied back and forth, between the group favoring and the group opposed to fraternities. The atmosphere became more and more heated. Once the president was asked whether he was not going to allow the fraternities a chance to defend themselves, and got the reply, "They have no defense." (This report the trustee in question wrote in years later.) At length Judge John E. West offered a compromise resolution:

Whereas: In view of the fact that the Board of Trustees has learned that a majority of the faculty of the University feel that fraternities should not exist in the University of Wooster; and

Whereas: In the opinion of the Board of Trustees of the University of Wooster it would be for the best interest of the University to prohibit the further growth and extension of Fraternities and Sororities among its students, therefore be it Resolved: by the Board of Trustees of the University of Wooster that it is the sense of this Board that the further initiation of members by fraternities and sororities among the students of this University be prohibited on and after this date, and that the Faculty be intrusted with the execution of this action.

Be it further resolved: That the Executive Committee of the Board of Trustees is hereby instructed to assume any land contract that any or all of the fraternities may have entered into before December 20, 1912.

And in taking this action the Board desire to place on record the fact that it is not influenced by any monetary consideration whatsoever.

The vote was taken at 11:30 P.M. and the motion was carried 13 to 10. Those voting in its favor were: Heron, Watson, Wishard, Cobb, Allen, McClellan, A. G. Palmer, Shupe, Hills, Weir, Severance, West, Holden. Those voting against it were: Criley, Foss, Taggart, Wick, Krichbaum, Meese, Schwartz, McClure, Moderwell, S. S. Palmer.

At the end of the meeting Mr. McClure of Youngstown, Mr. Moderwell of Chicago, and Mr. Taggart of Wooster resigned. The next morning the official announcement was read in chapel. Thereupon the students "cut classes in a body. There were parades and bonfires. Prexy Holden was burned in effigy." [7]

Of course somehow the word had gone out the night before that the vote was probably going against the fraternities, that they would probably have to turn in their charters at once. The four sororities met in groups in the dormitories in high excitement. They weren't thinking at all of rules just then or of certificates to be got from the dean; they were thinking of their pledges about to be deprived of membership. The Pi Phi's consequently initiated at once. The Kappas and Thetas waited until after the official announcement and then initiated and so made themselves liable to the charge of "flagrant insubordination." All three had indeed to turn in their charters to Dean Hughes at once, and to proceed to dismantle their chapter rooms. The new initiates were not allowed to wear their pins until after graduation. The Tri Delts had taken a chance and so won. They retained their charter and as soon as commencement of 1916 was over, they initiated their pledges of the winter of 1913.

The date of matriculation this year had been carefully set for the fifteenth of February. Each entering student was given the alternative on that day of signing the matriculation pledge or of receiving honorable dismissal from the college. The pledge was worded:

Whereas: I have voluntarily presented myself to the faculty of the University of Wooster as a candidate for all the rights and privileges of the student body of the institution over which it presides, and

Whereas, I have been made acquainted with the fact that the Board of Trustees has seen fit to prohibit any initiation of members by fraternities or sororities among the students of the University after February 13, 1913,

Therefore, I herewith give my promise to comply with the action and policy of the Board of Trustees; and I agree, without debate, to forfeit all rights and privileges of a member of the student body, should I in any way unite myself with, or seek

to maintain such an organization in the institution as long
as I am a member of it.

The pledge was signed by all but 11 freshmen, and "most" of these
"did not appear for matriculation."

The faculty, however, were still suspicious of what might have
happened among the men; they therefore required *all* members of
the fraternities to take an oath not only that they would obey the
order of the Board of Trustees but that they had not been a party to
any initiation, directly or indirectly since February 13, 1913. They
were required to take an additional oath:

I solemnly swear that I take the above oath without any mental
reservations and that no oath taken by me in the past is inconsistent with
the fulfillment of this oath.

The major storm was over, but it had left in its path an aftermath of
bitterness among many alumni that would take years to overcome
and heal. In the April, 1913, Wooster *Quarterly* at the head of the
story of the trustees' action Mr. Notestein had written:

Let us plead, not for harmony of opinion . . . ; but for a unanimous
tolerance of opposing judgment; for a recognition of our common falli-
bility and a patient waiting for clarity of vision in ourselves or in those
who oppose us, or in both of us in equal measure.

Yet the bitterness was not that of a moment; it went deep. Had the
trustees' action been framed to take effect at the end of the college
year, and not now at the moment of matriculation, the resentment
would still have been real, but the fraternities possibly would not
have felt tricked to the same degree. They had worked hard to choose
their new members; their disappointment and the disappointment of
their pledges in not being allowed initiation was real. Yet this quick
demonstration on the morning of February 13 was only a token of
what was going on in the minds of these young people, and as the
months went on there was no easing of resentment. All the logic that
"Compy" had tried to instil in their minds was but a whisper beating
on deaf ear drums. The college had allowed itself to be bought out,
they felt, not even for a mess of pottage, but only for a smell of

pottage floating in at the window. The fraternity men went to classes as usual, but otherwise they were as if on strike. They resigned all class offices; they absented themselves from all inter-class banquets and class parties; they withdrew from the teams. Why should they win for Wooster? Their loyalty was as if a dry stick tossed into a flame.

Of course there were exceptions. In fact, reading *The Voice* for these weary months one gets an impression that faculty and community were trying their best to put on an air of nonchalance. In the first day after spring vacation every classroom door in Kauke Hall was hung with a bunch of trailing arbutus, though by whom nobody knew or was telling. On April 12 Westminster Church had a dinner and reception in Severance gymnasium for the whole college. Nearly one thousand persons were there. Chalmers Martin was the toastmaster. Mr. Weir, the pastor, of course spoke, also Professor C. G. Williams of the Ohio Agricultural Experiment Station, and Clarence Bahler, president of the Student Senate, a fraternity man. The glee clubs sang and Mr. Lean gave a humorous reading. On another night, Mrs. Samuel Morris gave a "brilliant" piano recital in the chapel. The Girls' Glee Club was allowed to take a trip into the west-central part of the state during the Easter vacation. Twenty-two students went to Cleveland to see *Robin Hood* at the Euclid Avenue Theater. A new tea room had been opened at 658 Beall Avenue serving tea and chocolate every afternoon from three to five. Miss Hughes entertained the seniors at Holden Hall along with the Holdens and the Kelsos. On the night of March fourteenth the Forensic League had scheduled an all-college dinner at Kenarden (admittance fifty cents) where Chef Nissen outdid himself. That night Wooster had defeated both Pittsburgh and Allegheny in debate. The team from Pittsburgh were guests. Mr. Gould was toastmaster. Mr. Lean, in a sense the hero of the occasion, because he had trained the teams, spoke. There was a general jollification that went on until after eleven. Special permissions had been granted.

The world seemed to go on as usual. Barnum and Bailey would be coming later in the spring; the calliope and elephants, and the great red wagons full of animals and clowns would parade all the way from the Pennsylvania Railroad station along Liberty Street to the Fair Grounds. In Columbus Billy Sunday had been preaching—

"Teakettle" Davis had heard him and had written a commendatory article a column long in *The Voice*. The students at Ohio State had "come out against the new-fangled dances," notably the Turkey Trot. At Oberlin the attendance had been limited to one thousand. And at Wooster the Intercollegiate Prohibition League, a chapter of the national organization, had made its debut; and a few moustaches had appeared among the students.

Routine work and routine play went on. This winter, however, there had been some new courses, one in household chemistry, one in Oriental history, and one in Greek and Roman art. For this last the college had been accumulating slides and photographs of the masterpieces of antiquity. Down at the conservatory a victrola and records had been bought. The girls at Hoover at the call of Mrs. Crawford, the matrons got together and voted almost unanimously for self-government. The basketball season had been good. Wooster had defeated Ohio University, 41–23; Kenyon twice, Denison and Miami. In baseball she had scored over Oberlin 2–0. Ralph W. Fulton had taken the state intercollegiate tennis championship. At a track meet in Columbus, J. E. Moore had run the two-mile course in 9 minutes 41.6 seconds, and Carl Bischoff, '14, had won the Cleveland *Press* race against 100 competitors.

This was the year, it seemed, when everything happened. One light case of smallpox was discovered in Kenarden. Fourteen had been exposed. All of these men were moved to the Kauke house east of the conservatory. Happily no other cases developed. One night the girls of Holden Hall turned the tables and went serenading; after all it was leap year. "Jackie Black," who in addition to teaching geology, for years had been training all the youngsters of the community how to tell a phoebe from a peewee and where a hermit thrush might most readily be found, organized a class in bird study for the college students. They met on Wednesday and Saturday behind Kauke Hall at 5:15 A.M. In chapel one morning, May seventh, Dean Compton offered President Holden special felicitations. It was his fiftieth birthday. The students rose and gave him the chautauqua salute.

In the meantime, under the guidance of the Student Senate, plans were going ahead for the greatest Color Day yet. It was to be an Old English May day, and Mary Mateer, '14, had been elected queen. In the evening after it was all over Wooster would be entertaining the intercollegiate oratorical contest with orators coming from Muskingum, Monmouth, Depauw, Gustavus Adolphus, Beloit, Olivet, and William Jewell. Muskingum was sending up a delegation of fifty persons as guests of the college. The dawn of May 16 was made for a queen. It was perfect. The dew was still on the grass when at eight o'clock Mr. Erb at the organ of the chapel began playing the "Pilgrims' Chorus." Then the Conservatory Association sang "The Legend of the Chimes" from *Robin Hood*. President Holden was on the platform and read a telegram from Mr. Severance:

Not forgetting the men and women serving valiantly in foreign lands or filling spheres of usefulness at home, may I add to the pleasure and good cheer of this Color Day by presenting for the future efficiency of Wooster's sons and daughters a new and more complete athletic field?

In response to this the following answer was sent, signed by "The Assembled Friends of Wooster":

Mr. L. H. Severance
Waldorf Astoria, New York, N.Y.
The students, alumni, faculty, trustees, and friends of the University of Wooster send their most cordial greetings to you on this best of all "Color Days" and desire to express their deep appreciation of your splendid gift of a modern and much needed Athletic Field. Our hearts go out in thanksgiving to our heavenly Father for all that He has inspired you to do for our dear old college. We have missed you today, but we give three hearty cheers for the best friend Wooster has ever had, and wish you many, many happy years with us.

Mr. Holden then told the audience that for several years the trustees had been thinking about a new field. Mr. Severance had looked around and had decided that for this purpose ten acres northeast of Holden Hall should be bought. The cost of the new field, when finished, was estimated as between $20,000 and $25,000.

The pageant on the quadrangle was memorable. At the call of rain drops and sun the flowers of the springtime, violets, bluebells, buttercups, roses, poppies awakened; then trumpets sounded the coming of the queen preceded by heralds, crown bearers, flower girls (Dorothy and Lorna Dunn, faculty children), and followed by her eight attendants. After her crowning by last year's queen, she watched from her flower-bedecked throne the dances and spectacles in her honor. Milkmaids and chimney sweeps, Mother Goose and all her children, King Cole, Jack and Jill carrying a tub, Three Black Crows with pointed beaks and long flapping wings, Little Miss Muffet and her spider, Humpty Dumpty, and the Man in the Moon—looking down from the top of Kauke Hall—they were all there. There were a tournament and dances, and an opera of Julius Caesar, in which Roman citizens in their togas appeared, Caesar, Brutus, Mark Antony, Cassius, and Caesar's ghost, Portia and Calpurnia also. Then just before the end came the rose wreath drill and the winding of the Maypole. The queen riding in a white chariot drawn by black horses led the grand parade off the quadrangle.

In the afternoon Wooster defeated Kenyon in baseball. Before the oratorical contest in the evening—which Muskingum, Ohio's representative won—Mr. Erb gave a twilight organ recital. It was the most ambitious and well-ordered Color Day Wooster students had yet attempted and it set a pattern for the future.

In a growing college new patterns were always being set, old ones discarded. Wooster had long since realized that it was not a university despite its corporate title. It did not so aspire. The title was not only inaccurate but pretentious. The faculty in February had asked the trustees to consider making a change from university to college. The latter had consequently at the midwinter meeting appointed three lawyers from their number to study the recommendation and report later. Many years before the medical school so loosely tied to the college had gone its separate way. The Bible and Missionary Training School founded by Mr. Severance was after all but a department to which no degree was attached. In its earlier days the conservatory had given a degree but since 1899 only a diploma. This year of 1913 it was once again giving a bachelor of music to five or six persons, yet most of its work was in private lessons in voice, or piano, or organ to such college students as requested these.

The faculty this spring had voted another innovation. Hereafter the symbols used in their grading would be alphabetical. This was a move in the right direction. The numerical system had been inaccurate, for who was wise enough to say whether a student rated an 89 or a 90, a 74 or a 75? A, B, C, to be sure, were approximations, yet grades anyhow were only guesses by men more or less experienced in interpreting the student's mind and application to his subject.

Commencement of 1913 passed without incident. A class of 71 was graduated. The Corporation Lunch was served for the first time in Severance Gymnasium; the basement of Kauke Hall was no longer adequate. There were several announcements. Lester Wolfe, the registrar, had resigned. Regretfully at this time the college was bidding goodbye also to J. Lawrence Erb. In his place as director of the conservatory Victor Vaughn Lytle would be coming. He was a graduate of Knox College with his degree in music from Oberlin, where also he had been teaching. He was an Associate of the American Guild of Organists. An announcement of special interest, however, was that Miss Gingrich and Miss Pendleton had been granted leave of absence on salary for a year. Without any break they had been teaching at Wooster for twenty and twenty-three years respectively. Both would go to Europe. From there Miss Pendleton would go on to India to visit old familiar places, for as a young woman she had taught in India; thence she would go to Ceylon to visit her sister. The Comptons also were bound to Europe though for the summer only. Soon after commencement President Holden and four other citizens of Wooster, two of them trustees, would be leaving for Portland, Oregon, as delegates to the World Christian Citizenship Conference. It would open on June 29.

Then on the twenty-fifth the blow struck. A message from Cleveland told of the death of Louis H. Severance. He had attended commencement, had chairmanned as usual the trustee meeting. He had seemed happy and well. He had closed that meeting with a simple, humble, and moving prayer which they all remembered. The day after his return to Cleveland he had been out on one of Cleveland's golf courses, then on Monday he was gone. Everyone was thunderstruck, President Holden, of course, most of all, for to him Mr. Severance had been both friend and counselor. He had kept Severance's picture over his desk at his office, on his chiffonier at his home. He suddenly felt alone in a weary world. His dreams had faded. He went to the funeral at the home of Solon Severance, spoke at the memorial service at Woodland Avenue Presbyterian Church. Later, on July 8, such trustees as could come met in their room in Kauke Hall to honor the man who had given so much of his time and life to Wooster. They voted that a memorial minute to him should be printed in the next college catalogue. In early October a formal memorial service for him was held in the chapel.

Louis Henry Severance was a person of many and strong interests. He had been a titan in business but he had been much else in his seventy-five years. Of English ancestry he had grown up in Cleveland, the son of a drygoods merchant. He had attended Cleveland's public schools, and then at seventeen had gone into banking. During this apprenticeship—though it was considerably more than that—he did his hitch of 100 days in the Civil War. In 1864 he was enticed, however, by the oil industry, in which he found himself much interested, to Titusville, Pennsylvania. At length, in 1876, he returned to Cleveland as treasurer of the Standard Oil Company of Ohio, a position he held until his retirement in 1894. From that time on he was a free agent, traveling and developing other business and later philanthropic interests. Sometime in the 90's he formed with Herman Frasch, Frank Rockefeller, and F. B. Squire, the Union Sulphur Company, which became one of the major producers of sulphur in the world. Frasch had invented a new method of mining sulphur by injecting superheated steam into the sulphur-bearing rocks and pumping out melted sulphur. Severance had other investments, too, in both steel and salt. His philanthropies were far-reaching, extending to China, India, and Korea. He believed ardently in Christian missions and in training the leaders for them, and for this, though he was not himself a college man, he looked to the Christian colleges. This was his hobby. In this he found his soul's satisfaction.

VI

An Interpretation and a Variety of Angels

> For I also am a man set under authority, . . . and I say unto one, "Go" and he goeth; and to another, "Come" and he cometh; and to my servant, "Do this," and he doeth it. *Luke* 7:8.

PRESIDENT HOLDEN had a kind of magic touch with men of wealth. It is astounding that in his first interview with Andrew Carnegie he had won an invitation to come back and call whenever he was in New York, that on his first visit to Henry Clay Frick he had won for the college a library building, that on his first meeting with Louis H. Severance in Cleveland he had so impressed him that two weeks later Severance, with the Reverend Mr. Hiram Haydn, was on the grounds looking over the institution.

If one reads Holden's memoirs of these occasions, one soon becomes aware that they were all of a pattern. Of course he had admired these men at a distance, had made himself familiar with their careers and interests, but that knowledge or that admiration was not alone the magic formula that unlocked their pocketbooks. Not at all. Instinctively he understood their motivations and their manners. He was sometimes blunt; so were they. They were used to giving orders; so was he. He talked the same hard-hitting language, looked them in the eye, sometimes even telling them wherein their thinking was all wrong—as when he remarked to Carnegie that he might better have built libraries not for small towns but for the smaller colleges where every chair would have been filled from dawn to dark. He at once established a relationship of mutual respect. It was easy to turn away a man who expected to be turned down. But one who met you as an equal, who behaved as if he were a director of the company, to turn him down was harder. Carnegie had once said to Holden, "I like a man who believes in his cause whether I agree with him or not." It is clear that Holden had seen in his call to Wooster the fulfillment of a dream. He believed in Christian education. He believed in youth. He believed that under God he had a work to do. He believed in the man to whom he was talking; otherwise he would never have wasted time on him.

Holden had first met Severance in the spring of 1901,[1] having been given an introduction by the latter's brother, Solon Severance. As Holden entered the office in the Old Arcade, Severance greeted him with:

"So you are the new president of the University of Wooster! Well, sir, you have got a hard job before you, and you are built for the task. What did you want to see me about?"

I replied, "Mr. Severance, I have come to ask you a question. May I ask it?"

"Yes," he said, "certainly, what is it?"

"I hope you will not think it impertinent, but I would like to ask why you are not interested in the University of Wooster."

Holden told him that he was familiar with his philanthropic and religious interests, knew that he was a trustee of Oberlin and of Western Reserve, and an elder in the Presbyterian Church. Why indeed was he not interested in the Presbyterian college of Ohio?

There was no beating about the bush in this approach. Holden had been direct, even audacious. He had startled Severance, had struck him where he was most vulnerable. At that moment, whether by accident or arrangement, Mr. Haydn, pastor of Cleveland's Old Stone Church, had walked in. Severance quickly shifted gears. "This is the man," he said, "for you to interest in the University of Wooster," and turning to Haydn, asked, "Have you ever been down to Wooster, Dr. Haydn?" The upshot was, of course, that before Holden left the office a visit had been arranged for both these men. When they came, they saw the students in class and in chapel, looked over the whole plant, even talking with Bennett down in his basement laboratory and seeing the X-ray machine with which he was then experimenting. As the two men left, Severance said to Holden, "Young man, you are going to have a fire here some day, with that Chemistry department in the basement. . . . I would advise you to keep it [the building] well insured." It was on the following December 11 that Old Main burned to the ground.

In Holden's approach there was always the direct question at the beginning, later the unexpected something in the conversation that subtly flattered, or piqued the curiosity,—though one would say that by nature Holden never leaned toward flattery:

". . . if you live ten years longer," he had said to Carnegie on that first visit, "I prophesy that . . . you will be one of the greatest givers to Christian education the world has ever seen. . . ." He said this even though by this time Carnegie had explained that he was not a member of any church, and that he had no intention of ever giving a cent to a Christian college.

"This is strange, very strange," Holden said on his second visit, having just been turned down on his request for money for Wooster's rebuilding. And there follows immediately Holden's own sleep-walking scene [2] in which he relates to a now curious Carnegie the parable of the man who fell among thieves on the way from Jerusalem to Jericho, and of the good Samaritan, now turned business man, who after the priest and Levite had passed by, came to the rescue of the "sandbagged" traveler, bound up his wounds, put him on an ass and took him to the inn. And Holden went out with the pledge of $100,000 conditioned on the raising of the rest in the next sixty days.

And to Mr. Frick when he had just announced to Holden that it would do no good to talk with him, that he was not interested in Christian education, he parried,

I think you are greatly mistaken, Mr. Frick. I listened to President Eaton . . . for a half hour defending your stand with labor, as a business man and manufacturer, . . . can it be that the colleges of this country can command their students to listen to their presidents set forth your interests as business men when you are not interested in them?

In the end they were all left with a friendly feeling for this intrepid young man who saw in the man he was addressing possibilities that he himself had not known he had. In addition to the $100,000 toward the rebuilding, Carnegie in 1907 had given $50,000 to Wooster for endowment. Severance's gifts were everywhere. He had been Wooster's angel.

There were, of course, lesser angels whose interest also he had won, and some who had come of their own accord to lay their gifts before this president. There was that morning of his first commencement at Wooster. It was a June day, in the old gymnasium. The makeshift platform had been built in the north end and decorated with spruce boughs, and mock orange in bloom. The doors were open to the east and west to let whatever air there was pass through. All morning the graduates of 1900 had been giving their orations while down below the packed audience seated on hard camp chairs fanned and sweated and squirmed. In that audience on her first visit to Wooster, from Chicago, was the aunt of one of the younger faculty and cousin of one of the year's graduates, John Frame (who was later to spend his life as a medical missionary in Persia). Toward the end of the long session she sent up her card to President Holden. On it was her name, Sarah Frame Davidson, and beneath this a pencilled message, "I will pledge $15,000 for a chapel on condition that $15,000 more shall be subscribed for the same purpose." [3] By the next commencement her conditional offer had been met. So it happened that when the great fire occurred Memorial Chapel was already in building.

There is no question that President Holden really believed in all the men he was approaching for money. They may have been business tycoons, but to him were friends. Years later after he had been long gone from Wooster, he returned to make the town his home and to educate his two children at the college. One day he was attending a seminar for local ministers who wished to have explained some of the economics of the great depression. Some of these men, outraged by the tales of pyramiding and other machinations of the period, were lambasting the whole race of big business men. Holden listened for a while, then could take it no longer: "They aren't evil men; I know them; some of them were my friends; they were praying men." At that, one of the ministers leaned over and touched the shoulder of another in the group. "On whom were they preying?" he muttered.

Though President Holden counted big business men among his friends, he was just as familiar with college professors and students, with architects, as plans were drawn for buildings, with contractors who put them up, often with workmen on the job. He was always inspecting,[4] often checking to see that all the materials necessary were on order. One late summer afternoon when Kenarden Lodge was nearing completion he walked across the campus to show a visiting friend the new dormitory. Work was over for the day and a watchman on guard. Holden asked permission to go in and was refused; the watchman had orders to let no one in. In the end,

Holden explained that he was president of the University. This statement made no impression. The watchman would not have let in the President of the United States if he had applied; he was under orders. The two men turned away. A few days later, however, Holden made a point of hunting out that watchman, commending him for his fidelity, and assuring him that if he ever wished a job on the campus crew he would personally see that he got it. So it happened that Angelo Santoro from the local Italian colony was for thirty-six years a trusted and loved employee of the college.

Little by little, Angelo came to feel that he owned the campus, and he was proud of his position and of his workmanship. He mowed lawns, cleaned off snow, plastered in the dormitories, pointed out with amazing accuracy where the underground steam lines ran, gave advice to painters, plumbers, and carpenters. But most of all in his later years he delighted, bricklayer and mason that he was, in pottering about the walks watching out for every broken or frost-heaved brick lest it become a public hazard. Through the years he was called on for many jobs beyond the line of duty, once removing a skunk from the window well of the president's home without leaving even a tell-tale scent. Occasionally of an evening he was asked to drive away the starlings from the pine grove in Galpin Park. Then he would bring a whole posse of his countrymen from down beyond the railroad tracks; they would bang boards and thump buckets till anyone would have supposed that there was an old fashioned belling in the neighborhood. On Hallowe'en nights he and others patrolled the campus just to make sure that no cows strayed onto the porch of Hoover Cottage or no ammonium iodide crystals were strewn down the aisles of the chapel. For that occasion he came in uniform, that of the village band of which he had been cornetist in his native Abruzzo. He brought his cornet, too. One blast from it sent any mischief-minded students scurrying. Among his fellow workers he at length felt himself a kind of elder statesman responsible for their behavior on the job, especially if they, too, were Italians. One day in high dudgeon he appeared at the door of the director of maintenance. "Mr. Dick," he said, "just look at that John—just look at him! . . . That John he buys overalls just like mine—now he lean on shovel —don't work—people look at him and think it's me!"

When the time for retirement came and he was told, he just could not understand what was meant. He had always worked; he expected to keep right on, and did. But one day he was told that he was to come to the chapel service the next morning, that the president wanted him there. The next day he sat on the platform along with President Lowry and President-emeritus Wishart. He was introduced to the faculty and the students and his story was told and then he was presented a certificate: "The College of Wooster gratefully recognizes the faithful service of Angelo Santoro for 36 years." His fellow workers, too, were there and through a representative gave him a watch. Then Angelo himself made a little speech. At the end he pulled from one pocket of his coat a tiny flag of the United States, from a pocket on the other side an equally small banner of The College of Wooster. These he held above his head and waved. "Under these two flags," he said, "I have served"; and then he sat down amid an uproar of clapping. Finally he knew what retirement meant. This was it. It was a great day, a great day to remember. But it was all over, and he went home. The next year in December he died of a heart attack. In the lobby beside the president's office in Galpin Hall there hang the photographs of some of the various benefactors of Wooster. Among them is one of Angelo Santoro, once of Collepietro, Italy, friend not just of one but of four of Wooster's presidents.

Integrity, loyalty, gentleness—they are attributes of greatness wherever found, in working men or millionaires. Angelo had them. So had Louis H. Severance. Once aroused, his interest in Wooster had grown rapidly. He had come on the Board of Trustees in 1901; he became its president in 1905 and so remained until his death in 1913. He had given thought and time to Wooster's needs, as well as more than half a million dollars; and he had stood behind President Holden like a rock. In a statement (see page 58) made to the Board in 1910 Holden spoke of the "intimate relations" existing between them. He was right. He was right also that Severance had been a praying man. He had been in fact deeply religious, and had said over and over again that it was Wooster's "Christian aspect" that he valued above all else. To be sure, he had been the retired treasurer of Standard Oil of Ohio, had been so closely identified with the Rockefeller interests that twice, in 1907 and 1910, he had matched the conditional offer of their General Education Board to Wooster dollar for dollar. On the proposed third drive, that Board had been but waiting for his word that he would do so again before offering $200,000 more to Wooster toward another million of endowment. He had belonged to the era of the dominance of big business. He was used to weighing seriously the pros and cons of any situation, and then, to arriving at a decision that thenceforth was binding on all concerned. In this he, too, had been but following a familiar pattern, the business pattern of his time. Everything he did for Wooster he had thought of first in terms of Christian service. He had set up for five years the Florence H. Severance Bible and Missionary Training School at Wooster. It was named for his deceased wife Florence Harkness Severance. This he had believed in wholeheartedly. In 1907–1908 he had made a trip around the world, visiting especially Presbyterian missions. He had built and equipped the Presbyterian Hospital at Seoul, Korea, of which Dr. Avison was the head. (Dr. Avison had three children at Wooster.) He had been interested also in helping the Presbyterian Hospital at Chefoo, China, where Dr. Oscar F. Hills, son of Wooster's O. A. Hills, was in charge. As he had gone around he had seen the work of many of Wooster's sons and daughters in missionary service, and many others, too. He had seen in India the untouchables for whom life held nothing but poverty and disease save as Christian missionaries ministered to them, and he had seen the Brahmins, the aristocrats of India. He had been revolted by the inequities of the caste system. As President Holden had said at the dedication of Severance gymnasium, Mr. Severance had not built the gymnasium that the boys might win more games but that their bodies, that were the "temples of God," should become pure and clean and strong, the better to serve the Kingdom of God. He had offered in 1910 a "liberal donation" toward the erection of Y.M.C.A. and Y.W.C.A. buildings on the campus because he had believed so utterly in Christian democracy.

He was religious and he was generous. Aside from his larger gifts he had added at least $30,000 toward the building and equipping of Holden Hall and he had paid for three missionary furlough homes at Wooster. He had looked around for little things to do that would make more pleasant or less rugged the paths of various persons in the college community. Some of these little gifts came anonymously but no one really questioned long from whom they had come. There was, for instance, a set of *The Expositor's Bible,* in many volumes, to one of the faculty, pictures for the walls of Holden Hall, and a fine young horse to one of the older professors who because of a heart condition could no longer walk to the college. He was thoughtful and courteous, truly a gentleman of the old school.

On the occasion of the unveiling at the college of Mr. Severance's portrait, Mr. Grumbine had read a sonnet of his own composing in honor of Wooster's benefactor:

> With courtly grace he walks the busy ways
> Of kingly daring and of great emprise
> Where traffic unto traffic multiples
> And argosy with argosy repays.
> Sweet Labor laughs to hear the lusty
>   phrase
> Of high command; and industry replies
> With quick obedience till her shuttle flies
> In sounding cadence through the singing days.
> Captain of commerce, —where he bids men go!
> Not only this but where he calls they hear:
> The hurt are healed, the rude are led to find
> The paths of peace, the young are brought to know
> The ways of knowledge, and the skies revere
> His shining name, "A Lover of Mankind."

Even within academic halls that voice of authority had been sensed.

VII

Hurricane Boreas

IF Hurricane Alpha had long and far-reaching effects, Hurricane Boreas was even more disastrous, because it struck people down; they lost their sense of humor; they lost their tolerance; they lost their perspective; and some of the younger generation literally lost their religion as they looked on, and saw friendships that had lasted well on to a lifetime torn to bits and scattered to the winds. Each tornado gained in destructive power, and this was but the second of three in quick succession. If persons of a Christian college could so behave, on whom could one depend?

John Howard Dickason, principal of the academy and director of the summer school, had for years been a somewhat controversial figure. He had thousands of warm friends over the state. Teachers of high schools and elementary schools loved him.[1] He had the common touch. He knew how to meet them. He spoke their language. He was sympathetic in their difficulties. He offered the helping hand; he went the second mile. The farmers all over the countryside knew and loved him. He could milk a cow with any of them; he could plow a straight furrow. He went to their institutes and talked to them of education for their children. He was one of them.[2] He, too, was a deep believer in Christian education, interested in promoting the work of the church wherever there was opportunity, and both the Wooster academy and the summer school offered the opportunity. He had great organizational skills,[3] and he was a hard worker, up before dawn and on his way. However, he was essentially a school man rather than an academic. His background was limited to the farm and small midwestern communities. He had an innate courtesy because of the goodness of his heart, but he did not have the polish demanded by the great world. Many of Wooster's faculty found him just too folksy, too unsophisticated, too willing to compromise academic standards. In the academy at Wooster it was "'Aunty Pen,'" not "Dicky," who brought students to book, who insisted that goals be reached. For the academic person, his advertising for the summer school was crude; it savored of the middlewestern public square on a Saturday afternoon rather than of a college:

A man with an education has the consolation of knowing it can't blow off like a woman's switch.

The proverb "Take the bull by the horns," is one that a sane man never follows twice. However, if the question at issue is that of attending Wooster Summer School there is no danger. Hundreds have been elevated thereby and no one hurt.

There are a good many young women who will get to heaven all right, who can't bake a decent loaf of bread to save their lives. A domestic science course in the Wooster Summer School would be a boon to the men who are to be their husbands.

Talk about the long sleep of Old Rip! There are several thousand teachers in Ohio, too, who have never learned to open their eyes. If they would join a nature study class at the Summer School, their peepers would snap.

"The proof of the pudding is in the eating." There are literally hundreds who have attended Wooster Summer School the past few years who have doubled their salaries and reached positions they never would have attained without such training. You are invited to a seat at the table next summer. Then you'll smile, too.

There are a lot of people who would sing better in the Golden City if they had spent a term or two studying music in the Wooster Summer School.

A small pup at a political convention recently by nosing around dislodged a hornet's nest from one of the benches and created more of a stir than the party platform did. Those who attend Wooster Summer School will never think themselves in a hornet's nest, though they will find themselves in the center of stirring activities.

Wooster extends to you the glad hand. Its grip is so hearty that it makes you wince, but you will never forget it.

The trouble was that this type of glad hand did make academics wince, and they didn't forget it. It was cheapening Wooster, they thought and said. This was the rural Middle West at its worst, and no group of men hailing from the East or the cities could stomach it. The college itself was suffering the growing pains of sophistication. The president had after all been bringing in men from Princeton, Johns Hopkins, Yale, and other universities and colleges far from the smell of new mown hay. The faculty blushed to find Wooster represented by such advertising. Some had seen something of the great world; some just wished they had, and fell in quickly with the captious crowd.

The situation was not helped by the local advertising carried in *The Summer Breeze,* the hot weather counterpart of *The Wooster Voice,* edited by a former college student. There appeared not only the simple sample cards of the various merchants in town:

of Craighead's, the Students' Caterers. Crackers, Fruits, Candies, Pickles, Onions.
of John Saal, Dealer in Fresh and Salt Meats.
of Nick Amster, the One Price Clothier.
of Laubach and Boyd, Druggists.
of Ira Droz: Picnic Wagons, Cab, and Baggage Transfer.
of Dawson, Leading Photographer. Opposite the Archer House.
of Hunsiker's Bakery.

but there were the notices of other dealers who had attempted to tune in to the mood of the agricultural center in which they did their business, so that as one turned the pages of *The Summer Breeze* one came upon not only the pictures of Wooster's "white city on the hill" but what some ardent local copy writer had to say of Pinkerton's Steam Laundry:

> Untidy men, brace up and change that dirty shirt—
> Don't you know you're looking tough, covered o'er with dirt?
> Ten cents will make it clean—white as the driven snow—
> At Pinkerton's Wooster laundry, where all the people go.
> There is where the travelling man has his washing done
> Likewise every business man, every mother's son.
>   . . . . .
> The mother sends her finest goods, her linen and her lace,
> Because the work is neatly done, with ease, dispatch, and grace.
>   . . . . .
> Country folk who would look nice and citified,
> Patronize our laundry—the bridegroom and the bride.—
> Fair damsels, dressed in white,
> Who want to catch a beau,
> Patronize the Wooster—where all the people go.

This was in the Souvenir Edition that the summer school students bought to take home with them to show their friends what Wooster was like. In the same issue, to be sure, was an article by Sylvester F.

Scovel, former president of Wooster, on the "Final Aim in Education." That final aim, he stated, was not physique, not intellect, not
the aesthetic faculty—though all of these were important—but character: "that substance of soul which determines beforehand what a
man will do in given circumstances. It is that indefinable something
which makes sure that he will do the thing that ought to be done. It
is a habit of soul. Character is to the man what ripeness is to
vegetation, what proportion is to architecture, what exactness is to
mathematics; it is her perfection."

The Wooster summer school had had a long and honorable history. It had been opened in 1876, really to supplement the academy
or preparatory department; so many students seeking admittance
were lacking a credit or two. By coming the preceding summer they
could make up these deficiencies and enter with full freshman standing. This was desirable from their point of view and from that of the
college, which did not wish to get a reputation of allowing students
to enter who were not fully prepared for the rigors of college work.
The summer school at the beginning had been under the personal
direction of the president. Through all its early years he chose its
small faculty, most of them from the teaching staff of the preparatory
department and the college, whose proficiency he knew. The program, though only eight weeks long, was intensive, six days a week
with classes for two or more 55–minute periods a day. Examinations
were strict and credits were earned. In the beginning there had been a
need especially for courses in the languages, including English grammar and spelling, in Latin, Greek, German, and later French, in
algebra and geometry, even sometimes in arithmetic, occasionally in
geography and history. Soon, too, students who had failed a course in
college came back in the summer to try to make it up so that even
some work of college grade was gradually added, physics, chemistry,
biology, geology, and advanced languages. There were certain frills,
of course, to add to the attractiveness of the program: gymnastics
with special application to the laws of health, a six-weeks' course in
"elocution including gesticulation," individual training in oil and
china painting especially for the "young ladies," music—vocal,
piano, or pipe organ instruction—and a special course in bookkeep-
ing and penmanship. At Mr. Kirkwood's instigation, also, some

attention had, as early as 1879, been accorded to teachers and to those looking forward to teaching in the public schools. For Wooster to help in this way was just an expansion of its educational and Christian service.

President Taylor and President Scovel had given the summer school their blessing but had done little advertising. The attendance ranged from forty to sixty persons. In time, however, the president turned it over to the direction of John G. Black, adjunct professor of mathematics, an exacting and humane scientist with many strings to his bow. He was a superb teacher, clear and definite, and nobody fooled him. He was a delightful companion as well for young and old; he knew birds and animals, trees, plants, fossils, and rocks. He saw in the contours of the hills where the glaciers had been and had receded; he pointed out the peneplain on the far horizon. And on Sundays or in daily chapel he could stand in the pulpit and read the scriptures and talk with quietness and humility to the Lord and Master of all. Though many thought him severe in the classroom— and he was—he was nonetheless the soul of patience and understanding.

In 1895 there came a change. President Scovel named as principal of the preparatory department a graduate of the class of 1895, a man with high scholastic standing, of unbounded energy, and bubbling with ideas. John Howard Dickason thought nothing of bicycling to Savannah, Ohio, about thirty miles away, and back over the week end. Mr. Black at once brought him in as his assistant in the summer school. The next year, 1896, he became director of the summer school, and Mr. Black superintended only the work for college credits. Things now began to happen. In 1895 attendance at the summer school had been 49. In 1896 it was 140; in 1897, 210; in 1898, 285; in 1899, 350; in 1900, 436; in 1901, 438; in 1902, 420; in 1903, 447. It continued to mount until in 1914 it was very close to 1500.

Through all the early years even into President Holden's administration it had had the enthusiastic backing of the Board of Trustees. They saw in it a chance to help many young teachers of Ohio; they saw in it, moreover, a feeder for the college, for if these young teachers went away from Wooster enthusiastic, as most of them did, they were sure to speak glowingly of the college to prospective students and to their parents. In 1900 the trustees had taken action as follows:

Whereas the Summer School held in the University buildings has been conducted with conspicuous success by two of the professors of the Preparatory Department of the University for the past few years and is to be conducted during the coming year,

Resolved that the Board of Trustees of the University hereby endorse this movement, and regard it as an invaluable adjunct to the educational forces of the institution. We hereby grant the use of the buildings and apparatus of the University, under the control of the Executive Committee and Faculty, and request an annual report of their work to be presented to the Board at its winter meeting.

The next June they took further action:

The Board recognizes the receipt of the report of the Summer School and records its hearty appreciation of the labors of those who have borne the burden of conducting it, of the signal success which has attended their endeavors, and of the substantial help that is thus being rendered in advertising and building up the University.

In 1902 at a meeting of the Board, Professor Rayman of East Liverpool:

introduced the subject of a Teachers' College and dwelt upon the importance of establishing such an institution in connection with the University. A committee was appointed [President Holden, Mr. Rayman and Mr. Work] to consider the feasibility of such a project, and to report at the next meeting.

In February, 1908, the Ohio Legislature was considering the establishment of two state normal schools, and the Board at Wooster considered the possibility of having one of these located at Wooster.[4] There was, however, no action.

Wooster seemed almost an ideal location for a summer school. It had a woodsy campus and, since the fire, beautiful buildings, surroundings that beckoned for walks and picnics. In the valley of the Little Applecreek there was Highland Park, with great trees, high banks, and a pond. Until 1912 when the dam broke in a heavy storm and it was all washed out, there was also Reddick's dam to the north and west, actually the city's reservoir for fire protection, surrounded by trees. And there was always the Ohio Agricultural Experiment Station on the hill south of town, with an arboretum, much to see of interest, and picnic tables in a grove. Wooster was a small town of only six or seven thousand but accessible by the Pennsylvania Railroad, with four passenger trains a day. A train a day on a small fork of the Baltimore and Ohio Railroad also whistled its way down Killbuck valley from Lodi to Wooster to Millersburg, stopping at one crossroad to pick up a load of logs perhaps, at another a passenger or two. If a brakeman was left behind by chance, all that was needed was a good sprint and a jump and he was aboard again. The Cleveland and Southwestern Interurban ran cars to Cleveland every two hours or so. And over at Orrville, ten miles away, the C.A.&C. (Cleveland, Akron, and Columbus) Railroad had a train or two each way per day. Though only Hoover Cottage was open for the summer, there were many rooming and boarding places in town. Rooms with bath and telephone privileges ran from $1.00 to $2.50 a week (as late as 1904), and boarding from $2.15 to $3.25 a week. There were many boarding clubs—the Roth Club, the Bender, the Todd, the Kieffer, and others. Tuition had been for many years only ten dollars for eight weeks, with a dollar for incidentals.

The summer school offered some eighty classes a day, the first one at 6:45 in the morning—after all the sun was already up, and so was Mr. Dickason. In fact he had already milked the cow, fed the chickens, had breakfast, held family worship, and was in his office writing letters, ready to talk with all who came, and to dispense that famous "Dicky smile." No longer could the Wooster University and preparatory faculty do the job alone. To be sure, Dickason used as many of the local staff as were willing to be drawn in. Sylvester Scovel during his lifetime would occasionally give an advanced course in civil government. John G. Black taught geology and botany, and Mr. Behoteguy occasionally offered work in French. Mary and Frances Glenn were instructors in piano and vocal music, George Foss Schwartz in violin, and for one summer at least, Bessie Thorne, a 1900 graduate in music and daughter of the director of the Experiment Station, gave lessons on the pipe organ. Claribel Durstine, and before her Emma Sonnedecker, continued in the summer to help students achieve their ambition to do charcoal sketches or simple sylvan scenes in water color. Emeline McSweeney guided her wheel chair along the campus walks and lifted herself on crutches up the few steps to her classroom that she might teach Latin and German —later also Greek—to aspiring students. Robert Chaddock, '00, who was teaching Greek and history in the preparatory department, was also persuaded to stay for the summers and earn an extra few dollars toward the graduate work he was planning. Dickason employed other recent graduates if they had made a notable record or displayed proficiency in some field, Eleanor Ewing in vocal music, Murray Frame, one of Wooster's most brilliant young men (destined to lose his life from typhus on the mission field), John D. Fackler, '00, and in elocution Eleanor Blocher of Dickason's own class, an Amazonian young woman who, suitably enough, came from the huge house with the tower in Bloomington just above the Dickason home. Dickason sought his instructors everywhere, the most competent he could find at the price he could pay. In 1914 the pamphlet describing the facilities of the school said that on the teaching staff were persons from Mt. Union, Kenyon, Wooster, the Boston Conservatory of Music, from Chicago University, Harvard, Northwestern, Case, Cornell, Ohio State University, Adelbert, Lebanon, and Ada. This did not mean necessarily that they had come from the instructional staffs of these institutions, though some of them may have, but that at some time they had studied in these colleges or universities. He searched the countryside for principals or superintendents with some special professional skill. He brought on Lottie Everhard from the Anderson School of Gymnastics at New Haven, Connecticut, Ella Truman, principal of the Armstrong School of Sioux City, Iowa, to demonstrate the "Spear Method," Margaret Sutherland of the Columbus Teachers' Training School to teach methods in primary and grade school work. For them Dickason set up a model school with local pupils so that teachers could see how best to handle the problems they themselves encountered, problems of discipline, of inattention, of lack of interest, of the finding of attractive illustrative material. Afterwards in a give-and-take discussion they could share their experiences and come to sound conclusions. He brought in J. E. Woodland from Peddie Institute, Hightstown, New Jersey, to teach physics and demonstrate new developments, B. C. Barnard from Geneva College, Beaver Falls, Pennsylvania, for biology.

Yet many of the instructors came from small towns or villages, from Madisonburg, for instance, Fredericksburg, Millersburg (the Hon. J. A. McDowell, former Congressman, who taught English grammar), from Shanesville with its brick kilns down beside Sugar Creek, from Canal Dover, Savannah, East Liverpool, and Alliance. Such a list did not look impressive to the Wooster University faculty. Who was holding the measuring stick on credits? Were these good or bad? The summer school was overshadowing the college by its very numbers. And these hordes of people went out over the state blithely stating that they had studied at Wooster. The total effect, they felt, was to lower Wooster's standard in the minds of the public. Few people realized that the summer school had long since become a private enterprise with no official standing save as the university lent its buildings for the project and a limited number of its faculty chose to teach in its departments. Some of its credits were undoubtedly good, but which and how many? Yet on the annual announcement or catalogue the picture of the president was prominently displayed.

On the other hand, the summer school was doing a great service. Many school teachers who would have loved taking a year off for further study at some college or university were paid so little that that day of high privilege never came. But a summer session or two combined with vacation gave them refreshment both of mind and body. They could take a few courses, talk their problems in teaching over with others, get new ideas and suggested methods; and they were better for the experience both in their teaching and in their morale. Besides, Mr. Dickason had instituted an agency of his own for teachers, for which he made no charge. Within a few years of the beginning of his principalship he had become well known to schoolmen in Ohio; they liked him and trusted his judgment. They frequently wrote to him for recommendations for vacancies, and he gladly supplied them. For Dickason remembered people, remembered their names and faces; he made it his business to get acquainted with them; and he was glad to do his bit toward their advancement.

There were other features, a Y.M.C.A. meeting once a week, classes in missions, a training department in Westminster Sunday

School, for Mr. Dickason truly wished, so far as possible, to pass along to these students the Christian ideals and practices for which Wooster University stood. For entertainment he arranged for what could almost be called a small chautauqua. Every week an entertainer or a lecturer was brought in for an evening. Once William Jennings Bryan came. He was at his oratorical best, and he fulminated against the theory of evolution; he was most impressive.[5] Once Booker T. Washington spoke, once Helen Keller. Sometimes there were organ or piano or violin recitals, dramatic readings, or a lecture on some natural wonder such as the Mammoth Cave. There were oratorical demonstrations occasionally or an art exhibit by the students themselves, and there were several receptions during the summer. Then almost at the very end came "Dicky Day" when the "summer-squealers," as some of the faculty children mockingly called them, expressed their gratitude and affection to and for the man who had planned their wonderful summer. There were brief tributes, yells, one or two of the Wooster college songs, and at the end "The Song of the Summer Schoolers" written especially for the occasion (by one of the college faculty). One year it was arranged to the tune of the "Battle Hymn of the Republic":

> There is no one else like Dicky, big of heart, and clear of brain;
> He thinks more of helping others than he does of sordid gain;
> Tho' he does a lot of smiling, he smiles not because he's vain—
>   Sing on for John Howard Dick
>
>   . . . . .
>
> Then shout, ye summer schoolers, and ye teachers shout once more:
> We are marching on to vict'ry and our Dicky goes before;
> There are left good things behind us, but the best is yet in store,
>   And Dicky leads the van.

All summer the campus was flooded with these elementary and secondary schoolteachers. Many of them came with a glint in their eyes, eager to better themselves, as doubtless they did. They were everywhere, all over the porch of Hoover Cottage, in the library, around the Rock, under the trees, sometimes with books and papers spread out before them, sometimes just chattering away, sitting on the steps of every building, having their pictures snapped to send back home. Some of the faculty of the college felt that their domain had been invaded by a flock of starlings. Surely something had to be done about all this, and in June of 1911 the Board and faculty had come to a kind of compromise arrangement with Mr. Dickason. And so the matter rested, though uneasily.

As the summer school continued to grow, the president and faculty became more and more critical. Then a new state ruling on the granting of teachers' certificates provoked a crisis. Even the college graduate, if he aspired to teach in a high school, must present credits in professional courses in education far beyond what Wooster was now offering—though it had recently increased the options in this field. To meet the new requirements one fourth of all the college work of the prospective teacher would have to be in education. This was an impossible situation. The elementary and grade schoolteachers were in an even worse plight; they could not win a teacher's certificate without two years of normal school training. This posed a serious problem for the college. One third of all Wooster's alumni were teachers. One half of the last class graduated were teaching. Many of the women graduates taught a year or two before they married. Many others interrupted their college training to teach a while in grade schools till they could earn enough to go on. What could the college do? Must it lose all these men and women who were so large a part of its clientele? Was it fair to the Presbyterian youth of Ohio and to the leadership of the church to send them off to state universities and state normal schools? But what of the summer school? [6] Might it not now be an answer to Wooster's problem? Then it was discovered that its work would not be accredited by the state unless it was the summer extension of an established normal department of a college or a university.

Mr. Dickason was asked to study the question. He reported to the faculty that to meet the need Wooster not only would have to take the summer school under its wing but would have to establish a two-year normal department as a part either of the college or of the academy. This he thought could be done without harm to the institution. The college already had several courses in education. The summer school could take up the slack, allowing certain students to accumulate some of their education credits in this extra session. Wooster already had a precedent in the Severance Bible and Missionary Training School for work in which diplomas but no degrees were given, yet its courses were accredited in the department of religion. Many persons studied music in Wooster without completing the work for a diploma, let alone a degree. But the faculty looked askance at this solution; they would have none of it. Wooster was a liberal arts college; no other liberal arts colleges in the state were proposing to meet the problem in this way. To establish a junior school of education would be a lowering of Wooster's standards. Wooster, if it allowed this to happen, would soon be known primarily for its normal school. The tail would be wagging the dog; and many of them feared that it would be a mangy tail at that. They had not forgotten the country school atmosphere that prevailed on the campus in the summer. Most of them would welcome the elimination of the summer school. This they said among themselves. President Holden, moreover, was bitterly opposed.

Faculty meeting followed faculty meeting. At their order the curriculum committee brought in a report to be sent to the Board expressing their opposition. The faculty vote had been 18 to 5. The minority asked for and was granted the privilege of presenting their report as well. This small group felt that in not meeting the challenge Wooster was missing an opportunity and letting down the Presbyterian youth of the state. The group was led by Mr. Notestein, who, jealous as he was of the high standards of a liberal arts college, a teacher and an exemplifier of the "habit of mastery," could not forget another day when as a youth he had looked on while a small group of men met in prayer on this hilltop under the oaks to establish this college. He had later known several of these founders and was deeply conscious of their hopes for moulding the youth of the church. Surely to teach the teachers was part of the responsibility of a church college. The burden was on this institution to find a way and still to hold its excellence as a liberal arts college. Standing beside him were Bennett, Black, Dickason, and the newest member of the faculty of the Severance Bible and Missionary Training School, Clinton Tyler Wood. The stance was not easy for any one of the minority. Their ideals and their motives were questioned. Their position was considered virtually treasonable by the opposing faction.

The local Executive Committee read the majority and minority reports, and, though generally favoring the normal department, refused to take a stand and waited for the meeting of the big Board on

February first. When that day came several minor actions were first taken. L. C. Boles was elected director of athletics, and "Cully" Wilhelm a supplementary coach for the baseball season. Kenarden, it appeared, was not fully occupied, and it was decided that rent should be lowered. The financial secretaries for the college also were to be let go as of July first. It was recommended also that thirty acres of college land be put under cultivation to help in supplying the dormitories, and that a college steward should be hired as soon as possible to have charge not only of the campus but of all the purchasing for the dormitories, and of their domestic arrangements. At this meeting there was for the first time some concern also for the inadequate social life among the students, and the idea was broached of some sort of interchange of meals between the dormitories.

Finally they came to the subject uppermost in everyone's mind. The majority and minority reports from the faculty on the proposed junior school of education were argued till bedtime and throughout the next day. Finally a committee (White, Krichbaum, and Work) was appointed to formulate a motion and in time they came in with the following statement:

Resolved: 1. That the two-year Normal Course be adopted;

2. That this department be organized on a basis separate from the college proper; that its Committee of Control be responsible for its work, pass upon the merits of the credits to be given, and certify to the State Superintendent the work done.

3. In order to bring about a closer relationship between the Summer School and the College of Wooster, be it resolved that a committee, consisting of Dean E. Compton, Dr. J. O. Notestein, and Dr. J. M. Vance representing the faculty, and Dr. Heron, Dr. Weir, and Dr. Wishard representing the Board of Trustees be appointed to have charge of the selection of the teachers, both of the Summer School, and of the Normal Course, the giving of credits, the use of the buildings and apparatus, and any other questions of internal administration that may arise;

4. That for the present the students of the Normal Course be assigned to College classes for such work as the normal course may require.

The vote was fourteen to seven in favor of the adoption of this resolution. One member had had to leave early before the vote was taken. The decision hit President Holden between the eyes. He hadn't thought it possible that on an educational issue the Board could go against the judgment of the majority of the faculty. He took it, as any self-respecting president in his circumstances would have done, as a vote of no-confidence, and at once went to his office to dictate to his secretary his resignation, and then returned to read it to the Board:

Through the providence of God, it has been my exceptional and blessed privilege to finish with this collegiate year a period of twenty-six years of unbroken service to Christian education; first, as teacher in my own Alma Mater, where I spent ten most delightful years, and secondly, as President of this noble institution, over which you, as a Board, have the honor of presiding. During all these years I have been deeply conscious of my own defects, but I have felt justified in continuing my service to this institution, owing to the peculiar circumstances through which the institution has been passing. I have felt keenly your support and patience through all our difficulties.

The time has now come when the institution has finally reached the opportunity of an open sea, and you are permitted to choose the direction in which you sail your bark. The time has come when the Synod has acknowledged its duty toward the institution [7] and has assumed to support it more generously. The Board has entered upon a new educational policy, for the successful carrying out of which you need a different type of leader. Doubtless you foresaw such possible changes and generously provided that the President, after a service of not less than fifteen years, might retire with honor.

I therefore herewith avail myself of [*sic*] this privilege. "With charity toward all, and malice toward none," I pray that you accept my resignation from the Presidency of the College of Wooster, to take effect at your own pleasure, not later than the close of this collegiate year, the sixteenth of my administration.

With my constant prayer and best wishes for the future of this institution, I remain,

Very sincerely yours,
Louis Edward Holden, President

It was a dignified statement, written, it must be, under high tension. Still standing, he moved its acceptance, and "urged his

friends, Dr. Hudnut and Judge Krichbaum, to do him the courtesy of
seconding the motion." This they did, at his "earnest request." He
asked that his opposition to the introduction of the normal course be
recorded and stated that the action of the Board necessarily created
"an impossible situation for an executive elected for leadership to do
his best work for the institution." The Board was completely taken
aback. Some of them suggested that they would like to recall their
votes and wished that the acceptance of the resignation be postponed
so that a committee could talk things over with him. But it was too
late. This was final. He would not change his mind even though the
motion just taken were to be rescinded. He asked that his resignation
be accepted at once. It was put to a vote and passed unanimously,
though reluctantly. President Holden was out, or would be at the end
of the college year. Deep gloom settled over the campus. The faculty
was stunned. Maybe they did not all love President Holden—what
college president ever was loved by all his faculty? He sometimes
was rough-shod and overbearing; but they one and all respected and
honored him. He had done magnificent things for Wooster, and they
knew it.

On February 5 the faculty met and addressed to the president a
long statement, which they had recorded in the *Minutes:*

The recent proffer to the Board of Trustees of your resignation as
President of the College, and the Board's acceptance of the same, has
brought us, your colleagues in the faculty, into a state of stunned dismay
which almost precludes our expressing ourselves suitably with regard to
the matter. We are unwilling, however, that this meeting should pass
without our having adopted some minute expressive of our esteem for
you and our sorrow that we are soon to lose you as our leader. We know
that you desire no perfunctory and fulsome resolution of commendation;
but we know equally well that you would be the last among us to value
lightly a sincere and manly expression of affection and esteem. It is this
that we offer you. Some of us were here to see your heroic courage and
unshaken faith in God when Wooster's hopes seemed to lie buried in the
ashes of the great building under whose roof nine-tenths of her daily
work was being done. It has been the privilege of others of us to be
associated with you during two splendid and triumphant campaigns for
increased endowment, and to learn that no discouragement could daunt
you, and no completeness of success inflate you; and all of us have

wrought together with you long enough to be conscious that you daily set each one of us an example of noble and unwearying diligence, which has stimulated us also to do our best.

We cannot forget that you have honored us by seeking our counsel and leaning upon our help; that the evidences of your solicitous concern for our welfare are written large in the plan for Retiring Allowances which you have inaugurated, and stamped upon the physical conditions under which we do our daily work. It has been a joy to serve under such a leader, and long after you have ceased to be our leader we shall still be inspired by the memory of your leadership to more faithful efforts in Wooster's behalf. We do not know your plans; and neither we nor you know whither God may lead you, or what worthy work He may give you to do; but wherever you may go and into whatever work you may enter, you may carry with you the assurance of our admiration, our esteem, and our affectionate regard.

The *Minute* was adopted unanimously.

Yet the story was far from finished. Bitterness mounted. As a mark of loyalty to President Holden Mr. Grumbine resigned, as did Miss Riggs of the conservatory somewhat later. Little groups of faculty gathered to vent their venom. Names were called, sometimes with a slightly theological flavor, "whited sepulchre," "Jesuit."—After all, this was a Presbyterian institution.—Many of the faculty quite sincerely agreed with the president that to add a normal school to Wooster was "educational suicide." Wooster could not and ought not to compete, they thought, with state universities or state normal schools. They had lost the first round in the skirmish; they were determined in the end to win by whatever means. The magnificent record of President Holden was played up, as well it could be. The local trustees were accused of having yielded to pressure from the town. The summer school, of course, had brought the town a pretty penny. If it were closed many widows would be deprived of room rent they had counted on; many boarding clubs would be closed. All summer long the town would be dead. There had indeed been a petition signed by four hundred townspeople asking for the retention of the summer school and the addition of the normal course, but it was not based on monetary considerations—though one can hardly doubt that these entered into the thinking of some of the signers— but rather on the fact that many of their own children would otherwise have to go elsewhere to get the training they would need. Other petitions, strangely assembled and of unknown origin, against the "Junior School of Education" were published. Letters and editorials appeared in the church weeklies. Circulars went out to members of the Synod. The alumni were deliberately stirred up. It was a question of loyalty or disloyalty to the president; a question of Wooster's survival as a liberal arts college; or it was that Dickason had been profiting unduly from his summer school, which he had been running autocratically even though he used the facilities of the college; or it was an open dislike for everything he stood for, for his lack of academic standards, his lack of sophistication, his "hail-fellow-well-met" manner. Every ugly aspersion that anyone could think of was hurled about. There were only a few who kept their heads, their manners, and their Christian outlook.

The local trustees flatly denied the charge that they had been influenced by local pressures. The same trustees, they pointed out, had several years before approved the building of Kenarden Lodge, knowing well that its existence would cut the income of many a local citizen. As for Mr. Dickason's profiting from a private venture, while using the facilities of the college, the trustees had more than once passed resolutions indicating that the college was greatly benefiting by the presence of the summer school. Moreover no one ever saw then or later any evidence of Mr. Dickason's affluence. Indeed Mrs. Dickason sometimes worried when she found that he had been giving money to someone in need, money that she thought might be better spent on his own household. The tuition charges for the summer school were low. Thousands of dollars must have gone to the paying of his instructors, other thousands to the recruiting of lecturers and entertainers. William J. Bryan, the Hruby Bohemian Orchestra, and others, one may be sure, did not donate their services. Unfortunately the quarrel had degenerated into a question of personalities; and the would-be sophistication of the East was pitted against the down-to-earth Middle West. Yet essentially the argument turned on an honest difference of opinion on what Wooster's function was within the Presbyterian Church and whether, or how, it could fulfill this function and still keep and advance its status as a liberal arts college.

In the meantime five trustees had requested a special meeting of the Board to be called for May 18 to discuss Wooster's situation. For presentation at this meeting the faculty had formulated a counter proposal "as to the future Educational Policy of Wooster." In this they advocated "avoiding of all distinctly professional and technical work," putting the college department of the summer school "under the immediate control of the College Faculty," and "a gradual reconstruction of the educational work of the College so that our classical and literary work" will "approximate the Princeton or Bryn Mawr standard" and in science "attain the standard of the theoretical work in science in the Massachusetts Institute of Technology." "Wooster" they added, "should not be content to compete merely with the local Ohio institutions. Her aim should be to make the amplest provision for those who desire a general education, either for its own sake or as a cultural basis for graduate work in a university or professional school." They then proposed that by the fall of 1916 there should be inaugurated a system of freshman preceptors, in seven departments, for those who were unable to keep up with the standard of work required; that new professorships at $2500 each be established in botany, astronomy, archaeology, and history of art, Romance languages, psychology, economics, jurisprudence, and associate professorships in English literature and in history. They urged that the campaign for a million dollars, already voted,[8] be pushed to a successful conclusion and that none of this money be used for buildings, but that $100,000 should be endowment for the library, $350,000 for the endowment of the seven new professorships, $50,000 as endowment for the two new associate professorships, and $100,000 of endowment for the seven preceptors.

In the last paragraph the memorandum said:

We as a faculty firmly believe that the proposed policy is the surest method of effecting an increase not only in the quality of our students but also, eventually, in their number; and of enhancing our reputation and influence for good.

It was an ambitious proposal and one to which in its general principles they have since sought to adhere. When it was presented, however, it was tabled till the June meeting in favor of more urgent matters.

For John E. West came to the meeting with a brief showing that the action of the trustees in February establishing a junior school of education was illegal. They had set up for that school and for the summer school a committee of control consisting of three members of the trustees and three of the faculty. This was contrary to the Statutes of Ohio governing the *Charter* and to the *By-Laws* of the institution, for credits could be granted only by the faculty and no trustee could be a member of the faculty. Besides, if they had intended that this should be an amendment to their *By-Laws,* they had not had the necessary two-thirds vote of the full membership for its passing. It would still be illegal. The February action was at once rescinded unanimously, but not the action accepting President Holden's resignation. The president himself had made sure of that. He had gone to the pre-General Assembly sessions at Rochester, New York, to address, on the nineteenth of May, the College Board and the Association of Presbyterian College Presidents. He had obviously been aware of what was pending at the Board meeting at Wooster and had sent a letter to the Board saying that "there is to be no reconsideration on my part, even if such opportunity were given me." And so for the second time in two years a failure in timing had brought a seeming disaster to the college. At this meeting in May, in addition to the rescinding of the action of February 2, the Board asked the faculty to submit a working plan for the control of the summer school. This they did, presenting it in printed form in October.

In the meantime the faculty and the now-disqualified committee of control had set up certain requirements for the summer of 1915. In the fall of 1914 Mr. Dickason had submitted to the Executive Committee of the Board his proposed list of instructors for the summer of 1915. These had been approved. He had accordingly gone ahead and made contracts with them. When the issue came up again in the winter after the meeting of February 2 establishing a committee of control for both summer school and the junior school of education, and he was asked by this new committee to bring in the list, he came with the names of twenty-four instructors who would be offering courses for college credit. Much as the committee might have liked at this point to make changes, they felt legally bound by the contracts that had been made. It was too late to cancel these. The summer school would go on for the coming summer but within certain safeguards.

It would be in three sections, college, teacher-training, and academy, each with its director. For the college the director was J. G. Black. He would tolerate no nonsense. The faculty had already laid down regulations. No one could accumulate more than eight college credits in the eight weeks of the summer school and for each of these there must be sixteen hours of recitations or forty-eight of laboratory and field work. No additional work even without credit would be sanctioned. Every student of the college section had to be "certified by the entrance committee of the college faculty" as having the prerequisites for the course as specified in the college catalogue. At the end the instructor in charge must submit his examination lists to the director of the college section, must report the student's grade, the actual number of hours the student had spent in recitation and in laboratory, the number of excused and unexcused absences, and the material actually covered in the course. If this were less than the standard for the winter, the credits would be reduced accordingly. The problem of high school and grade school teacher-training posed by the state had not been answered. It seemed, however, to make no difference, for the attendance reached its all-time high, 1551 students. Of these 235 were taking at least some courses in the college section. The fury was somewhat abated, yet it had not spent itself.

While all the storm was going on, there had been notable changes within the college. The University of Wooster was no more. The College of Wooster had come to be. In early 1914 the state legislature had acted to allow the change; in October the Synod had ratified it; the seal now bore the name it should have had from the beginning. This June the faculty had voted, also, to put commencement hereafter on Wednesday rather than Thursday morning. The commencement season had been too long.

There were new faces among the faculty. A year ago Mr. Lytle, director of the conservatory, had resigned and in his place Neille Odell Rowe,[9] F.A.G.O. had been appointed. He came direct from Muskingum where he had been teaching for a year, to begin a service to Wooster of thirty-one years. In 1912 he had gone to Paris to study organ with Charles Widor and Joseph Bonnet, to work also with Albert Roussel and Isador Philipp, the composers. It was a year that changed his life in more than one way. For there he met Mr. and Mrs. Behoteguy, and this meeting led later to his coming to Wooster. Under him music at Wooster was to thrive and come into its own so that finally in 1929 it became an accepted major toward a B.A. degree. He was happy as an organist, and in his direction of Westminster choir and of the oratorio chorus, which this June of 1915 would be singing Haydn's *Creation.*

Robert Caldwell, too, had resigned in 1914 to accept a position at Rice Institute in Texas. He would be long remembered at Wooster as an excellent teacher and a congenial companion. As the new Hoge instructor of political science, William Estabrook Chancellor had been brought in. He was enthusiastic and stimulating, sometimes erratic, however, and not always as tactful as one might wish. A graduate of Amherst with his Master's degree also from that institution, he had written several books on education and two others of which he was especially proud, for they had been published also in Braille, *Our Presidents and Their Office* and *A History of the Government of the United States.* He would be teaching some economics as well during the coming year. For several years past Mr. Dickason had been using him as instructor, chapel speaker, and lecturer in the summer school. He had had sixteen years of public school experience in Patterson, New Jersey, Norwalk, Connecticut, and Washington, D. C., had taught briefly or lectured at New York University, University of Chicago, Johns Hopkins, and George Washington University.

In the summer of 1914 Mr. Dunn, head of the department of rhetoric and English composition, had taken leave to Glasgow for two years to complete the work for his doctoral degree. Walter Edwin Peck, a brilliant young student while at Wooster and a graduate of Hamilton, had been brought as an instructor in that department, and was filling in for Mr. Dunn and would continue for a while. H. William Taeusch, '14, had for the past year been winning his spurs in the same department and would continue through 1917, accumulating money toward his contemplated graduate study at Harvard.

Wooster had been growing in nearly every direction. Six hundred students were enrolled from twenty states and fifteen foreign countries. Three were Persians, six Chinese. The faculty numbered

twenty-four professors, two assistant professors, and eleven instructors in addition to those teaching in the department of music.
Though for nearly a year every newspaper had carried headlines of
the war in Europe, the impact of the war on the campus was still
relatively slight. To be sure, Miss Bine Holly in the summer of 1914
had had a harrowing experience in getting home from Germany. The
students and faculty, too, had contributed $200 toward Belgian re-
lief. Hamilton Holt, editor of *The Independent,* had come to lecture
on world peace, and John R. Mott in the spring had stirred his
hearers by an address on the world situation and the war in Europe.
New courses had been added even in German. Physical education
was now required for all those entering below the junior year, and all
men must prove that they could swim the length of the pool. There
had been introduced a course in machine drawing, and as soon as
they could find the money they would like to offer one in domestic
science. Wooster had a distinguished alumna at the head of this
department at the University of Illinois, and so was conscious of this
new field for women. In the Board there had been some talk even of
a course in agriculture. Wooster's endowment now stood roughly at
a million and a quarter. By the end of 1914 all debts and deficits had
been wiped out, thanks to the Severance estate. The trustees had
raised the tuition and incidentals from $78.50 to $100 a year. In
June of that year there had been organized an Alumni Endowment
Union with the objective of encouraging alumni gifts. The class of
1914 had made the first of these—$50. There was talk, too, of
employing eventually an alumni secretary and of establishing in
various cities local Wooster clubs.[10]

The physical plant was becoming more impressive. Mr. John
Severance and his sister, Mrs. Dudley Allen, had honored Mr. L. H.
Severance's promise of a stadium. It had been built, playing fields,[11] a
running track of a quarter of a mile, jumping pits, a corner for
hammer and discus throwing, and sturdy bleachers to the north and
south to accommodate about two thousand persons. The whole project had come to $60,000, considerably more than Mr. Severance had
anticipated. There had been some outside help of interested friends.
The site was perfect. From the Beall Avenue entrance one looked
across to green fields and woods and hills. To the north the steep
banks left by the excavation would soon be a mass of rambler roses,

and the fields immediately beyond would be planted with a grove of elms, and in the foreground an orchard specifically for the students. In spring it would be white with the bloom of apples and pears. In the fall there would be fruit. As of 1914 the campus encompassed 100 acres. The care of this would be the responsibility of the new college steward, A. K. Miller. He would take office on August 15.

Students as usual were presenting occasional new problems to the faculty. In January they petitioned for a branch of the International Socialist Society. The faculty shied away from the name but answered that they would not object to a study of socialism "on other lines." Several speakers had added to the breadth of student experience. Mr. William Henderson of Columbus, alumnus and trustee, came to talk on the "Modern Conception of the Atom," and Dr. Banks of the University of Chicago lectured on the Hittites. This was the year, too, of the first Gum Shoe Hop in addition to the traditional formal Washington's birthday in the chapel.[12] Washington would probably have been the first to approve the change, and in gum shoes (to protect the floor of the gymnasium) would have led off the Virginia reel. It was gay in every way for both students and faculty: an obstacle race between freshmen and sophomore men, a basketball game between junior and senior women. Even the faculty forgot their dignity. "Tubby" Gould and William Taeusch chewed two ends of a long string to reach the candy in the middle. Other faculty ate dry crackers and then competed in a whistling match. The girls had prepared box lunches and sold them from corner booths.

Color Day on May 22 was a pageant of Wooster's own history, with particular honor accorded to the retiring President Holden. Scenes showed the choosing of the site, the cornerstone laying, the early days of romance and struggle, the fire that reduced the Bitters Bottle to a pile of brick and ashes, the tense but finally triumphant campaign for the rebuilding, and the magic of renewal. In the afternoon Wooster played Case, because of rain a four-inning game, in which the score was 1–0 in Wooster's favor. And in the evening in the swale to the south of Hoover Cottage the Coburn Players put on *Midsummer Night's Dream.*

Soon afterward commencement came. At an earlier meeting the trustees had made provision for President Holden. For the coming year he was voted $6,000 so that he might travel and be leisurely; he had never in all his sixteen years sought a sabbatical for himself. For the years thereafter until he should take a comparable position to the one he had resigned, he would be pensioned according to the formula he had himself helped his trustees to set up in 1911. The trustees passed also a *Minute* of deep appreciation of his services. Regretfully at this meeting they received the resignations of the Reverend Mr. Robert Laidlaw, the Reverend Mr. Eben Cobb, and of Mr. John Severance. The latter had been a member but one year. He did not come to the meeting but sent a letter in which he asked the privilege, as administrator of his father's estate, of placing an undesignated amount in his father's gift account ($75,000) to the credit of Wooster's pension endowment fund. Doubtless he was wondering whether Wooster actually had the money to pay President Holden the pension to which he was entitled; perhaps, like Kirkpatrick, he was making "sicher."

On Sunday afternoon President Holden preached his final baccalaureate, a simple and direct sermon on "Christ, the Sure Foundation." At the end of the exercises of graduation on Thursday [13] he spoke briefly and without dramatics of the privilege of his work at Wooster. A little better than a year before at the 151st General Assembly he had received on behalf of the Board of Christian Education the Distinguished Service Award in Christian Education. Now quietly he was stepping down. Nine hundred persons came to the Corporation lunch just afterward, paying thus their tribute to his years of leadership. Then at 4:45 he and Mrs. Holden boarded the trolley car to Cleveland. Thence they went to Clifton Springs for the summer. They both needed rest and peace, time to think, and to renew their spirits. So indeed did everyone. Compton and Behoteguy went to Otsego Lake in Michigan, Lean to Waupaca, Wisconsin, Kelso was off to Chicago University to study, and Gould across to England and the continent to see and feel something of history in the making. The year had ended. A notable administration had ended. Summer was here, though the wind still "blew cool over the oats-stubble."

Hurricane Calliope[1]

J OHN CAMPBELL WHITE, who was to become the fifth president of Wooster, was a man of grandiose visions. He was not an
academic in any sense. He had grown up on a farm to the east of
Wooster, had been reared a member of the then still psalm-sing-
ing United Presbyterian Church and at twenty had been graduated
from Wooster with the class of 1890. He was tall, personable,
earnest, and dedicated to the idea of doing good. His first job had
been as Y.M.C.A. secretary visiting colleges, his next with the
Student Volunteer Movement. He had attended Xenia (Ohio) Theological Seminary for two years, but before he had completed his
training there or had been ordained,[2] he had an opportunity he could
not resist, to serve the World Y.M.C.A. as missions secretary for
India, with headquarters in Calcutta. There he met many kinds of
people, British Army officers and civil servants, American, British,
and Dutch missionaries, Indians high and low—Hindus, Moslems,
Buddhists, and others. He was appalled by much that he saw, on the
streets, in the temples, on the riverbanks, appalled at the hordes of
people, poor, and hungry, and sick, and hopeless. Why had the
nations of the West in their comparative affluence and comfort failed
through so many years to meet this challenge of bringing to India
and other hapless lands salvation of body, mind, and soul? It was for
these western nations to provide a new, more comprehensive, and
vigorous Christian leadership. When he came home after ten years it
was with the idea of promoting such leadership. He first accepted a
position within his own church, then one in the Laymen's Missionary
Movement for all the evangelical churches. He had been in the thick
of this when he came to Wooster.

He had first served on Wooster's Board of Trustees as an alumni
member in June of 1913. He became active at once. He had made
the motion in the winter of 1915 setting up the junior school of
education. He wanted Wooster's sons and daughters to go into teaching, into the ministry in greater and greater numbers, into the
Y.M.C.A. and Y.W.C.A., into medicine. He was interested in their
spiritual growth and their training in the practical arts. He would

have Wooster give courses in domestic science, even in agriculture; he would have a farm to supply the dormitories. In working on that, boys could help to support themselves through college and learn something that might well prove useful in later life. He rejoiced to learn that Wooster still had evangelistic teams of students going out to villages nearby, and a group that taught a night school in the Italian district in town. It was the spirit he wished most to see in Wooster's young people. He believed that "character is caught, not taught."

The manner of his becoming president was unfortunate. He had been appointed as one of a committee of five trustees to hunt a new president. Ever since Holden's resignation there had been an undercurrent of rumor, however, that White himself was being suggested as a possibility. The committee had been in existence scarcely a month when it brought into the Board a recommendation. They had considered, they said, the qualifications of fifteen men; they had consulted with faculty members and others, seeking advice and suggestions. Actually, they had talked with a group of three faculty, Compton, Notestein, Kelso, questioning them about the necessary qualifications of a president, but had mentioned no names (AAUP Report). The faculty as a whole had not been approached. When the committee had reported their nomination of Mr. White to the Board, he was present; and though he offered to leave the room while the vote was taken, he was told to stay to discuss the matter with them and to tell them something of his hopes and aspirations for the institution. He was elected unanimously, but he asked for time in which to make his decision. When the faculty heard of his election, they were aghast. They knew he had qualities of leadership but they thought it was the wrong kind of leadership. He was not an intellectual, not trained at all in the academic discipline, and not familiar with academic mores. They had just put themselves on record as wishing to make Wooster a high ranking liberal arts college comparable to Princeton or Bryn Mawr or in science to Massachusetts Institute of Technology. They had had as president a business man, though one drawn, to be sure, from academic ranks. They had hoped for an educator; they were being offered a promoter by nature and an evangelist.

Immediately Mr. White called together the faculty and asked their advice as to his decision. It was a gracious gesture. Mrs. White came along to listen to what they had to say. The faculty lacked the courage to tell him there in public what was in their minds—that they did not want him, that his training and experience had not fitted him for this kind of position. They proposed rather that he talk with some of the individual members, the dean and others. This he did, and they laid it on the line: outstanding as he was in his own field, he was not the person for the place; and he had been too closely identified with the recent storm. Though they did not say it, Mr. White in reality had much in common with Mr. Dickason. He had, however, been exposed to a more cosmopolitan life; and his surfaces were consequently smoother.

In hoping to persuade him not to accept the presidency the faculty were overlooking the fact, or unaware of it perhaps, that Mr. White was cherishing a world vision for Wooster; if properly guided it could take its rightful place as a great center for the evangelization of the world. From the beginning the college had embraced wholeheartedly the missionary cause; this could be developed and a great host of young persons could here be trained to carry the Christian message to the far corners of the earth, or through their influence inspire others to go. Wooster could become the glowing coal from which many a lesser ember would catch the spark. He would as rapidly as possible accumulate a faculty in sympathy with this ideal. He would bring in as speakers the great men of the church both ministers and laymen. He would broaden the scope of its education. By scholarships and projects for self-help he could draw many more young people in to share the vision he had himself experienced.

He dreamed up other possibilities. In summer he would bring to Wooster religious conferences with delegates from everywhere. He would talk with the Wooster Board of Trade—and did within the first few months of his administration—about the feasibility of making a lake at Wooster and building on its edge a large summer hotel; there was no reason why Wooster should not be a summer resort like Chautauqua or Winona Lake in Indiana. He talked also to the Board of Trade about a factory where students might work half a day, using five years instead of four to complete the requirements for graduation. Many more boys could thus become self-supporting; and hundreds could then afford to come. He saw in the old gymnasium a place for starting a student laundry; indeed one of the gifts he received before he was inaugurated was $4,000 from Mrs. Livingston Taylor of Cleveland for this purpose. All the time he was looking at the stars and they seemed to be falling into his lap. After several weeks of prayerful cogitation, he accepted Wooster's invitation to become its president. It was an earnest of what to expect. This president was obviously not going to listen to his faculty, not even to his dean, with whom he had family connections.[3]

Mr. White's opening address in September as he welcomed the students and faculty was good; and it was well delivered.—In his college days he had won the Ohio intercollegiate oratorical contest. —*The Voice* went so far as to state that it had been "in all probability the most significant and important ever heard in the college chapel." He talked about the well-rounded personality. He stressed athletics; he would have every student learn to play at least one game well; physical education was of prime importance. He stressed the intellectual life; students must learn to think, clearly, and responsibly about life's problems and the problems of the world. He stressed most of all the developing in each one of a vital Christian purpose, for in whatever field they eventually chose to enter Wooster's graduates must be Christian leaders. "The solving of all problems of the world depends on leaders" and "the college is a factory of leaders." He did not bring to his presentation any really fresh ideas or any new slant, yet it was an excellent address. It warmed the hearts of the students, and sent them out brimming over with thoughts of their own potentialities. Each student, freshman or senior, in the secret recesses of his own heart, no doubt as he listened could see himself in later years a stalwart in his own community, perhaps the brilliant young doctor, the loved teacher inspiring youth, the minister, maybe a missionary in a far-off land, a scientist discovering new things, developing new processes for the benefit of mankind. But the faculty —many of them—went out relatively cold. Was this their new intellectual leader? Where would he put the emphasis? With all their misgivings they must wait to see, and in the meantime go about their business of teaching.

At the start he had won the students. He loved young people. After all, he had five of his own. One was still at Rutgers, and had made quite a record in athletics. A freshman daughter and a sophomore son were enrolled at Wooster. Two younger daughters were in the academy. It was proper that he should be interested in athletics. When he was in town, he attended every game, the enthusiasm meetings in advance, the bonfires or consolation gatherings afterwards. In the late afternoon he was often on the field watching the practice games. When he was away he made a point of sending to the coach and team before a game a telegram of encouragement. November of that first year one morning chapel was extended forty-five minutes to allow for the celebration of a football victory over Ohio Wesleyan, the first such in six years. It had been one of the most exciting games of the season; the first half had been scoreless; in the second half fullback Roderick had made an 80-yard run. Student enthusiasm had carried over to president and faculty.

Mr. White's interest in young people showed itself in other ways. Almost at once he offered prizes of $10.00, $5.00, $2.50 (2), and $1.00 for the best 1000–word essays on the habits underlying (1) physical efficiency, (2) mental efficiency, (3) spiritual efficiency. Another series was to go to students submitting the best ideas for self-support. At the midwinter meeting of the Board of Trustees he proposed a plan, which was adopted, for one hundred $75 scholarships covering full tuition for prospective freshmen, sophomores, or juniors coming from high schools or colleges anywhere in America. He hoped by this to nationalize Wooster's reputation. The awards would be on the basis of moral character and scholarship, each worth three points, and physical development and qualities of leadership, each worth two points. Preference would be given to those planning to take a full four-year course, and no person who used tobacco in any form would be eligible.

Of course Mr. White's major concern—and Mrs. White's as well—was for the religious welfare of the students. This, after all, had been his compelling motive in coming to Wooster. Through every resource at his command, chapel addresses, direct counseling of individuals, through the leaders of the college Y.M.C.A. and Y.W.C.A., the Christian Endeavor Society, and the Volunteer Band, he was seeking to strengthen the religious faith of the students and to foment among them the personal urge to evangelism. He expected in his faculty a like spirit and a like sense of responsibility. One Sunday evening two young instructors were invited by the president and his wife to supper. They were set down to servings of milk and corn flakes. Regrettably, they were hungry. As soon as they could with any politeness make their excuses, they fled to a restaurant in town. Bidding them a gracious goodbye, Mrs. White remarked, "We like to give our guests spiritual food." The remark was symptomatic. Evangelism was the keystone of Mr. White's overall plan for Wooster. Already in the first month after the opening of college he had gone to Columbia, South Carolina, to deliver a series of six lectures to the students of the Southern Presbyterian Theological Seminary. From there he had gone to Newark, Ohio, to attend a meeting of the Ohio Synod, thence he had taken off to Chicago for a Laymen's Missionary Conference, to choose, he said, speakers for the fall and winter at Wooster. The week of prayer had already been set, early this year, for October 24 to 31, and the speakers for it arranged. They were, for the women, Miss Maud Kelsey, traveling secretary for the Student Volunteer Movement, and for the men, the Reverend Mr. G. C. Mahy, secretary of the General Assembly's evangelistic committee, and the Reverend Mr. H. W. Foulkes, secretary of the Presbyterian Board of Ministerial Relief.

So far as the faculty were concerned the year opened with a pleasant round of parties. First, the Bennetts entertained for the Whites, and the faculty all came in their gayest mood and best bib and tucker. Shortly afterwards the Hutchins had a picnic for the faculty and trustees with tugs of war and other games. Then the Samuel Morrises held a masquerade party at which 'Tubby Gould" —to use the students' nickname for him—and William Taeusch distinguished themselves, the former coming arrayed as a southern mammy, the latter as a scarecrow. Everyone had fun.

The first faculty meeting was another thing. The new president came in with a carefully prepared list of his committees, committee members, and chairmen. The faculty had expected some changes but not these changes. The president obviously needed guidance, and this time they were not slow in telling him so. The membership of most committees had been kept much the same from year to year to year, in experienced hands, and younger and newer members had been trained in gradually for these posts. On the religious life committee, for instance, White had failed to name Martin and Vance, long-time professors in the Bible department, and he had put on Weir, pastor of Westminster Church, a logical choice to be sure, but for the fact that no trustee could double as a faculty member.[4] The by-laws of the institution had settled that point as most of the faculty and trustees had discovered the preceding spring. What worried them still more was the personnel of the curriculum committee, one of the most important in the college. On it White had named five members of what might be considered the minority group, including himself, Dickason, and the new professor of education, and only three from the former majority group. The president, of course, had not had time to familiarize himself with such matters. He conceded the point and at their suggestion appointed a committee to advise him on committees—Compton, Yanney, Wood. They met and the problem seemed to be solved to everyone's complete satisfaction. Yet in the president's absence his revised list was presented, and though additions had been made to pertinent committees so as to change the balance between majority and minority groups, the faculty still felt the lineup unsatisfactory. At the next faculty meeting as soon as Mr. White returned, Mr. Compton rose and told the president that he must accept the changes the advisory committee had made; otherwise the faculty would resume its former prerogative of electing its own committee members.[5]

In the meantime all the latent suspicions had come to the fore. Was White trying deliberately to stack the committees in favor of the junior school of education? They asked him bluntly whether he was about to reopen the issue. He in turn answered flatly that the trustees had settled that question the previous spring. Yet from this time on, the ghost of what had seemed a dead issue kept reappearing to haunt the faculty, always in a slightly different form. The trustees at their meeting in May, 1915, had not really settled the matter; they had merely rescinded an action as illegal without establishing a clear-cut policy for the future. The faculty recognized this, but the trustees, in their consternation over President Holden's resignation and their consideration of a new president, had gone blithely away assuming the question forever settled. Even the faculty's "proposal as to the future educational policy of Wooster," concerned as it was with objectives for the campaign for endowment, had been allowed to wait.

The trustees had at that time, however, asked the faculty for a plan for the summer school. This they had worked out. Now early in October it seemed wise to print this in official form. They recommended that the summer school should henceforth be called the Summer Session of the College of Wooster. It was to offer courses:

(1) For students of college grade who wish to take advantage of the summer vacation to do further work towards a degree or to make up some deficiency.

(2) For high school teachers and others of college grade who wish to pursue courses in Education and other college departments which will better fit them for high school teaching or supervisory work or which will enable them to meet the state requirements. Many of these teach in the winter and have no chance to take such courses.

(3) For students who wish to take high school branches such as are required for entrance to the College of Wooster.

Then on October 27 the dean presented to the faculty the following proposal which was carried unanimously:

Resolved, that it is the sense of the Faculty that it cannot in justice to itself or to the College as a whole be asked to assume responsibility or give credit for work done at the College of Wooster but not under Faculty's control and supervision, and that any Committee appointed to exercise control and supervision of such work must be appointed by the Faculty and be answerable to the Faculty, if the work is to be credited or certified by the Faculty.

On that same day at the fall meeting of the Board on motion of Mr. Henderson the trustees voted that the summer school be put under the control of the college faculty and that a committee be elected by the faculty to have charge of all work offered in the summer school and to recommend the instructors employed. A few days later the faculty at a special meeting elected such a committee to be in charge of the summer session: Compton, Yanney, Hunter, with Kelso to serve as dean of the college section.

As we have seen, the troubles of the college of the preceding year had been widely publicized, especially the part played by the local Executive Committee. Much had been broadcast about their having dominated college policies. It is true that out of thirty members of the Board, ten were residents of Wayne County, and these constituted the Executive Committee with power to act between stated sessions of the full Board. The Synod of Ohio had not been unaware of the situation at Wooster. Consequently at their October, 1915, meeting they were in a mood to ask questions of the new president. Mr. White made a plausible and reassuring statement about conditions at the college. The Synod was impressed by him and passed a resolution pleading for understanding and patience as the new president gathered up the limp reins, and for time for him to find his way before judging harshly. None the less they asked that a committee be appointed from their body to study and recommend possible changes in the charter of the college so as to make any such domination, real or imagined, by an Executive Committee impossible in the future; this committee would report in a year.

In late fall the faculty committee in control of the summer school was apprised of a new development; the local Executive Committee had made the faculty committee subordinate to a new Summer School Senate, consisting of White as chairman, Notestein, Bennett, Remp, the new professor of education, Platt, also new and as yet only as instructor in education, and Dickason. To this Senate the names of instructors and courses must be referred for approval. Quite naturally the committee considered this action an affront and intolerable. They promptly resigned and advised the faculty to elect a new one. This they did, naming for it Black, Notestein, and Olthouse, a committee equally desirous of maintaining the standards of the college, but one perhaps more acceptable to the Senate. The new committee in turn appointed Black as head of the college section, Knight as head of whatever preparatory courses were to be offered, and Remp for the courses in education. Dickason was to be overall director though without power in any of these three sections. He in turn had been shorn of most of his prerogatives. So the matter rested for the summer sessions of 1916 and 1917.

All fall and early winter rumors had been floating about. Mr. White, it was said, had been writing to alumni asking advice as to what changes should be made in the faculty. "Heads," it was intimated, "would soon be rolling." To whom this applied, if to anybody, no one knew or cared to speculate. Yet even the students, in time, became vaguely conscious of tensions in the air. Then on the first of January, 1916, Miss Hughes received a letter from Mr. White and his Executive Committee indicating that they considered her work as dean of women unsatisfactory. It was a staggering blow. She had had no suggestion that her work was not acceptable; Mr. White had not called her in to explain wherein he felt that she had been failing. She asked questions, but these seemed to get her nowhere. Evidently the letter was really intended as a dismissal. Yet she was in no mood meekly to offer her resignation. She was in her fourth year at the college. She knew that President Holden and the dean had approved her work. She assumed that she had tenure, though perhaps nobody had ever referred to her status in exactly those terms. She felt, and her friends on the faculty with whom she consulted felt, that the administration owed her a hearing.

No one knew for sure just what Mr. White and his Executive Committee had against her. It was true that Mr. White and Miss Hughes had been in college at the same time, he in the class of 1890, she in 1891. Maybe he had not liked her then and had harbored this feeling of dislike through the years. It was probably true that she was the high-strung, fidgety type; the college girls often did have fun "taking off" her mannerisms; and yet taking off their instructors and superior officers had always been one of the indoor sports of college students. To be sure, she was strict with them, enforcing standards of behavior that they were not always used to; and they may have resented this interference with their accustomed ways. In his many conferences with students Mr. White may have heard some of these complaints and may even, without intending to do so, have encouraged their talking about her. It may have been that the matrons of the women's dormitories had resented her presence, had felt somewhat displaced, and they may have been critical of her to the president or to individual members of the Executive Committee. It may have been that certain of these local trustees had taken exception to her handling of certain cases among the girls; at least in the records there are many references to a mysterious Case X. It may have been that she was not altogether in sympathy with the rather overheated religious atmosphere of the Wooster of his time, and he thought her not all-enveloped in the odor of sanctity, not lending her influence sufficiently toward personal evangelism. No one could doubt, however, that she was a loyal churchwoman. Probably very few at that time knew the inwardness of her dismissal. Surely still fewer, if any, persons now living know the answer.

Maybe she was nervous; maybe she made mistakes in her handling of young women. But she had standards and convictions, had had experience in two of the best women's colleges in the East, and had had an opportunity to observe what was expected in a dean of women. To most of the faculty she seemed to fit well into the scene. She was a responsive and gracious hostess, and for the girls who studied the history of art under her—the first such course that Wooster had ever offered—she opened up a new world as she pointed out in the illustrative prints brought to the classroom, beauties of theme, of line and color, of light and shadow, of proportion and space. By and large, Wooster's first dean of women had been a success. And in one meeting toward the end of the year her colleagues went on record in a resolution expressing their confidence in her and asking for her reinstatement.

At the midwinter meeting of the Board of Trustees (February 1, 1916) the case of Miss Hughes came up for review. She was not invited to come in to state her case. Instead, they appointed a committee chaired by the Reverend Mr. Robert Watson of New York and including President White to confer with her as to her best procedure. Mr. Sheldon Parks, a Cleveland attorney, who in 1913 had been elected to lead off in the contemplated drive for endowment, made an "impassioned" speech in her behalf, and fell over with a stroke. Tragedy it seemed was being piled on tragedy. As for the committee that had been appointed, they apparently made no effort to go into the case but advised Miss Hughes that she would be given a hearing in June before the full Board if she still so wished.

In the earlier part of the same midwinter meeting the ghost of the junior school of education once more showed its head. During the Holden administration a by-law of the institution had been consistently ignored—or perhaps not yet discovered—which stated that the voting members of the faculty must be specifically so designated by name by the trustees. Everyone had been voting at faculty meetings even down to the humblest instructor. Now for clarification the president asked his trustees to name the voting members. They named twenty six, professors and assistant professors, including the principal of the academy, and Miss Pendleton. The dean of women, the director of physical education, the registrar, and several others were not named and thereby disfranchised. Reelections and promotions were also validated for the year of 1916 to 1917. One or two instructors were raised to the rank of assistant professor. Certain others who had served just as long and had equal or better academic attainments were not advanced. Once again there was a cry that the faculty was being stacked for a purpose. At the end of the year several of those who had been disfranchised left, having found themselves appointments elsewhere.

The next few months were probably the worst in Wooster's long history. For a year tensions had been mounting, first over the summer school and the proposed junior school of education, then over the case of Miss Hughes. In Board and faculty Wooster was a house divided against itself, even though on both sides there were those who sincerely were trying to seek the best for the college. Morale was at its lowest. Nerves, already taut, were stretched almost to the breaking point. The year before in 1915, protests had come from individuals, and from the presbyteries of Cleveland and Marion about the junior school of education. Now an anonymous pamphlet was being widely circulated. Everybody was distrusting the motives of everybody on the opposite side. Some faculty wives stopped even speaking to other faculty wives. In the midst of all this Mr. Vance of the Bible department, realizing something of what was happening to otherwise well-meaning people, suggested a faculty prayer meeting to be held monthly on the Friday after the faculty meeting. This they solemnly voted and as solemnly observed. Here surely they could meet on common ground. There had been false witness; there had been cruelty. Many unfortunate things had been said on both sides, innuendoes, cruel and untrue, born of unthinking anger. There was much to be forgiven and forgotten. Indeed they might all have prayed in deep humility: "Create in me a clean heart, O God, and renew a right spirit within me." And mayhap they did.

All through this weary spring while robins came back and crows flapped their black wings overhead and cawed, a faculty committee was completing plans for the inauguration of President White. It was to be a great occasion, perhaps the most elaborate Wooster had yet seen. Mr. White had set it late, on May 12, to allow for preparation well ahead. It with Color Day would occupy most of four days. Delegates were being invited from many universities and colleges. Distinguished speakers were coming from everywhere, most of them named by Mr. White. Sherwood Eddy would present "The World Situation as a Challenge to Wooster Students" on Wednesday evening, May tenth. Robert E. Speer would follow the next morning, speaking on "God's Need for Men." On the afternoon of the same day there would be an educational conference in which President W. W. Boyd of Western College for Women, Shailer Matthews of Chicago, E. O. Lovell of Rice Institute, and Dean W. F. Magie of Princeton would take part. That evening there would be a pre-inaugural banquet in the gymnasium with a toastmaster chosen from the alumni. On Friday morning, the twelfth, the inauguration proper would occur with all the usual academic accompaniments. In addition to Mr. White's inaugural address, President Thompson of Ohio State University and the Reverend Mr. Ross Stevenson of Princeton Theological Seminary would be speaking. At the inaugural lunch to follow in Kauke Hall still others were to address the guests, among them President Thwing of Western Reserve University, the governor of Ohio, and Dr. George W. Crile, distinguished Cleveland surgeon, who had been a Wooster medical graduate in the class of 1887 (at a time when the medical school in Cleveland was attached, however loosely, to the University of Wooster. The Color Day that was to follow on Saturday was, of course, an affair of the students, but at Mr. White's suggestion, its pageant was to portray the various aspects of student life on the campus. And on Sunday morning Mr. George Luccock, pastor of the Oak Park Presbyterian Church of Chicago, an alumnus, would preach in Memorial Chapel. On Sunday afternoon the program called for nothing—and there was nothing but exhausted sleep and bread and milk for supper. The trains carrying away the guests would long since have closed their doors, whistled their way around the corners and up and down the valley of Little Applecreek and Killbuck.

On Monday morning the college community would once more awake to its own heartbreaking problems. In the spring at the urging of some of her colleagues Miss Hughes had finally appealed to the American Association of University Professors. It promptly appointed a committee to investigate. On May 31, the first member of this committee arrived from Cleveland. He spent four days on the campus and was later assisted by other members of the committee. They went into the long background of Wooster's situation: the summer school as a source of faculty irritation, the proposed junior school of education, President Holden's resignation, Mr. White's election and qualifications, his apparent aims and ideals for the college, the part of the local Executive Committee of the trustees and its relationship to the town, the divisions within the faculty, and finally the case of Miss Hughes. They made every effort to arrive at the facts, reading back for accuracy to each person interviewed the notes made at that interview.[6] It is a sorry tale, and reading it today, one would like to bury it deeper than ever King Midas tried to bury the secret of his ass's ears. In the summer this report was published in pamphlet form.

In the meantime commencement had come and gone. The Board had met and granted, at her request, a hearing to Miss Hughes. The charges were made against her, and she was given a chance to answer them and to state her position. After she went out, however, other letters were read which were not in her favor. In the end the Board sustained the Executive Committee in their former action. Miss Hughes was not reinstated.

The report of the AAUP when it did come out was really not greatly beneficial to anybody, not even to Miss Hughes. Though it had cleared her of every charge but one derogatory comment about the president, the fact of her having been involved in such an uproar made it difficult for her immediately to find a place elsewhere. It had not brought about Mr. White's withdrawal, for which doubtless many persons had hoped. It blackened the name of the college, and may have postponed for ten years or so the winning of a chapter of Phi Beta Kappa. That Wooster was not ready for such a chapter was the verdict of Phi Beta Kappa's national officers, and in this they had the backing of one of Wooster's trustees [7] and possibly of one of the faculty also.

All this controversy and all this publicity had, however, led to one good thing: it had made Wooster once and for all aware of the right of tenure, something badly needed. President Holden, even before President White, had transgressed in this matter, dropping precipitately at least one person who had served the college for many years, a person guilty of no misdemeanor, calling for his resignation utterly without a hearing. Faculty and president would now know where they stood. At the end of their meeting in June, 1916, the Board had voted that the method of dismissing instructors without a hearing is in itself wrong. They went further in adopting the so-called Pennsylvania Rule that a professor or assistant professor might be removed only after conference with a committee consisting of five representatives of the faculty chosen by the faculty and with a committee of five members of the Board and the president and after a report of this conference between the two committees had been submitted to the Board for consideration.

The incident, however, was not yet closed. Mr. Sheldon Parks of Cleveland had by June 5 recovered sufficiently to send a letter to every member of the Board saying that he would be a candidate for reelection by the Synod the following October, that in doing this he was calling for a reorganization of the Board at Wooster, the abolition of the summer school, and a restoration to the faculty of their powers and the exercise of these powers. He wrote that if the Board through its nominating committee failed to recommend him to the Synod for reeelection to the Board, it would be evidence that "the Board is unalterably opposed to these reforms," that if the Synod refused to reelect him he would know that the Synod was also opposed to these reforms. He sent a similar letter to the Synod accompanied by a 16-page document. Mr. Parks was not nominated and not reelected.

The Synod, however, heard the committee it had appointed a year before to study possible changes in the charter of the college. This committee recommended that the trustees from Wayne County be limited to seven; that the committee passing on the discharge of teachers be empowered to pass also on their employment, promotion or demotion; that the College of Wooster seriously consider discontinuing the preparatory department; that "the College of Wooster be supported to the end that the aim of the fathers be realized and that an institution under the auspices of the Presbyterian Church may be attained and maintained with such standards of education as will make it second to none." So quietly, without fanfare, or serious argument did the Synod take action.

The last session of the summer school was in 1917. The preparatory department closed in June of 1918. As Mrs. Dickason wrote years later to *The Wooster Record,* the preparatory school [or academy] had served well its era but with the multiplication of high schools in rural areas, its era had passed. So also with the summer school. As normal schools grew throughout the state and departments of education flourished more and more in the colleges and in the great universities there came a time when there was little need for the summer school. Mr. Dickason found his place as an assistant secretary of the Presbyterian Board of Temperance, a position which suited him well. Mr. Painter, the assistant principal, went downtown to a position in a savings and loan institution.

Wooster could remain now, as it always had been at heart, a liberal arts college, a place where the study of the classics of all literatures, of history, science, and the social sciences flourished, in an atmosphere of Christian harmony. As for Miss Hughes, one need only remind the reader that at her death in 1955 she left a bequest of $5,000 to Wooster College.

It is a long, long time since the day of Petrarch, but a sentence he once wrote seems here peculiarly applicable: "To pardon offenses is a most beautiful revenge, but to forget them is still more beautiful."

Reaching Out

PERHAPS all this controversy had been a necessary irritant, a kind of mustard plaster for the brain. In the last two years the faculty had given much thought to what they really wanted for Wooster, what kind of faculty, what courses, what Wooster's diploma should mean, what modifications should be made in entrance requirements, what requirements for graduation and special honors, what brakes might be put on student activities and social life, what endowment should be sought for attaining these goals. Their imagination had been quickened. There had been and would continue to be a kind of reaching out in many directions, much of it, to be sure, by individuals rather than by the faculty as a whole. Mr. White himself, talking as he so often did of a world vision, was seeking something beyond himself and his immediate environment.

At the beginning of Mr. White's first year there had come several new faculty members, Mr. Holden's appointees, who were to make each his own contribution. Two of these were in the music faculty: James Husst Hall and Daniel Durkee Parmelee. Both of them were graduates of Oberlin and Oberlin's Conservatory. Hall in his senior year there had instructed also in piano, and in the year following had been kept as an instructor in the theory of music. He was an associate also in the American Guild of Organists, though his main field was the piano. Though young and relatively quiet, he had the versatility and that creative human quality that make a true musician and a true teacher. He knew how to touch the keys so lightly as to make them sing; as he looked at the score before him, he could make others feel what he felt, see what he saw, hear what he heard. And with it he had a puckish humor. He was to be only seven years at Wooster, but persons who knew him in these years still hold him in affectionate esteem.

Daniel Parmelee was not so reticent, was more generally outgoing. As Chalmers Martin mingled with the townspeople on the golf course, so Dan Parmelee was soon to gather around him all sorts of persons with a pining for musical expression. Within a few months of his coming to Wooster as instructor in violin he had sought out in the town as well as in the college those who played orchestral instruments. On the ninth of December of 1915 he organized the Wooster Community Orchestra of twelve charter members in the Board of Trade rooms over the old Citizens National Bank. Among them were a shoe dealer, a farmer, a barber and justice of the peace, and a printer, as well as a Wooster music teacher and a senior in the conservatory. On that occasion he told the aspiring group: "It may well be said that no city may be called musical until it encourages or maintains an orchestra, the members of which are striving to understand and interpret lasting compositions, for their own education and development, as well as for that of their hearers." The rehearsals of this new organization were first held in the conservatory once a week. Soon it grew to twenty-two members. And on May 8, 1916, it gave its first public concert, in Memorial Chapel. It was an ambitious performance including, among other selections, Elgar's "Pomp and Circumstance" and Mendelssohn's *Concerto in E Minor.* This was the beginning of an organization that grew steadily in numbers and skill of performance, and still carries on today, a real link through the years between town and gown. Mr. Parmelee after graduating from Oberlin had taken off in the early summer of 1914 for Brussels to study there under Cesar Thompson. When the war broke out that summer he had to leave for home. Back in this country he found a position teaching at the University of Idaho. From there he came to Wooster in the fall of 1915.

That same fall Martin Remp came back to head the department of education at the college and to make his home in Wooster until his death in 1947. Of the years since his graduation in 1904 he had given five each to Huron College, South Dakota, and Hastings College, Nebraska, both young Presbyterian colleges. In each place he had charge of the work in education and had served also as dean. In the interval, too, by studying summers he had won his Master's degree in education at The University of Nebraska. Before he entered Wooster he had had experience teaching in the public schools. In college he had majored under Mr. Compton—though technically there were yet no majors or minors in Wooster's curriculum. He had indeed much in common with him, the same calm, judicious temperament, the same thoughtfulness, the same love of his students, the same meticulousness and thoroughness. Yet he often had a far-away look in his eye as if he were scarcely cognizant of the present. He often had the students in his home, and discussed with them their individual problems of studying and thinking. And in later years he was in charge of the psychological testing program. For ten years he was a member of the teaching staff committee, and for years too in charge of arrangements for public occasions. He did not speak often in faculty meetings, but when he rose his colleagues gave him close attention. He had great common sense, and his were never snap judgments.

At a glance one would have recognized Lawrence Caspar Boles as Wooster's new athletic director. He was stocky, blond, and bespectacled. He was no hail fellow yet a genial soul with a broad smile. Since sometime in 1914 a committee had been on the lookout for a new coach. When someone suggested Boles, they agreed that he was worth watching. In his nine years of high school teaching[1] and coaching after his graduation from Ohio Wesleyan he had almost consistently turned out championship teams. In addition to his coaching he had taught also chemistry, history, and physical education, and he had a way of inspiring boys. The upshot was that the president had sent Lyman Knight to Cleveland to talk with Boles.

Knight had been since 1908 the faculty manager of athletics and knew Wooster and Wooster's teams and record like the back of his hand. He had been responsible for helping to make the schedules for the games, arranging transportation for the teams, managing the financing. He had always been interested in athletics, and believed in them but because of a stiff leg had never been able to play. The boys in affection called him "Skippy Knight." From the first Boles and Knight liked each other, and when Knight brought back his report, the matter seemed almost settled, save for the question of salary. But then Knight turned the trick, giving up at his own suggestion the little extra the college had been paying him for his athletic duties so that they could make the coach a better offer.

In September Boles was on the ground ready to start training the boys. Wooster had its attractions. It had a brand-new stadium to be opened on the second of this October. It had a fine gymnasium, only a few years old, with excellent facilities. And for Boles college coaching was one step up the ladder. He found that all of last year's football team were back. At once he set up a training table at

Kenarden for them, the first such in Wooster's history. There they would be allowed no fried foods, no pastries. Soon, too, he had his cross country men at work. Of a late afternoon one could see them running up and down the lanes and byways around the town.

It was a surprise to everyone that the new coach had never played on a varsity team; his father had been unwilling to sign the permit for him to do so even though the Ohio Wesleyan coach had one weekend made a special trip to Blanchester, Ohio, to try to persuade him. It was not that Boles' father was opposed to sports. He had built on the farm a tennis court for his three sons. He had allowed them, when there was opportunity, to swim, and to ride the horses. But one day in jumping, Lawrence had badly strained a muscle in a leg with a resultant severe case of sciatica. The father would have no part of his son's playing on a varsity team.[2] At college, however, the boy had gone out for the practice team and for the intramurals where he had shown his quality; and he had taken all the courses in physical education that were offered. He was naturally competitive, played bridge and a good game of chess. In his college career he had especially enjoyed the courses in history and the sciences. He wanted to know what made things tick, why and how they were what they were. He had imagination, was always thinking up new approaches to a problem. Yet he was essentially an outdoor person. He loved green grass under his feet, fresh air, and exercise. He stirred in boys also the competitive spirit, but he showed them that to win there must be teamwork, fair play, and straight shooting. Everybody liked him from the start. The first game of the season was with Heidelberg, in the stadium on the day that it was opened. Fifteen hundred persons, from both town and gown, the best crowd to date in Wooster's athletic history, were there.[3] Unfortunately Wooster was defeated, 13–6. Yet it had been a good game; they had lost only in the last thirty seconds. The next two games thereafter were also defeats. Then the tide turned. Wooster tied Wittenberg, defeated the University of Akron, and Kenyon, tied Case, 0–0, and finished by winning from Ohio Wesleyan 21–7. Wooster was third in the Ohio football conference. Thirty years later President-emeritus Wishart was to say of Boles' career at Wooster: "He was a great coach because he was more than a coach."

In President White's inaugural address in May of 1916 there was a somewhat similar sentence: "Our first question about a new teacher in this institution is not, How much does he know about his subject? but, How much does he know in addition to his subject? How much does he know of that vast world of knowledge that lies behind his subject? . . . Only that teacher deserves to be intrusted with the delicate and dangerous task of directing the thought of young men and women, who is a true interpreter of life's deeper issues and significances." White was speaking on "Neglected Elements in Comprehensive Education," and he was stressing first "the most important qualities of leadership—accuracy, thoroughness, system, initiative, and expression. . . . True education," he said, "includes not only the unfolding of the powers of the intellect but also the development of the motives and the will, and the disciplined control of all these powers in the service of humanity. . . . The training of the mind is vital, and deserves the combined wisdom of the world. But the cultivation of character is of primary importance, and without it all other education is a comparatively small achievement. . . . There is no antagonism between scholarship and religion. On the contrary, religion stimulates and assists to the very highest scholarship. Vital religion sets free the mind as well as the soul of man. It provides the most powerful motives for thoroughness. It develops qualities of concentration, patience and persistence. . . . The College of Wooster was founded on a frankly and positively Christian basis. Instead of this being a limitation or a handicap of any sort, we glory in it as our greatest asset and inspiration. We are firm in our conviction that we can have higher standards of scholarship on this basis than on any other, for we know that vital religion enriches, beautifies, and glorifies everything it touches." Then reciting in its entirety the Apostles' Creed, he went on: "Our central controlling purpose in this College is to help men and women to live the largest life open to human beings in the world, and to lead them to cooperate in the largest possible way with the Infinite Forces of the universe in establishing the eternal Kingdom of God over all of life and over every life." In these words he stated the platform of his administration. There was no recognition here of the scholar's ideal of truth for its own sake, no basic pattern for the promoting of intellectual mastery; and though one could not quarrel with most of the statements, the address left the impression on many minds of having somewhat missed the point.

The president after nearly one college year at Wooster was still using the language of the world Y.M.C.A. secretary; he did not yet understand the academic vision.

To all appearances Mr. White had carried the students with him during his first year. He had been much among them, in their chapel services, in their contests, in their religious activities. They had been in and out of his house on Beall Avenue, the welcome guests of his children. He looked on them with affection.

The faculty, however, must have raised their eyebrows at the word in the inaugural address that the College of Wooster did not ask first of all a candidate for teaching how much he knew about his subject. The faculty did ask. More and more, beginning with Holden, they were putting emphasis on advanced degrees for new members; these must prove their thirst for knowledge and their adequacy in their specific subjects by at least some training in a graduate school. Waldo Dunn was completing his study at Glasgow. Walter Peck and William Taeusch would this year or next be going east to continue or begin graduate studies. So Lyman Knight [4] felt the urge, of a summer, to go east for courses in advanced mathematics and later for a year to Columbia to complete his Master's degree, and Mr. Yanney of the same department was some time later (1923) to seek and win his Ph.D. at the University of Chicago. So Martin Remp as he was shifted gradually from education to psychology went for several summers to Columbia or Chicago and finally also for a year. And Perry Strausbaugh, who had served an early apprenticeship as an assistant sometimes in biology, sometimes in botany, was before long making a notable record for himself in graduate work in botany at Chicago. Even the older professors, some of whom had come to Wooster early without graduate degrees, were forever trying to improve themselves and their teaching by private study in their fields. They no less than the younger men believed in the intellectual life as a prime necessity to which all other qualifications were to be added. More than anything else it was Mr. White's failure to appreciate as fundamental, academic values and purposes that made him unpopular with his faculty. One morning in chapel, for instance, he had incidentally downgraded the place of science in man's total equipment. Nothing was said at the time except in private. A week or two later, however, it was Mr. Bennett's turn to lead the morning chapel service. He took as his theme the great benefits of science to humanity, ending in his characteristic dramatic way with the words: "I love Science!" He was openly and privately applauded by the faculty.

Yet this emphasis on graduate work was but one of several ways by which the faculty were seeking to improve Wooster's academic status. In the late fall of 1915 or early winter of 1916 they passed a new system of quality points to stimulate intellectual effort on the part of the students. Up to this time a given number of credits was required for graduation; yet a student could slide along with "C's" and "D's" and still technically fulfill requirements. Now he must have 124 credits and 92 quality points. An "A" in a course would yield him three, a "B" two, a "C" only one, a "D" none. To attain sophomore standing he must have 24 credits and 15 quality points, to become junior, at least 56 credits and 40 quality points. For senior status he must show 88 credits and 66 quality points. This marked a distinct raising of the level.

Along with this new system the faculty had authorized twenty-two honor courses.[5] For these forty per cent more work than in the regular courses was required; and at the end of the year an aspiring student must submit not only to a comprehensive written examination but to an oral as well, before a specially appointed committee of faculty. Seventeen students applied for these courses in the first year. Those who passed them were entitled to wear gold chevrons on their academic gowns at graduation. At the same time a local honor society was authorized to include all those who attained general honors (*cum, magna cum, summa cum laude*), or these special honors, all faculty giving honor courses, all alumni who had won special or general honors.

The next move was to strengthen the entrance requirements. Hereafter the college would accept only those in the upper two thirds of a first-class high school. Those without the proper scholastic certificate would be admitted only after examination, and in some instances they must show also a special letter recommending their "character, diligence, punctuality, and likelihood of success in college work." Such a person, notwithstanding these advance precautions, would be limited to twelve hours a semester, for which, of course, he would receive only twelve credits.

While the faculty were promoting scholarship on the one hand, they were feeling the need of curbing in some way the multiplying student extra-curricular activities. Because of these distractions some students were failing to make the most of their abilities; some others were flunking out quite unnecessarily. Fortunately the Student Senate, themselves aware of the situation, willingly made a study not only of the activities but of every student's participation in these, compiling an index by classes and setting a value for each activity of one or more points according to the time involved in each. Thus the presidency of the Athletic Association in the year of a minstrel show rated eight points, in other years only six. If a student was working his way, five hours of outside work a week rated one point. So each was given a value: a cabinet post in the Y.M.C.A. or Y.W.C.A. or the C.E.: each class office, membership in the Student Senate, on the house committees of the dormitories, the editorship of *The Voice, The Index, The Literary Messenger,* membership in the glee clubs, the oratorio chorus, the choir, the Wooster Orchestra, the band, participation in forensics, whether debating or oratorical contests, in dramatics, etc. Seniors were allowed twenty-four points, juniors twenty-two, sophomores twenty, freshmen only eighteen. These limitations were then rigidly enforced.

Two of the major changes affecting the curriculum itself came during the White administration. In the fall of 1916, the Student Senate, feeling that it had come of age, recommended to the faculty that the Ph.B. degree be discontinued and only the B.A. and B.S. given; and that thenceforth the candidate for the B.A. degree be allowed a choice of one modern language and one ancient language in place of the two classical languages heretofore required. The curriculum committee took the proposal under consideration. There seemed considerable sense in following a trend already being set by various other colleges of like standing with Wooster. The distinction between the B.A. and Ph.B., though real, meant little to most persons. On the other side, might the lowering of the requirements for the time-honored B.A. degree be lessening the real value of Wooster's diploma? It had been the traditional degree of English and European universities, even of Harvard and Yale, where Greek and Latin had been regarded as basic in the background of the educated man, the foundation languages of modern civilization and institutions. Besides, these languages were in their mastery a discipline in themselves, different from yet comparable to that of science. The arguments went back and forth but finally those for simplification won and in 1917–18 the Ph.B. was dropped. The B.A. degree, however, still required that of the fourteen to eighteen language credits accumulated, two languages must be included, and one of these at least must be Greek or Latin.

The other innovation was in the requirement of a major and two minors for graduation. Of the three one had to be in a foreign language, one in natural science, and one in some department of neither the preceding categories. Besides these, there were still pre-scribed courses which could not be counted toward a major or a minor: in Bible, English composition, history, science (biology, chemistry, or physics), mathematics, philosophy, and psychology, and physical education.

In other ways there had been a growth and change in the specific courses offered during the administrations of both Holden and White so gradual as to be hardly noticed, the natural result of an increase in enrollment and in the teaching staff. In earlier years when the faculty was small, the individual member had to be responsible for his whole department if not for a department and a half or two departments. He had to be a man of versatility and wide horizons, ready on occasion or in emergency to turn from chemistry to French perhaps, from Latin word analysis to Spenser and Chaucer, from college algebra to geology, from advanced psychology to a course in daily themes. He often grew along with his students as he read widely in fields in which he may have had little or no specific training. From time to time there had been much shifting around. The Hoge Profes-sorship, for instance, was at first that of morals and sociology and all that could be included within those ample terms. Later it became that of political science and still later of economics. Until in the middle nineties whatever training Wooster had given in public speaking had usually been termed somewhat disparagingly "elocution." Then it was finally dignified by the name of oratory and became a depart-ment, and so remained until in 1917–1918 it became speech. With the coming of new instructors and professors not only did the nomen-clature change but there was a burgeoning of new courses. The first two decades of the century were a time of change and ferment everywhere, at Wooster, in education in general, and in the world.

In 1903, the reader will remember, with the founding of the Florence H. Severance Bible and Missionary Training School, two new professorships had been established, one in the Old Testament, one in missions. Immediately these opened up a wide variety of courses. Heretofore the student could win his eight credits in Bible by taking a semester of study in New Testament, another in Old Testament, and one in apologetics. Now with some limitations as to grouping he could choose electives according to his taste, from primitive religions, Hebrew poetry and wisdom, to the history of missions before the Reformation, city evangelization, or the methods and practices of religious education.[6]

Mr. Kelso joined the Greek department in 1911. He became one of four or five outstanding professors in the Wooster of his day. His interests ranged from athletics to aesthetics. Music he loved, for his wife was a skilled pianist. He walked much, sometimes with faculty, sometimes with students. He read avidly, knew what was going on in the world, balanced the pros and cons of every situation. Not always right, of course, he was nevertheless a person whose ideas were reckoned with. Besides, he was personable, approachable. In his teaching he gave more emphasis to Homer, to both the *Iliad* and the *Odyssey* than had been given, to Greek drama also, offering separate courses in the tragedies of Sophocles, in the works of Aeschylus, and of Aristophanes. He read Herodotus with his students and Lucian's *Dialogues,* gave courses in Greek lyric poetry, and in Greek art and architecture. For those students who knew no Greek he listed a background course in Greek civilization that they might come to realize the contribution of this ancient world to modern thought and institutions. So also later, after World War I, he added a course in Italian painting and sculpture designed especially for those who were contemplating travel in Europe. Some of these offerings were for a semester only; others were given in alternate years, a practice followed more and more as demands multiplied. It was a long time now since any Wooster student at graduation had delivered a Greek oration, yet many students from high schools came to college prepared in Latin, a few even in Greek, and at Wooster they found the ancient classics still in high favor.

Wooster was in this day probably one of the few colleges east or west that taught Latin as literature rather than just as a discipline in linguistics. Mr. Notestein loved Latin as a language, its roots, its inflections, its packed phrases, but he loved also its literature and the far ranges of Roman history. For him language and literature and history were really one package. To teach Roman history, he did not rely on standard histories in the library, though often enough he sent his students to these in the preparation of special papers; rather he made it come alive by reading with them portions of Livy's books, or sometimes of Sallust. In Tacitus' *Annals* there was revealed the life of Tacitus' own period, in his *Germania* the current Roman conception of the fierceness of the Germanic tribes to the north, in his *Agricola,* there was reported the story of Tacitus' father-in-law during the Roman occupation of Britain. In Pliny's *Letters* he found impromptu comments on things and places and personalities: "Nevertheless Regulus did well in dying, but he would have done much better had he died sooner." [7] In Cicero's essays there was much homely wisdom as true in the early 20th century as it had been 2000 years ago, and in his orations passages that would have reverberated across the years no matter what their language. As he taught the comedies of Plautus or Terence or the tragedies of Seneca he was quick to point out expressions often comparable to our modern slang, stock situations and characters long familiar in the drama of various countries. So at times he taught some of the lyric poetry of Catullus, or Tibullus, or Propertius, calling attention to their meters, the singing quality of lines. To these he added occasionally a selection of Latin hymns. Most of all he loved Horace and Virgil. With both he had much in common. Both poets had known and loved the land, its rivers and springs, its fruits, and rugged people. Mr. Notestein had himself been a son of a farmer-teacher, and had grown up in the country close to a little stream.[8] He had looked on the countryside of Virgil's boyhood, knew something also of the Sabine Hills and the "rushing Anio" at Tivoli (Tibur). Like Horace he blessed the quiet of his own "Sabine Farm" north of the campus. In Virgil's *Georgics* and *Eclogues,* he followed the countryman's life, the changes of the seasons, the movement of the stars, the cultivation of the vines and fruit trees, the harvesting of the honey—he had four or five hives of Italian honey bees in his own backyard. Most of all, perhaps, he loved his course in the literary study of the *Aeneid,* loved to trace its backgrounds, to compare it at times with the *Iliad* or *Odyssey,* to examine the accuracy of its phraseology and the beauty of its rolling hexameters, to interpret for his students Virgil's philosophy of life and his conception of immortality. From year to year he offered different combinations, different selections from a given author, not always Plautus' *Captivi* or *Trinummus,* but perhaps his *Mostellaria,* not always Horace's *Odes* and *Epodes,* sometimes his *Satires* or *Epistles.* Occasionally, too, he would read the tenth book of Quintilian with one of his classes. When he finally came to have an instructor in the department he allowed him to give a course or two of his own choosing, and to share in the teaching of the ninety or more students in freshman Latin.

There were various influences, of course, bearing on the modification of the curriculum from 1910–1920. The new age of science was just beginning, the age of the multiplication of industries, of advances in medicine, in agriculture and plant breeding, in the study of textiles, in food processing, in transportation, in the development of natural resources throughout the world. Research was being called for in many fields. Young people were looking forward to careers in college teaching and in research in chemistry, biology, physics, geology, botany, or in the practice of specialties deriving from these fields. The attaining of a Ph.D. required at least a good reading knowledge of two languages besides English, usually French and German; and the man with more than a smattering of Latin or Greek found himself with a further advantage when confronted with the scientific terms of learned treatises. Thus about this time the French and German departments were strengthened by additional courses not only in the appreciation of their literatures but for increased facility in the reading of the languages themselves. A course in scientific French had been offered as early as 1908–1909, and French conversation in 1911–1912; and at about this time a French club of a few members was organized among the students, though discontinued later, and again organized. Additional courses appeared in 19th century French literature, in Victor Hugo's works, for instance, or in some French dramatist, Molière, perhaps.

A similar expansion occurred in the German department. German had flourished through the years under the devoted tutelage of Gertrude Gingrich. With shining eyes she had shepherded the willing and unwilling student through carefully selected works of

Goethe, Lessing, Schiller, had added, as seemed best from time to time, other courses, in the history of German literature, for instance, in prose composition, or scientific German. All along, however, the college had a ruling that no course could be offered for which fewer than ten students were registered. From 1914 on, German courses became more and more the victim of the growing hatred of all things German, engendered by World War I. Though many of the faculty felt with Miss Gingrich that the present sins of a nation should not be held against its language and literature, there were nevertheless fewer and fewer persons signing up for these courses. Besides by the spring of 1917 military training and the courses in science and mathematics in any way related to war service were in demand. A few German courses were offered through the year of 1919–1920, but in the college catalogue of 1920–1921 there is a note that the German department had been temporarily discontinued. This added, however: "The College is prepared, whenever the demand justifies it, to offer necessary work in the subject."

At about the same time that German was lagging, interest in Spanish was picking up. Europe, everyone was saying, would be bankrupt after the war, but the continent to the south of us would be ripe for commercial development. Those who learned Spanish now would have a chance to be on the ground floor of the boom. In 1916–1917, consequently, Wooster employed an instructor in Spanish, who offered a beginning course, a second year course, and a full year in Spanish-American literature. This included the writing of commercial letters in Spanish. After one year this instructor disappeared and Mr. Olthouse, who had been studying Spanish, in the summers, at the University of Michigan, was asked to add a beginning course in Spanish to his repertoire. Nothing more of the sort was offered until 1919 when, as authorized by the trustees, a full-time assistant professor of Spanish came on the campus.

As might be surmised, the sciences were on firmer ground during this period. Rutherford Hunter in physics had gone far beyond his immediate predecessor in developing his department. In addition to fundamental general physics, physical measurements, and electricity that had been given, at one time or another, he offered courses in heat and light, in mechanics, magnetism, in dynamo-electric machinery, in the theory of alternating currents, in physical optics, as well as in advanced heat and advanced laboratory physics. He was rather a rough and ready person, yet with an eagerness for truth that was contagious, and what he lacked in advanced training he made up in enthusiasm. Students thought him a good teacher, though some commented long afterwards that he had been perhaps a better engineer than physicist. Among his colleagues, he was respected as a man of ability.

In biology the courses had remained for years much the same. Mateer had carried the full load, with laboratory assistants. As a practicing physician he had long been aware of what the student looking toward medical school or other advanced work in this field would need in preparation. Beyond the freshman courses in biology and zoology, his electives had been pointed in these directions: mammalian anatomy with its detailed dissection of the cat; histology with its microscopic examination of tissues, and the making and interpretation of slides; vertebrate embryology with a comparative study of the embryos of the chick and the pig; human physiology. His students, the best of them, went off sometimes to teach biology for a while in freshwater colleges, or to enter medical schools where often they won honors. Then in 1918–1919 Clarence Turner came, first to serve as acting professor in Dr. Mateer's absence, then to remain as assistant professor. New courses were then added in neurology, in personal hygiene, and in laboratory physiology (1920–1921).

For years only one generalized course had been offered in college botany. Then in 1913–1914 when Mr. Black had finally been relieved of all responsibility for freshman mathematics and had also been granted some assistance, he felt free to branch out and to offer beginning courses in forestry and plant uses, in ecology and plant physiology, all of which would be valuable background for those looking toward graduate study in forestry, agriculture, horticulture, or their related fields. In alternate years he had been offering also two courses in geology. When Mr. Strausbaugh finally returned to take over the whole field of botany [9] Mr. Black was finally free to devote his energies to the field he loved the best, geology. Gradually he began to split up his former offerings into historic and economic geology, meteorology, mineralogy and fossil geology, two courses in physiography, and in 1917–1918, "the great ice age." In all these he delighted, and from him his students learned to read the landscape wherever they went in later life. Here close by in Wayne County were rounded hills and deep valleys now partly filled and probably holding buried lakes. These were the carvings of the glaciers. There were round boulders, too, worn down and smoothed by ice. And where the glaciers had ended a few miles south there was the terminal moraine, and higher, more pointed hills never reached by glaciers. Occasionally there were a few fossils to be found, insignificant but interesting. Even the flora spelled history: in rare spots one found a yellow birch, a mountain laurel or two, a clump of closed gentians, left over from those that had followed the melting of the glaciers as they moved south. Geology took one back to Genesis.

Mr. Bennett had had for years an enthusiastic following. Many had gone on from his elementary courses in chemistry to qualitative and quantitative analysis and to organic chemistry. With more help in his department he, too, added more technical courses in quantitative analysis, organic analysis proximate and ultimate, in chemical calculations (1913–1914), and physical chemistry (1918–1919). He enjoyed these; they posed more problems. For him even the simplest experiment carried dramatic overtones, and when it came to those in the more advanced courses, the student often felt that he was about to discover a flake of gold or that he just had a bear by the tail and but narrowly escaped. Mr. Bennett was still full of oh's and ah's and what-might-have-been. Even his daily life had a Shakespearean quality. He had always been happy in the number of college girls who took his courses; he made rather a special bid for them; and in 1912–1913 he began offering sanitary and household chemistry: "devoted to the sanitary study of water, food material, the chemistry of cookery, preserving, cleaning, bleaching, dyeing, disinfection, textile fabrics, etc." For a few months of 1918–1919 in that confused period of war, fuel shortages, S.A.T.C., Spanish flu, and demobilization, Wooster had offered experimentally three courses in home economics: in the practical aspects of food and its preparation, in textiles, and in household administration. At that time Miss Amelia Doddridge had come to serve as acting dean of women, trained and experienced in domestic science. After she left, this work was dropped, though Mr. Bennett and his successors for some years continued household chemistry.

All this time there had come to be a growing awareness among Wooster's teaching staff of the place of the small liberal arts college as a feeder for the graduate schools, and particularly for the medical and engineering schools. They believed in what they were teaching as first of all a wide and necessary cultural background but also as preparation for what for many persons would be specialization. It was not, however, until February, 1919, that a formal arrangement took effect whereby pre-medical students at the close of their junior year at Wooster could be given leave of absence for their senior year, and on certification of the satisfactory completion of the first year of their medical course (assuming that this was taken at a first class medical school—class A as rated by the AMA) be granted their baccalaureate degree from Wooster.

In mathematics the offerings were for some years almost stationary, save as Mr. Thomas and later Mr. Williamson developed the field of applied mathematics. In addition to that in machine drawing, they gave courses in analytic mechanics, in the mechanics of materials, with the cooperation and assistance of Mr. Hunter. In connection with this last course there had been set up in the basement of Kauke Hall in April, 1917, a strength of materials laboratory over which Mr. Thomas reigned and for which he had made several pieces of equipment. In this course problems of tension and torsion, compression, elasticity, etc. were treated. The laboratory was "equipped for the making of all the standard tests of steel, iron, wood, concrete, required by the American Society of Civil Engineers." There was, as noted by *The Voice* (April 19, 1917), a large universal testing machine weighing 5000 pounds. There was also a Barry strain gauge which measured to the one hundred thousandth of an inch, an adjustable transverse indicator, a compressometer, a deflectometer, and many other highly technical pieces of equipment.

In September of 1916 the faculty *Minutes* show that they had authorized a course in descriptive astronomy "as soon as it is feasible." This was given that same year by a Mr. W. I. Ferguson, from Missouri Valley College, who came as assistant professor of astronomy, to teach also a course in Greek. At the same time Mr. Yanney was teaching spherical and practical astronomy, in which he included a study of observational methods with practice in mathematical manipulation of the data.

This was a time, too, of ferment in the whole field of education. It was a period of experimentation and fresh theories. There was much debate, for instance, about how best to bring up children, to discipline them in the old-fashioned way or to give them their head to follow their inclinations. The old principles were being challenged and new methods introduced. There was, for instance, the Montessori school. At Columbia John Dewey was leading a whole new movement. Nearly every magazine carried a popular article on the new education, and every women's club nibbled at theories of education along with Nabiscoes. Suddenly the old adage that teachers were born not made was in the ashcan. Normal school courses, if not fully fledged normal schools, were being hatched all across the nation, even though there were many academic noses that turned up slightly and sniffed at their mention. In Ohio the new school law governing the certification of teachers for primary and secondary schools had for a while nearly disrupted the college. Yet even before this the problem of training teachers had been acute. Wooster had, already by 1913–1914, not just a course or two in education but a full-time instructor, later a professor, who gave work in the history of education and its principles, in methods of teaching, in the organization and administration of a high school, in educational psychology, and even sometimes and in a somewhat tentative fashion, in observation and practice teaching. There had also been listed in the catalogue supplementary courses in nearly every department in methods of teaching a given subject. With the coming of Mr. Remp and Mr. Platt in 1915 there were added courses in genetic psychology, in modern educational theory and a survey of European school systems. The Wooster graduate if she majored in education could win an Ohio temporary certificate for high school teaching which after a certain period of actual teaching experience could without examination be transmuted into a life certificate. It was only the primary teacher, after all, whose needs Wooster was not meeting.

With the return of Mr. Dunn from Glasgow in the fall of 1916, now to be professor of English language and literature, that department took on new life. The courses in advanced composition and short-story writing in which he had made his reputation as an inspiring teacher he promptly relegated to others. He took over instead the work in Shakespeare. He kept, too, for a while a survey course in

English poetry. From time to time he would offer a course in Milton; in Browning, or Tennyson or both; in Dr. Samuel Johnson, or in the evolution and development of English biography as a literary form. This had been the subject of his thesis at Glasgow.[10] To others in the department, as they came, fell other courses according to their interests or training: Old English and the history of the language, Chaucer and his century, pre-Shakespearean and contemporary Shakespearean drama, the romantic movement of the 19th century, classical influences in English literature, American literature. Never before at Wooster had English literature covered so wide or seemed so fertile a field. Mr. Dunn had made himself felt in the faculty in other ways. With the end of the first semester after his return, he had persuaded them through the curriculum committee to make written composition for freshmen a full year course. He was determined that Wooster students should learn to express themselves clearly, should be able to write good sentences and orderly paragraphs. Besides he was chairman of the catalogue committee, a member of the graduate work and honors committee, and in another year or two would have a place also on the library committee.

A similar growth became apparent when Clarence Gould as a young instructor had taken over the newly established Michael O. Fisher chair of history. Up to this time history had been treated much like an orphaned child, save for a brief period when Robert Caldwell had been teaching it (1909–1911). It had been too often handed around, and had not been dignified as an entity. Gould, however, saw it as a world in itself, with ramifications stretching out into political science and law, economics and the social sciences, art, and literature. To this wider view he introduced his students; they too were soon looking beyond their own little world and asking questions of what they saw. He required much correlative reading in the library. His were no snap courses. For the first year he followed the pattern already set: two courses in European history, medieval and modern, one in English history, one in American history. But for the several succeeding years he outlined a wide selection, eleven possible courses, four of these a series in American history: the Colonial period (1492–1763); the Revolution and the Constitution (1763–1800); Slavery and Disunion (1800–1861); Reconstruction and Imperialism (1861–1913). There was also a general course covering the entire period. Besides there were three courses in English history, one in Oriental history, one in the Reformation and one in the French Revolution. Later he was to give one also in economic history. He himself read widely, watched the turns in foreign affairs and domestic, sought to understand and interpret them. In the summer of 1915 he had visited France, Italy, Switzerland, and England, and had come back to report to his classes of the war from behind the scenes. His successor after the war added courses of his own choosing, one in English governmental institutions, one in the World War, tracing its origins, its character, its economic, social, and political effects; and still another course on Great Britain and its dependencies since 1832. By this time, however, and even before, the burden did not fall on one man; an instructor or two had been added.

In the years from 1910–1920 Wooster had come a long way in the segregation and development of individual departments. In 1908, for instance, Sylvester Scovel was head of the department of history, morals, and sociology. Happily by the fall of 1910 history had been divorced from this department. Yet Mr. Scovel until his death that autumn had remained the head and sole incumbent of a strange department listed as morals, and sociology. It included such courses as Christian ethics, comparative government dealing with theories of the State, development of existing governments, the history of political opinions, and one semester of international law, an elementary course in political economy in which, according to the catalogue, an effort was made "to relate the principles of the science to our national life and our intercourse with other nations," an advanced course of the same title apparently limited to the problems of labor and immigration, and a course in sociology which began with a consideration of the theory of human society and the practical questions of reform and administration, went on to the study of the amelioration of conditions of dependent and delinquent classes, and ended with a study of socialism. No wonder Mr. Scovel was tired and stooped and walked with slow and measured steps—yet his eyes still shone with the hope of a new day to come when peace and righteousness would triumph in all the world. Out of all this dizzying amplitude grew gradually the departments of political science, of economics, and of sociology.

With the coming of William Estabrook Chancellor to the faculty in 1914–1915 definite problems in some of these fields were sorted out. Courses appeared in money and banking, in taxation and public finance, and in the family, poverty and crime. Within the next few years others were offered in American government—federal, state, county, municipal; in the organization and function of political parties, questions of American foreign policy; in English and American industrial theory. However erratic and lacking in judgment Mr. Chancellor may sometimes have been, he was nothing if not stimulating to the student mind. He got students to thinking and asking questions of many kinds, and they liked him. He had been one of the finds of Mr. Dickason for the summer school. Even then he was not always following the well-beaten path, for it is recorded that once in making his plans for the following summer Dickason felt it wise to have a frank talk with Chancellor (one gathers like a Dutch uncle) and having ascertained that Chancellor was really in sympathy with Wooster's ideals, reemployed him. Chancellor had made a sufficient impression meanwhile on President Holden that in 1914 the latter appointed him to the college faculty as Hoge instructor in political science. In 1919 he became the Hoge Professor of Political Science. He was always doing the unusual. Once he brought in Jeff Davis, the hobo king, to talk to one of his classes. On the occasion of the reelection of President Wilson he arranged for a special wire with election returns, at his home, every two minutes all night and invited his students in to listen. At the jubilation that followed he announced: "Four years from now the protective tariff will be a dead issue." Such statements were part of his stock in trade. He was instrumental, however, in organizing among the students an economics club "to discuss live questions" in that field, and it was during this period that both Republican and Democratic clubs sprang up among the men of the college. On the faculty he served on the committee for community service, student publications, publicity, and for a period also on the library committee. In the town he was active, speaking on many occasions, serving on the town council, and writing letters to the newspapers as the spirit moved him.

Mr. Compton had long exemplified the principles of logic that he taught. It was in his psychology and advanced psychology classes, however, that he seems most to have impressed the students in the earlier days. William James' writings in this field were for them as they became acquainted with the doctrines of realism, idealism, pragmatism, an expanding mental discipline, and when Compton touched on those borderline experiences like hypnosis and telepathy and all extrasensory manifestations he had then all agog. Yet all the time he felt his own field really to be philosophy; for this he had constantly been reading and studying; and to this he gradually shifted. Even his young children had early recognized his interest, for as the Notestein all-black spaniel was named Pluto, so the Compton black and white terrier answered joyously to the call of Plato. Anyhow Mr. Compton had long been giving two introductory courses in the history of philosophy, one in the ancient and the medieval period from Thales down the years, one of the modern period of Descartes, Spinoza, Locke, Kant, Hegel, and others, and still a third course in metaphysics, the aim of which in its second semester was "to find a view of the world, man, and God which will commend itself to the thinking man of today, and which he can apply to religion and life." Later, by 1916–1917, that course was to reflect Mr. Compton's own growth in this field as "the quest for a consistent theory of reality" involved "a class study of the basal concepts of all our thinking, such as space and time, being and relation, change and identity, matter and energy, cause and purpose, nature and life, law and freedom, mind and will, truth and goodness, in terms of which we interpret the world." Some of his students were going on to graduate work in eastern universities and to theological seminaries. Some took what they saw before them and what they heard, never questioning. Some others, however, were stumbling along as in a thicket of logs and underbrush, trying to discover their own philosophy of life and calling everything into question. If Mr. Compton found a student inclined to stray from Wooster's orthodoxy, he was quick to try to point him back, often referring him to James' *Will to Believe.* He was still at heart the missionary who had longed to go to India.

In some of the other departments, even though the changes noted in the curriculum had not been marked, the work itself had been distinguished. This was notably true in the field of oratory.[11] During the years since his coming to Wooster Mr. Lean had won for himself and for his department the respect of his colleagues, of his students, and of Wooster's sister institutions over the state and beyond. Up to 1919 under his training Wooster's debating teams had won twenty-two out of twenty-eight intercollegiate matches. And of the six that were lost—all out of town—no one of them was by a unanimous decision. Besides in oratory Wooster's men in the ten years had won six state and interstate intercollegiate contests, and in twelve others had come out second. In addition to the coaching of the individuals for these contests, Mr. Lean conducted classes in interpretation of literature, extemporaneous speaking, in public address, the writing of orations, as well as in debate. There was much class work, but to the individuals in these courses he was giving almost unlimited attention, to briefing, style, delivery, to control of the voice and proper enunciation, to posture while speaking as well. With a sense of humor and a gift of patience he was often able to develop strength where there had been weakness, confidence where there had been timidity, proficiency where there had been only eagerness.

In physical education, in which no more than four credits could be counted toward a degree, there was of course much group work. By the end of two years of general gymnastics nearly everyone had fitted into some sort of recreational sport, swimming, tennis, soccer—for soccer was being played at Wooster as an intercollegiate sport as early as 1914—track, football, basketball, baseball on the varsity team, the second team, or in the intramurals. Even fencing was listed in the catalogue. By 1914–1915 a course was being offered in the theory, organization, equipment, and management of a playground, and another in the theory and practice of gymnastic and athletic training.

In music most of the work was individual, though the college choir, the glee clubs, the oratorio chorus provided much training in choral work and in musical appreciation. By 1913–1914 courses for which college credit was being given were in elementary theory, harmony, simple counterpoint, and history of music. By 1915–1916 more advanced courses in some of these subjects had been provided; and in 1918, a course in musical aesthetics, for which two credits were allowed, was authorized by the faculty.

Yet all this growth, desirable as it was, was costing money that Wooster did not have. In January, 1914, a committee of the trustees had been set up to initiate a campaign for a million dollars and for the simultaneous wiping out of the deficit. This they had needed badly for new professors and instructors, for the raising of salaries all

along the line among faculty, the administration, and the maintenance staff. Though the president at that time was drawing $5000 a
year from the Willis James endowment for the president's office, the
chef at Kenarden was getting $600 a year and the head electrician,
James Bryan,[12] $840. In all the turmoil of those years the campaign
had never even started. Now in the fall of 1916, the faculty were
restive. The time had come for action. President White well knew
that something spectacular was expected of him. The college advertised its assets as $2,600,000, which included its campus of 100 acres
and twelve buildings. It had 36 faculty members "with degrees from
25 different colleges or universities," a library of 40,000 volumes,
756 students (including those of the preparatory department) from
27 states and 17 from foreign lands. The fee for tuition, room, and
board ran to approximately $300 a year, which was but a token
payment of what this actually cost the college. Yet Wooster had an
enviable record. Already in these forty-six years it had supplied
twelve college presidents, sixty college professors or instructors.
Twenty-five per cent of its graduates had been ministers or missionaries—it had done well for the Presbyterian Church. In this fall of
1916 there were 217 freshmen. The town, too, had grown to seven
thousand persons. The fiftieth anniversary of Wooster's charter day
would occur on December 18, 1916. It would be fitting if a great
Jubilee Campaign could be launched on that day. And what more
fitting if this would close on the fiftieth anniversary of the laying of
the cornerstone, in June, 1918.

As usual Mr. White was at the head of the line suggesting plans.
The campaign must begin in Wooster and Wayne County. After this
initial effort had been won, it must spread to the seventeen presbyteries of the Synod with meetings and canvasses in each, to the alumni,
to the far-flung real and potential givers on the outside. This could be
a studied campaign in education and in finance for the Presbyterians
of Ohio. First, President White must establish in their minds the
unique place of the Christian college in training leaders for the
church, and the obligation of stewardship. He would set forth as
cogently as possible Wooster's financial needs as of the moment. By
presenting the cause in its proper framework he would hope also to
discover and enlist one thousand new leaders in the service of the
church. In October, on recommendation of Wooster's Board, the

Synod heartily endorsed the campaign. Twice already the faculty had given the idea their official blessing, once in early 1915, again recently. To the end that the public might be informed a 100-page brochure about the college was got out. It was elaborately illustrated with pictures of donors, trustees, faculty, students, buildings, even of the towers of Kauke Hall by moonlight, and of the Pennsylvania Railroad station. Here were a summary of Wooster's assets, a record and setting forth of her most pressing needs. The most urgent of these were for seven professorships each to be endowed for $50,000, for two assistant professorships and two instructorships; for increases in salaries of existing faculty to the extent of $75,000 in endowment, and for a pension fund as well. Needed endowment for the library was listed as $250,000. The desirability of more funds for student aid was also mentioned, for equipment of several of the scientific laboratories, for the music department, and for the enlargement of the chapel, the religious education wing of which, though provided for in the original plans, had never been begun.[13] The time had come also for a small college hospital, the building of which would require $10,000 and its endowment an equal sum. The college hoped also for another women's dormitory to include a women's gymnasium; and they were looking ahead to a possible physics building. In the brochure there were also testimonials from alumni of what the college had meant in their lives. Mr. White went further. He had prepared and circulated to Presbyterians throughout the state a brief study in four lessons of the Christian doctrine of property. These he suggested should be used by individuals or organized classes in place of four of the officially published Sunday school lessons. In this he was rather over-estimating the religious dedication of the Presbyterians of Ohio, for though they had glowed with enthusiasm over the founding of the college, they had through all these more than forty years all but let it die on its feet for lack of adequate financial support.

The plan for Charter Day had been well made. It was a notable occasion. December 18 fell on a Monday. On Sunday the Rev. Mr. John A. Marquis, president of Coe College in Iowa, and Moderator of the Presbyterian General Assembly, preached. In the afternoon in the chapel Mr. Rowe directed the college choir in the Christmas vesper service. Monday morning in the chapel Mr. Charles F. Wishart, president of the General Education Board of the Presbyterian Church, U.S.A., spoke. The special program was set for three in the afternoon. As the principal speaker Mr. White had brought on the Hon. James Alexander Macdonald, managing editor of the Toronto *Globe.* In a moving wartime address he appealed to the young men and women to remain true to the North American ideal of the right of a free people to govern themselves and to protect liberty, justice and law. "These two republics" (Canada and the United States), he said, "are Europe's second chance. . . . Let them give back to the father and the mother countries not only their men but their ideals. . . ." Preceding this address Mr. T. K. Davis, veteran librarian, spoke from memory of the events leading up to the founding of the college, and Mr. Notestein, also from first-hand experience, of the life and spirit of the college through the years and of the loyalty and self-sacrifice of so many persons that had made it what it had come to be. At the evening banquet many persons spoke, and with enthusiasm of the coming campaign, pleasant things everyone liked to hear: "Wooster is a city set on a hill; it cannot be hid, must not be hid." "I had not even dreamed what you had here at Wooster." "One ninth of the wealth of the United States is owned by Presbyterians, and yet they give less to their colleges than any other denomination. . . . Our church ought to have thirty to fifty million for education in the next ten years." And Moses Breeze, director of the Presbyterian Forward Movement in Ohio: "Nothing will withstand the prayers and appeals of six hundred young men and women . . . the work of raising the fund will be done before it is begun." There were others, of course: the moderator of the Ohio Synod, the president of Alma College in Michigan, a Wooster alumnus, Wooster's own George N. Luccock of Oak Park, Illinois, and again Mr. Charles F. Wishart, who recalled hearing here many years before the "sweet music" of Karl Merz, and who referred to President White as "one of those men who never knows when he is beaten." The jubilation ended and the work began.

Preparations for the campaign in Wooster and Wayne County had been going on for some time. Since the middle of November the newspapers had been giving almost daily bulletins of the progress of the plans: in fact Albert Dix, editor of *The Republican,* and chairman of the Board of Trade, had consented to be general chairman for the local drive. *The Daily News,* however, was not far behind in its backing: "Wayne County citizens," it said one day, "don't appreciate the standing of the college throughout the world. It is really one of the great educational institutions of the day, notwithstanding that it is not one of the largest," and then went on to remark that the British ambassador in Persia had spoken "particularly of the frequency with which he encountered Wooster graduates." Even *The Orrville News* wrote that "Wooster College is Wayne County's greatest asset, and the campaign should have the sympathy and support of every citizen." Pastors of churches in Rittman, Fredericksburg, Congress, Dalton, West Salem, Creston, Sterling, Orrville, Apple Creek were giving it their support, and in some instances holding union services to stir up enthusiasm. The goal for Wooster and Wayne County was $50,000. Headquarters were at first above the City Shoe Store on the southeast side of the public square. The trustees had employed an experienced money raiser, Mr. Alfred Hoffsommer of Harrisburg, Pennsylvania, to take charge, and to assist him Harold I. Donnelly, '11, former instructor in the preparatory department. The slogan was: "Boost Wooster and Wayne County by boosting Wooster College." The campaign had been endorsed by the Board of Trade, by Wooster presbytery, by the local Women's Federation, by just about everybody. It was pointed out that fifty years before when T. K. Davis "almost singlehanded," undertook the campaign among Presbyterians of the county and vicinity, raising the fund that assured the existence of the college, the Presbyterians had averaged, including chidren, ten dollars per member.

On December first a citizens' meeting was held at which Mr. White outlined the purpose of the campaign and its specific objectives. In 1888, he said, neither Harvard nor Princeton had had more than four millions of assets, and now they had each more than forty millions. If Wooster raises this million for endowment, it, too, would have nearly four millions in assets. He predicted that the college would have ten millions in ten years, and could establish a standard for the Christian colleges of the world. Others spoke, notably Mr. Chancellor. He estimated that there were eighty millions of assets in Wayne County, that the college community probably spent an average of $1000 a day in Wooster and Wayne County, not excluding Sundays. He wisely pointed out also as an economist that every college building needs a productive endowment equal to its cost. In the local newspapers within a few days letters from him appeared showing Wooster's productive endowment and her tuition costs in comparison with other colleges of like standing. At the citizens' meeting also Judge L. R. Critchfield spoke, saying that the college was just as good as or better than a factory, and Mr. Fred Heim spoke for the farmers and the people of the county.

Committees of leading citizens had been appointed: for the Board of Trade, Mr. Critchfield, Dr. R. A. Biechele, and John A. Myers; for the college, W. D. Foss, George Schwartz, Superintendent of Schools G. C. Maurer, and Herman Freedlander. The campaign started with a dinner of all team captains and workers at the American House on Tuesday evening, December 26, and was to last five days. Each noon the ten captains reported at lunch at the American House. Each of these captains had chosen five assistants. Besides these were three teams of women under the chairmanship of Mrs. William Annat. The next morning a large clock was affixed to the west wall of Alvin Rich's hardware on the northeast side of the square to show the progress of the campaign. Its hands moved slowly. Thursday afternoon they indicated a little more than $13,000 pledged. By Friday afternoon the $16,000 mark had been passed. By Saturday night nearly $20,000 had been subscribed. The canvass was held over. By the following Tuesday the total had reached $21,584. The headquarters stayed open until Wednesday, for those in charge were still hopeful of several large contributions. In all fewer than 300 persons had contributed. The college seniors had undertaken to pledge $1000; so had O. A. Hills, president of the Board of Trustees, and Mrs. C. M. Yocum and President White. One hundred dollars had come in from the Wooster Preserving Company, another one hundred from Shreve, and among the contributors was a Negro barber from Wooster. Mr. Alfred Hoffsommer took off for Pennsylvania. Harold Donnelly maintained an open office through January.

Around the campus gloom was outlined on every face. What had gone wrong no one knew. War, of course, was in the air. People were uncertain of what lay before them. It was possible that too much stress had been put on Presbyterianism and those of other denominations were inclined to hold back. One can only speculate about the feeling of President White. When after his election to the presidency of Wooster in June of 1915 he had gone back to the home of his family on Bowman Street, he is reported to have been as white as a sheet; and one of those present is said to have remarked to him that any president who followed Holden would be sacrificed. He must now have thought of that remark. But yet, what had Mr. Charles F. Wishart said on the occasion of the Charter Day banquet?—that he "is one of those men who never knows when he is beaten."

X

On Campus

TO be sure the going had been rough the first year and one half, rough for Mr. White, rough for many other persons, but not all had been lost by any reckoning. There had been achievements and advances, happy occasions to remember, things to make him proud of the college of which he was the president.

Undoubtedly many new friends had been made for Wooster and were being made in the church at large notwithstanding the controversies and disappointments. In the summer of 1916 the college had entertained the Ohio Synodical School of Missions on the campus with speakers from New York and from the South; men and women from all over the state had come, many of whom had never before seen Wooster. At the inauguration in the spring eighty colleges and universities had been represented. Both that event and the Charter Day celebration just past had brought distinguished churchmen. In the long run all these new friends would make other friends for Wooster. He was laying the ground work. The campaign for endowment in the presbyteries must go on as planned even though Wooster and Wayne County had not lived up to what everyone thought they could and would do. After all he was seeking not so much growth in plant as in the inner structure of the institution and in its spirit, and of this there was continuing evidence, especially among the students.

Now at the turn of the year of 1916–1917 as he looked out over the campus there among the elms still stood the life-size bronze statue of Abraham Lincoln, solid on its seven-foot stone base. The dedication of this had taken place more than a year ago, soon after he had come. It had been a happy occasion in which both town and gown had shared. The local Board of Trade band had furnished the music that rainy afternoon. The Lincoln had been given by William H. Mullins, '76, of Salem, Ohio, and presented on that day formally by his father, Wooster's own James H. Mullins. Judge Charles Krichbaum, '83, had given the address on Lincoln the ideal statesman and citizen, and though Mr. White had of course accepted the gift in the name of the college, the president of the Student Senate had spoken

also of how much this statue would mean to generations of Wooster's students,[1] a cherished symbol of greatness of spirit, to which all
might aspire. The statue was Lincoln to the life, in the build, the
facial expression, even in the stance and the crumpled shoes. In the
left hand was held the Emancipation Proclamation. Underneath on a
bronze plaque were inscribed his memorable words: "With malice
toward none. . . ." The sculptor had been one of Mr. Mullins' own
workmen in his plant in Salem, gifted though generally unknown.[2]

Over across the way in the old gymnasium the laundry equipment
was now in, all but a pulley. Soon nearly twenty-five boys and girls
would be busy there helping by their work to pay for their education.

There had been during the year many minor occasions worth
recalling—when Clinton Scollard, the poet, came, for instance, to
talk of "Tendencies and Phases of Modern Verse":

> . . . Why is Memnon mute,
> Whose voice was tuned as is the silvery flute
> When Thebes sat queenly by the Nile's low shore?

or John A. Lomax on another evening with his "Cowboy Songs." In
December of that first year when autumn was over and the snow
once more flying there had been a banquet, an annual affair, at which
the football men at long last broke their training table rules and
indulged in roast pig with all the trimmings, including speeches and
a general post mortem of laurels and losses. At the end the captain
for next year's team was named and the outstanding players received
their *W*'s. There had been also, in the spring of the year, a Forensic
League [3] dinner at Kenarden at which gold medals were presented to
the winning debaters of the year. One day in March of 1916 the new
honor society had been officially organized, and in June had held its
first dinner meeting with Mr. Kelso moderating, and an alumna and
alumnus giving the addresses. There had been another time that
stormy spring when the faculty had thought to forget for a night
their provocations and honor their president on his forty-sixth birthday. In February the college had had occasion to observe two other
birthdays. When Dean Compton announced in chapel one morning
that W. Z. Bennett had reached his sixtieth milestone, the students
rose, gave him a special salute and called for a speech. Touched, he

reminisced briefly of his thirty-five years at Wooster, incidentally recalling how in his first class there in the basement of Old Main next to the coal bin, among the fourteen students had been one Elias Compton. In early February one day, T. K. Davis, librarian emeritus, had been invited to lead chapel on his ninetieth birthday. He was still hale, still walking on occasion from his home at the corner of Beall and Pine to the public square and back. Knowing that he would be asked to what he attributed his long life and happiness, he answered by reading the 34th Psalm:

O magnify the Lord with me, and let us exalt his name together. I sought the Lord, and he heard me, and delivered me from all my fears. . . . What man is he that desireth life, and loveth many days, that he may see good? Keep thy tongue from evil, and thy lips from speaking guile. Depart from evil, and do good; seek peace and pursue it. . . .

He ended with emphasis and looked up. His desire was at all times to praise the Lord, no matter what the occasion, and when one had reached ninety the occasions were likely to be all too few.[4]

The scholastic year of 1916–1917 had started auspiciously with 517 students registered at the opening, and by October 549. Though the freshman class was large, there had been a significant dropout; only seventy were enrolled as sophomores, and the juniors numbered fewer than 150. Classes this year had been limited to from fifteen to thirty; every instructor or professor had a chance really to know his students.

From the college community there had been several withdrawals. In the spring William F. Weir had resigned the pastorate of West-minster Church. Within the next few months they would be welcoming in his place the Rev. Mr. George N. Luccock, with his common sense, his abounding humor, his understanding of human nature, and his devotion to his calling. Herbert Archibald, the registrar, was now gone, and had been succeeded by acting registrar, Charles R. Compton, brother of the dean, and a meticulous man for detail. Emery Bauer and Berenice Wykoff, the directors of physical education for men and for women, had not returned. Samuel Morris, an instructor in chemistry for more than three years, highly esteemed by his colleagues, was leaving as of the first of January, 1917.

Clinton Moffett had been added this year to the English department, to handle, along with William Taeusch, the various courses in English composition. He had had a year of advanced study at Princeton, and some teaching experience. The new Miss Florence Jenney,[5] who had come in the fall of 1916 as instructor in vocal music, was proving already to be an acquisition. She was in her early thirties, well trained, with several years already of teaching experience. She was gay and generous with her voice.

Mr. Dunn was back and had taken over the chairmanship of the English department with gusto, as well as his share of committee work in faculty. Now in academic processions he could wear his gorgeous Scottish doctoral regalia, the envy of all who looked. The juniors and seniors remembered him of course, his shock of blond hair which he kept sweeping back, his habit of reading aloud in the classroom in a manner almost of boredom, his sardonic comments on occasion. Yet somehow in all this lay buried a deep enthusiasm for literature and learning, and this he transmitted to a host of his students. His elective in Shakespeare numbered forty. All semester they considered with him but one play until they knew it backwards and forwards, its origins and parallels, its characters, its phraseology, the world in which it was born, its dramatic construction. It came alive; they would never forget it.

To be the new dean of women Miss Ruth Marshall had come from Minneapolis. She was still in her twenties, yet she had stature in every way. She had come not only from a large city but from a great university where as an individual she had stood out, not only for her scholarship, but for her warm personality, her poise, her natural dignity. Instinctively people respected her, looked to her as one they could trust. With an M.A. in history and a year of experience of teaching at the University of Minnesota, she had also an additional year of graduate work at Bryn Mawr. She was well able to take over a course or two in history along with her work as dean. She was awake, responsive, and full of ideas. In the two years she spent at Wooster besides giving a sense of peace and stability to the women of the college to whom the discords on the hill had inevitably communicated themselves, she was instrumental in securing for Wooster membership in the National Association of Collegiate Alumnae, and, for the local self-government association of the girls, membership in the International Self-Government Association. Self-government among the women at Wooster had been functioning since 1914.[6] Now it could feel itself no fledgling, but a part of a great community of responsible young women from whom they could get and with whom they could share pertinent information.

Throughout the fall of 1916–1917 nothing much happened on the campus. There were exciting football games; there was for the first time a Thanksgiving vacation from Wednesday till Monday, cause for special rejoicing among the students. But for the most part it had been a time of considerable reorientation, of getting acquainted not only with new personnel and their ways of working and thinking but with one's own attitudes. It was in November of this fall that Mr. Kelso, who had long since made his reputation as a teacher, as an adviser, as a courteous gentleman and delightful companion, and as a stickler for academic justice and standards, moved in faculty that "we proceed to elect by ballot a committee to consider dismissals, promotions, and demotions in accordance with the action of the trustees last June and the recommendation of the Synod at its recent meeting." For the moment the motion was laid on the table; there were other things in the offing on which they needed to concentrate; yet it remained in the back of everyone's mind.

Then after the holidays, the stubborn cold of January settled over campus and town. In such weather the power house was eating up 150 tons of coal a week. Prices were rising and the administration was already alerted to the possibility of a coal shortage. Classes in Taylor Hall were moved to other buildings and schedules adjusted to suit, thus saving approximately five tons a day. By the middle of February the shortage had become alarming. The gymnasium was shut down save for games and practice schedules. The library, open all day and three evenings a week, was kept "fairly warm" for study. Lights went out at nine o'clock in the dormitories. In 1915–1916 the college coal bill had been $10,000; this year of 1916–1917 it threatened to reach $20,000.

When the trustees met in February, they considered a probable deficit of $15,000 for the year. In the face of this they voted, though regretfully, to raise the price of boarding from $3.50 to $4.00 a week.[7] At this meeting the individual trustees reported on the various conferences being held for Wooster's endowment in the presbyteries.

Eleven thousand circulars had been sent out. Lantern slides had been made to show the campus and college activities. Mr. White and his helpers had been speaking all around the state. In spite of an impending deficit, however, the trustees took positive action to make it a part of the permanent record that one professor should each year be granted leave of absence on full salary. This year the leave went to John C. Boyd, instructor in German and Latin, through many years in the preparatory department. At this meeting, too, Oscar A. Hills presented his resignation as president of the Board, an office he had held since the death of L. H. Severance. He had known four of Wooster's presidents, had worked with three of them as a trustee for nearly thirty-two years. Though he had as a member of the local Executive Committee come in for much criticism, he had long been a benignant figure on the campus and in the town, generous both with himself and with his money.[8] As president of the Board he was succeeded by the Rev. Mr. John Timothy Stone of Chicago, who had been a member of the Board for some months, and a visitor to Wooster on several occasions before that time.

The students in the meantime had been taking everything in their stride, the cold weather, the fuel shortage, the good and the bad. When the death of Mrs. L. E. Holden was announced in chapel they promptly voted to send to the former president an expression of sympathy. When the cold was at its worst in January, one Saturday morning they took off for an all-day skating party to Chippewa Lake, having arranged to have the old hotel there opened and ready with coffee and wieners. The seniors, too, had one night displayed their hiking ability by a progressive party from one town member's home to another, stopping at each place long enough for sandwiches and songs and a general "warm-up." They finally wound up on South Grant Street. There they were treated to a grand finale of ice cream. Their appetites somewhat appeased, they sprinted back to Holden Hall to deliver their dates just before the last bell. They were a robust and happy lot, these Wooster students; one had but to listen to their campus sings on the library steps on Friday nights spring and fall.[9]

All in all, student attitudes and activities, in which the faculty had no small part, during the four years of Mr. White's administration were satisfying despite minor breaches of discipline from time to time. At Mr. Kelso's instigation Color Day in 1917 had been planned as an all-college production, not of classes, as in former years, a pageant commemorating the 400th anniversary of the Reformation. The Student Senate had arranged for a professional from Pittsburgh to come over for five weekends to help them. It was all to be photographed by Hearst-Pathè. The music faculty more than ever before were entering into college and community life. Their recitals were memorable occasions. The Boys' Glee Club in the spring of 1916 had made its most ambitious trip so far through parts of eastern Ohio and Maryland, ending with a concert in the Metropolitan Presbyterian Church of Washington, D.C., the church of which Mr. Paul Hickok, Wooster trustee, was pastor. For the spring of 1917 they planned a trip from Dayton and Cincinnati as far as Kansas City and possibly Des Moines, returning via Detroit. The conservatory students had organized among themselves a Fortnightly Musical Club "to foster the desire for musical education" by the "study of the lives and compositions of the great music masters of the world." In the spring of 1917 the new Wooster Orchestra, now grown to twenty-five instruments, gave its second public concert under the direction of Daniel Parmelee. Not only had this enlisted the local music enthusiasts, but the college had extended its community benefits by offering to the young children of Wooster and vicinity two preparatory courses in piano and in violin at special rates.[10]

The literary societies were functioning much as they always had. In April of 1917 there came an innovation. Athenean and Castalian presented at the Opera House Sardou's *Scrap of Paper* in a joint cast. No longer did the girls have to wear bloomers and pretend that they were men. The more exclusive literary clubs, Stratford, Quadrangle, Ruskin, Franklin, still existed but their activities had become more and more social, less and less literary. There had sprung up, however, a poetry club for the encouragement of those who wished to toy with writing verse and to practice various verse-forms. In the second annual literary contest with Hiram College in 1916 Wooster had won the decision in three out of four entries: the reading, the short-story, the oration. They had failed, surprisingly, in debate. During all this period *The Wooster Literary Messenger* kept struggling for existence financially. Once its managers had sought outside help and had brought on a lecturer on Negro spirituals. In the spring of 1917 three members of the faculty, Miss Jenney, Mr. Dunn, and Mr. Lean gave for it a benefit performance. In debating Wooster's teams had kept their record of never losing on the home floor. They were now petitioning for a chapter of the national forensic fraternity, Delta Sigma Rho. In this again Mr. Lean was a prime mover. Every spring on Memorial Day for some years he had been inviting all his debaters and orators to his home for a "sumptuous" breakfast.[11] Around the tables they usually talked till noon, talked of everything, of Wooster, yes, but of much else, national and international questions inspired by their investigations of the year as they had prepared their briefs. It was a kind of final bull session of the year for them, and one that held its place as an annual and cherished custom.

Mr. Lean always dreaming up ways to improve the college literary and forensic activities had suggested in the fall of 1915 to twenty-one men, most of them juniors and seniors and all of them leaders in various student activities, that they form among themselves a Toast-masters' Club for the practice of after-dinner speaking.[12] In November of that year they had organized. Every six weeks thereafter they met at a formal dinner at the Archer or the American House downtown. One of them was toastmaster; six others spoke. Everyone thus had a chance to speak twice a year. Each program was built around a theme, sometimes serious, often humorous. At the final spring meeting Mr. and Mrs. Lean were special guests, and each member was allowed to ask a young woman. The first dinner occurred in January, 1916. Mr. Lean served as toastmaster. The setting they had chosen was New York on the occasion of the return of Henry Ford's peace ship. J. H. Millar, impersonating Mayor Mitchell, gave the address of welcome. Wilbur M. Smith, as Henry Ford, responded. Hubert White took the part of Thomas A. Edison speaking of war and modern inventions; Paul Patton talked of paper warfare, R. S. Alexander of modern war and the international scene, and Harold Collins told of the trip from the point of view of an accompanying Oberlin student. The next dinner in late February took the form of a political symposium in the Statler Hotel before the Cleveland Board of Trade. Each of the six speakers presented the name of a candidate for the presidency of the United States—including a suffragette and Gus Eberly.[13] Another occasion represented a meeting of the Wooster Alumni Association in the year of 1942, and yet another, just before the Charter Day celebration in 1916, purported to be a meeting of the Wooster Board of Trustees discussing how best to use the million dollars about to be raised. They had obviously studied some of the campaign literature. Once they impersonated the village fathers of Smithville met together to discuss the general state of the town. Johnny Appleseed Miller, editor of *The Smithville Fizzler* extolled the advantages of life there. So they went on. Yet sometimes they could be serious, too, and were. The Toastmasters' Club was at least for that generation the club of clubs. It and the Congressional Club were honor clubs to which any man in college would be proud to be elected.

There were many other student groups of course. As fraternities had disappeared, the sections in Kenarden in a way had taken their place. Each had its loyalties and its own parties, sometimes at the Dolly Madison on Beall Avenue, sometimes elsewhere; and as seniors were graduated others by invitation took their place, and these new members were duly initiated. The gregarious instinct sometimes brought together individuals with only a regional loyalty. Some years before, the Trans-Mississippi Club had been constituted from the small group of students from the western states. Now those coming from Michigan had formed the Wolverine Club. There was even the Columbiana County (Ohio) Club. More seriously, the thirty-seven students from seventeen foreign countries had organized a Cosmopolitan Club to familiarize themselves with the problems, political, social, economic, of other nations, and "to further the aims of the Association of Cosmopolitan Clubs." The Scientific Club had now for years been meeting to listen to serious papers or talks on scientific subjects. Mr. Chancellor's Economics Club usually serious, sometimes indulged in a lighter moment; once it transformed itself into a sample New York stock exchange. Mr. Remp, too, encouraged a teachers' club which brought in an occasional speaker. The students were alive, talking and thinking of many things. In all of this there was manifest perhaps the beginnings of an intellectual ferment. Undoubtedly this had already existed among small coteries of students as they came flat up against ideas they had never before met, but now perhaps it was more widespread, as conditions favorable to its growth arose.

Though many things were argued in the sections of Kenarden—

religion, politics, philosophy, social relations—and in Livingstone Lodge, as time went on, the center for such discussion, where girls, too, were involved, was possibly The Shack. Just off campus, on Pine Street, halfway between College Avenue and Beall, it was becoming more and more a student institution. Started in 1910 by Fred Collins, '13, as a way of adding to his straitened budget, it was a crude, one-storied, frame building which the operator advertised as "The Club," though before too long everyone else had dubbed it "The Shack." Here the students could buy cokes and ginger ale, candy of all sorts, and all the truck one usually finds in a simple confectionery. Then in 1915 along came William K. Syrios and George Stavropolis, two young Greeks, who took over, renamed the place, quite unsuccessfully, "The Sugar Bowl," and gradually transformed it.[14] Before long Stavropolis dropped out, and Syrios [15] alone carried on. He gave the place personality and made it what it became during many succeeding years, a kind of embryonic student union. There the rebels of the college came to expound their ideas. There they dreamed up all sorts of plans, analyzed their professors over coffee and a piece of pie. Eventually "Bill Shack," as everyone called Syrios, enlarged the place, added booths, tables, more chairs, more to eat and drink, and homemade candies. Around these tables as the years passed, especially in the twenties and the thirties, many a student found the place where he could let go and say what was churning in his mind. A personal letter from a Wooster student of this somewhat later period tells the story of campus life as viewed from the Shack:

It (The Shack) certainly was, sometimes in ways not looked on with favor by the Administration, a vital center for a good many students. I was told, though I never knew it for a fact, that Bill Shack not only knew his clientele so well that ten years after graduation when you walked into the place he unhesitantly yelled "One lime coke coming up," but he also quietly slipped a few bucks to students who were really on their uppers. And certainly his relaxation about the staggering bills in the little black book back of the cash register was astounding; he practically never entered the charge himself, almost always trusting us to mark down ourselves what toasted cinnamon rolls and cokes we couldn't pay for. . . .

Not everyone went there. In fact, one of the few really valid ways you could divide up the undergraduates in my day was into Shack and not

Shack. I would guess that the former group was larger, though only slightly. It was not homogeneous. Perhaps the only thing that its members had in common was that they all went to the Shack. If you were a butterfly, you went there. If you dated, you went to dances on weekends, but during the week you had a rich choice—the movies (changed twice weekly), the Stadium (overpopulated and risky), or the Shack. The great thing about a Shack date was that it cost the boy ten cents, the price of two cokes, and if you could find a place to sit you could stay all evening. A girl who had snared a date with someone really worth flaunting would insist upon at least ending up in the Shack.

Then there was the bridge group. There was a marathon bridge game at the Shack, beginning at opening time in the morning and continuing until Bill turned out the lights. The players changed but never the cards, which were unbelievably limp and barely legible. The Shack was also the place where you could make all sorts of noise. There was an old phonograph (no jukebox) and a stack of scratchy records—Dwight Fiske, "Marie the Dawn Is Breaking," lots of Tommy Dorsey, not much Guy Lombardo—but noise.

During the day, the Shack was perhaps more important because less the place to show off a new boy friend. One of my most vivid associations with the place is this. I took Vergilius Ferm's introduction to Philosophy in the afternoon—and that was a course which shook a fair number of students out of the magnolias—and most of us had no classes after that. A large group from the class, ten or a dozen, fell into the habit of adjourning from Kauke Hall to the Shack and continuing the discussions there, those heated wranglings about the nature of reality which came almost to blows and which constitute so important a part of anyone's education.

It was also a place where you could find a political argument any time you wanted one. The place where the campus communist (later to die in Italy rescuing an officer) took on the Franco apologist (still comfortably alive in Barcelona)—and where the boy who was about to drop out of school because his family had just gone on relief stood around listening and saying nothing and wishing someone would pay for his coke.

The people who didn't frequent the Shack, anyway some of them, thought it a bit risque. It was our Dome, our Left Bank. The fine thing about it was that it was filled with majorities of one, some pretty intolerant, some pretty phony, and some pretty weak. . . .

Sometimes student interests took a practical turn. On Mr. White's first list of faculty committees he had named one on community service with Mr. Wood as chairman. He wished to encourage a greater participation of both faculty and students in efforts toward bettering the community. In February of his first year, College Hall had been opened. It was just across the bridge over the railroad tracks from Little Italy and had been built by Westminster Church with the help of some other interested citizens as a neighborhood house for the local Italian colony. The college had always a very friendly feeling for these Italians, some of whom had been on its payroll as workmen about the campus. Here Toni and Nicolo and Giovanni, and no doubt Angelo and his friends could come in their leisure to enjoy music and games and good fellowship and perhaps also to join the boys in a class in manual training or in one to improve their own English. For some time men from the college Y.M.C.A. had been going two evenings a week to Little Italy to conduct such a class. Girls, too, from the Y.W.C.A. had been enlisted. For the Italian wives and daughters whose opportunities had been limited there were classes in sewing and cooking; and for the little tots play classes; and on Saturday afternoons a college girl gifted in story-telling was there to weave for them wonderful tales of make-believe. On Sunday mornings there was a Bible class and in the evening a simple, informal preaching service conducted usually by Mr. Wood.

This project constituted, however, but one of several ways by which the college, the Y.M.C.A. and the Y.W.C.A. were extending their service to a wider community. Occasionally groups of boys and girls, as many sometimes as twenty, were going out to the Wayne County Orphans' Home north of town to teach classes or to put on some entertainment for the lonely youngsters living there, deprived for one reason or another of a normal home life. Others, small groups of the more zealous, conducted, usually by request, religious services in outlying villages, Creston, Congress, Nankin, New Pittsburgh, Shreve, or at country schoolhouses. Mr. Knight, who was much in sympathy with these activities, often drove them to their destinations and brought them back. He knew many of them well, knew some of them on the playing fields, knew them in his home, where now and again of a Sunday evening a group congregated around the piano to sing. They were by and large young people brought up in homes where such activities were usual. As election time drew near in the fall of 1917 college teams comprising often a quartet and two or three speakers were going out to Burbank and West Salem and other villages within Wayne County to help rouse interest in the dry campaign. College girls, too, did their stint in Wooster itself.

More and more town and gown seemed to be finding common ground. Time was when the city Opera House had been out of bounds for student performances. Now the literary societies and glee clubs, singly or jointly, used it for their plays or concerts. Townsfolk were coming up to the college for lectures or other entertainments. As early as October, 1915, the college had invited the business men of the town to make free use of the gymnasium facilities on Tuesdays; and of course they flocked to the games in Severance Stadium on Saturday afternoons, and on winter nights to the basketball games in the gymnasium.

From the first Mr. Boles' coaching had brought results in building up Wooster's teams. He was just as firm as Wooster had ever been in requiring a strict observance of all the rules, rules of the game and rules of the college; there must be no smoking, no drinking among his players, no self-indulgence, no profanity, no loose talk. Good sportsmanship there must be at all times. In games, as in social life, or business, one must learn to think quickly, to practice not only self-respect but respect for the other fellow, teammate or opponent, to take the rough and tumble for what it was worth. Through all his career he tolerated no hint of professionalism. He welcomed the good student, rejoiced to find a baseball captain who was also a captain of a debating team. The brains, the quick thinking that made him excel in the one field made him strong also in the other. Yet despite the rigor of his training, he inspired confidence and loyalty. They loved him; from the start they followed his lead.

In his first season of football Wooster's team had registered third in the Ohio Conference. Though they had lost to Oberlin, they had tied Case, and they had shown good blocking and tackling and a strong offensive, especially in a game with Kenyon. To be sure, there had been casualties, one broken leg, two fractured shoulders. The next fall, 1916, however, the team topped Wooster's record of many years; only in 1905 had it been matched. They had lost only to Miami and Case; and at the end of the season *The Cleveland Press,* and *The Plain Dealer, The Cincinnati Enquirer,* and *The Columbus*

Dispatch singled out Wooster men as worthy of places on the All-Ohio team. It was their proudest moment, save for the next year, 1917, when they rose to first place in the Ohio Conference; out of nine games played, three were ties, six victories.

In baseball the record had not been so spectacular. In the spring of 1916 Wooster's team opened the season in the rain, at Cleveland, by winning from Case 4–2; and at home on inauguration day, with Mr. White pitching out the first ball, they won from Otterbein. It was the first baseball game played on the new field. That year they lost only two games, both close: to Miami 2–1, and to Ohio Wesleyan 4–3. In the spring of 1917 Wooster lost only to Ohio State University and to Western Reserve. Twice she defeated Case by large margins.

In basketball in the winter of 1916 Wooster won eight out of twelve Conference games, never losing one on the home floor. That year the game considered the most exciting was that in which they defeated Western Reserve by a score of 27–25, but the one that called for a snake dance and a great celebration afterwards was the triumph over Wittenberg, the champion of the year before. For some years, beginning in 1916–1917, there was held at Wooster an annual track meet in which sixteen to eighteen northern Ohio high schools participated. The other athletic event was an athletic carnival, occasionally two such, put on by the Y.M.C.A., with wrestling and boxing bouts and sometimes an intramural basketball, or a volley ball game.

The alumni in these years were becoming steadily more active. Several Wooster clubs had sprung up, in Wooster itself, in Cleveland, in Toledo, and in New York. The class of 1915 on graduation had established an award, a silver cup, to the class that could claim the greatest number proportionately, of living graduates back for commencement. A committee had been appointed to advise on class memorials, and the class of 1917 was soon to endow an annual lecture at the college. There was no alumni secretary, yet the desirability of having one, as soon as finances would allow, was accepted. A new alumni catalogue needed to be compiled and published. A young woman of Wooster was employed to work on this. She at once conceived the idea of drawing into the alumni group the many former Wooster students who had never gone on to graduation. Many of these, she was confident, still had Wooster in their hearts and should be recognized. No record of them had been kept through the years. Listing these by their original home addresses as given in the annual catalogues from the beginning, she tried first to trace them through their classmates or through fraternity or sorority rolls. If these clues yielded nothing, she next approached local postmasters in the towns from which they had come, to find traces of their whereabouts or of relatives. Postmasters in that day were still allowed to be cooperative, and many of them were. The result was that in a period of months she gathered some 1500 of these addresses out of a total of 2400. When the catalogue was published, these names and addresses were included as ex-students at the end of the roll of each class.

In every direction it seemed Wooster was growing, in personnel, in awareness of the world, in education, in athletic prowess, in alumni relations, in community life, in every direction except financially and perhaps also for the moment in faculty solidarity. In these negative respects there was still a long trek ahead.

War

THROUGH all these months since August 1914 the college had carried on as usual as if Europe were not soaked in blood. Classes, parties, games, concerts went on. Everyone, to be sure, read the morning papers with distress, hoping against hope that all this carnage would end in victory for the Allies, and went on about his daily routine. In the fall of 1916 students and faculty had pledged $1200 for the relief of student-soldiers caught in the prisons of Europe, yet for the most part the war seemed very far away in this middlewestern community. There were those with some familiarity with England and the Continent or with friends abroad who doubted in their hearts Wilson's policy of "peace with honor." Others thanked God that the U.S.A. was not yet involved. Slowly the pinch, however, was beginning to be felt even in Wooster, manifest in the coal shortage and in rising prices. Yet as late as the evening of February 7, 1917, Clarence Gould speaking to the students at the behest of the Y.M.C.A. had stated in the chapel that he seriously doubted that this country would ever become an active partner of Britain in the war; it was our responsibility none the less to keep the seas open for her, to see that her ships and ours were regularly plying back and forth with food and supplies.

The Imperial German Government, however, had been making other plans, not that they wanted us in the war, but that they inclined to think us chicken-hearted, and that even should we eventually come in on the side of the Allies, they could probably bring Britain to her knees before our impact became at all serious. After all, in May of 1915 they had sunk without warning the British passenger liner, *Lusitania,* with more than 100 U.S. citizens aboard. Wilson had protested several times without effect. Again in 1916 after the sinking of the *Sussex,* he had issued an ultimatum indicating that we would enter the war if the Germans persisted in unrestricted submarine warfare. This had brought in May of that year agreement as to a cessation of the policy, but as of the last day of January, 1917, they once more announced that they were resuming such warfare as of the next day.[1] As a consequence, within a few days we cut off diplomatic relations, still hoping, however, that we could act as mediator between the warring nations. Presently word came through the British Intelligence that the German government was inciting Mexico against us, and the Zimmerman note proving this was released by the State Department. Before the middle of March orders had been given to arm U.S. merchant ships. Four days later three American cargo ships on their way home were sunk by German submarines. Congress was called by the President to meet in special session on April 2. The whole college came, as it were, to attention. On the fifth of April, realizing that we were on the eve of war, they passed a resolution of loyalty and sent it to President Wilson. The men of the college, too, at a mass meeting requested of the faculty compulsory military training. On the sixth came the official declaration of war. Immediately trustees and faculty offered to the government, for whatever use it might desire, the plant with its facilities including laboratories and the services of the faculty. A few students wishing to show somehow their venom toward the German government managed at night to climb through a window into the German room; they tore down Kaiser Wilhelm's picture on the wall, and beheaded him then and there.

Within ten days military training one hour a day, five days a week, had been substituted for required physical education for men. One credit was allowed. Commandant Whitmarsh was secured to take charge. Before his arrival, three of the faculty already familiar with military orders, Gould, Moffett, Boles, and the director of the physical education department undertook the preliminary training of the company leaders. A new schedule was arranged. Each class was shortened by ten minutes. Lunch now was at eleven o'clock. By the 26th of the month all the men, not just the seniors as at first, were drilling on the athletic field. The girls, too, wished to do something. They voted to have established, if possible, a Red Cross training department; and at their annual spring gymnasium exhibition the advanced class already "distinguished itself by its marching tactics."

Now everyone was living more or less from day to day, and everything took on a patriotic aspect. Every concert or significant meeting opened or closed with the singing of the "Star Spangled Banner." The boys at the "Beer Garden" [2] had a party with red, white, and blue decorations. The Scientific Club heard Mr. Bennett on "Science and the War." The Toastmasters' Club at their final banquet of the year took the national situation as their theme. By the third of May the Reformation pageant, for which the cast had been chosen and work begun, was called off. The girls this year must take over Color Day. They could at least have the crowning of the queen, the rose wreath drill, the winding of the Maypole. As it turned out they actually did put on also an operetta, "The Garden of Japan," and a special folk dance. Forty-eight men of the Wooster Battalion executed a military drill.

Throughout the nation there was a back-to-the-farm movement to supply food both for ourselves and for our Allies. Among Ohio colleges, Oberlin, Otterbein, Ohio Wesleyan, Ohio State University, led in this. All men were to be given full credit for the semester if they would work till the end of the summer on the farms to which they went. Dean Marshall arranged that the girls would be given similar credit if they could prove that their work was adding to the national food reserves. Already by the third of May, seventy college boys had left for farms. Three of them had rented fifteen acres near Shreve and were about to plant onions there. Other men were signing up for military training in the camps. On the eleventh of May an all-college farewell party was staged for those leaving, in whatever capacity, for patriotic service. The flame of gaiety burned brightly for a night. By daylight, faced with reality, they were all back on their jobs. It was about this time that by unanimous vote students and faculty sent President Wilson a telegram "earnestly" petitioning him "to recommend to Congress the prohibition of the manufacture and sale of intoxicating liquors during the war." By the end of the month the new physical education director had himself taken off for one of the military camps.

With all this going and coming, this shifting around of personnel and schedules, the faculty as well as the students, began to feel themselves so many marionettes in a whirligig. Perhaps this was the inspiration for the final faculty party of the year. They celebrated with a Maypole dance of their own and a burlesque pageant of the Reformation. How many of them would still be here carrying on next year no one knew nor how many students would be on campus. They were concerned about many things here at home, the discipline committee especially by the apparent increase in smoking among the

men. A new regulation was consequently passed: every person wishing to live in Kenarden Lodge must hereafter sign a pledge not to use
tobacco in any form while a resident there. Alarmed, too, by the
mounting deficit and the disappearing likelihood of much help from
the campaign out in the presbyteries, they voted a committee to study
possible administrative economies.

Examinations loomed ahead, that time when faculty and students
were tying up all the loose ends of the year, and then commencement. Eighty-eight seniors were to be graduated. This year the final
exercises were to be held on Wednesday morning instead of on
Thursday, to be followed immediately by the alumni banquet in
Kauke Hall instead of the old corporation lunch. The commencement calendar seemed to be closing like the folds of an accordion.

In the fall of 1917, 400 students were enrolled, a drop-off of 28
per cent. Sobered by the national situation students were serious and
attentive, poised for work. During the summer at Fort Benjamin
Harrison eleven undergraduates and alumni of Wooster had been
granted second lieutenantships. The military training at Wooster,
however, was in abeyance; there was no longer a commandant. Two
of the students with some military experience were drilling the men
two days a week in setting-up exercises and close-order marching in
place of the regular class work in the gymnasium. The students
found other changes. The laundry, for instance, which had the preceding winter been running full speed ahead, was no longer operat-
ing. The student manager had gone; anyhow with so few students it
could not function satisfactorily. Several of the faculty were not to be
seen. Mr. Vance was on leave for the year. Mr. Cletus Van Voorhis,
'14, instructor in physics since 1914, had accepted an appointment at
Northwestern, and Mr. Meyer of the Latin department had taken a
business position in Canton. William Taeusch had enlisted.

In late September the trustees met for three days to consider what
could be done to alleviate the existing financial stringency. Receipts
from tuition of course were down; costs were rising everywhere, for
food, fuel, for wages for maintenance personnel and all service, for
chemicals used in laboratories. A similar stringency was pinching
everyone. There was no use at present in continuing the Jubilee
Campaign. The minds of people everywhere and their emotions were
occupied with war, not with education. To be sure, not all the

conferences that had been held across the state had been wasted; they had acquainted many persons with Wooster, her ideals, her purposes, and her needs. Yet now there were too many distracting influences to think of pursuing any active solicitation. The Synod in October took action appealing to all the Presbyterian churches of Ohio to put Wooster in their regular budget for one fifth of their annual benevolences. How this would result was anybody's guess.

It was in September of 1917 also that the faculty took off the table the motion made by Mr. Kelso the preceding November and elected a committee to consider all dismissals, promotions, demotions. They voted as well a committee on appointments and one on the budget. Though such matters would continue through the years to require ratification by the trustees, the faculty were at last claiming for themselves the right to initiate such actions. They had thereby attained a new authority and a new academic stature. No longer could a president completely dominate a situation.

Throughout the year of 1917–1918 town and gown were to be brought more and more together in a common effort for the war. In October Mr. Chancellor and Daniel Funk, '17, who was teaching political science in the high school, were, each, speaking on the war issues twice a week for four minutes at the local movie houses. They had been appointed respectively president and secretary of the Wayne County organization of Four-Minute Men. They spoke also once at least to the crowds at the Wayne County Fair. Topics, outlines, and material for these speeches were furnished to them weekly by the U.S. Government. Mr. Kelso later addressed the business men of town explaining the background and the urgency of the war. Toward spring Mr. Lean's class in extemporaneous speaking, all fifteen of them, took it upon themselves to appear twice a week at the movies to boost the sale of War Savings Stamps. The college, too, joined the town at the Opera House in a successful drive to raise $20,000 for the work of the Y.M.C.A. in the training camps. The students themselves collected $500 and they contributed 2800 books for the libraries of the camps. With the financial backing of the Board of Trade, the Boys' Glee Club spent four days at Camp Sherman entertaining the boys in camp and in the camp hospital. At home under the same auspices they gave a concert and turned over the proceeds of about $100 for war work.

To acquaint the students with the underlying concepts of the warring nations and the general background in philosophy, economics, and politics, the faculty undertook, beginning in November, a series of lectures at morning chapel on Mondays and Thursdays. These would be the result of careful study and were planned for presentation later in outlying towns. Mr. Kelso, for instance, lectured not only on "Terms of an Enduring Peace," but on Prussianism, tracing it historically and showing that essentially it was a cult of militarism; Gould on "Anti-British Prejudice in America," outlining its causes. Chancellor spoke on "International Law and Christianity" and later on "Economic Phases of the War."[3] Wood and White in separate lectures outlined British policies and achievements in the colonies, Wood citing what the British had done in Egypt and in South Africa—this he had seen for himself—stressing their standards of justice, fair play, liberty, and their efforts to uproot slavery and the slave trade, White speaking of their achievements in India, in education, medicine, sanitation, in trade and in government. These he, too, had had the chance to observe. Compton, quoting Nietzsche and Kant, explained the German doctrine of the superman, and of the State as above morality and all international law. Remp developed the German methods of training the young in these doctrines, to a life of obedience to the State. Dunn outlined the concept of the freedom of the seas and went on from there to show how the British naval power in all crises had proved to be the "ultimate bulwark of liberty." Lean talked on what was to be done with Turkey after the war, Notestein on the problem of Alsace-Lorraine, Mateer on the effect of the war on medicine, and so the series went on all through that winter and spring. No examinations were required on these chapel talks, yet they must have been an illuminating experience for many of the young people from the small towns of Ohio and Pennsylvania. In addition there came in February the annual Washington's Birthday celebration. The Congressional Club had asked W. E. Wenner of Ashtabula to give the address. His topic was the testing of the nations. This testing, he said, was not as to which nations would be the winners, but rather whether in all of this conflict we could save our own souls and those of the world.

Just before the end of the term in December, a large service flag which had been ordered by the Student Senate and to which several of the girls of Holden Hall had affixed the stars, was put in place in the chapel. Already there were two gold stars. R. R. Boor, *ex* '18, had died of pneumonia in France soon after his arrival there. C. Ian Forman, *ex* '18 had but recently been killed in action. He had gone over early in the Canadian Expeditionary Forces, in the air service. The war was beginning to come home to Wooster.

By this time, too, the coal shortage had made it necessary to lengthen the Christmas vacation until January 16. The faculty hoped that by abbreviating the spring vacation this time could be made up. The students came back in January to a shortage in both coal and water. By the fifteenth, it was reported that there were only four inches of water in the huge college tank. Showers in the dormitories were disconnected. A pipeline was built from a small well east of the gymnasium as a temporary measure until more wells could be drilled. On Monday classes were not held while all sorts of adjustments were being made. The boys in Kenarden were moved to the first three sections. Everybody hoped for a January thaw, but there was no thaw. The thermometer played up and down around zero. It was the coldest January on record at Wooster's Ohio Agricultural Experiment Station. Gas stoves were installed in Severance Hall. The library was closed at four in the afternoon. For heat they were relying on two car loads of coal that had finally come and the promise that more were on their way. Freight trains, one after the other, roared past the Pennsylvania Station carrying war materials to the coast. Wooster's coal was somewhere sidetracked. Yet eventually it did come and college went on even if it was only from day to day.

One by one at intervals of ten days or so boys were leaving for the camps. Even the faculty were taking off. Leon Parsons of the chemistry department had gone before Christmas to Washington as a first lieutenant in the Sanitary Corps. Gould was offering his services to the Navy and in February would be taking examinations preliminary to a commission. Clinton Moffett in English went to be Y.M.C.A. secretary at Camp Sheridan. Seboyar, also of the English department, had been taken by the draft. Ross Thomas, who had built up for Wooster excellent courses in applied mathematics, took a position with the Woodard Machine Company making war materials. Rutherford Hunter went to Pittsburgh to help in the testing of materials for airplanes. Mr. and Mrs. Vance had joined a Red Cross unit, and having made their way precariously by ship around the Cape of Good Hope, were now in Jerusalem,[4] behind the British lines, working with the people. In late January word came through that Gordon Enders, *ex* '18 who had gone to France in the spring to join the American Ambulance Service and who had later been in training in the American aviation school in France, had fallen in his plane 3200 feet. After the first 1000 feet, with one wing gone, the plane circled and he came down alive though "considerably shaken up and bruised."

There had been no official military drill on campus this year, and in February it was too late to make a satisfactory arrangement. For the most part the men had had to content themselves with the regular gymnasium classes and with sports. With attendance steadily dropping, it had been hard to find enough men for a basketball team. In baseball in the spring of 1918 Wooster's gains and losses were about evenly matched. Recently the government had been asking that a course in telegraphy and signalling be arranged. Twenty men now signed up for this. It was under the general direction of Mr. Remp and Mr. Wertz of Western Union. In the fourth section of Kenarden a telegraphy room was fitted up. The course included two two-hour lectures a week, five hours of individual laboratory work, and an hour on Saturday afternoons of company work. Later there was added field work in flag, smoke, and flare signalling.

Early in February the trustees met again. Mr. White having been urged to go to France for the Y.M.C.A. asked for leave for three months. The Board refused to grant the request in the light of the serious deficit. First this must be cleared. This time they voted to discontinue also the summer school, though expressing hope that at a later time it could be revived. Miss Pendleton presented her resignation, but the Board postponed its consideration until June. She had served the college well and faithfully since 1890, for the most part in the preparatory department. Who knew but that they might need her again during the present emergency.

Already by the fall of 1917, as we have seen, there were more women than men among the students; and as the men continued to disappear into some kind of war service, the women were feeling the urge to train themselves for kinds of work they had never really seriously thought of before. In this Miss Marshall was ahead of them.

With the backing and assistance of the Women's Advisory Board she arranged in the spring of 1918 a vocational conference for women, the first such in Wooster's history. In this the faculty cooperated, excusing the girls from classes to attend. The speakers were a dozen or so men and women, all specialists in their fields. One woman described social service in the community, in business, in industry, even in the public schools as an inviting field for the idealistic young woman of these tumultuous days. The war was of course opening up many opportunities, not only in nursing and secretarial work, but in vocations formerly almost reserved for men, in dentistry, law, real estate, insurance, journalism, as well as in civilian relief. A professor of botany from the University of Cincinnati explained women's possibilities in agriculture, in both plant and animal husbandry. Other opportunities were discussed, in library work, in the management of lunch rooms, in chemistry, in textile and costume designing, in interior decoration, in commercial art of all sorts—advertising, poster-making, the illustrating of magazines—and in many other fields. Employment bureaus, it was pointed out, were being set up in industrial institutions. The speakers urged, however, that girls remain in college to get all the general training and background they could get before specializing. To many girls this conference was a great eye-opener. Miss Marshall undoubtedly had recognized that a small college in the country could not provide a show-window on the world in the sense at all of a great university of varying colleges set in a booming industrial center. In presenting such a conference to Wooster women, she was doing what she could to compensate. No doubt she had found Wooster and its small-town clientele provincial in many other ways, but if so she kept the secret well to herself.

By the end of March several students in advanced chemistry had gone to Washington where they were sworn into the Army to work in the field of poison gas and its preventives. Clarence Gould was now at Pelham Bay, training potential officers in the Auxiliary Reserves. He had won his commission as an ensign in the Navy. His classes here had been taken by colleagues, those in European history by Miss Marshall, those in American history by Coach Boles, who had made American history something of a hobby; besides he had been enrolled in one or more of Mr. Gould's classes and had known something of his plans. Spring vacation was late and short, lasting only from Thursday noon to Monday noon. Then on March 31 the town, like many other communities, had in the interests of the war adopted daylight saving. But recently the borders of the eastern and central time zones had also been shifted, and Wooster had fallen within the eastern sphere. It was rather a jolt, therefore, for both faculty and students to find themselves two hours ahead of their accustomed schedule, hurrying across the campus for 7:30 classes by the light of the moon. The world seemed more and more unrealistic. Food substitutes began to appear on everyone's table, and one was supposed to find them tasty. Indeed at the suggestion of the government Mr. Bennett was lecturing once a week on these and on the more general subject of food conservation. By late April, seven of the teaching staff and 202 of the students were in the war. A benefit for the Red Cross, in which many students had a part, was arranged, and $500 was raised. Soon word came of another war casualty among Wooster's students, at Camp Sherman. Then a girl in the senior class died suddenly. By the end of the month cheering word came, however, from Washington; in all probability the college would in the fall be granted a unit of the S.A.T.C. Men in such training would not be called for active service until they were twenty-one, unless there were to be a military crisis.

This year only fifty-one were to be graduated; ten were in the service and of these only two could make it back to receive their diplomas. For the June oratorio chorus Mr. Rowe had chosen appropriately *Jeanne d'Arc*. In another way this was rather a special commencement, the fiftieth anniversary of the laying of the cornerstone of Old Main. On Tuesday afternoon they celebrated this occasion with the forty-year class in charge. George N. Luccock presided. David Ross Boyd, president of the University of New Mexico, and Ella Alexander Boole, president of the W.C.T.U. of New York State and vice-president at large of the National W.C.T.U., made the addresses. There was a special reason for thankfulness; the deficit had been wiped out. The Synod had surprised everyone, had "rallied" to the college emergency rather "better than ever before." The Jubilee Campaign had ended if not with a flourish at least with a faint whistle.

By the fall of 1918 Wooster, along with many other colleges, was assured of an S.A.T.C. This meant some changes in existing courses to adapt them in content to the needs of the Army, some new courses, and additions to the teaching staff. A course in war issues, demanded by the government, fell for the most part on Mr. Kelso, though a faculty committee was in general charge. Others took over accounting, sanitation and hygiene, economic geography, military law and practice. Of the S.A.T.C. itself and its military training—Lieutenant Schwartz was in charge. On Tuesday morning, October first, the 300 men, who had already been sworn in, marched from Taylor Hall to the athletic field and there were passed in review. Short speeches were made by the Lieutenant and by President White. Then to the strains of the "Star Spangled Banner" the flag was raised and the pledge of allegiance repeated. Messages from President Wilson and others followed, and Judge Weiser addressed the men on behalf of the citizens of Wooster.

Hardly had students and faculty settled to their new routine when the mayor shut down all civilian classes in town and college. Public gatherings were banned. The Spanish influenza had struck. Only the men of the S.A.T.C. attended classes, pending orders from the War Department. Soon, however, Kenarden Lodge was virtually a hospital. People remember the next few weeks as a nightmare. Sometimes whole families were down. People fainted at the slightest exertion. Those who did not succumb marketed and cooked and nursed for the rest. Doctors were kept on the run. Nurses were practically unavailable. Many of the students went home right at the beginning, there to be sick if they had to be sick. One sophomore boy and one junior girl died. Twenty girls who elected to stay in Wooster during the siege were stranded in Holden Hall under the watchful eye of Amelia Doddridge, instructor in domestic science and now acting dean of women. Theirs seems rather to have been for the most part a pleasant interlude. It was not quite like being sequestered in Boccaccio's villa —though one can be sure that many tales of a sort were told—they could venture forth and did and an occasional man was admitted (once six together), though dates were few. Miss Doddridge put herself out arranging for their recreation. There were tennis and rook, hayrides, wiener roasts, small barn dances in local homes that were flu-free, a wartime sugarless candy party, a picnic supper in the Holden Hall gymnasium, and on Sunday evenings tea was served in the parlors; then they all gathered around the piano for a vesper song service.

Football games went on as scheduled. The men of S.A.T.C. had been encouraged to take part in intercollegiate athletics so long as practice periods were limited to an hour and a half a day including the time for showers and dressing, and provided that games away from Wooster were within easy distance. The team was lucky to have Hartman and Ben Roderick back. Wooster won six out of the seven games.

Concurrently with the new courses being demanded by the Army, there had been something of a hegira of faculty. Dean Marshall had resigned to continue her graduate work at the University of Minnesota. Dr. Mateer had suffered a fractured hip during the summer in Labrador. A sail-yard had suddenly come about and hit him. Moore, Homer Crain, and more recently, James H. Hall were all off to the war. Once more the college had to make adjustments within the faculty. Miss Pendleton was to teach three divisions of freshman English, Miss Georgia Field [5] from Minnesota was brought especially to teach the S.A.T.C. divisions in English. There was one long-range appointment also in English, Mary Rebecca Thayer. With increased emphasis on French by the Army, two new instructors were brought in, one man and one woman, a native of Alsace with much experience in teaching the language. Other instructors were found in chemistry and mechanical drawing. It was a time when the small college had to hunt along the highways and hedges, and to capitalize on personal loyalties to get teaching staff.

Gradually the influenza epidemic passed its worst, and one began to hope that order would succeed chaos. Though most of the S.A.T.C. boys had been in Kenarden, the officers quarters had been in Taylor Hall. Then on the night of October 24 a fire broke out in the fan room of Taylor, probably the result of crossed wires. It spread rapidly, filling the halls with smoke and destroying the only stairway, a central one of wood. The 150 officers and boys, awakened, all escaped, some by ladders, some by expertly climbing down the spouting, some by tying sheets and blankets together and sliding on these to the ground. Some managed to dress, others came down in pajamas and bare feet. Five minutes after the alarms, however, the roll was called and everyone was there. Meantime Coach Boles and Wooster Fire Chief Snavely had managed to get in to search the building to make sure that no one had been left behind. The fire was soon got under control. For the rest of the night the dislodged men rolled up on the floor of the canteen in the basement of Kauke Hall and allowed themselves to be served hot coffee. Later they moved their belongings, some to the Y.M. rooms in Scovel Hall, some to the canteen room. Damage to the building was assessed as between three and five thousand dollars.

College reopened in late October. Hardly had they got well under way when on Monday, November 11, the bells all over town began to ring and the whistles to blow. Never had the custodian pulled the bell rope in the chapel tower more jubilantly, nor had the McKinley bell [6] sounded more triumphant. The war was over. People rushed from their classes—which were subsequently dismissed. Even the S.A.T.C. men were released from their formations. In the afternoon at the chapel the college community and many townspeople met for a service of thanksgiving. Mr. White, who presided, chose passages from the 9th and 89th Psalms: "For thou, Lord, hast not forsaken them that seek thee. . . . Justice and judgment are the habitation of thy throne: mercy and truth shall go before thy face. . . . For the Lord is our defense; and the Holy One of Israel is our king." Then the Rev. Mr. T. K. Davis prayed out of the fullness of his heart. In his more than ninety-two years he had known the end of the Civil War, of the Spanish War, and now of this World War. Various members of the faculty spoke, the president of the Student Senate, also, and Lieutenant Schwartz. Kelso pleaded for Christian magnanimity as we were beginning the "reformation" period; the United States and England were trustees for the world. He hoped devoutly for a League of Nations. Mr. Hays stressed that we were celebrating "the victory of one system over another. Our greatest hope," he said, "is to show the German people that might does not make right, and that the greatest thing is righteousness." In the evening all the students marched to town for a celebration. However great their rejoicing everyone was conscious of the problems ahead, and of those also who had lost their lives in the conflict, especially of those from the college and community. One of the most recent of these was Mr. White's nephew, Wilbert W. White, who had fallen in France in

October in aerial battle, bringing down also the enemy plane he had rammed.

Though the armistice had come, the S.A.T.C. was to be continued for the present. In fact, the uniforms of the men had never come. A Y.M.C.A. secretary for the Corps was due to arrive from France before the end of the month, S. W. Foster.

The week of November 11 to 18 had been set aside all over the country for the United War Work fund campaign. The goal was $17,500,000. This was for the war activities at home and abroad of the Y.M.C.A. and Y.W.C.A., the Knights of Columbus, the Jewish Welfare Board, the Salvation Army, the American Library Association. The College of Wooster's quota was $3000. The cause was presented in chapel one morning. At once $2100 were subscribed, and within a few days, more hundreds were added. Though the shooting was over, there would for months be work of many sorts in many places to be done. Before the armistice the girls in the dormitories had made plans to furnish a hostess room in the basement of Kauke Hall for the S.A.T.C. For this they needed money. They decided to give an original play for the college community and sell tickets. A senior girl wrote a burlesque, *In Flew Enza,* and the others put it on in Severance gymnasium on the evening of the sixteenth. It was a hit.

Now that the war was officially over, the faculty decided that it would do their Calvinistic souls no harm to indulge themselves in half an hour more sleep in the morning; they consequently moved the first class of the day from seven-thirty to eight. At length toward the end of the month the long awaited uniforms came and the men were fitted out. Lieutenant Foster, too, arrived. By this time the tenth gold star had been stitched to the service flag. Then along with a secondary outbreak of flu in Wooster came the orders for demobilization. Every man by December 21 would have a medical examination, be vaccinated, inoculated, and discharged. Through all this period of confusion regular college classes had been continued. Several girls in Holden and Hoover were down with the influenza, though in Kenarden there was not a case. Private homes in town where cases occurred were quarantined. All receptions were called off. Town girls continuing to attend classes were required to live on the hill. All boys had by this time been moved back into Taylor Hall, and temporary makeshift quarters were fitted up in Scovel Hall for the girls from town. Miss Doddridge, in the meanwhile, had had to leave because of illness, hoping later to return. (She never did.) Mr. Behoteguy, too, became seriously ill, and did not meet his classes again till spring. So the first term ended.

Then on the day before Christmas in his 93rd year, T. K. Davis, librarian-emeritus and patriarch of the college, died, holding in his heart even in the last week of his life the interests of the college. He had been born in Chambersburg, Pennsylvania, on February 11, 1826, had been graduated from Yale in 1845, the orator of his class. A boy in the horse and buggy era, he had lived to know the day when men shot each other down in the skies. His death for Wooster marked the end of an epoch.

XII

Readjustment

THERE is a time between dark and dawn, neither night nor day, when the world around one is suffused in a gray transparency, when no star shines, when hardly a leaf quivers, when only a bird or two may utter an audacious and hesitating tweet, when standing alone under the sky one is almost afraid to breathe. So came in the New Year of 1919 to a torn and bewildered world. No more, no less was this true in the college community. They would be starting anew after all the turmoil of the last few months. Dormitories would go back to the old uses. Taylor Hall would once more be converted to classrooms. Even tablecloths and napkins would again appear in Kenarden Lodge. The specialized S.A.T.C. courses would no longer be needed. Others would be re-arranged. Boys fresh from war with a new seriousness would for some time keep trickling in. There would be some returning faculty, too, and new faculty with whom in all the passing hub-bub one had scarcely become acquainted. Back and beyond all this was a new world everyone hoped was in the making.

As if to emphasize the changing scene and the relentless procession of the years, there occurred on January 9, 1919, the death of the Rev. Mr. O. A. Hills. A native of Indiana, graduate of Wabash College, he had lived in Wooster since 1885 when he began thirteen years as pastor of the First Presbyterian Church. In 1898 he became pastor at Westminster, and the next March moved up close to the college into the house he had just completed. Always meticulous in his dress and his person, almost frighteningly solemn in his mien he walked the strait and stony path that his conscience and his upbringing had dictated. Though individuals at the college may often have differed with him strongly on policies, he had nevertheless been a staunch friend at all times. Once at the grim end of a campaign when President Holden still lacked $10,000 in meeting a challenge goal, Hills had, never looking back, reached into his reserves and saved the day.

On the faculty there were still the old standbys, Bennett, Compton, Mateer (walking about now with a cane, though still on leave),

Notestein, Black, Behoteguy, Gingrich, and the appointments of a later date who had become stalwarts in their own right, Martin, Dunn, Lean, Kelso, Olthouse, Vance—though the latter was still away in the war zone. Dickason had gone off to Pittsburgh to his new appointment in the spring of 1918. Gould would not be back, nor would Hunter. There had come others, additions or replacements in the falls of 1917 and 1918. Some of these were temporary; some were to stay a period of years, perhaps a lifetime at Wooster.

One of the latter was Frederick Wall Moore, '14, whom Mr. Dunn had had his eye on for some time. He had taken his Master's degree in English at Ohio State University and had been retained there for a year as an instructor. He had hardly finished a year of teaching (1917–1918) at Wooster till he, too, was off to war, but now he would be coming back to teach courses in English composition, and to add one in American literature to which he gave his whole heart. He was a born teacher, sensitive and perceptive. Under a quiet exterior was something akin to the soul of a poet. Nothing escaped him, the green of the grass that would so soon turn brown under a burning sun, the aroma of well-made coffee, the delicacy of a cup, a star sinking into the shadow at the horizon. He could fan the imagination of the young boy or girl just waking to a new world of literature. On the other hand he was impatient of trifles, absented himself whenever possible from faculty meetings where persons who ought to know better talked endlessly about things that would never get anybody nearer heaven.

In the same fall new persons appeared in the department of music and in physical education for women. Homer Crain would soon be returning from the war: he had taken the place of Daniel Parmelee as instructor in violin and conductor of the Wooster Orchestra. Ruth Conrow trained in the Sargent School at Cambridge, Massachusetts, was giving new impetus to her department and to athletics among the women.

It was in the fall of 1918 that Mary Rebecca Thayer first came to Wooster, as assistant professor of English, fresh from teaching for four years at Vassar. She was young and excited by life, ready to take on almost anything. She had grown up in Maryland, had been graduated from a small college in the western part of that state. Her mind, however, was on fire, and she promptly went on to Cornell to take a second B.A. and then a Master's in English and a Ph.D. Even to this day she likes to say that she was brought to Wooster as a war measure. In that she was doubtless right, for men available for teaching were surely then in short supply. Happily, however, she found herself at home in Wooster, and Wooster found itself at home with her, and she was not tempted after the war to go elsewhere. She liked her colleagues. She liked her students, and she was familiar with a small-town background. She fitted in. She found here a place where the classics still were cherished, and students did not shy away from Latin and from Greek; she loved the classics. Her Ph.D. thesis, published by the Yale University Press, had indeed been on the influence of Horace on 19th century English poets. Her training made her not only a stickler for exactness in scholarship and in diction, but a person with a wide appreciation of beauty of many sorts, in personality as well as the arts. Through her many years at Wooster her favorite course was the one she gave in classical influences. She was a wistful person who loved to walk in the woods and fields in the spring, to identify flowers, to see ferns unfolding. She was a person, too, of deep loyalties and convictions.

William R. Westhafer, professor of physics, came that year, too. An Ohioan and a graduate of Ohio Wesleyan, he had taken his Master's degree in physics at Harvard in 1909. Thence he had gone for several years to Amherst where he attained the rank of associate professor. Feeling the desire and the need for further graduate study he had then gone to the University of Chicago. Wooster was to claim him from September of 1918 on till the end of his life. To look at, he was small and unimpressive. It was only when he was mingling with students or talking to them from the chapel rostrum that one felt the quality of the man. He was not brilliant; neither was he commonplace. He was down-to-earth, and met students halfway; they were people he liked to know. He was religious, became an elder in the church. He was first of all, however, a teacher, demanding, yet always clear, and always interesting. He could make a student with no real taste for mathematics warm to the mysteries of physics. Yet he was over all practical and human with a guiding sense of humor. Reared on a farm, he was used to rising before the sun; it was no hardship, and no rare thing, for him to be at work in his laboratory two hours before the first class in the morning.

Then there was Miss Emeline McSweeney. Everyone knew her. For years she had been teaching in the academy. She seemed to have a gift for languages. Soon after finishing college she had spent a year studying in Berlin. Now in 1918 she had been transferred to the college where she remained until 1942. There in a few years she added French to her repertoire, becoming an assistant professor of French in 1924, a full professor in 1928. She had spent several summers studying at graduate schools, three at the University of Chicago, two at Western Reserve, one at McGill in Toronto and had had at least two summers in France, one of these at the University of Bescançon in Burgundy. A victim of polio at four or five, with both legs encased in steel braces, she had lived all her life in a wheel chair, always an uncomplaining and gallant soul. Her wheel chair, in her later life a motorized one, took her everywhere, to classes, to church, to lectures, to concerts; and her spirit did the rest. She read much, loved especially poetry,—for she knew both suffering and joy—and loved people. In her home she had, to be sure, a housekeeper, yet she always had a student or two living there as well to do chores and run errands and sometimes to push the wheel chair. These like many others became her great admirers. She was a great-great granddaughter, of General Reasin Beall,[1] whose home had once been just around the corner on Bowman Street.

Frank Winfield Hays came from Grove City, Pennsylvania, that same fall to be professor of history, and two years later to become the Michael O. Fisher professor of history, a position he kept until his death in 1930. Having in his young manhood held several pastorates in Pennsylvania, he finally turned to teaching. He became a professor in Grove City College (Pennsylvania) where he was already well known. When he came to Wooster he found himself the only member of the history department. He demanded much of his students. With a ministerial background he was interested in them also as human beings. They came to him often in his office, often to his home. He was a quiet man, sincere, kindly, with a resounding laugh. He walked much with John B. Kelso—loved to walk and talk. He loved the outdoors, his garden and his trees. A wild cherry, still standing and grown now to be sizable, is evidence enough. Most persons building a house and developing walks and a lawn would have cut the young thing down as a nuisance. Instead he graded around it, letting it stand on a hump by the street straight in front of the house, and he led his front hedge across the hump. His sympathies were broad, and that broadness perhaps entered into his capacity for understanding and teaching the wayward turnings of history.[2]

The chemistry department during the war years had suffered seriously; instructors one after another had left for the war or war industry, or for other teaching positions—Samuel Morris, Leon Parsons, Cary Wagner, and now Amelia Doddridge—leaving Mr. Bennett to shoulder alone the work in a field in which the war had been making heavy demands. It was not just a temptation to seek out one's own best students of the years just past and to lure them back before they were well entrenched elsewhere; to do so was almost the only possibility in recruiting staff for a small college. Thus in the summer of 1918 Bennett sought out and was fortunate in being able to engage for the ensuing year Roy I. Grady, '16, who, having finished his M.S. at Ohio State University, was now working as a chemist for the Ohio Agricultural Experiment Station on the other hill. From the beginning though interested in research, his mind was set on teaching. So it remained, though at a later time when he succeeded to the chairmanship of the department he showed himself also an able administrator. Then little by little he built up his department in its personnel, in its library, and eventually had the satisfaction of knowing that among liberal arts colleges meeting the requirements of the American Chemical Society in undergraduate chemistry Wooster was ranked at the top. Mr. Grady had none of the dramatic qualities of Mr. Bennett; he interested himself very little in student activities as such, but was always a helpful member of the community. He was thoughtful, slow-spoken, weighing the evidence as if it were so many grams before making up his mind on any question. He was often called upon, as also Mr. Bennett had been, to make analyses for court cases, and for years he analyzed all the local water supplies. His classes and electives were always full; and in the faculty he was a man to stand up and be counted.

These were all men and women who were to occupy distinctive niches in Wooster's history. The others brought in for a year or two, however effective their service, would only have rung the bell and left their calling cards inside Wooster's door. So Miss Doddridge flitted away in only a few months. Mary Brookfield Lowthian, a widow with a Master's degree in English and the record of having attended also the Divinity School of the University of Chicago, followed her in late February as dean of women. She finished the year at Wooster and then she, too, was gone.

Student life, however, soon became normal after the holidays. One could be human again with a clear conscience now that both military orders and the influenza were things of the past. Only 166 of the former S.A.T.C. boys came back to continue their college work. Fifty others returned from the Army and the Navy. There was a rush for places on the debating teams; twenty-two men were trying out. James Kirk and Warren P. Spencer were the captains. The Congressional Club for Washington's Birthday brought on J. Knox Montgomery of Muskingum who spoke on the price, the purpose, the path, and the power of true greatness, using as illustrations incidents from the lives of George and Booker T. Washington. In the evening there followed the Gum Shoe Hop. In early March Wooster entertained the Student Volunteer Conference of Northern Ohio, 182 delegates from 18 colleges. The Girls' Glee Club was scheduled for its first annual out-of-town tour. In April the Toastmasters' Club was finally able to put on its first banquet of the year. The simulated occasion was a mass meeting at which the possible removal of the old gymnasium and observatory was discussed. One speaker supposedly representing a faculty member suggested that these be replaced by an agricultural hall "to supply the demand for such an innovation in our progressive institution." (Tongue in cheek?) Student representatives spoke, one favoring the retaining of the buildings, the other their removal "for aesthetic reasons." The alumni, regarded as "ancestor worshippers," were of course represented in favor of keeping the buildings.

It was indeed a full spring. Zillah Pocock was elected May Queen, and Color Day was arranged as a Greek festival. The girls of Hoover put on a Japanese party complete in every detail, including the presentation of a Japanese fairy story written and directed by one of the girls. The Holden girls also entertained. Athenaean and Castalian gave a musical comedy for the benefit of *The Index* with "catchy music, and special costumes, and graceful dancing." There were picnics at Reddick's Dam, a Memorial Day program in the chapel in the evening with an address by Col. James McQuigg, '88. The four small literary clubs had a supper party back of Taylor Hall with tables set up under Japanese lanterns. There were swimming meets by both men and women in the gymnasium.

All year, it seemed, the girls were taking a special interest in athletics. Early in the fall they held an athletic rally with the slogan, "More athletics for girls, more girls for athletics." They were allowed even to wear Varsity *W*'s. Intramural women's basketball teams were organized, and one of these had its own training table. Every once in a while groups of girls would hold a hare and hounds race across the fields and over the hills.

Never before had so many persons attended the basketball games during the winter. The season, however, had not been good. Only two men on the team had heretofore played the game. Nevertheless under skillful coaching they won from Baldwin-Wallace 32–11 and 28–15, from Mt. Union 26–23, from Kenyon 21–19, from Ohio Northern 29–14, and from Case 11–9. In baseball with Ben Roderick still pitching, Wooster won twice from Case, once from Denison, and tied Akron. Unfortunately it lost four games, one of these the first of the season on the home field.

In sports other than football, baseball, and basketball during the years of Mr. White's administration Wooster's record was not distinguished. It was weakest of all in tennis. Soccer had been played only occasionally, in 1914 and 1915, and Wooster had lost in all instances. Though it had scored in long distance running, its record in track was nothing to brag about. Once it lost to Ohio Wesleyan 53–51 though winning the relay race by four yards. Once again it won the triangular track meet with Oberlin and Case by just one-half point. In the fall of 1915 it ranked third in the cross-country meet of the Ohio Conference at Columbus. It never rose above that rank. Yet in these years it had had one of Wooster's most distinguished athletes in Ben Roderick. When only a sophomore, he had scored 18 points and won his *W* in track. In the preceding fall he had won it also in football. Once that season he made a 98-yard dash through the lines of Case for a touchdown. He had won his *W* in baseball also that year and in basketball. Only one other man in Wooster's athletic history thus far had achieved such a record, A. Worth Collins, '13, in his senior year.

It was now, in the spring of 1919, six years and a little more since the fraternities and sororities had been ousted by the trustees. Murmurs were beginning to be heard among the students and occasionally a word in *The Voice* suggesting their reinstatement. Just why is uncertain. Yet many persons in college during the war years may have lost something of their sense of continuity. Everything had seemed in flux. One made a friend and presently he was gone; one joined a club and half its membership may have shifted in a year. Courses were changed. Faculty came and went. One couldn't even be sure where one was eating next or sleeping. Kenarden, home of the student sections, had during the period of the S.A.T.C. become a bunkhouse, its dining hall a study room. One had been lucky if one had not had to live in Taylor Hall or Scovel on a cot. Now that the background was again rather normal, perhaps some of the students felt the need to close ranks, to make solid relationships, wanted to belong. Yet when a vote was taken only one third came to the polls, and only 38 per cent of these favored a revival of fraternities. At least there seemed no urgency in debating the issue despite the fact that a good many of the alumni had been watching the movement with more than a curious interest.

Still other changes were already in the air. In late February 1919 President White had gone west for three weeks at the invitation of some of the interchurch leaders. Before long it became known that he was being offered an Associate General Secretaryship in the Interchurch World Movement of North America. He would be one of five men to form an advisory committee for the executive secretary. In that capacity he would himself be in charge of the lifework department of the movement, "to cooperate with all existing agencies in discovering, enlisting, and training an adequate supply of qualified leaders for the enlarging program of all Protestant churches of North America in their work both at home and abroad." This was an irresistible call for Mr. White, who felt that his sojourn in Wooster had but fitted him the better for such a position. He resigned the presidency asking the trustees of Wooster, in a called meeting on the first of April, to release him on the earliest date possible. This was set for May first. He spent the month of April closing up administrative details. In Wooster he had always worked under a kind of shadow knowing that he was not in full rapport with his faculty. When he had cast off academic robes, he could be freer, and happier.

He would still be in touch with the young, the young of many institutions. He would still be following the star of his world vision. It was better for everyone that way.

The trustees named Dean Compton acting president until a new chief executive could be found. On him now rested a heavy responsibility. Appointments were to be made, someone to replace Mr. Hutchins, who was leaving to accept a business position, a professor of economics to be found, an assistant professor of Spanish. He was happy indeed that the summer school, which was to be revived this year on a strictly collegiate basis, was to be under the direction of Mr. Dunn and that the instructors were all members of the existing Wooster faculty. In this there would be no problem. The trustees had their own committee scouting for a new president. There was a welcome bit of news within the faculty. James Hall would be back in the music department next fall; he and Miss Jenney would be married in June and both would continue teaching.

Commencement was late this year, Wooster's forty-ninth, marked by innovation. A speaker, William Lyon Phelps, professor of English at Yale, gave a commencement address in place of the usual speeches by members of the graduating class.[3] He spoke on "Culture and Happiness." Tuesday was now the official alumni day, with the banquet at noon in the dining room of Kauke Hall. The senior class had given at the Opera House their play, this year Goldsmith's *Mistakes of a Night*. The oratorio chorus had presented Mendelssohn's *Saint Paul*. The campus promised to be full this summer of other kinds of activity: Taylor Hall was to be readapted for the use of the physics department, because Severance Hall was needed for chemistry alone. In the Frick Library a second tier of stacks was to be installed. Wooster's books were overflowing their shelves. It was a good omen.

XIII

A Change of Seasons

C HARLES and Frederick safely landed. Not to go out of the family until Monday." Such was the cryptic telegram from Wooster received one August day of 1919 by Dean Compton vacationing in Michigan beside Otsego Lake. If the dean had not been such an undemonstrative man, he would have jumped up and down and let out a whoop. Recounting the incident, he reported only, "I had the best night's sleep in six months." All through the hot early summer he had been tied to his desk as acting president of the college. All the time he had been longing to breathe again the ozone-laden air under the hemlocks and pines, to taste blueberries he had helped to pick, to go fishing in the early morning while the loons were still calling across the lake. He was tired. When August came, he decided he must get away for a few days at least. Before he left, however, he instructed his secretary—who happened to be also his niece, Leila Compton,—to send him word at once when and if any message came from Wooster's president-elect. That answer had been long delayed. When it came on August ninth, it asked that no mention be made of his acceptance until after he had told his congregation on the tenth; hence the secretary's efforts to conceal the news from any talkative local telegraph operator.

Charles Frederick Wishart, pastor of the Second Presbyterian Church of Chicago, had been the unanimous choice of the trustees in June for the sixth president of Wooster. His had been a hard decision. He had been in Chicago for five years; he was happy there, and beloved of his congregation. That aside, he had to weigh the opportunity at Wooster against that of still another pastorate.[1] In Wooster he would have John Timothy Stone as president of the Board, a good friend on whom he could depend. Wishart knew Wooster but not too well. As president of the Presbyterian General Board of Education he had of course known something of its troubles in the last decade—who hadn't?—but fortunately he had not been in any way identified with them. He could be objective about the past and take a fresh look at whatever problems might arise. Wooster had a good scholastic reputation, a fine plant of fourteen harmonious buildings in a woodland setting, a faculty of 42, an enrollment of 550 roughly, about equally divided between men and women. The students came chiefly from Ohio and western Pennsylvania, with a sprinkling from other states and 12 from foreign countries. It had a good music department with 7 on its faculty, and winning athletic teams. He liked small colleges, had himself been graduated from Monmouth in Illinois, and in recent years had served on its board of directors. Moreover, Wooster had an excellent record in Christian service; its alumni were all over the world, ministers, teachers, physicians. It had furnished in this country a significant group of college presidents and college professors, as well as teachers in preparatory schools and high schools. To be sure, many alumni had been alienated by the events of recent years. He must meet this challenge and try to win them back before he began any campaign for endowment so badly needed. He had the satisfaction of knowing that in the past ten years Wooster's salary scale for professors had risen by 40 per cent. Yet its greatest need was still for endowment—and for peace.

In some ways, too, going to Wooster would be like returning home for him. He had roots in that rolling middlewestern country. His mother, Sara Irvine, had been born and had grown to young womanhood in the village of Fredericksburg, scarcely nine miles away; a grandmother, grandfather, and an aunt all lay in the cemetery there. As a boy he had once gone to Wooster to visit at the home of Martin Welker, whose wife was a cousin of his mother's, and he remembered the chapel of the old Bitters Bottle where he had been taken to a funeral. He himself had been born in the village of Ontario in Richland County, thirty-five miles or so to the west of Wooster. There his father had been the United Presbyterian preacher, and often they had had occasion to drive by horse and buggy into Mansfield seven miles away. What memories he had of those slow trips, what warming memories! Robins were "perched," singing, "atop some stake-and-rider fence. . . . Squirrels scolded . . . from neighboring tree tops. . . . Young rabbits whisked their white tails in and out of the grass. . . . To this day," he was to write years later, "we cannot hear the shrill call of the killdeer sweeping across the sky, or smell wood smoke in the open springtime, or listen to the rustle of the wind over the wheat . . . or catch the smell of new-mown-hay, or the scent of apples ready for the picking, without a certain indescribable longing. . . ."

To the Wooster trustees Wishart had seemed a natural. He was a distinguished preacher, in fact something of an orator. In Monmouth while in college he had won the intercollegiate oratorical contest in which representatives from ten states had been entered. He was widely known in the church. He was already familiar with many of the problems of a small church-related college. He knew something of administration and even of faculties. He had been a director of the Presbyterian Hospital in Chicago. Immediately on his graduation from Pittsburgh Theological Seminary and his ordination as a United Presbyterian minister he had thrown himself into the project of organizing the 11th United Presbyterian Church of Pittsburgh, and had become its first pastor. There he had stayed for five years, teaching also part time the last two of those years at Pittsburgh Theological Seminary. In 1912, however, he had accepted a full-time appointment at the seminary as professor of systematic theology. John Timothy Stone had felt that he was the man for Wooster. It was reputed, too, that Wishart had a sense of humor and the suavity of a diplomat. Perhaps he could bring real peace to Wooster. That he did not know the college intimately was good. He would be unaware of the latent hostilities within the faculty, and would treat all alike as Christian gentlemen and scholars. As the youngest of twelve children, he had early learned the art of holding his own while getting along with others, and the art of doing without, arts which required both stamina and grace. Besides he was a man of wide reading and wide interests, in history, in literature, and in music. He loved to play the piano, knew classical music, and yet could sing the old popular songs with the zest of a schoolboy.

When college opened he was on the ground. Wooster gave him an enthusiastic welcome. Even some of the townspeople came up to the opening convocation on September 17, 1919. Dean Compton presided reading the fourth chapter of Proverbs: "Hear, ye children, the instruction of a father . . . Get wisdom, get understanding: forget it not . . . Exalt her, and she shall promote thee: she shall bring thee to honour, when thou dost embrace her. . . . Take fast hold of instruction; let her not go: keep her; for she is thy life. . . . Let thine eyes look right on . . . . Turn not to the right hand nor to the left: remove thy foot from evil." —Let Solomon speak. What need of rules and regulations!— Then Mr. Compton introduced the new president. Wishart's address that morning had been well studied. Wooster's ideal should be, he said, "the highest academic standards of any religious center in the country, and the highest religious standards of any academic center in the country. . . . The fact that we are a church school should not be a cloak for any inefficiency. . . . Let us have fidelity to intellectual standards, fidelity to duty." He went on to describe what he felt constituted the soul of a college: first, "the play and interplay of minds" and added to this "the cumulative effects, the piled-up results of all the dreams and the thoughts of the college past." On Sunday, the first of the college year and the first at which Wooster's old and returning faculty and students had been together since the close of the war, he chose his text from Isaiah, prophet and poet. They were all soon to learn that one could almost count on this president's choosing of his theme from the Old Testament. This time it was from the beginning of the fortieth chapter: "Comfort ye, comfort ye my people, saith your God. Speak ye comfortably to Jerusalem, and cry unto her, that her warfare is accomplished, that her iniquity is pardoned: for she hath received of the Lord's hand double for all her sins." Beginning with the general appreciation of the Old Testament he established the pertinence of his theme by remarking that he would like Jonah on the brotherhood of man read in the U.S. Senate every day at noon, "during the present sessions at least." The appeal of the text he had chosen, he went on to say, is "Cheer up, the best is yet to come. . . . There is a meaning and limit to all life's tragedies. . . . This sorrow . . . has a limit . . . will not always endure. . . . Evil . . . can last but a season. God has all eternity. . . . 'Iniquity is pardoned.' It is in this pardon that we find the great comfort." The reference was obviously to the national and international scene. Yet possibly he intended also that this first sermon should have a dual pertinence. Anyhow in Wooster's history a new era was beginning. Writing in the October issue of *The Wooster Quarterly* Mr. Notestein remarked, "There is unity of purpose and a sense of advance in the air."

For both faculty and students it was a time of welcoming back those who had been away for a year or two and for greeting the new.

Chalmers Martin was again in his classroom after a sabbatical. He had spent the year in Princeton and came back with the enthusiasm of a man who has been living in the atmosphere of a great university where talk on many subjects flows freely and many points of view come in for questioning. The Vances, too, had at long last returned. For two years, first in Palestine, later in France, they had been at work with the Red Cross. Full of their experiences in mingling with many sorts of people, they came with freshened international understanding that gave piquancy to their lives and to his interpretation of the New Testament. Dr. Mateer was once more carrying a full schedule, quite recovered from his injury of the year before, and Clarence Turner, who had substituted for him, had been retained in the department as an assistant professor, pending the return in another year of Perry Strausbaugh from his graduate studies. Mr. Behoteguy, too, after his illness was back in the harness. James Hall, no longer in naval uniform, and Florence Jenney, since their marriage in late June and a summer in Wisconsin, would be giving new strength to the conservatory of music. Homer Crain, too, was back from overseas service. And so was Frederick Moore, of the English department. Miss Georgia Field had been continued in the English department, yet now became also the official dean of women. Mr. Compton had watched her, and had confidence in her. She was an able woman, firm and careful of detail, not at all so outgoing as had been Miss Marshall, never so close to the girls, a little stiff perhaps, yet respected by her colleagues.

This should be an interesting year, especially with a whole flock of new personalities on the faculty. Herbert Simpson from Ohio University was the new professor of economics. He was a graduate of Princeton, with a Ph.D. in economics from the University of Wisconsin, where also he had served for three years as an instructor before going to Ohio University as a professor.

John Thomas Lister had come as head of the Department of Spanish with the rank of assistant professor. He was a man of parts. A specialist in Spanish, and incidentally in Old French, he enjoyed deciphering Old English manuscripts. He played golf and soon joined a faculty group playing volley ball in the gymnasium. In college he had played football all four years, and had been named for the mythical All-Indiana team for three of those years. He had also been a weight thrower. His particular antipathies were poetry and the making of speeches. He warmed especially to the teaching of young men; some years before he had lost his only son. He had taught in the University Schools of both Cleveland and Chicago, and soon after coming to Wooster, he sought out the president one day and arranged with him to pay, anonymously, the tuition of some promising boy (the choice of Mr. Wishart) in college.[2] He had sandwiched in his graduate study between sessions of teaching at Olivet College, Colorado State Teachers' College, and Northwestern University. In 1901 also he had spent a while at the University of Geneva. He was a native of Indiana, had grown up on a farm, had won his B.A. from Butler College in 1897, his M.A. from Chicago in 1916, and in June just past had completed his thesis and won his doctor's degree from Chicago. In 1917 with Professor Owen of the University of Kansas he had edited a Spanish drama, *La Conjuracion de Venecia.* With Miss Richardson, he was to edit also for college use Cervantes' *Rinconete y Cortadillo,* and in 1927 Florencio Sanchez' *La Gringa.*

This was the year, too, when Charles Owen Williamson began his long career at Wooster. He came as instructor in applied mathematics from Western State Normal College of Kalamazoo. He had taught for five years also at Ohio University, from which he had been graduated, and had spent the years from 1916–1918 in graduate study at Yale. He was tall and gangly as if he had lived on cornstalks all his life yet full of humor and given to philosophizing. Even on a bitterly cold night under the open dome of the observatory, one of his students has related, as he pointed out the constellations he was busy talking not only of the glories of the universe but of their Creator.

Olla Fern Kieffer, '95 joined the English department in the fall of 1919 to teach three divisions of freshman composition, a field in which she was very much at home. She had always been an avid reader, in literature and many other fields and had a sense for words. Little and quick on her feet, she was equally quick in her mind, always questing and always questioning. She was sometimes likened to a wren. An excellent conversationalist; intelligent, informed, and perceptive, she could flit from international politics to international literature without ever losing her direction. Moreover there was always a glint in her eye, no matter how hard her life sometimes proved to be, and as a teacher she was exact and exacting. She had taught for eight years in high schools and colleges, before coming back to Wooster to look after aging parents.[3]

The time had now come for the appointment of another instructor in physical education. The choice fell on Ernest (Mose) M. Hole, '18. His special responsibility besides routine class work would be in coaching the freshmen in basketball. For three years in college he had played on the basketball team, becoming in his senior year its captain. He was more than just that, however; he was an all-round athlete, one of Mr. Boles' stand-bys. He shared Mr. Boles' ideals for Wooster's teams and lived up to them. He had moreover a humorous twist, which made him much in demand as a speaker. Through the years much was to be heard from and about him.

College had opened with every room in the dormitories filled. There were nearly 200 freshmen. There was also some gain in the upper classes because of men returning from the war, some of them formerly outstanding men in college. They would once more add strength to the organizations and activities, to athletics especially. Taylor Hall now housed all of physics and some classes in mathematics. A minor improvement had come in the installing of a drinking fountain just to the south of the chapel in a spot convenient to all. It had been the gift of the Student Senate of 1918–1919.

Late in October when the Wisharts were settled in their home on Beall Avenue, the faculty staged a dinner at Holden Hall for them and for all the newcomers. Everyone had been asked, wives, ex-faculty living in Wooster, local trustees and the Women's Advisory Board. Miss Gingrich with her usual love of woods and fields had decked the parlors with brilliant autumn leaves and berries. After dinner, Chalmers Martin as toastmaster took over. From then on the party became almost as gay as an Irish wake. All summer long it seemed, everyone had been collecting stories against this time, from the college halls of Princeton and Columbia, the woods of Wisconsin where six of the faculty had spent their vacations, the streets and offices of Chicago, the sociables of small middlewestern towns. There was music too, provided by Mr. and Mrs. Homer Crain. In early December the Mateers followed with a reception again honoring the Wisharts, and Assistant Professor Turner with his bride of a few months. Former President Holden, too, stopping in Wooster for a day, was present. Two to three hundred persons including some townsfolk passed in and out of their doors.

Any college president is overwhelmed in his first few weeks—and never ceases to be overwhelmed thereafter—with all he needs to know and do and be. Mr. Wishart once put it succinctly when he wrote: "A college president needs to be a statesman, an orator, a diplomat, a financial promoter, a scholar (but not losing the common touch), a business man, a social leader, with much *fortiter in re* and also much *suaviter in modo,* and a dozen other qualifications which have never yet existed in any one human being." He must get acquainted with faculty, trustees, students, alumni, friends of the college, in this instance also with the Presbyterian Synod of Ohio, and the townspeople as well. He must study the various rules and regulations, the statutes and the charter, find out the past of the institution and what would be pending in the immediate future. He must raise money in the meanwhile to keep the college going, preach sermons, counsel the young, keep open house for their parents when they come to visit; he must know what is going on in the world, particularly in the educational world. He must go to all the games and attend the student rallies; he must be Santa Claus and Lord High Executioner especially if he lived before the day of multiple deans. This year he had to see in early November that the college had enough coal to weather a coal strike of uncertain duration in a season when temperatures might sink low and furnaces be eating from sixteen to twenty-five tons a day.

In October he attended the meeting of the Ohio Synod, there made two addresses, and was enthusiastically welcomed. During the fall and early winter he had spoken or was still scheduled to speak at alumni gatherings arranged in his honor at Cleveland, Toledo, Youngstown, New York, and Chicago. At home the Student Senate had planned and issued invitations to the first of Wooster's Homecomings attended by nearly 100 alumni and former students. It had been an auspicious first, for that afternoon in the stadium Wooster's team "walloped" Case 26–0 before a crowd of 2000 persons gone shouting wild. At the ensuing bonfire the president, of course, spoke. That night in the gymnasium the Homecoming entertainment continued with student performances of various kinds, a farce taking off the faculty as they appeared in chapel, a spiritualistic medium in action, a number by some of the Girls' Glee Club dressed to represent maids of the Orient, a serenade by a string quartet. There was no end to the student activities into which the president was directly or indirectly drawn. He was elected, for instance, an honorary member of the freshman class of 1923, and felt obliged to attend the freshman-junior banquet. There he spoke as an honored guest, but for the most part was listening to the students and taking their measure. One in particular attracted his attention, a boy from Portsmouth, Ohio, obviously a born speaker with a gift of humor.[4] Young as he was, this boy was trying out also for a place on the debating team.

What the president saw of student life on campus pleased him. On the football field Wooster did not lose a single game even when once the team had to play in almost a sea of mud and water. The game in Cleveland against Reserve, which Wooster won 13–7, was notable in that the Reserve team was much heavier on the average than Wooster's, yet Wooster made two touchdowns in the first eight minutes, and though the second half was harder going, those seven points were the only ones against Wooster made by an opposing team in all the season. The Cleveland and Southwestern had run an extra car that day to carry the crowd to Cleveland; about eighty of the students had made the trip. To their elation the men of Case in attendance joined in the shouting on Wooster's side and in the snake dance. That day a happy coach could be seen striding along the sidelines with a huge yellow chrysanthemum on his lapel.[5] On the return to Wooster the team was met by a brass band; and they all adjourned to the old athletic field for a victory bonfire. In the past five years out of thirty-eight football games played Wooster had lost only four; twenty-nine were victories; five were ties. If this record spoke well for the players, it spoke well also for the coach; and the students were not slow in recognizing this fact. On the day they played Akron (score 19–0), again Boles was wearing a big yellow chrysanthemum, sent him by the senior class, for this had been designated as Coach Boles Day. The Board of Trade band was on hand to play for the game. There was a little ceremony that day, and for it Earl Dunbar, '21, one of the team who was known for his good "booting toe," and his skill at breaking up forward passes, made the speech on behalf of the *W* Association. They had passed a resolution, which read:

Lawrence C. Boles has distinguished himself for five years as Coach of our athletic teams and, whereas in that time he has won the admiration and devotion of the entire student body through his Christian leadership and unselfish interest in our welfare, we, the members of the W association of The College of Wooster, do hereby award him the W certificate for all branches of intercollegiate sport and with it a token of appreciation [6] which expresses our loyalty to him, our faith in him and our stand by him.

Several of Wooster's men had again been singled out by the sports writers as worthy of places on the All-Ohio team. Ben Roderick known for his speed, his punting, his skill in changing pace and direction, and for his general good nature, was mentioned again, as half-back, full-back, even as captain, of this team, Allen Snyder as quarter-back, and Walker as tackle on the second team. Wooster was proud. In cross country it had not fared so well, having been defeated by Oberlin 19–7; it had come out third in the Big Six meet in Columbus in November. Even the girls had caught the athletic fever. They were no longer merely shouting spectators, but participants in battles of their own. The girls of 1920 had set the pace; others had followed their lead. This year a tennis tournament was played off in November, and hockey teams were driving the puck fast and furiously past the opponent's goal. Two more girls had been awarded their letters by the Women's Athletic Association for excellence in various sports, points won in swimming, tennis, hiking, and in basketball.

The president had been delighted, too, to find such interest among the students in the more literary activities, in debate and public speaking of various sorts, in current affairs, in science, and in music, as manifested by the many extra-curricular clubs. Twenty-two persons, including two girls, had tried out for the college debating teams; forty members of the young Honor Society had spent an evening at the Kelsos hearing Mr. Kelso lecture on the Allenby campaign and entering into the discussion afterwards of Palestine and its problems. A new literary society among the girls had sprung up, Pembroke, named, at Miss Thayer's suggestion, for the Countess of Pembroke, Sir Philip Sidney's sister, who in her day had been a patroness of literature. Both a mathematics club at the instigation of Mr. Yanney and a physics club on the prompting of Mr. Westhafer had been organized.

There were times of course when students took things more or less into their own hands. There was Armistice Day, for instance. Classes had been dismissed for the third and fourth hours and the chapel period extended to allow for a special service. The boys in Kenarden who had been in the war decided, however, that they were having a celebration of their own preceding this. They cut the classes of the first two hours. Forming themselves into a company they marched past the girls' dormitories, then down Beall Avenue toward town. At the Korner Klub they picked up a large U.S. flag to head the procession. On the public square they formally reviewed the colors. Then some wearing German helmets that had been lent them by the Citizens' Bank, they paraded back to the campus, and marched into the chapel in time for the service. There, after the "Star Spangled Banner," and "In Flanders' Fields" sung as a solo by Mrs. Hall, John A. Baird, president of the Student Senate, who had served as a First Lieutenant in the air service,[7] spoke as representative of the men who had served overseas, Earl Dunbar for those who had never been sent across. Then as Mr. Crain played Chopin's *Militaire Polonaise,* and Mr. Compton read the names of the sixteen Wooster men who had died in the war, the service flag was lowered. It represented 692 Wooster men and women.

Sometimes the students could be both gay and earnest, as when the Y.W.C.A. put on the Dingling Sisters Circus, complete with animals —the bear, giraffe, tiger, and elephant—and a variety of sideshows including the fat lady and the tallest one on earth, a scene depicting the death of Cleopatra, one in the Garden of Allah, a troupe of tight-rope walkers, and a chariot race. It was all for the benefit of a school in Tokyo, for which they thereby raised $135.

And sometimes they posed serious questions demanding an answer. Soon after Mr. Wishart came he was waited on by a delegation asking his position on the reinstatement of fraternities. A petition for such reconsideration had gone to the trustees the preceding June and had been at least temporarily shelved by being referred to a commit-

tee for study. Mr. Wishart assured the delegation of his open mind
on the subject; he was, however, unfamiliar as yet with the local
situation, and it would take time and study for him to form any
opinion. With that the matter rested, yet it was to keep coming up
more than once during the next few years before everyone decided to
let the *status quo* remain the *status quo.*[8] Mr. Wishart, years later,
once stated that he had always felt that his first mission at Wooster
was to bring peace to the institution, and he could not at least in the
early years of his administration risk restudying so controversial a
policy.

Two new, seemingly minor but really significant policies, however, were voted by the trustees with Mr. Wishart's blessing within
the first few months of his coming to Wooster. One was the establishment, on a very small scale, to be sure, of a press bureau to handle
college news going out to the newspapers of Ohio and elsewhere,
especially to the towns from which the students came. Surprisingly,
they put in as director of this Arthur Murray, a senior and war
veteran who had been editor of *The Voice* before going off to war.
He was an athlete, too, one of Coach Boles' trainees, who could
report Wooster's prowess in athletics sympathetically to catch the eye
of high school students across the state. He was given an assistant
and a basement room in the library as headquarters.[9] The other
innovation was the appointment of Miss Emeline McSweeney as
acting alumni secretary; her first assignment was to start work toward a new alumni catalogue. Mr. Wishart felt all along that one of
his major efforts should be toward a real consolidation of Wooster
alumni, and for this he needed full and accurate records. He had
already a minor but appealing project in mind toward which the
alumni could help.

However, all thought was now turning toward December 9 when
Wooster's sixth president was to be recognized officially with all the
fanfare accompanying inaugurations. Town and college had long
since taken him to their hearts. The day for him began long before
the hour appointed. He was sleeping when at 3 A.M. he was startled
wide awake by loud and persistent shouting under his window—
Speech, speech, SPEECH! By the arc lights from the street he could
see about 200 men gathered under the trees. For a moment he was
angry. This was an outrageous bit of thoughtlessness toward a man

who was tired and faced with a heavy day ahead. With boys one was always walking a tight rope. He must keep his balance. An old story flashed through his mind, and the first speech of the day was ready. "Boys," he said, "there was once a farmer who had a bull, and the bull was anxious to try out his strength against a railway engine. The engine severely and permanently wrecked the bull. The farmer came to view the remains and soliloquized, 'Bull, I admire your ideals, but darn your judgment.' Goodnight." So the boys went home and Mr. Wishart back to sleep. On campus that morning the story made the rounds, with appropriate changes, to be sure.

It was really a great occasion on that early winter day, a warm and friendly day. It was an academic occasion first of all with processions both morning and afternoon from Kauke Hall to the chapel, led by girls in white carrying large United States flags. Fifty delegates from sister institutions over the country were there to symbolize the great academic community. Former President Holden, Dean Compton, and President Thomas McMichael of Monmouth, Wishart's own college, had a part in the early program. Then President Henry Churchill King of Oberlin, fellow administrator, made the major address of the morning, on "The Challenge of the Present World Situation." It was a day of congratulation and commitment also for the Presbyterian Church, and its representatives had their own formal places on the program morning and afternoon: President J. Ross Stevenson of Princeton Theological Seminary, the Rev. Mr. Paul Hickok, '97, Washington, D.C., and the Rev. Mr. George N. Luccock, '78. As it was a church and alumni occasion it was also something of a family day, for two of Mr. Wishart's brothers were present.

It was to the afternoon service that all looked with greatest expectation, for after the devotionals, the Hallelujah Chorus sung by the Oratorio Society, the swearing in of the new president by the Rev. Mr. John Timothy Stone, president of the Board of Trustees, there followed the inaugural prayer by the president's brother, the Rev. Mr. John L. Wishart of Xenia (U.P.) Theological Seminary, and the inaugural address. Mr. Wishart had chosen as his title, "The Search for the Golden Mean." At once making it clear that by golden mean he did not mean any wishy-washy compromise, but rather the fine balance between fixed persistence and progressive change, between conservatism and radicalism, he found the educational ideal of the

Christian liberal arts college to be "to put the color and warmth and glow and splendor of the religious life into the stern and rigorous forms of mental discipline." The College of Wooster, he said,

dares not neglect the fixed principles of the intellectual life. It must always deal with truth in the persistent, unchanging forms that come to us through logic, through pure mathematics, under the white light of science and philosophy. [Yet] . . . sheer intellectual training ought to be balanced by the emotional, inspirational and imaginative development of the human heart under the influence of religion . . . physical science . . . is always conservative, fundamentally because it is dealing with fixed laws. . . . The vision of faith, however, . . . steps far beyond the limits of logic and the tests of the senses. . . . It is . . . the essence of liberalism. . . . Religion has always been the handmaid of democracy. . . .

To preserve that fine balance we must have the personal touch. [It] can never be done in an institution where the numbers pass beyond the point of personal contact between teachers and pupils and between the scholars themselves. . . . where, substantially speaking, the Faculty cannot know the whole student body . . . and every student does not have more or less vital contact with all the others. Hence I suspect that if in Wooster during the next five years we shall reach eight hundred or a thousand students we shall have gone practically to the point of safety so far as our particular function is concerned. I should like to see about that many,—with a waiting list. . . . our . . . task here is to train the picked leaders . . . and our first aim should be the quality of this leadership rather than the numerical quantity of our output.

It will be necessary, too, that an institution doing this work should have a certain willingness to be unique. If we are striving after form we shall of course be likely to conform to the cast and custom of the average school. But if we are seeking after color, after individuality, we shall strive not so much to imitate as to differentiate between our own and institutions doing different work by different methods. . . . We are striving, and I hope shall strive, for simplicity, and for an after-the-war reconstruction program of Christian democracy. We have been, and I hope shall be, frankly Christian in every phase of college life. . . . That the golden mean between piety and true manhood can be found is, I think, assured by our record. . . .

. . . . .

If you ask me whether any existing features of college life could be changed or improved I reply "Undoubtedly yes!" If you ask me whether they should be changed or improved at the expense of discord and upheaval I reply "No!" Our first and crying need is for the ability and willingness to see eye to eye and to play the team for the good of the whole. Whatever the experiences of the past have been may we not now launch upon a great adventure of balance?—of Christian brotherly balance?

Then risking an anticlimax, he spoke of Wooster's financial needs, estimating them, at the moment, as two million dollars.

And so quietly and without demonstration he answered many questions.

That evening at the inaugural banquet in Severance gymnasium almost 900 persons were present. No longer was the mood one of an almost austere solemnity. It was rather a time of relaxation, of gaiety, and reminiscence. Governor Cox was the main speaker welcoming Mr. Wishart back to the state of his father and grandfather. Many others followed. Former President Holden told of some of his experiences as president of the college. J. Ross Stevenson talked of the great value of such institutions as Wooster to the total work of the church. One hundred Wooster men, he said, had gone out from Princeton Theological Seminary. George N. Luccock in his quiet, humorous way reminisced about all six of Wooster's presidents. It was only President Lord whom he had not known well and personally. Mr. Pomerene, United States Senator from Ohio, on whom Wooster had in the afternoon conferred a degree, spoke in his turn, and Chalmers Martin from the faculty, the Rev. Mr. W. I. Wishart from Pittsburgh, the president's brother. In the intervals the college glee clubs sang. By the end of the day Charles Frederick Wishart had been safely and happily landed, and all the world could know it.

Enlarging Vistas

FOR a long time Highland Park had been a happy haven for students and many others. Close to, actually but a mile away from the college, one nevertheless felt there as if one had reached deep country hidden by the hills and woods on either side of the meandering Little Applecreek. Sunday schools and churches had often picnicked there. Hare and hound races had sometimes been scheduled to Highland Park and back by circuitous routes. Boys took innocent freshmen to the valley for snipe hunts, and left them holding the bags. College classes meeting at the Rock or library had occasionally walked down en masse carrying baskets of food and coffee pots, and maybe a guitar. More often a wandering couple or two escaped down the hill to talk over something important. One could build a fire in a bare spot and cook. There was a shelter where one could set things if it rained. And there was the creek where one could wade and over which one could pick one's way precariously on stones protruding from the water. Besides, above it, forty or so feet, rose a steep bank of loose clay and stones known to the students as the "devil's slide." Young boys were always climbing it, dreaming that they were climbing mountains, usually letting loose a minor avalanche behind them. Once on top, however, they found woods. Some years before, a twister had passed through and laid low many forest trees and transformed this patch of ground into a tangle of fallen logs and sprouting underbrush. There chewinks could nearly always be seen—or heard, and perhaps veery thrushes, and in the migrating season many kinds of warblers. Squirrels frisked in the trees, garter snakes were not a rarity, and an intruder was always starting a rabbit from its form. In all this region in the spring, wild flowers bloomed, in the valley especially, buttercups and violets, hepaticas, and white anemones, and on the grassy slopes farther down where the sun blazed, yards of bluets. On the edges of the woods wherever there was both light and shadow whole colonies of May apples spread their green umbrellas. Except for Clear Creek several miles away or spots on Christmas Run where long wild grapevines hung from beech trees, Highland Park was nearest to being a place of enchantment in all the country around.[1] Besides, there was a so-called lake, really an old millpond, where one could skate in winter, or in the open season row around an old flat-bottomed boat. Willows clustered along one bank and in the late summer tall black-eyed Susans bloomed there too. The millpond had not so many years before fed a water mill, belonging to a farmer, Kline, located across the little dirt road that threaded the valley. To that mill farmers had brought grain to be ground and apples to be turned into cider. Yet the pond had its grim story, too, for, now years ago, a young man of the neighborhood, a farmer's son, swimming there, had been drowned.

There were other stories too, grim and not so grim, that hovered in this valley, twenty rods or so to the north where the dirt road north and south met the road to east and west. At the foot of the hill, on a knoll stood an ancient frame house, black, desolate, gradually falling apart, haunted, it was said; at least strange sounds issued from it at times and strange lights shone in the windows. It was a likely place for a ghost, but no one had ever seen it. Anyhow the boys of the community, including an occasional student, prowled about it and through it, climbing the half rotten stairway, from which several of the steps were gone, opening closet doors, peeping into the cellar, wiping spiderwebs off on their clothes as they went, and always threatening to come back and spend a night there "just to see." True, the old glass in the windows caught and reflected the evening sun as in a mirror; maybe that was all there was to it; or perhaps the ghost kept only business hours from sunset to sunrise and spent the day sleeping in the old graveyard [2] just at the other side of the valley as one started up the hill.

Close by the haunted house lived a character of the community. Lily was his name, and Lily had a temper. He owned the land north of the bridge beside the creek. There was a deep spot there in Little Applecreek which the boys sometimes used for swimming. When they came, they always made a point of singing at the top of their voices, "O the lily of the valley, the bright and morning star. . . ." He would then come down the hill boiling with rage and order them off. And once he came a little too soon armed with a long blacksnake whip while one of the group was still in the water. At the top of the long hill not far from the old pike,[3] Lily finally gave up the chase, and the late swimmer put on his clothes which the others had rescued from the bank as they all took off. The singing of the Lily of the Valley on occasion had become almost a "must" among the younger generation just north of town.

But all such events were long in the past. The present owner of Highland Park had shut off the land for picnic purposes, had indeed recently put up "no trespassing" signs and meant them. It was his purpose to clear the land and make it into fields. Then he hesitated. He would sell forty acres for $100 an acre if anyone would give him the price, and then he would leave everything as it was. This was prime recreation ground for the college, and Mr. Wishart was not slow to consider the proposal seriously. He consulted alumni, faculty, and the local trustees and found a general acceptance of the idea if it could be financed. The physical education department and the botany department could use the place to advantage. Mr. Knight, who knew the value of land such as this in Wayne County, was empowered to look into the matter, and the Student Senate to take it up with the students. Early in February an option was taken on the land consequently, and in late February the deal was closed. It was understood that the students were to raise one fourth of the money for the project; they would be expected also to take over much of the cleaning up of the park itself which had been allowed to run down, and to help also with the reviving of the little lake. From the beginning they had been enthusiastic and in chapel one February morning had subscribed $744 toward this, which soon grew to $786. Others interested were invited to send in checks to the president of the Student Senate or to Mr. Knight. Later in the season the biennial Castalian-Irving play was put on at the Opera House as a Highland Park benefit performance. Management of the park was to be left in the hands of the athletic and the scientific departments and the Student Senate. By late spring the college was already making use of it. Mr. Strausbaugh's classes were botanizing there. On that gala May day, declared officially as a holiday when Earl Dunbar, '21, came home from winning the interstate, intercollegiate oratorical contest, all the students with "Prexy" and many of the faculty went there for a picnic. Though not exactly an inauguration of the park, it seemed so to everyone. Later adjoining plots of ground, offered at reasonable prices by neighbors, were added to the holding.

In his first year Mr. Wishart was moving cautiously, though definitely and in the right direction. The students and faculty he had already, as it were, in his pocket. But there were others. Within the first few weeks of his coming to Wooster he had announced to a group of Presbyterian ministers in Cleveland that the college must have two million more in endowment for salaries if it was to move ahead. This he had reiterated at his inauguration. Yet he knew as well as he knew his own right hand that to be successful in any campaign for money he must have the prior backing of Wooster's alumni; otherwise his work would be just as futile as the cow's jumping over the moon. He knew also from the persistent proddings of some of the old alumni, almost from the moment of his arrival on the scene, that these men were still bitter over the ousting of fraternities in 1913.

At the February meeting in 1920 he had asked his trustees for a more closely knit alumni organization and for an executive alumni secretary, full-time. Wooster had had a Central Alumni Association since the early eighties. Once a year it met attended by those alumni who came back for commencement. They listened to a report about the college, made nominations for alumni trustees from the floor, attended their class reunions at noon, the alumni banquet in the evening—a kind of glory meeting where the president made a speech and sometimes interesting announcements; and then they went home for another year or five years or maybe ten. The rest they left to an executive committee who sent out the ballots for the election of the trustees, gathered them in when they were returned, and notified the college officials of the results. Otherwise the alumni had little contact with the college, direct or indirect. During their life at Wooster the fraternities and sororities, it is true, had furnished much of this contact through their continuing organizations. It was true, too, that *The Wooster Quarterly* through the years had been a binding force, but it was by subscription and only about a fourth of the alumni at any one time took it. There was no disaster pending— the president devoutly hoped—no great dramatic moment that would of itself inspire the gathering of the clans around the college of their memories. They needed someone who would by letters and personal contact and whatever means he could dream up make them

Original campus grove as it appeared in the 1930's, looking south to the back of Kauke Hall.

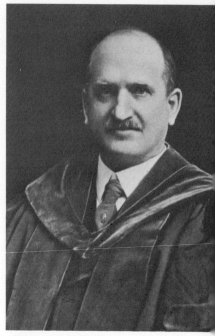

John Campbell White,
President 1915–1919

Louis Edward Holden,
President 1899–1915

Charles Frederick Wishart,
President 1919–1944,
with Matthew Arnold

Memorial Chapel. Erected 1901.

Commencement 1930—re-enactment of 1912 Color Day with Wooster's first May Queen.

Warren Poppino Spencer, Professor,
Department of Biology

Aileen Dunham, Chairman,
Department of History

Mary Zelene Johnson, Chairman,
Department of Political Science

Delbert Giles Lean, Chairman,
Department of Speech

Elizabeth Bechtel, Librarian

William Zebina Bennett, Chairman,
Department of Chemistry

Lawrence Casper Boles, Chairman,
Department of Physical Education

John Bolton Kelso, Chairman,
Department of Greek

President Wishart speaking at his last commencement, 1944.

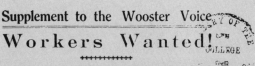

Page from an early advertisement for summer school.

Supplement to the Wooster Voice

Workers Wanted!

Wooster The City of Progress

W—orthy
O—riginal
O—ld fashioned
S—erviceable
T—horough
E—arnest
R—ising

U—nselfish
N—on-exclusive
I—mproving
V—irile
E—ducative
R—estful
S—ane
I—ntensive
T—actile
Y—oung

S—prightly
U—nselfish
M—iscellaneous
M—oderate
E—nergetic
R—efreshing

S—anguine
C—ollege centered
H—onest
O—rganized
O—pportunity-full
L—arge-hearted

A school that's growing better every year. Can you say as much for your self?

A school that's different

At Wooster Summer School
WOOSTER, OHIO

Bring your brains and have them sharpened while you wait.

Do you want inspiration? It is on tap every day in the week at Wooster Summer School.

Do you want better preparation? The school was organized to meet your wants.

Do you want a better position? Three thousand dollars every week in the year is the business done through the Summer School Teachers' Agency

Do you want to hear the best platform talent? Wooster will give it to you for almost nothing.

Do you want a wider outlook? Wooster is on a hill-top from which you can look off to every portion of the world.

Do you want every-day work for every-day needs? Wooster is built on the ground where people live and work and love and die.

Do you want your hard questions answered? Wooster will try to help you answer them.

Do you wish any special work? Wooster is organized to give it in almost every line.

Do you wish strictly professional training? In Methods and Pedagogy alone Wooster employs a faculty of not less than twelve; all of them thoroughly versed, some of them specialists.

Do you wish the most enjoyable summer you have ever had? Wooster promises this to its patrons, and it keeps its pledge.

Do you wish to form an alliance that will always help? Hundreds date their success from the time they became acquainted with Wooster Summer School.

Hoover Cottage, Freshman Women's Dormitory. Erected 1895.

One of Coach Boles' winning football teams from the early 1920's.

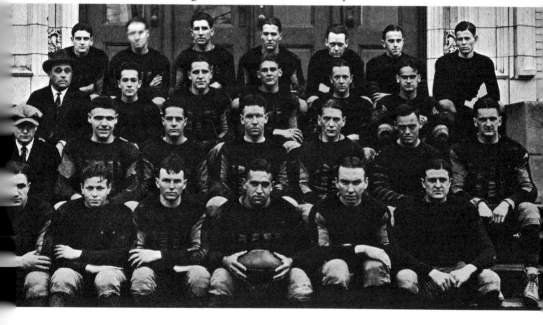

Henry Clay Frick Library. Erected 1900.

feel that they still belonged here, that the college needed them, someone who could supply enthusiastic leadership as a dean did for faculty and students. The alumni needed to be told, not just once but frequently, of the needs of the college, of its frustrations and of its triumphs. There was a place waiting for a man who could weld the diverse elements within a far-flung alumni body in a common loyalty. The trustees considered and authorized the seeking of such a person.

Through all that long winter and spring of 1920 Emeline McSweeney had been preparing the copy for a new alumni catalogue, the first since 1916. It was needed, for the war had intervened, and not only had four more graduating classes been entered on the rolls but many of the old addresses had been changed. Now on June first of 1920, the copy was ready, the rolls themselves, the geographical and alphabetical index, the lists of former faculty, trustees, and officers of the college. They had used this list in sending out the 3500 invitations to the Jubilee Commencement.

It was a great commencement in terms of alumni participation. Of the thirty-four students entering in Wooster's first year, nine were back. Mrs. A. A. E. Taylor, widow of Wooster's second president, was there, still gay, still beautiful, still with the grace of an angel. Elsie Scovel Barnett, daughter of Sylvester Scovel, sent a telegram. President White had come. Louis E. Holden, but recently become president of James Milliken College, was busy with his own commencement there. Paul Shorey, head of the Department of Greek of the University of Chicago, made the commencement address.[4] At the alumni business meeting discussion centered on how to finance the new office of alumni secretary authorized by the trustees but with no provision for its expenses or the salary. Pledges toward expenses were then solicited and a life membership fee in the Association set up. Three hundred and sixty-five pledges were made. These amounted to about $3000 for the immediate needs of the Association and $2000 in life memberships which were to become an endowment fund, from which only the interest could be used. With these pledges as an incentive the executive committee went about hunting their victim. It would be his responsibility to develop so strong an *esprit de corps* among the alumni as to assure his own salary. So he was told, at least when interviewed in the summer by the president of the Alumni Association, John McSweeney, Jr., and by the treasurer of the college when he arrived on September 7, 1920, to begin the job.

The choice had fallen on John D. McKee, '17. He had come back from the war,[5] had married a classmate the year before, Ola Weygandt, and had settled in business in Barberton. He was young, enthusiastic, and energetic, and he had the advantage of having had his whole Wooster experience in the post-fraternity era. Though his background, save for his war service and the year in Barberton, had been Smithville and Wooster, he had a generous and amiable disposition which he would need through the years in fending off complaints; and he was a go-getter. In college he had been outstanding, an able debater, winner of a Fackler medal, a member of both the Congressional and the Toastmasters' Clubs. He knew something of organizational procedures and could stand on his feet and speak.

In accepting the appointment he took a gambler's chance, betting on himself and on the alumni. He had been in Wooster for the Jubilee Commencement, and had attended the Denison-Wooster game, which Wooster won, the senior class play, the alumni business meeting, and the banquet in the evening. There he had witnessed, and shared, the enthusiasm of the old grads and the young for the new office of alumni secretary. He had been pleased with the president and had been thrilled with the announcements of that evening. A campaign for a million dollars of endowment was being launched, for professors' salaries primarily, had indeed been already launched, for one morning in the spring Mr. Wishart had been called out of bed by the long distance telephone. It was E. P. Douglass, '77, of McKeesport, Pennsylvania, one of his trustees, offering him out of the blue the first $25,000 toward the new endowment fund. Wooster had made an appeal again after so many years to the Rockefeller General Education Board. It had offered in answer $250,000 provided Wooster could complete the million in cash and guaranteed pledges by June first, 1921. To the alumni of an older generation this seemed indeed like old times. In nine years the growth of the college in attendance and in faculty had been marked; in endowment there had been little or no change. The need was urgent.

When John D.—for that became his name to everyone thenceforth—reported in to President Wishart that September day of 1920, he was greeted warmly, but told that as yet there was no office available for him. Temporarily he was set down in the trustee room adjacent to the president's office in Kauke Hall, without instructions, without assistance, without any office equipment, save the table and the chairs in the room. He soon discovered, however, that the proof was coming through for the new alumni catalogue. This he must read at once. Correcting proof was fortunately no new trade for him. He had been editor of *The Index* in his day in college. Soon he was informed that it was now his chore to mail out the ballots for the election of the alumni trustees nominated in June. This he did, gathering in the answers and reporting to the executive committee of the Alumni Association. With a rented typewriter he next sent out penny postal cards to all the 3500 alumni and former students listed in the forthcoming catalogue, inviting them to a Homecoming on October 23. Before doing so, however, he consulted with the Student Senate, Coach Boles, and others, and arranged that a special section in the bleachers should be reserved for the alumni that day, that President and Mrs. Wishart would hold open house after the game, and that Mr. West of the Department of Oratory would be staging a rollicking farce,[7] at the Opera House for the occasion. Evidently the invitations had had the proper touch, for on the great day 300 alumni were on the campus, and John D. was moving among them like an old hand. The game that day was with Oberlin, Wooster's perennial enemy which had not been defeated for two years. Their team came accompanied by 500 students, a band, and cheerleaders. Four thousand persons, it was estimated, were on the field to watch. The Board of Trade band played for Wooster. Captain Walker, according to *The Voice,* did that day a "sensational job of tackling." Wooster won 19–0 and the shouts of jubilation could be heard for a mile around. The Cleveland *Plain Dealer* reported that Wooster had won "because it had by far the best team." There was still another victory, however. Before the big game, had been the 4½ mile cross-country meet with Oberlin. Wooster won this too. Her top runner came in in 27 minutes and 3 seconds. In the evening at the Opera House before the curtain rose on "Polly in Politics" several students with special talents entertained with readings, a violin concerto, and vocal numbers. All in all it was literally a day and a half.

In the meantime Mr. McLaughlin, assistant treasurer, who was taking over more and more the duties of a non-existent business manager,[8] studied where to put the alumni secretary. Before many days after his arrival carpenters were at work on the second floor of Kauke Hall dividing and redividing the old art room, to the left as one climbed the stairway, giving a part to John D., another to the registrar's office as an addition. John D.'s room was #214, and Alumni Association was blazoned on its door. Then came the task of collecting furniture. A table was found in the basement of the library and several old chairs in Irving Hall. Jesse McClellan pulled out from somewhere some old cabinets for files; Chalmers Martin lent a golden oak desk and chair. A telephone was put in.

Two tasks, John D. knew, now awaited him, that of keeping records of names, addresses, death dates, and the other more pleasant one of keeping the alumni in touch with Wooster and each other, of building up their group and individual loyalty to the college. This perhaps might best be done in two ways: by enticing them back to the college on special occasions and by cultivating alumni groups wherever sufficient numbers lived to allow for some sort of regular get-togethers, even though these might be only once a year. He had already ascertained that a few local alumni clubs were or had been in existence off and on, notably in Cleveland, Chicago, New York, Pittsburgh, Cincinnati, and Columbus. In Cleveland the men had a regular luncheon monthly in the dining room of the Chamber of Commerce. This he and Mr. Wishart attended in late October. In November they went to alumni dinners in both Boston and New York. On the way John D. made a point of stopping in the alumni offices at Massachusetts Institute of Technology, at Yale, and at Princeton to get ideas on how these were run. He had no compunctions about asking questions, for Wooster had been a charter member of the Association of Alumni Secretaries since 1913, even though it had had no secretary. The whole movement was new, for until Wooster came in, Ohio State was the only college in Ohio with a functioning secretary.

In early December the alumni catalogue came out. It was mailed to all alumni save those in Wooster. The college refused to pay the postage for those here at home. "You can get a little express wagon," said Jesse McClellan to John D., "and deliver them yourself on Saturday afternoons." [9] This he did. Anyhow the new catalogue made each community aware of the other Wooster men and women in its vicinity, speeded up and simplified the alumni organization meetings in Ohio and elsewhere. In January Wooster clubs in both Youngstown and New Philadelphia were organized. Toledo alumni met at Grace Smith's invitation at her Tea House in the suburbs and effected an organization. So gradually the flame spread. Indeed in the winter John D. made a trip to the south and southeast in Ohio organizing groups in East Palestine, East Liverpool, Bellaire, Cambridge, and Mt. Vernon. His budget wouldn't allow him to go far afield. In the first few months of 1921, fifteen meetings of Wooster alumni were held. In Wooster 125 persons came to the meeting at Memorial Hall. In the annual meeting in New York at the Waldorf in the spring more than 100 were present. Soon some of the clubs began playing host to the Boys' and Girls' Glee Clubs on their trips, arranging dates for them at the local Presbyterian churches, and entertaining them for dinner or overnight. Sometimes they were asking for special guests in addition to President Wishart, Earl Dunbar, Wooster's orator, for instance, or Coach Boles and possibly a member or two of his team. (Coach Boles was known now all over the state not just by Wooster men but by all sports fans.) The Wooster women of Cleveland had a dinner honoring Mrs. Wishart and Mrs. J. M. Vance, director of the Girls' Glee Club.

Of course all this enthusiasm had been given impetus by the campaign for endowment already under way. The college in the meanwhile had brought in F. N. Riale, '81, of the General Education Board of the Presbyterian Church, to assist in raising money. The college was little more than a name in most of the 51,000 Presbyterian homes in Ohio. It was time for Wooster to rouse itself to the dramatic possibilities in its own everyday life and to let the people of Ohio, particularly the Presbyterians, know what of real interest was going on in this small but active college. To be sure, Wooster had made one or two attempts at getting more publicity, yet had come to little. Happily, the Rockefeller Board had consented, because of the serious financial depression, to the moving of the deadline for the completion of the campaign to June of 1922; that gave time for beating the bushes near and far for contributions. The trustees had allotted $250,000 to the Synod as its share, and had assigned to the alumni an equal amount. There was need of a news bulletin to apprise the alumni from month to month not only of their responsibility but of how they were meeting this. On April first of 1921, consequently, the first issue of *The Wooster Alumni News* appeared. It was edited by John D. McKee, under the supervision of the Executive Committee of the college, was a four-page, three-column folder on inexpensive paper, and carried important items about the college, administration, faculty, and students, the campaign, the alumni, and the alumni clubs, as well as an editorial or two. It went out to all alumni and former students without charge. This first issue carried also a letter from President Wishart in which he told

of a man who had been very, very sick and whose room had been literally filled with flowers from affectionate friends. There came a time when the sick man . . . approached convalescence, and demanded sustenance. The flowers kept on coming, however, and the old colored butler, with an eye to the psychology of convalescence, said to one of the callers, "De time for flowers am past. De time for grapefruit am done come."

So in alumni relations. In the last two years alumni have had a lot of pleasant things to say and we have welcomed them. . . . But I do not mean exactly that we do not relish the flowers and seek all of them you have to give, but I do mean that the time for definite activity has arrived. The old institution needs more than flowers. It demands sustenance. It seeks the active cooperation of all the alumni toward the building up of its resources—academic, physical, and financial. Now or never is the period of "grapefruit". . . . I believe the continuity and activity of every Wooster alumni chapter will depend on its assuming a definite responsibility for a fixed objective, and getting every member to work upon it.

Our supreme need is your supreme opportunity. We are depending on you.

> Charles F. Wishart
> March 29, 1921

The continuity of Wooster's alumni clubs did depend on their having work to do, some focal point of interest and activity. In the past in several instances, clubs that had started with apparent enthusiasm had withered away. The new alumni secretary had indeed been busy this year in a work of resuscitation as well as of acting as mid-wife to other clubs at their birth. Reminiscences were delightful at reunions but offered no incentive toward continued existence. Now the alumni had something real toward which to strive.

In the spring the executive committee of the Central Alumni Association met again taking stock of the situation thus far. Expenses had been heavier than expected during the year, and pledges toward these had fallen behind. It seemed wise, therefore, to establish annual dues of $5 and life memberships of $50. The new alumni secretary had done well. Not only had he seen the alumni catalogue through publication and inaugurated a news bulletin, but he had compiled files (three sets of them on cards) on all alumni and all former students for whom he had or had been able to find exact information. He had written personal letters to forty-three of the classes, had looked after arrangements for Homecoming, and was planning a dinner in June for all class secretaries at which he intended to outline their responsibilities and opportunities. Early in the spring he was already making sure of the alumni arrangements for commencement, an occasion to which he looked forward with some trepidation. There would be a hospitality committee to meet all trains, rooms provided, if reservations were made ahead, in dormitories and if necessary in private homes. A thousand details confronted him as he thought of plans for the reunion classes and the alumni banquet. Besides, he must justify his existence by his report at the alumni business meeting.

When it was all over, however, he felt that something new in alumni relations was shaping up. At the business meeting of the Association, a temporary alumni council had been set up consisting of the executive committee of the Association and one member from each of the existing alumni clubs. Several new ones had been recently added, Los Angeles, Seattle, Mansfield, Canton-Alliance, Lorain, and even a club of four or five in Salt Lake City. This gave the Association more national scope. A committee chaired by Elias Compton, '81, had been appointed to draft a new constitution. One of the aims of this commitee was to find a procedure for the nomination of alumni trustees. They were interested, too, in the possibility of using alumni clubs in the discovery and directing toward Wooster of promising students in their local communities. The Association voted that a brochure showing Wooster, at its best of course, be got out for use in high schools, and that *The Voice* also be sent to a selected list of these. They had recommended also that five alumni or alumnae representing different fields be brought to the college every year for life-work conferences with students. Of course the expenses of the past year were reviewed and the fact recognized that to function at all adequately the Association should have for the next year a budget of from $5000 to $6000. The class secretaries, as John D. had hoped, had met and effected their own organization.

The college had ended its year (1920–1921) with an accumulated deficit of nearly $45,000 of which $15,000 had been incurred during the past year. However, preparations for the campaign were well in hand, and at the end of June the new campaign manager with his dramatic flair was on the ground. He was R. Arthur Basham, Welshman and ex-coal miner, immigrant to Canada (with ten dollars in his pocket), and member of an ambulance unit in the Canadian Expeditionary Forces. He had managed somewhere along the way to acquire a college diploma, a Reverend in front of his name, and a wife. He had been an assistant in a church in New York City, a pastor in Buffalo and Columbus, had raised half a million dollars in four months for Wesleyan College in West Virginia, and had lately been employed by the Presbyterian Board of Education to raise money. He was in short a kind of whirlwind; he moved so fast one could hardly trail him save by the smoke from his large pipe. When he came, the total pledged toward the three quarters of a million yet to be raised stood at $84,000. It had happened one May day in chapel that faculty and students had been so carried away in a burst of revival-style enthusiasm that they had pledged $27,000, more than they had any reason to believe they could ever pay. There had been miscellaneous gifts totaling $33,000 and the town had thus far loyally come through with pledges of $24,000. In three days in July Mr. Basham raised this latter figure to $53,000. It was a brave beginning. But his major work right now was really that of planning. Of course there were minor indications here and there of activity. A few more alumni clubs were formed; others held summer picnic meetings, attended by Mr. Wishart, John D. and a faculty member or two. One alumnus sent in a check for $10,000. The Cleveland alumni had set themselves a goal of $50,000, and of this the men of their financial committee had already, to start the drive, pledged $10,000. Ten persons would be working for Wooster in the churches of Ohio. Mr. Wishart and Mr. Basham would be seeing the possible large givers. The alumni would be divided into forty districts, each with its chairman. John D. would be giving most of his time during the year to the development of this work. To cover the existing deficit and the necessary expenses of the campaign, $100,000 over and above the million dollar goal would have to be raised. By the first of October a total of more than $150,000 in pledges had come in, exclusive, of course, of the Rockefeller challenge fund.

In October of 1921 there was another Homecoming, another game, with Case, attended by some 300 alumni, another reception at the Wisharts', and another play in the evening, given by the Student Senate at the Opera House. This time, however, Cleveland alumni had brought down with them for their first visit to Wooster 200 members of the Cleveland Presbyterian Union. Arrangements had been made with John D. that these visitors were to be given lunch at Kenarden, would then be taken on a brief tour of the college and the town, would have seats reserved for them at the game, and would afterwards be given a snack at Holden Hall before their return to Cleveland. This was but the beginning of many such visits to Wooster through the years.

At Homecoming this year the temporary alumni council [10] held its first meeting, with fourteen members from Wooster clubs in attendance as well as the executive committee. They approved the observance of Wooster Day on December 11, the anniversary of the fire and of the subsequent dedication of the new Wooster. They recommended that on this day Wooster clubs everywhere meet in an expression of their common loyalty. In this its first year, 1921, meetings were held on that night in sixteen cities or towns. Wooster Day was recognized also in the services of 200 Presbyterian churches.

Mr. Wishart on the eleventh had been speaking in Cleveland at the Church of the Covenant—he was speaking every Sunday at some church. A few days before, Earl Dunbar, '21, had been chosen from among forty-one candidates as the Ohio Rhodes Scholar to go to Oxford University. It was only natural for Mr. Wishart to mention this and to go on to tell something of the story of Dunbar, the boy from Tennessee, who had come to Wooster equipped, financially speaking, only with a scholarship for his freshman year and $50 in his pocket. During college he had won one prize after another, one oratorical contest after another, until in the spring of 1921 he had come back from South Dakota, winner of the interstate, intercollegiate oratorical contest. To put himself through college he had done almost everything, had served as janitor in Kenarden Lodge where he lived, had waited table, had sold shoes downtown, had pitched hay for a farmer, had scrubbed floors, and peeled potatoes. One day in his senior year, to encourage other boys to take the risk and come to college he put down in the form of a letter to a friend how he felt about taking such a chance. He ended his story in this way:

And it hasn't been a grind. I've had time to play a little tennis, a little baseball, a little football. [Actually he played on the winning Varsity team.] I've gone out for debate every year. [He had been on one of the college teams.] I've had my share of dates. I've been to most every class party. I was president of my class one year, and even had time to dunk the freshmen! It hasn't been a grind, but a glorious game and one that pays. And I'm glad now that I didn't have any money when I came to Wooster, for when I walk down the aisle next June and get that diploma, I will know that it is something that I have worked for.

He hadn't mentioned that he had been a member also of the college Congressional Club. After the service Mr. Wishart received various pledges to the college endowment fund and along with them a note from a woman in the congregation asking him to call on her the next day. When he appeared, she said not a word about his address, but only "That was a wonderful boy you told about yesterday"; whereupon she handed him, for the college, bonds amounting to $50,000. It was in the Severance tradition, and she was a Severance, Mrs. F. F. Prentiss.

In general, large givers in this campaign had been few. The after-the-war depression had shaken the confidence of many. Men and women were holding tight to what they had. At their midwinter meeting the trustees had taken note of this fact, and offered as individuals to go out to try to shake loose money from various potential givers. They had added strength, too, to their organization by the election of two new Cleveland trustees, A. C. Ernst and Whitney Warner of the W. H. Warner Coal Company, director of The Union Trust Company and of The Morris Plan Bank. By the first of February, 1922, the total, including the initial challenge fund and nearly $117,000 from alumni, stood at nearly $600,000. By the first of April this had risen to nearly $700,000. By May first another $100,000 had been added.

An every-member drive among the alumni was set from May 15 to June 1. The alumni issue of the college *Bulletin* of May first carried an editorial headline: "YOUR ALUMNI DOLLARS—NO MATTER HOW MANY YOU CAN SPARE—MUST BE PLEDGED." And it quoted from the speech made by Senator John Sherman at President Lord's inauguration:

If you would have this institution of learning rise from the stone and brick in its foundation to the ideals of its founders . . . if you would have it the true Alma Mater of thousands . . . who will look back to it as the foundation of their usefulness . . . you must by study and persistent efforts endow it amply, so that literature and science may here have their ablest Professors.

By June first the alumni had raised $214,000 of their quota. John F. Miller, '81, had offered to pay the last $10,000, yet they still had a considerable sum to raise. During the first ten days of June, however, alumni gifts came in at the rate of nearly $1000 a day. This was not enough. The campaign had been scheduled to close on commencement day, June 14.

A $50,000 general drive in Wooster and Wayne County was consequently arranged from June 5–8, with Thomas Prosser as chairman. Eighty canvassers worked steadily for the three days. At the dinner meeting on the night of the eighth they were several thousand short. When this was announced several men led by Donald Dickason rose and pledged the difference. Wooster had come through again. In the meantime $16,000 more had been found in Cleveland.

By Tuesday morning of commencement week, alumni day, nearly everyone who arrived for the meeting of the Alumni Association was on tenterhooks. The announcement soon was made that the total now stood at $1,064,134.04. The challenge fund and the clearing of the deficit were covered. Yet there remained almost $36,000 before the goal of $1,100,000 would be reached, and the expenses of the campaign also covered.

It was in a mood of hopefulness that the Association that morning transacted business. The continuation of Wooster Day was approved, the Dix plan of class reunions also. Dues were reduced to $3 annually, $5 for husband and wife. The budget for the alumni office for 1922–1923 was set at $6000, two thousand of which was to go toward the expense of enlarging the monthly College of Wooster *Bulletin,* Alumni Number. The major work of the morning, however, was the ratification of the new constitution proposed after much study by Mr. Compton and his committee. Hereafter alumni trustees were to be nominated by a committee, and elected in the spring by an orderly procedure. The constitution provided for an Alumni Council with full power to determine the policies and regulate the activities of the Association. This was to be made up of a representative from every class (term, five years), a representative from each club having a membership of twenty-five or more persons (term, one year), and members at large elected at the annual meeting of the Association (term, one year). This Council was to meet twice a year. At the alumni banquet in the evening the announcement was made that only $12,000 were lacking in meeting the final goal.

All through the morning of commencement day the campaign office was busy. At the end of the formal activities in the chapel Mr. Wishart sent for Mr. Basham and asked the audience to wait for his report. Wooster had once more gone over the top. Mrs. Cyrus McCormick of Chicago had sent in her pledge for $10,000. Mr. Basham read the names of those whose pledges came in at almost the last moment, and many of them were alumni giving for a second or even a third time. At the end Mr. J. E. Harris, *ex* '82, had telephoned to ask how much was still lacking and when they told him $1000 he pledged it. Altogether some 7000 persons made up the roll of contributors. The class of 1921 had won the silver trophy cup given for the class with the highest percentage of contributors. Like Earl Dunbar they had been betting on themselves and their ability to make good all their pledges by 1925. And so commencement ended with jubilation.

Interlude

M R. WISHART had come to Wooster convinced that his role was to be that of a peacemaker. Yet all his life as president, as later he once said, was one of minor skirmishes. His first year had been a happy one of making new friends everywhere, of being wined and dined, at home in Wooster and as he went about the country, speaking and preaching, listening, too, hearing the good word and passing it along. The summer, too, of 1920 had been peaceful. Mr. Knight was building a house in Bloomington, and Mr. Dunn was deep in writing the life of Donald Grant Mitchell. Everybody else, nearly, had taken off, including the president, who spent part of the summer in cool Colorado.

In June, 1920, however, he had lost several members of his faculty. Clarence Turner, assistant professor of biology, was leaving for Beloit to become professor there. Mr. Behoteguy, professor of French since 1892, had been ill and felt that the time had come for him to retire. Warm and unassuming, he had through many years made almost a point of staying in the background, quiet, bright-eyed, loyal, and persistent, but inconspicuous. Miss Gingrich, since the war had deprived her of classes in German, was leaving Wooster to study at Northwestern until indeed the prejudice against the German language might have spent itself. John G. Black had retired to his home in Bloomington because of increasing deafness. But he would probably do a bit of preaching up at Golden Corners (Wayne Presbyterian Church), and he would still be picking up rocks and reading geology. Mr. Lean would be gone on sabbatical leave, to do further study at the University of California for at least part of the year. To take his place Mr. Wishart found Charles F. West as instructor in speech. He had studied at Harvard, and while in the consular service in Naples, studied also at the University of Naples. Henry Powell Spring from New York City, trained at the University of Toronto, would become assistant professor of French. Best of all Perry Strausbaugh, having completed with distinction his Ph.D. in botany at the University of Chicago, was returning to Wooster as professor of botany. Several instructors were coming in, among them, George Bradford in French.

The fall opened with more students than ever, 570 by September 20. The Juliana Long home for missionaries was taken over as a dormitory and twenty-five girls housed there. In their self-government association the boys of Kenarden voted new rules covering damage to college property. Every boy was required to make a deposit of five dollars with the college treasurer against such a contingency; and should any individual's balance fall below two dollars he must replace the full amount. A committee from the Lodge together with the student property manager for the building evaluated all damages. Students were definitely trying to accept their share of responsibility.

The football season had started with a whoop. The Wooster team had all the scores on the board: their opponents to date, Baldwin Wallace, Toledo, Hiram, Reserve, only frigid zeros. Saturday night celebrations on the old athletic field were the order of the day. In a triangular cross-country match Wooster had defeated Oberlin and Case, though in the Big Six meet (Ohio Wesleyan, Miami, Cincinnati, Oberlin, Case, and Wooster) it came out only in second place. Knappen and Campbell were its star runners. They could do a mile in near-record timing. The annual freshman-sophomore tug-of-war, formerly arranged so that the classes tugged one or the other through the waters of the Killbuck, took place on either side of the creek at Highland Park. A part of Little Applecreek now was theirs.

Another triumph in which the whole college took pride was announced in the early fall. Marshall Knappen of the senior class had won the Rhodes Scholarship for South Dakota, his native state. He had indeed spent his freshman year in the university there, but this was his third year at Wooster. Next fall he would be starting off for two years at Oxford University. Besides being a runner, he was a college debater, president of the Y.M.C.A, and a top student.

All fall the air was heavy with the breath of political campaigners, for this was the presidential election year. Governor James Cox[1] was running on the Democratic ticket, Senator Warren G. Harding on the Republican. It was likely to be a close race. Before the end of October Mr. Chancellor had already invited his students and some of his friends in town to his house for election night to listen to election returns, for he had again arranged for a special wire. He was a popular professor; his students felt him a brilliant teacher.[2] His colleagues found him occasionally extreme but delightful and stimulating. He was rated a local authority on political science. He was also a link between town and gown; he had incidentally served on the town council.[3] Indeed he had made himself a part of the community. Writing of him years later a local newspaper man said of him that he was "one of the most personally charming men I have ever met."

Soon after the Republican and Democratic conventions Mr. Chancellor went to Columbus on an errand, and on his way back stopped off at Marion, Harding's home town. There he turned up a story that had circulated off and on among some of the townspeople whenever Harding had run for office: that back two or three generations there was Negro blood in his family tree. Later Chancellor did some investigating with the result that he was inclined to believe not only the story but also jumped to the conclusion that this might well be a link in a chain toward Negro domination of the country. This idea became for him almost an obsession. Mr. Chancellor every once in a while had taken some extreme point of view, and had been given to making predictions on bases known only to himself and heaven. That tendency may well have been a factor in his student popularity; he was fresh and interesting and different. In Wooster's conservative background he may have seemed slightly, oh so slightly and delightfully, avant-garde, even though in this instance reactionary.

Anyhow he felt impelled to write what were, as he thought, his findings to several persons. Nobody yet knows quite what happened next. Some weeks later, toward the end of the campaign, however, the country was flooded with thousands of circulars, cheaply put together on flimsy paper and in clumsy English, over the printed name of William E. Chancellor, College of Wooster. The circulars attempted to trace Harding's lineage and to claim the existence of affidavits to prove Harding's Negro blood. One report said that 250,000 of these circulars were mailed from the San Francisco post office. A bomb had been dropped on Wooster. Mr. Chancellor was at once approached, and he denied authorship. He pointed to the "slovenly" language and the whole manner in which the sheet had been put together. He had a point; this was not the kind of circular one would expect from Mr. Chancellor's pen. It was nevertheless a shameful bit of political propaganda and it bore his name, and that of the college. Mr. Wishart in all his life had not been embroiled in so alarming and disgusting a situation. He was besieged with telephone calls, letters, telegrams from all over the country, from scandalized alumni (how could the college allow itself to become involved in such low-down political propaganda?) from reporters everywhere hot on the trail of a story, from politicians of both parties outraged and angry. Mr. Wishart, too, was outraged and angry. He did the only thing he could do, after talking to Mr. Chancellor; he telephoned the chairman of the Board, John Timothy Stone, and arranged with him for a meeting of the trustees to be called in Wooster. To those who couldn't come Mr. Wishart told the story as he knew it and asked what they would favor doing.

Wooster's Negro colony was small, self-respecting, and respected. The relations between them and the college had always been friendly. Occasionally there had been a Negro student at the college, the first one, Clarence Allen, was graduated in the class of 1892, and he had been treated just as any other person. Though most of the Negroes lived in the south end of town where they had their own Baptist church and their own minister, yet a few families lived also uptown near the college; nobody had called their presence there in question. Mrs. Follis, one of these, had cooked that first dinner for the Wisharts when they came to town, and she and her husband [4] cherished the ornate lamp which had been a wedding present from President Scovel. Westminster Church, too, through its women's associations had long contributed toward the Negro Presbyterian college in the south and toward the various schools and women's seminaries supported by the Presbyterian Church, U.S.A.; in fact a few of Wooster's graduates taught in these schools. In other words, whatever were Mr. Chancellor's prejudices, they were not shared by the college community.

At the trustee meeting on October 29, the faculty committee on tenure had been invited, for their own information and for their advice. Mr. Chancellor was sent for. They heard his statement and asked questions. He disclaimed having had anything to do with the circulars, though on being pressed he admitted having been in Marion and having given such information as he thought he had discovered to several other persons. The faculty committee felt as did the trustees that the question of academic freedom did not enter into this case. To a man the trustees voted to ask for Chancellor's immediate resignation. A committee was sent to break the news to him. He took it like a gentleman, said that he could understand the embarrassment of the college, but that he felt "in his breast that he had done nothing wrong or improper" and that he would "continue to have the kindliest feeling toward the college." The trustees,[5] however, had not finished but took further action. They declared the Hoge Professorship vacant, though continuing Mr. Chancellor's salary until January first, 1921. They recorded in their *Minutes* the further action as follows:

It having come to the knowledge of the Board that circular letters are being broadcast throughout the country with reference to Senator Harding, Republican nominee for the presidency, which letters are attributed to Professor William E. Chancellor, a part of which he admits to have been written by him;

And whereas such circular letters issued on the eve of the election are for the manifest purpose of appealing to prejudice and to influence the electorate of the country at the coming election;

Therefore be it resolved that we, the Board of Trustees of the College of Wooster, repudiate and denounce such political methods as utterly unworthy of our College and Country.

And be it further resolved by the Board that the College of Wooster indignantly disclaims all connections with, knowledge of, or authority for the making and issuing of any such circular letters.

Mr. Chancellor retired to his home on the northwest corner of Beall Avenue and Pearl Street. There remained for Mr. Wishart to break the news to the students at chapel the next morning, about the hardest thing, he said later, he ever had to do. In doing so he referred to Mr. Chancellor's part in the circular letter as "striking below the belt." Instantly there rose from her pew a young woman (a relative of Mr. Chancellor). "Yes, it was," she said, "and there are others who can strike below the belt." [6]

Yet the story had not yet reached its denouement. Harding was elected, but on that night when the returns were coming in, Chancellor was not listening to the returns in his living room but was in Kenarden. There had been ugly threats that he would be tarred and feathered. To protect him, students had spirited him away. Four students, well armed, were in his house determined to protect it.

Twice a disorganized mob from town came up on his lawn shouting maledictions. The young men sent word out that Chancellor was not there. One of the four was Howard Lowry, '23, and he was deputized by the others to go out and mingle with the crowd and shout with them yet to try at the same time to calm and disperse them. It was one of his early efforts at moral suasion. The students no more than the president and trustees sympathized with Mr. Chancellor's point of view or with the tangle he had got himself into, but they were going to protect him, his family, and his home from violence—and they did.

The Scripps newspapers had from the beginning refused to touch the story as had also the moguls of both parties. Mr. Doheny, however, a Democrat, sent to the Republicans a gift of $25,000 for the publication in newspapers of full-page portraits of Harding's father and mother in an effort to clear the record.

Mr. Chancellor moved to Columbus and busied himself with writing. The next year he published there a book entitled *Warren Gamaliel Harding, President of the United States. A Review of Facts Collected from Anthropological, Historical and Political Researches.* It was without copyright and was to be distributed only by agents. When word of it came to the ears of Harding's Attorney General in Washington, he sent his own agents out to gather in by whatever means all copies they could lay their hands on. They found many, some still at the printers. All these they burned with the exception of three which they took to Washington. Even the plates for the book were confiscated and destroyed.

For some years thereafter, Mr. Chancellor lived sometimes in Maine, sometimes in Canada. In 1927 well after Mr. Harding's death he returned to Ohio, to Cincinnati, to teach economics at Xavier University. After his retirement there, he lived at a home for the elderly in Kent, Ohio, and finally in his middle nineties, on February 12, 1963, he died in Wooster at a nursing home. So ended the story of a man who had written some twenty books, two of which had been republished in Braille, and one of which, *Class Teaching and Management* (Harper & Brothers), had been chosen by the Bureau of Education of the United States Government for use in the Philippines in normal schools and colleges of education; it had been adopted also in Japan for the teaching of pedagogy in English.

XVI

Quiet Again

THE years of 1910 to 1920 had measured considerable growth
in Wooster's academic life despite minor setbacks. The salary
scale, for instance, for faculty had risen forty per cent. The
number of faculty had been slowly augmented. A wider
variety of courses was being offered so that prospective graduate
students seeking to enter eastern or western universities could qualify.
In the classroom instructors were depending less on the textbook
approach, more on correlative reading in the library. The honor
courses had given impetus to this, as also had the debating activities
of the college, and indeed the clubs sponsored by the various departments. And of course the war itself had left in its wake an awareness
of national and international issues. In January of 1920 a poll was
taken in American colleges as to students' attitudes toward the
League of Nations. At Wooster the vote had been three to one in
favor of the League. Besides, it was to a rather serious-minded group
of students that Wooster was catering; more than one fourth of them
were earning at least a part of their way, forty-eight of them all of it.
Though Knappens and Dunbars—and Lowrys—were relatively
scarce, the average intellectual interest was fairly high.

The departure of Mr. Chancellor had left more than a little gap.
Whatever wrong leads he had followed, he had started his students
thinking of political, economic, and sociological problems, and to
enjoy that thinking. There was no one in that field at Wooster to step
at once into his shoes. At mid-term there was no one available from
the outside. Of all those around, Mr. West, who had come to Wooster to substitute for Mr. Lean, seemed the best qualified. He was
shifted to an instructorship in political science, though still coaching
the debating teams. Actually, since his undergraduate days, he had
taken some courses in political science and in sociology, the latter at
the University of Naples, where he had occasion to prepare various
reports and also to do considerable traveling in other European
countries. All this gave him at least some background. Mrs. West
had majored while in college in speech, and now took over temporarily the teaching of the course in interpretation of literature, and

along with others she advised student dramatic efforts. So a temporary arrangement was made.

Once more a relative quiet descended on the hill. There were classes to prepare for, reading to be done, meetings, lectures, games to attend, winning games when one shouted oneself hoarse, with bonfires afterwards, speeches and songs. Thanksgiving was not far away, then the end of the term with its rush and gaiety. Just before that on December 21 came the annual banquet for the football men. Mr. Knight, faculty manager for athletics, had planned this rather special occasion. Mr. Wood was toastmaster. "Prexy," Dean Compton, Boles, and Knight all spoke, and of course, at the end, the retiring captain of the team and the incoming captain. Merle and Bechtel Alcock were there to sing. After all, in four years Wooster had lost but one football game. And Allen Snyder, '21, generally recognized as the all-Ohio quarterback had been awarded a Templar sports car "for being the man most valuable to an Ohio Conference team." [1] The football men themselves were at last breaking their training table rules and having their fill of pig and pie and peppermints without so much as a quiver of conscience or indigestion. They were young and fit and proud, proud of their record, of Wooster, and of Coach Boles, who now by action of the trustees was to become professor of physical education with voting power in the faculty. Besides being a coach he had done much for Wooster. Once he had taught physics in the preparatory department; once history in college. For several years he had a Sunday morning Bible class but gave it up because so often on that day he felt it his first duty to go to see some recently injured member of one of his teams.

Not long after the holidays came Recognition Day at morning chapel for all those who had received honors and were eligible to membership in Alpha Delta Omega, the local honor society. This included also those who had won Fackler medals in debate the previous year and the winner of the Edward Taylor prize scholarship. The faculty for this occasion appeared in academic gowns. The list [2] of honors was read, then after a brief address by Mr. Dunn, the new members were welcomed. Observed for the first time in January, 1921, this became an annual custom. It was an occasion when all the college came to feel that scholastic honors had their high moments too.

New courses this semester were being offered in mineralogy, in labor problems and international trade, and in advanced physics. The faculty had been studying, too, how to fortify Wooster's academic standards. Under the new regulations, students who in any semester failed to make at least six quality points or failed to win enough credits or quality points to justify their promotion to the next class rank, went on probation. Probation meant that they could participate in no public activity; it meant also that if they slipped in attendance or in the quality of their work during this period, they were dropped from college. Freshmen of course were automatically on probation.

In March came the announcement of the resignation[3] of Elias Compton from the deanship. For all practical purposes he had been dean of the college, dean of men, and until 1911, dean of women as well. One thousand and one picayune details involving the college calendar, minor permissions, or student records came to him for determination or recording as well as major questions of policy and behavior. Some of these he could answer himself; for many others he was rather the clearing house recommending them to some faculty committee or to the faculty as a whole. Perforce he came to know every student and many of their parents. If a student fell violently ill, he must notify the parents and in the meantime see that the boy or girl had proper care; if a student's work fell below standard he must interview him and write the parents. If there had been a pajama parade that had gone too far, if some freshman had greased the flagpole, if a cow had been found on the porch at Hoover Cottage, or a young pig just inside the door at Holden Hall, if plans for a sneak dance had been discovered, or a scheme to put H_2S in the ducts of Kauke basement just before a banquet, if boys had been seen mounting the fire escapes of a women's dormitory, if the McKinley bell in the chapel tower rang unaccountably at three A.M., if the old Rock had been painted in stripes, he had to ferret out the culprits. He had to be detective, father confessor, judge, and one of the jury, day after day and month after month. And he had to be "the big ear" to listen to all the gripes of both students and faculty. In a period of twenty-two years he had served also off or on as chairman of innumerable committees including that of the curriculum. Besides he had carried almost a full load of teaching which at one time or another included psychology, logic, philosophy, education, and English composition

—he had once even given a daily theme course in which he delighted. Besides, in cases of emergency he had tried his hand at teaching mathematics, Latin and Greek, ethics, and English literature. Whether or not he enjoyed fully all that he was called upon to do is beside the point; he took it all in his stride and kept a poker face. It was his responsibility and the president's to keep the college running smoothly; it is hard to say who had the greater task. But now he was retiring to enjoy being a mere professor of philosophy; he could think about Pythagoras for hours together and maybe the telephone would not even ring.

Presently it was announced that John B. Kelso, professor of Greek, had been chosen by the faculty as the new dean and the appointment had been confirmed by the trustees. A second announcement followed soon. A dean of men had been named, J. Milton Vance. Both would take office in the fall of 1921. Mr. Kelso was ideal as dean, level-headed, experienced, sophisticated, familiar with academic policies and ideas, a natural leader. He was strong and the soul of courtesy; he would hold the line. A reader, a thinker, a gentleman, an excellent conversationalist, he would be a credit to Wooster wherever he went. Mr. Vance was also a happy choice. He could make distinctions; his mind was keen. He could laugh. He would consider all angles and be fair. Though he and Mrs. Vance had had no children, their life for two years in the Middle East war zone had deepened their understanding of human nature. Mrs. Vance, director of the Girls' Glee Club, was a great strength to him. The college would be starting in the fall with a new administration. One could look ahead with confidence.

Much else was just now in the wind. Wooster badly needed more dormitory space for women. Mr. Wishart was proposing to his trustees the immediate erection of an annex to Holden Hall to take the overflow. To be sure, there was no money for such an undertaking; it would have to be an act of faith, a faith that had permeated so much of Wooster's history. It could be a temporary building to last only until money for a permanent dormitory could be found, and it could be amortized in the meantime by room rent. If it were only two stories high and of frame construction it need not be expensive. The girls could be boarded at Holden Hall. The trustees agreed. By fall it was completed and fifty-three sophomore girls with one junior resident were housed there.

As spring came on and in early April the grass turned green there came a desire to freshen up everything. The boys in Kenarden had no general lounge in which to gather. President Wishart, the student government president at the Lodge, and representatives from each section put their heads together and made plans. The second still unused dining room in the basement could be turned into a lounge. The walls were to be painted, cretonnes put at the windows, a piano could be found somewhere and moved in, two divans in leather and several deep leather chairs were to be bought, a table, too, and a lamp for the piano. Again there was no money, but the residents said they would raise some. The result was a "high class vaudeville show" in the chapel one Friday night, with a magician from Ft. Wayne brought in, and admittance charged. Everyone cooperated. The girls put on the cat act from one of the glee club concerts. The faculty helped, supplying as a feature a double quartet. Wishart, too, performed with "vocal trombone slides," Martin added comedy "with winks and twists and little flourishes," and Mr. West impersonated Noah in his "little cruise in the Ark." It was an uproarious evening.

There were other respects in which faculty and students were working together. Among them they had managed—with the help of $700 from the college exchequer—to raise enough money for the support of a college missionary, $2250. They had chosen Ned Adams, '18, finishing his final year in McCormick Theological Seminary; and he had come and led chapel one winter day. In college he had been a football hero, one of Wooster's notable tackles.[4]

In the meantime in his spare moments Mr. Notestein had been quietly studying the catalogues of various English second-hand book dealers, seeking out at the lowest price possible source books in English history urgently needed by the library.[5] He had interested E. P. Douglass of the class of 1877 in giving $1000 toward starting such an alcove, and had eagerly sought the advice of specialists in the field as to what was most needed. Several hundred of these books had already come by the spring of the year, and others were on the way. New instructors were quick to know and evaluate Wooster's library in their fields. If Wooster's students were to have adequate preparation in this new day, if it was to keep instructors who knew their fields and could teach, it must work at building its library. When Mr. Notestein had gone with a plea for such an alcove, Mr. Douglass had been glad to contribute to it. When the latter had first been a student at Wooster, a poor boy who needed books and couldn't afford them, Mr. Notestein had found a way for him to have them. Now in a sense Mr. Douglass would be paying back with interest a debt. The two were long-time friends.

In early May of 1921 when spring was at its most glorious, Wooster, as has been noted, had one of its proudest days, that on which Earl Dunbar, '21, came home from Mitchell, South Dakota, as winner of the interstate oratorical contest. The whole college and part of the town were already at the Pennsylvania Station when the train came in. "Dunny" was led to the firechief's bright red car; then with the Board of Trade band and the Elks Drum Corps heading the procession he was paraded to the public square, on up Market Street to Bowman, across to Beall, up to University and to the chapel for the official celebration.[6] There were various speeches and at the last Dunbar himself spoke of the help of many persons, from Mr. Wishart and Mr. West, both of whom had coached him, to those who had sent him telegrams at Mitchell to boost his morale.

Not many weeks thereafter the largest class thus far to be graduated from Wooster, 104 of them—59 men, 45 women—were handed their diplomas and were gone. Kelso, too, was off to Europe with his eighteenth party for the summer. And Simpson settled in to teach and be dean of the summer school.

In 1919 at the instigation of Mr. Kelso and some of the faculty the summer school had been exhumed. The objectionable features had fallen away; only a skeleton was left. It was now strictly a collegiate "summer session." There were no frills, only a scattering of students, and just solid work for eight weeks in a limited number of courses. The trustees had reaffirmed the faculty position voting that this summer session be developed to the "highest pitch of efficiency" on the basis of "the academic standards of the college year." An overall dean was placed in charge. The remuneration for the five faculty teaching in it that first season depended on the number of students registered for the course each was giving. Hoover and Kenarden were kept open for the students.

Though Mr. Simpson stayed only four years at Wooster, he did much in organizing and developing the new department of economics. By the spring of 1922 twenty-five to thirty students were majoring in economics; the department had already more than 125 students, of whom eighty-five were in the beginning course, and the others in electives in business organization, business statistics, and in what he called industrial disarmament, such as the "Open Door" in China and the Kansas Industrial Court. He held the belief that "the wastes and losses of industrial conflict between nations, sections, and classes are perhaps fully as great as the wastes of war itself," and he felt that with the memory of the war still fresh, a proper approach could well be made to this subject. The next year he would give other courses in banking, foreign trade, and labor problems.

Another department that had been forging ahead rapidly was that of chemistry. Mr. Bennett, Mr. Grady as assistant professor, one instructor, and six student laboratory assistants constituted the teaching force for 237 students. Sixteen students were in the advanced course in physical chemistry offered this year of 1921–1922 for the first time. Ten courses in all were being given, including pre-medical organic chemistry. When it was requested by qualified students, a course was available also in inorganic preparations. Physics, too, was winning an unexpected number of students, twice those of last year. Mr. Westhafer had a gift of illustration that illuminated all his teaching.

The college, however, was growing now almost too fast. In the fall of 1921, 712 students were registered with a freshman class of 315. In October of that year Mr. Dunn writing editorially in *The Wooster Quarterly,* remarked that he felt Wooster would do well to limit its attendance to 800. "Our country needs," he said, "at the present more colleges content to remain small . . . eager to increase the quality of the human product that goes forth from their halls." And then he added as almost a postscript, "Already in the annex to Holden Hall the College has been compelled to depart from our uniform and beautiful plan of architecture." There were many who agreed with him. Yet the quality of the students still seemed good. Among the seniors there were thirteen majors in mathematics, certainly not a snap subject, as against thirty-two in English, always popular. Twenty-eight students this year had gone out for honor courses, including four each in the Departments of History, Chemistry, and Latin, three each in Economics, Greek, and English.

The year of 1921–1922 started without the new dean, Mr. Kelso, who had become ill in Europe. His arrival two weeks late was not so unfortunate as it might have been, for the new instructors this year were nearly all familiar with Wooster and Wooster's ways, either as former students or former faculty. Mr. Lean was back from his sabbatical, and Mr. West had been continued for another year in the Department of Political Science. Mr. Olthouse was on leave, studying at the University of Paris.

Then there was Walter Edwin Peck, who came back as assistant professor of English, fresh from his studies with Sir Walter Raleigh at Oxford University. In June of 1922 he would go back there long enough to take his final examinations and to receive from Oxford its rarely awarded Ph.D. He was brilliant, sure of himself, somewhat condescending, but nevertheless a teacher who awakened the mind of the student and set it to speculating and probing.

Warren Poppino Spencer, '19, was back too, as an instructor in biology. For two years he had been teaching biology in Assiut College, Egypt, a United Presbyterian institution fifty miles or so up the Nile from Cairo. There his already imaginative and inquiring mind must have been further inflamed by all that he saw, in this land old as the Old Testament, new as the polo fields on the Island of Gezira, in this land of stupendous ruins, mosques of surpassing beauty, of beggars diseased and forlorn crouching in the corners of the streets, of round cakes of hard-baked bread gathering flies on dirty doorsteps. What was the meaning of life? What its long history? He came back to teach, to study, and to go on to become in time one of the recognized geneticists of the country.

Kathleen Lowrie, *ex* '17, also came back as the new director of physical education for women. She had found out early what she wanted, and had been graduated from the Normal School of Gymnastics at New Haven, Connecticut.[7] She had directed physical education at the Y.W.C.A.'s of Indianapolis and Norfolk, Virginia. She was a natural leader, knowing what she wished and needed, and always willing to fight for it. (She was indeed a good bridge player.) not only the discipline but the delights of various forms of physical Under her, Wooster women perhaps experienced for the first time

education. Color Days, too, took on new meaning with her understanding of interpretative dancing, her willingness to follow through
to the last detail, and her regard for beauty in presentation.

While all these young instructors were getting their bearings, Mr.
Dunn [8] was deep in the finishing and seeing through the press of his
life of Donald Grant Mitchell ("Ik Marvel"). As a young enthusi-
ast at Yale he had one day written some verses commemorating
Mitchell's eightieth birthday. These had so pleased Mr. Mitchell that
he sent for the young hero worshipper, and the two became close
friends. In the summer of 1919 consequently he had been asked to
write Mitchell's biography and was invited to New Haven not only
to go through all the available source material but to stay in the
home just outside New Haven with the family and so to get the feel
of the background, a feeling so necessary for the writing of the life of
anyone anywhere. Since that time, aside from his teaching, to which
he gave the best that was in him, this work absorbed every daylight
hour and much of many nights.

It was in this year, too, that James and Florence Jenney Hall said
goodbye to Wooster. They had taken a leave of absence to go back to
Oberlin that they might study with Professor Edward Dickinson
before his expected retirement. Once there, however, Oberlin claimed
them and they never returned save for visits with their friends at
Wooster.

After four years as dean of women, it was in 1922 that Miss Field
resigned. She had been respected and trusted by students and faculty
alike. She was essentially a scholar immersed in detail. She had never
aroused antagonism, nor had she ever stimulated the enthusiasm
usually accorded a warm human being.

In October word came of Mrs. A. A. E. Taylor's death in Columbus. She had been at the Wooster meeting there only the week
before. Since 1895 she had been a member of the Women's Advisory
Board, the representative from Columbus. So another link with the
past was broken, a memory of Wooster's golden age, and to those
who knew her, a life, it seemed, "without a tarnish."

And then as of July first, 1922, Jesse McClellan, college treasurer
since 1885, resigned, and James McLaughlin reigned in his stead.
John McClellan, first treasurer of the college, and trustee as well
until 1892, had served for nineteen years, maintaining his office in

the McClellan bookstore on the public square. There indeed it remained until the building of Kauke Hall. To this bookstore, after
four years in the Civil War and a period of business training, Jesse,
his son, came back to help his father. In 1883 he became assistant
treasurer of the college, and two years later as treasurer took on the
full responsibility for handling the college funds. Thus the span of
their relationship to the college covered fifty-six years. In 1892 when
the father relinquished also his trusteeship, the son took over in that
capacity, as well, until 1917. For something over ten years he was
secretary to the Board, inscribing the *Minutes* in a longhand so fine
that they showed almost the delicacy of a "steel engraving." For a
period, too, he did the hand-lettering on college diplomas.

For years Jesse McClellan did much of the investing of college
funds, and he had the pleasure of seeing the assets grow from a few
hundred thousands to several millions. At the urging of Mr. Severance in the 1900's he changed the method of accounting from the
single to the double entry system. With the tenacity of the bulldog he
held on to every dollar and dreaded parting with it. And, whether by
intention or because of inattention, he was often gruff in his manner.
An instructor or even a professor appearing to claim his monthly
check could sense a kind of suppressed growl from behind the
counter as it was handed to him. It was a habit of his life. He had
another minor habit. On the window ledge just inside the door at
Kauke Hall, when McClellan was in his office, there could nearly
always be seen a partly burned cigar. This he retrieved as he went
out. He knew the college rules and he obeyed them—but he suffered.

The spring of 1922 seemed interminable. All attention was fo-
cussed of course on the financial campaign. Nothing else much
seemed to matter. In April a full-time nurse, Miss Dorothy Angell,
had been installed in that small section of Hoover Cottage set aside
as an infirmary for the girls. She was a graduate of Wesleyan Hospital, Chicago, where she had also been head of nursing in the surgical
ward. Though Wooster had been behind hand in making adequate
provision for sickness among the students, it now had taken a first
step, and would not be caught completely off-guard in an emergency.

In May the alumni organization brought the first of its own
vocational representatives, Miss Grace Smith, '08, owner and manager of Toledo's finest cafeteria, to address the students on the

opportunities and responsibilities of restaurant work.[9] In late May, too, Wooster was congratulating itself in having produced the winner for the second consecutive year in the Civic League Oratorical Contest. The decision was unanimous for Howard Lowry, '23. The other contestants were from Ohio Wesleyan, University of Pittsburgh, Allegheny, Colgate, and Washington and Jefferson.

Earlier in the spring Wooster's speech department had been notified that its petition for a chapter of Delta Sigma Rho, honorary forensics fraternity, had been granted unanimously. Wooster had been waiting six years for this; now it would have the 58th chapter in the national organization. It was the only one of the national honorary fraternities eligibility to which was granted on the basis of service to one's college.[10] Mr. Stanley B. Houck of Minneapolis, national president of the society, came for the installation on June tenth. After the official ceremony Howard Lowry, '23, was named as first president of the new chapter, and Craig McClelland, '23, as secretary-treasurer. Then by vote President Wishart, who was present as a guest of honor, was "recommended to the national executive committee as a member at large."

At the commencement [11] which followed soon after, 123 diplomas were issued. Wooster's alumni now numbered almost 2500. The annual tuition had reached $100 a year and the incidentals $50. This year the annual Willard-Castalian-Pembroke Public was held at 3:30 Monday afternoon under the trees near Hoover Cottage. The Congressional Club had a breakfast for their alumni on Tuesday at Kenarden. The four small literary socieites, Quadrangle, Stratford, Ruskin, and Franklin, had also a breakfast on Thursday morning at 7:30. Yet the real occasion this year was the address of Frank Aydelotte, the commencement speaker. His theme was "the importance of conversation among equals. . . ." "The educational value of conversation," he said, "is not in the acquirement of information but rather in the development of the ability to use one's ideas in action. . . . In free, equal open conversation a man must fight for his own hand. He comes in contact with the real universe where things are done, agreements made, beliefs changed, and the work of the world goes on. . . . If in college you have learned the art and zest of talk, you have one important qualification for success in the great university of the world in which you matriculate today."

XVII

Sophistication and Apathy

> . . . For what a college means to one is not just the events
> that mark its progress, those things which in time will compose
> its formal record—but rather its small concerns of every day,
> including perhaps its chronicles of wasted time.[1]
>
> HOWARD F. LOWRY

THE tumult and the shouting after the war had long since died, but the arguing and discussing went on and on, on campus, in town, in churches, in business offices, and in legislative bodies. The college generation that had served in World War I had its sights set; they had purpose and determination; and the spirit of adventure in them still lived. But after that followed a period of near-frustration. Nothing real had been settled. No one was sure where the world was tending. Nothing much mattered. The old idealism had been smothered; the new idealism spelled pacifism. There was a growing sophistication of a sort and a growing apathy. One cannot read the college publications in these twenty-five years of Mr. Wishart's administration without becoming aware of this changing mood in student life.

For a while in the early twenties college activities were nearly normal. College sings still took place of a Friday evening on the library steps. A new collection of Wooster songs was being contemplated, and prizes ranging from $25 down to $1 were being offered. Even the faculty were at liberty to compete.[2] The college band organized a few years back by Allen Snyder was in need of some new and gay and vibrant songs that suggested victory, not just something tuneful and nostalgic. The band was hoping before long to have new uniforms, too.[3] The Student Senate and the Athletic Association had each contributed $100 toward these; there had been some individual contributions, and the band itself had given a benefit performance at the Wallace theater to help the cause along. Bobbed hair had come in, evidence of growing independence among young women.[4] So had crossword puzzles, evidence of nothing much except of the public's inability to spell. Down on the corner of Bowman Street and College, the new First Presbyterian Church was under construction, and up on the hill a youth with his recently acquired "Tin Lizzie" was chugging along displaying the slogan: "Coach Boles for President." There was some reason for this, for from 1919 through 1923 [5] Wooster had enjoyed three undefeated football seasons and had lost only three games. Then in 1924 they tied Ohio State University 7–7.[6] Intramurals were booming: basketball, handball, volley ball, boxing, wrestling, swimming, tennis, and even horseshoe pitching. And the college girls were scheduling tennis tournaments, swimming, playing hockey, tennis, and basketball.

The ancient rivalry between sophomores and freshmen still went on. Once years ago this had taken the form of knock-down, drag-out fights; to these the faculty had promptly put an end. There had ensued the surreptitious fights after dark in the swale south of Hoover. Now these had become tame pole rushes or tugs of war supervised by Boles on the old athletic field. The sophomores still made freshmen wear beanies. The penalty for any minor malfeasance on the part of a freshman was to make him climb on the Rock and there sing any Wooster songs demanded. By the 1940's various forms of torture for freshmen had been invented. Once, for instance, they were sent over to scrub the long wide porch of Hoover Cottage with toothbrushes. The sophomore women devised their own ways of lording it over their underlings. One year they required the freshmen to slouch along to classes in stocking feet and rubbers, each one carrying a bag of peanuts with which to feed any hungry upperclassmen she met. When everything was in the doldrums, and the usual activities paled, nothing helped the boys more than a good pajama parade. One November night in 1922, for instance—it couldn't have been that year when the leaves froze on the trees and dropped—they thought the moment had come. Anyhow the Elks were holding a carnival downtown. Led by the band, still without their uniforms, the boys of Kenarden took off. Circling Hoover, they proceeded past Holden and on to town where they paraded through the Lyric and the Wallace theaters, then crashed the Elks carnival, before taking themselves back up the hill. One other time a group of students making merry in town came into conflict with the police and had to spend the night and until noon in jail. Yet in after years that experience had become no doubt just high adventure.

Social life in the early twenties was at a low ebb. To be sure, there had never been a lack of occasions for single dating, walks,[7] lectures, concerts, games. Occasionally a considerable group organized a trip, to see *The Student Prince* in Akron, for instance, or *Blossom Time.* The Shack, too, was busy from morning to night, and the students there were not always discussing philosophy or religion or the world scene. It was particularly busy at the chapel hour in the morning until the faculty allowed only twelve chapel cuts a semester. Without any kind of social center the students did not know quite what to do with themselves, except for the all-college occasions, such as the annual Gum Shoe Hop. The old class socials and interclass banquets had lost their attraction, and there was little to take their place except the open houses in the women's dormitories and the parties put on by the sections of Kenarden and after 1928 by Douglass also. Sometimes, in the open season of the year, there were picnics, too, at the devil's slide in Highland Park. The faculty were aware of all this and were studying the situation. Before the students all went home for Christmas in 1922 they consequently put on an all-college party for them in the gymnasium. Dean Root was full of ideas for broadening the outlook of the young women, vocational conferences, for instance; she even encouraged them to wear evening dress on guest nights in their dormitories; and on Monday night was talking to them on etiquette. The women were occasionally holding dances by themselves in the gymnasium.

Square dances had this long time been accepted at Wooster as harmless, but other mixed social dances were taboo. By 1925 murmurs among the students were becoming widespread. The students wanted two nights a week for recreation. They asked that the meetings of the literary societies be moved from Friday night, a time that for years had been almost sacredly reserved for them, to Thursday night. This was granted. The next petition, in 1925, was for social dancing. They had taken a poll among themselves. Four hundred and sixteen of them favored restricted dancing, meaning, one supposes, dancing in a suitable place and with suitable chaperonage. Only fifty one voted for unrestricted dancing, and two hundred and fifty others were opposed to dancing of any kind. For a while the students got nowhere with their request, but eventually strictly supervised dancing was allowed if in an acceptable place off campus, as in a private home. St. James parish house of the local Episcopal Church, too, opened its doors; and from then on until 1932 there were at least two student dances there a week, occasionally four. In 1932 a committee of two students waited on the deans for permission for an all-college dance on campus. It was then that the bars came down and stayed down. Then the Gum Shoe Hop became a real hop rather than a succession of vaudeville skits, or a home-made musical comedy. Thereafter Homecoming, Dad's Day, Color Day weekends all had their dances. By the middle thirties junior and senior proms had become a part of Wooster's student life. In 1939 there was a sophomore prom, and an all-college spring formal featuring Don Ricardo and his orchestra. The college had come full circle. Coeducation was on the move.

About the same time that dancing was beginning to be considered, murmurings began favoring coeducational dining. These, however, had little effect for many years. In 1937 the deans yielded to having the men and women together for Sunday evening suppers. Again in 1942 during the Navy Flight Training program and the accelerated trimester program, coed dining was for a brief while "a distinguishing feature." Yet again it disappeared and did not become an accepted custom until in Mr. Lowry's administration.

By 1930 social clubs among the women were appearing, which took the place, though locals, of the sororities of the old days. The Imps, the Peanuts, and the others had their own pledge days; these soon came under strict regulations. A few years later the faculty sanctioned social clubs for men [8] in Kenarden. Each had its constitution, and a continuing organization which chose its own members every year at the end of the first semester. In time an eighth section at Livingstone Lodge was added and a ninth in the old Chalmers Martin home on Beall Avenue. The section heads, each with its faculty adviser, constituted the Kenarden Council to which suggestions for the good of the whole dormitory could be brought for discussion and decision. At the same time a head resident with his wife was installed in the building for general oversight. These social clubs thenceforth flourished, and before long their annual initiations gave rise to what has since become known as "Hell Week." At first these took the form of "innocent merriment." In one of the first instances the pledges of one section were sent out to patrol all night long each of the dormitories, and at half hour intervals assured the inmates with cowbell and megaphone that "the Night Watch was on the job and the residents might sleep with perfect safety and peace." Sometimes, however, initiations were considerably rougher.

Many other changes in student life were evident during these years. One after another the literary societies, big and little, folded up. In 1920 Athenaean had celebrated its fiftieth anniversary with a dinner to which various members of the faculty had been invited. Mr. Wishart, remembering his days at Monmouth, felt that the work of the literary societies was one of the most valuable aspects of student life. Mr. Notestein reminisced about the beginnings of Athenaean and Irving. Mr. Compton, and Mr. Dunn also spoke, and several students. By the fall of 1925 Athenaean and Castalian halls were already being used as classrooms; in 1928 Irving hall was also taken over. The old literary societies really had no place to go that they could call their own. Athenaean merged with Irving; then both died. In 1930 Castalian disbanded. Willard soon followed. Pembroke and Emerson were left. Even the little literaries were fading out; only Stratford and Franklin continued, and they before long abandoned any pretense at studying Shakespeare or the American literati, in favor of dancing, roller skating, and bridge. Pembroke, too, underwent various changes before it left the scene entirely some time during Mr. Lowry's administration. In its final phase it became a club of upperclassmen for creative writing. Applicants for membership had to submit a short-story, a poem, an essay of some kind.

College journalism, too, was languishing. The college annual suffered least. Everyone wanted *The Index;* it was a memory book, a part of one's college record. But *The Wooster Literary Messenger* after two tries had finally given up the ghost; it had never been adequately supported. Sporadic humorous sheets featuring the foibles of college life had appeared from time to time, yet they had not caught on. By 1925–1926 it looked as if *The Voice* were succumbing to the current apathy. It had no sparkle, very little college news. The pages were filled with what one might call intercollegiate "boiler plate," jokes, occasional editorials or news items clipped from the journals of sister institutions, but very little reporting of the local scene except on great college occasions. It was, however, definitely interested in the position of the United States in international affairs.

At the end of its editorial on the Locarno Conference its editor wrote: "Has the sun begun to set for the United States because of the narrow selfishness of a few politicians?" For a while it carried a column week by week written by one of the history faculty on topics of international discussion, "The Fascists," "The Soviet Mind," or "The United States of Europe." *The Voice* was advocating also the sending of a delegate from the college to the Collegiate Conference on the World Court at Princeton in December of 1925. This movement was backed by The Congressional Club, which with the Christian Associations, the student government, and *The Voice* took a poll in November of student opinion on the World Court preparatory to sending such a delegate. Ironic as it may seem, it was probably true that the English and speech departments had become so influential as to lessen the need for some of these student organizations.

Wooster had still and would continue to have its college orators, who were winning firsts in either Civic League or state intercollegiate oratorical contests, and sometimes also in the regional meets. The winners were not without honor, but nothing short of the interstate intercollegiate contest excited mass enthusiasm. So it was also in debate.[9] Wooster was winning its fair share of these triangular matches, held sometimes with Reserve and Ohio Wesleyan, sometimes with Allegheny and Washington & Jefferson, occasionally with Oberlin and Denison; yet these no longer drew great crowds to the chapel. In the meantime the college girls had taken up debating and were vying with a similar team at Oberlin.

Despite what may appear as student apathy, there was no lack of intellectual interest among many of the students. This manifested itself in their professional clubs, in the national honor societies that were installed during these years, in the prizes being won, even in some of the Color Day pageants. In 1924–1925 forty-two upperclassmen were working for special honors, including nine each in Latin and history, five in mathematics, four each in Greek and French. The following year there were thirty-six with history leading with six, and five each in chemistry, English, French, and Latin. In the spring of 1930 two freshmen, one girl, one boy, won prizes of $500 each from the American Chemical Society in an essay contest.[10] In the spring of 1941, Betty Dodds, '41, won the second prize in *Vogue*'s Prix de Paris contest. This entitled her to six months of experience at a desk at the *Vogue* offices. Of the professionally inclined clubs, the ancestor of them all was the Congressional Club, one of the few that had survived the war. It had not been designed really to turn students into politicians or lawyers, yet there they were awakened undoubtedly to the possibilities of these professions as well as to thoughtfulness on legislative matters. The clubs in chemistry, physics, education, philosophy all tended in the direction of professionalism. Though these were especially attractive to the students looking forward to graduate study, their appeal was not always limited to such persons. The Philosophy Club, for instance, brought in as a speaker Joseph A. Leighton, head of the department at Ohio State University, to lecture on "The Influence of Philosophy in Civilization." "What we need," he said to a large group of students and faculty, "is a great awakening of the significance of quality rather than quantity, and a recognition of the value of the individual personality. It is necessary that we consider ultimate reality, and that we become active creative souls. Our present civilization has creative leadership . . . but no creative fellowship." The Philosophy Club was doing its part in trying here at Wooster to promote such creative fellowship. Begun long ago under the leadership of Mr. Compton, it was again active under Mr. Evans and Mr. Ferm. With the coming of a new assistant professor of biology in 1923, Ralph Bangham, a pre-medical club was set up for both men and women looking forward to entering schools of medicine, dentistry, or nursing. They brought in as speakers prominent physicians from the cities round-about as well as some of the local doctors. The O. A. Hills Club (later the Clericus Club) for those planning for the ministry or some other form of Christian service had been functioning for some years.

At this time the departmental clubs, if they had died down during the war, were once more revived. One by one they received national recognition. Delta Sigma Rho [11] in 1922 had been the first of these to win a national charter. There followed in 1924 that in chemistry, Theta Delta Chi, and in Spanish, Sigma Delta Pi; in January 1926, the same year in which Wooster's Kappa chapter of Phi Beta Kappa was installed, the national honor society in Romance languages, Phi Sigma Iota; in May of 1928 that in dramatics Kappa Theta Gamma, Kappa Phi Kappa in Education installed December 1930, in classics Eta Sigma Phi, in 1934, that in music, Pi Kappa Lambda, in 1941, later that in political science, Pi Sigma Alpha.

With their installation all these societies became increasingly active. In April of 1931 the Spanish fraternity celebrated Cervantes' Day with a gala dinner and speeches about the life and work of *Don Quixote*'s originator. A dramatic club had existed back as far as the days of President Holden, but it had come of age only in these later days. Now everybody was getting into the act. The seniors had put on plays at graduation time. Now the Student Senate regularly put on a play at Homecoming. The faculty had decided to give the students a run for their money by staging a play every year in the Opera House on the night before Thanksgiving. The first year under Frederick Moore's direction [12] they staged *Mr. Pim Passes By* with Mr. Lean playing the title role. The next year their choice was *East Lynne*, which put the audience into gales of laughter. Le Cercle Français, now dignified by its Greek name, presented Moliere's *Le Bourgeois Gentilhomme.* Eta Sigma Phi, when it was still the Classical Club, met one night to hear Mr. Cowles' own translation of Plautus' *Rudens.* In 1931 for the benefit of freshmen in Greek and Latin they presented Horace's *Bore* and Theocritus' *Festival of Adonis* and twice in the quadrangle under Mr. Cowles' direction one of Plautus' plays, once his *Menaechmi,* and the next year his *Mostellaria.* Mr. Lean's classes, too, on Dad's Day or the night of Color Day were giving such New York favorites as *Outward Bound* and *Journey's End,* for which they designed and constructed the sets. It was Kappa Theta Gamma that in 1930 first inaugurated the use of Taylor auditorium for theatrical purposes by transforming the old platform there into a little theater and presenting *The Mollusc,* and later Masefield's *Tragedy of Nan,* and once in Memorial Chapel *Everyman,* a morality play. Yet perhaps the climax came for everyone when, with a chorus of seventy students and an orchestra conducted by Mr. Parmelee, the glee clubs presented *The Mikado* at the Opera House with "Prexy" in the title role.

> In a fatherly kind of way
> I govern each tribe and sect,
> All cheerfully own my sway—
> . . . . .
>
> My object all sublime
> I shall achieve in time—

To let the punishment fit the crime—
   the punishment fit the crime—
And make each prisoner pent
Unwillingly represent
A source of innocent merriment!

Miss Eve Richmond and William DeVeny, both of the music department, were the directors. It was "a smash hit." Yet there were other uses made of dramatics. One year as a part of the Week of Prayer, Frederick Moore directed a miracle play, the *Shepherds.*

The pageants of Color Day, directed by Miss Lowrie, but written and put on by the students had become more and more elaborate occasions. Some of them had been based on fairy tales or variations of an Old English May Day, yet not always. Once the script writers had used *The Canterbury Tales* as a background; once Milton's "L'Allegro"; once in celebration of the 200th anniversary of Virgil's birth they represented his return to earth as poet and priest; once they went for their inspiration to Strauss's tone poems centering around the 16th century story of Tyll Eulenspiegel and his pranks, and once the occasion, dedicated to Miss Gingrich, was in commemoration of the 100th anniversary of Goethe's death, a pageant representing Goethe's theory of the art of poetry. That was probably the greatest Color Day [13] of them all, for Lou Henry Hoover (Mrs. Herbert Hoover) came, and at the end of the pageant in the stadium accepted from the college an honorary L.H.D. in token of her distinguished work in sharing with her husband in the translation of *De Re Metallica,* and also in recognition of "the administrative ability" shown by her "in the Boxer uprising in China." That day the Queen of the May, Elma Sage, had the honor at the end of the ceremony of handing her own armful of roses to the mistress of the White House.

Mrs. Hoover had come by special invitation, yet gladly, for she had roots in Wooster. Her grandfather, William Henry, had been one of the three founders of the town. For him Henry Street had been named. Her father, Charles Henry, had been born in Wooster; her mother, Florence Weed Henry,[14] had come from the village of Jackson, first called Old Hickory, in Wayne County, nine miles to the north. May Day of 1932 is memorable in the annals of the town as well as of the college. Mrs. Hoover visited the graves of her family in the cemetery, put a wreath on the Old Soldiers' monument on the public square, had lunch with the faculty, tea with women of the Federated Clubs, attended a pageant of the history of Wooster on the fair grounds, mailed a letter there to her husband, the first air letter to go from Wooster—by blimp—and finally, still smiling, entrained that evening on her special car.

There had been another great day in Wooster's history two years and a half before when Genevieve Rowe, '30, senior in both arts and music, had won the Atwater Kent award as the top amateur singer among the women in the country. There had been five regional contests, in the East, Midwest, the South, Southwest, and far West, and then the final contest when all ten regional winners, five men and five women, appeared on the Atwater Kent hour one Sunday night at 9:15. Genevieve sang first, the Shadow Song from Meyerbeer's *Dinorah*. At home on the hill nearly every radio was on, awaiting the end of the hour and the judges' verdict.[15] When it came, Genevieve Rowe had won first place, which meant a $5000 award and a two-year scholarship for study in New York. Then the doors of the dormitories "burst open," and the celebration was on. A bonfire was lit in front of Kenarden. The boys from both Douglass and Kenarden walking four abreast, started for the public square, where with the permission of the police, they serenaded the town. On the hill again, there was more singing, more shouting of "Rowe, Rowe, Genevieve Rowe," a snake dance, and a final all-college singing of "To Wooster U." Act II was to follow on Thursday morning when Genevieve alighted from the train at Wooster's Pennsylvania station. The Girls' Glee Club, of which she was a member, was there on top of the big red fire truck. John McSweeney, '12, who was always helping to give a boost to Wooster whenever there was opportunity, was on hand to marshal the parade, which wound up, of course, at the chapel. Many short speeches followed, by the mayor, the superintendent of schools, a member of the Wooster Orchestral Society, a student, by Miss Richmond, who had been Miss Rowe's vocal instructor, Mr. and Mrs. Rowe, a representative from the conservatories of Ohio, and finally by the slim, black-haired Genevieve herself, holding aloft her check and her certificate of scholarship. A week or two later WTAM (NBC's station in Cleveland) gave her a radio party and a jeweled wrist watch.

The glee clubs in the twenties began to feel the competition of the radio and talkies. In 1926, however, the Boys' Glee Club had the opportunity to sing in the Public Auditorium in Cleveland before 6000 persons.[16] The oratorio chorus, active and appreciated for many years, in 1931 ceased to exist. The college choir, robed since 1925, which had grown in size and in proficiency in a way took the place of the other chorus, presenting, for instance, *Messiah*, Brahms' *Requiem*, or Gounod's *Messe Solonnelle*. The Wooster Orchestral Society,[17] once again under the direction of Daniel Parmelee since his return to Wooster in 1924, had been growing in numbers (sixty-nine in the spring of 1931), in experience, and competence. In June of 1935 they played over WTAM in Cleveland, the first college orchestra ever to be so scheduled. The next year they were invited back. (Mr. Herman Freedlander, always a generous and loyal townsman, had their instruments trucked to Cleveland for them.) As Mr. Parmelee through the years had been leading his orchestra through increasingly difficult and sophisticated selections, he had been training also the taste of Wooster's audiences, both town and gown. Besides, Mr. and Mrs. Parmelee as a team (she was a pianist, he a violinist) had been going out of their way to give recitals in neighboring towns as a way of encouraging a taste for good music in the public.[18]

The class of 1930 had given impetus to all of this by establishing as a memorial a concert fund to bring a musician or musicians of note to the college in recital. The Cleveland String Orchestra was one of these attractions, Joseph Lhevinne another. Later in the thirties a Cooperative Musical Association (college and town) was organized to bring other musical attractions, such as Gregor Piatigorsky, or Mozart's Boys' Choir of Vienna.

Though music had had its place as an accredited college department since 1929, in 1934 additional courses were added leading also to a degree of bachelor of school music. No one, however, received such a degree until 1936.

The Student Senate and the student self government associations were to assume from their first appearance to the end of Mr. Wishart's administration a variety of functions. Just how these kindred organizations meshed is at times a little hard to determine. The Student Senate not too long after its organization took over the management of Color Day, then of the Gum Shoe Hop, the purpose of which was not only college entertainment but the raising of money to defray the expenses of Color Day. Since then it had taken over the student part of Homecoming and Dad's Day. It had drawn up and put into practice an honor code, and in 1925 joined with the men's and women's self government associations inaugurating a student vigilance committee of fifty members to discover any cheating which might be on the campus and to report this to the Honor Court. The Senate also supervised the sophomore court that determined punishment for freshmen offenders, and had power to veto the court's decisions. It had given money for landscaping some of the banks of the stadium, had helped with the student financing of Highland Park, and it had once turned over approximately $600 toward the modernizing of the lighting in Severance Hall. In 1933 it was occupying the dean's former office in Kauke Hall (the administrative offices of the college had moved to Galpin Hall). And in 1937 it was enlarged to sixteen members. On the other hand the primary purpose of student government associations seemed to be disciplinary. In 1923 the men's student government was determining true bills, and with the assistance of the presidents of the Student Senate, the Y.M.C.A. and the senior class, of the editor of *The Voice,* of the *W* Association, and of two members at large, was meting out fines, expelling boys from Kenarden on occasion, recommending to the faculty, on sufficient cause, the dismissal of a student from college. Yet the self government associations were also in charge of the separate chapel service for freshman men in Kauke on Wednesday mornings and of that for freshman women in Taylor auditorium on Mondays.[19] And in 1941 they chose the speaker, in this instance Bernard Iddings Bell, and arranged the program for the Week of Prayer.

There was undoubtedly need for a closer relationship between students and faculty. In 1925 consequently a faculty-student council was set up "to enable student opinion to be presented to the faculty in concrete form, and to provide a means of common discussion of campus problems." The students were busy sizing everything up. They complained in *The Voice* that there were not more courses in the appreciation of art. One of them wrote advocating independent study (Mr. Lowry was at this time an assistant professor of English at Wooster) and comprehensive examinations in one's major subject. They were rating also the professors. In 1930, too, one of Mr. Lowry's freshman classes, at his suggestion, started an English book-

shelf in the library; before the year was over they had contributed
ninety-eight volumes.[20]

All through President Wishart's administration religious activities
persisted though with some falling off of attendance and interest and
some change of direction. Each year several days before the opening
of college the cabinets of the Y. M. and Y.W.C.A. came back and
held their own "retreat" at some cabin in the country, to consider and
prepare for their program of the year. They fostered a big and little
sister movement for the incoming freshman women, a big and little
brother movement among the men, made plans for get-togethers of
various kinds, and discussed their budgets and their projects. In some
of these all-college projects, the two Christian Associations joined
with the C.E. under the name of the Big Three. Once they had
arranged an all-college date night as a general "mixer," for the
college was slowly growing larger and not everybody knew everybody else, as in earlier years. There was no longer the evangelistic
urge of an earlier period; even College Hall had been given up. With
enthusiasm, however, in 1920 as has been noted they had undertaken
with faculty help to support their own missionary in Korea, but in
subsequent years they had failed to meet their budgeted quota. Since
then they had forwarded annually instead a flat sum of $1200 to the
Presbyterian Board of Foreign Missions. Now in the fall of 1931 the
Big Three was raising money to send a Wooster representative,
William McAfee, '32, for a three-year term to Ewing Christian
College,[21] Allahabad, India. Sam Higginbottom, well-known mis-
sionary-agriculturalist from Allahabad, came to Wooster and spoke
in chapel to give a boost to this drive for money. This was the
beginning of a project that was to go on until the present day. A
promising boy is always chosen from the senior class. Once at Allahabad, he lives in one of the dormitories, associates with the student
boys, does a certain amount of teaching and often some coaching of
athletics. At intervals he reports by letter to the student publications
at Wooster, and on the completion of his two-year term he comes
back to speak directly to the students at chapel. In time the Big Three
became the Big Four, adding the Volunteer Society to its group, with
a single annual drive for money, a single budget, allocated as seemed
best.

Surprisingly, the Y.M. and the Y.W.C.A. sponsored the International Club. This had at the beginning as its three fold aim to aid

foreign students financially, to help student Volunteers to become better acquainted with the lands and peoples to which their life mission would take them, and "to serve as a general stimulus to interest in foreign affairs." Students were becoming somewhat more socially conscious. As years went on a whole dormitory perhaps or a group in one or two of the small residence halls would arrange to eat a rice-dinner or some inexpensive meal that the money so saved could go to some worthy cause.[22]

The International Club was still flourishing as the calendar changed from the twenties to the thirties. Yet the wave of pacifism had not yet reached its crest. In 1931 the Congressional Club for its Washington's Birthday celebration sponsored Norman Thomas in a lecture in the new high school auditorium. In the spring of 1932 there was added to Wooster's organizations the Peace Society. Its first meeting was attended by seventy-eight persons, students and faculty. Its purpose was "to provide an informal center for students interested in the movement and to cooperate with related student groups in other colleges."

Everyone knows what happened with the advent of Hitler in 1933. From then on, every agreement or treaty to which Germany was a party, one after another, was repudiated by the German Chancellor. Italy took over Ethiopia. Franco and the communists fought it out in Spain. Munich happened. Mussolini and Hitler drew together. Czechoslovakia and Poland were thrown to the dogs. Nobody seemed able to cope with the situation. All the while the United States was watching from across the Atlantic. She had herself in the years from the fall of 1929 gone through the economic wringer. People were poor and apprehensive.

Wooster was in the agricultural, industrial, isolationist Middle West. Through the thirties in their classes, in the newspapers, in the lectures, even in some of the sermons students were hearing war talk till they could not face the future—nobody could; they felt themselves in the front lines. Students everywhere in the country were crying out for peace in the world, peace at almost any price. Twice during the period Wooster students joined the national student demonstrations. One April morning in 1936 they gathered around the Rock, summoned there by bugle and drum, and listened to many speeches, against war in general, against the R.O.T.C. in particular, for which Wooster had not even applied. The whole campus had been plastered with placards bearing such slogans as "Future Gold Star Mothers Demand Bonus," or "Buy Your Own Wreath Now." Again in 1938 they held a torchlight parade and burned War in effigy.

Through all this period not only had the International Club flourished, but political interest of all kinds was strong. Twice the students held mock political conventions, once in 1936 nominating Arthur Vandenberg for President; in 1940 for their convention they brought on as their keynote speaker Senator Rush Holt. Once one hundred or so students paraded in the public square to protest the sales tax. It was a time of many lectures. Valentine Williams, journalist, talked of the Spanish situation. Jacob Meyer of Western Reserve discussed national sovereignty and world peace. Hugh Dalton, under the auspices of the class of 1917, came to analyze the experiments in economic planning of the United States, England, Italy, and Russia. The classes of 1932 and 1934 by their memorial funds made the major contribution through their annual institute of foreign relations. The general themes were Spanish America, Central Europe, the Italian-Ethiopian conflict, the tensions of the Far East, the challenge of dictatorships. The speakers were such persons as Raymond Leslie Buell of the Foreign Policy Association of New York, Sir Herbert Amery, G. H. Blakeslee of the Fletcher School of Diplomacy, and Abram Leon Sachar of the history department of the University of Illinois. Each gave two evening lectures and two or three seminars. They were plied with innumerable questions, after the lectures, at the seminars, at luncheons and dinners in the dormitories. Blakeslee, it was estimated, spoke to a total of 2000 students during his stay though he came when March was at its worst with heavy slush on the ground, and the rushing season on at Kenarden.

During this time Wooster had a young history professor who was being heard day after day in the classroom. Aileen Dunham had come in 1923 fresh from taking her doctorate at the University of London and from a summer in Italy studying art and the backgrounds of the Renaissance. She was a Canadian, a graduate of the University of Alberta. She had stopped in Chicago on her way home from Europe, had been interviewed by Mr. Kelso, had accepted the appointment as instructor in Wooster, and had begun teaching almost at once. Wooster has rarely, if ever, been more fortunate. She was young, enthusiastic, analytical, astute, and fearless. She loved to read, to talk, and to teach, making great demands on her students and on herself. She combed the newspapers and magazines for sidelights on her subject, read every new book in her field as fast as she could get hold of it. Her success was immediate; students flocked into her classes in European history. She rose to an assistant professorship, then to a professorship.

Miss Dunham had been an undergraduate during World War I, a graduate student in England during its aftermath. She had come home a pacifist. But as tensions tightened in Europe, as she watched the rise of Hitler, the crushing of Czechoslovakia, the threat to all Europe, to England, and the world, she saw clearly, that there was no way out except war, that the non-Axis nations must unite to save Europe and the world from utter disaster. This she said. Wooster students were not prepared for such an attitude. In 1938 a poll had indicated that seventy-nine per cent of Wooster students and faculty "favored embargoes as means of enforcing a strict policy of neutrality by the United States Government." [23] The students put up posters all over the campus, on trees, in buildings, demanding her resignation; she found these placards in her classroom, in her desk; they dropped out of her wall maps. She was accused by them of being a British agent. She was summoned to a meeting of the Congressional Club to defend her position.

Then in December, 1941, Pearl Harbor came. Everything changed at once; her position was vindicated. All along, however, there had been some of the more intelligent students who had remained her friends, who even sought her out at her house on Monday evenings to discuss things with her. This Monday evening discussion became in time a kind of seminar, based on their reading beforehand, as preparation, of the daily and Sunday issues of the New York *Times*. Finally, indeed, it became so well established and so well known that it was granted college credit. Now in retirement she looks back to that class as one of the joys and achievements of her teaching career.

Yet one must not get the impression that these were the only interests of the students. They came to the chapel also to listen to poets, to Carl Sandburg, to Edwin Markham (brought by John D. Overholt), to George Russell, who talked of the modern Irish literary output as influenced by the ancient Irish culture. They listened to distinguished preachers, Henry Sloane Coffin, Bishop Francis McConnell, and others. The geology department introduced them to Douglas W. Johnson of Columbia, who explained something of the emergence and submergence of shore lines over the world.

There were still other palliatives, however temporary, for all this war fever. The students could take it out on the playing fields or in the swimming pool or even in watching the activities there. In 1923 Carl Munson,[24] who had come in 1921 to Wooster's physical education department, "led" his team in the first intercollegiate swimming meet in Ohio. Two years later he succeeded in making swimming a requirement for graduation for both men and women, and he put in also a Red Cross lifesaving course. Before long he was making an annual trip during vacation to Ft. Lauderdale where his boys could really stretch their muscles and their lungs. By 1935 Wooster's swimming team won eight out of ten matches; in 1938–1939 they took second place in the Ohio Conference.

In cross country meets, too, Wooster ranked high. It did not need to look to past laurels; it was winning them. In 1930–1931 Wooster won the mile relay race, taking the Conference championship. Twice Chegwidden, '37, won the two-mile race in the Big Six Carnival, and in the 5000-meter Olympic trials he had won by three yards; his time 15 minutes 58.4 seconds. Frank Knutsen, it is recorded, had been beaten only once in twenty-four starts. In 1937–1938 Wooster had a record in cross country of being unbeaten, with Bruce, '39, and Lehman leading off. In 1937 Berny Bishop made a record for the high jump at 5 feet 11¾ inches, and George Watson scored a first in shot and discus. In a meet against Case, Wooster won the discus shot, the 100-yard dash, and the 120-yard high hurdles, and the high jump. Wooster had both speed and endurance in its men, and technique as well.

In the winter of 1926 "Mose" Hole took over the coaching of basketball. He had gone out to study various techniques, and he trained his men in what came to be known as the "Spray and Pray" offensive. In 1930 Wooster won twelve out of thirteen games, eleven of them with Ohio Conference teams. Mt. Union was proving in the thirties to be one of Wooster's toughest opponents in basketball, yet in 1935, thanks to the team's speed and punch, Wooster twice defeated this rival. In both 1939 and 1940 Wooster's team won the

Ohio Conference championship in basketball. In fact, at one point for thirty-five consecutive games Wooster suffered no defeat. They were all good basketball players, but Nicholas Frascella, '38, was a star. So much appreciated was he that after his final game as a senior the students presented him with a Hamilton watch.

The Wooster *Alumni Bulletin* in an article in 1930 remarked that athletics in Wooster "had passed its expansive period," that it was now the mode among Wooster students to seem blasé even though they might attend the games. Yet clearly not everyone chose this attempted sophistication; many of them were still reaching for the ball with enthusiasm. The record in baseball, it is true, does not show up so well, yet after all baseball comes in the spring of the year when everything is crowding for a place.[25] In all the sports there were bad seasons and good seasons. Once in football a succession of injuries incapacitated some of Wooster's best players for weeks. In 1930 Ray Miller, '31, as end, was listed on the all-Ohio team by the Associated Press, the United Press, and the International News Service. In 1933 Nussbaum and Pryor,[26] both of the class of 1934, were given place on this mythical team as guard and halfback, by the Associated Press, and Foley, '35, was named first as tackle by the International News Service. Weisenbach, '34, was on several lists. Case, and especially Muskingum in these years were opponents to watch. They were strong. When in 1937 Gotshall, '38, returned a Muskingum punt sixty-five yards for a touchdown in the third quarter, there was cause for shouting. He and Arthur Pomeroy, '38, were both tagged by the Cleveland *Plain Dealer* for the all-Ohio team. The next year, 1938, was the best year of all, for then the team was undefeated for the sixth time in Boles' twenty-three years. That year they tied Case, Muskingum, and Washington and Jefferson. They won from Oberlin, Ashland, Denison, Mt. Union, Heidelberg. But not all the credit goes to Boles, part also to Arthur Murray, who coached football part of the time, and to Swigart. It goes, too, to Hole and Munson. They all worked as a team, a team in physical education and a team for Wooster, and they will long be affectionately known as "Wooster's Five Horsemen."

"If I Take the Wings of the Morning"

WHEN in 1919 they were hunting a new president for Wooster one of the trustees is said to have remarked that what they wanted was "a luminous spirit on the campus." Mr. Wishart was a leader; he was a conciliator; yet the students who knew him best over the twenty-five years of his administration would say, I suspect, that most of all he was a luminous spirit. To be sure, he was often tired to the point of exhaustion, sometimes deeply worried, yet he knew delight and gloried in the minor adventures that life put in his way. His whole experience from boyhood on had brought these qualities of his spirit into being. "Not so much common sense," he once said, "as the sense of the uncommon can save us from life's monotony." He had both; as the youngest of twelve children, he had needed both.

It must have been a very simple home in that village of Ontario, Ohio, that numbered, including dogs, not more than one hundred inhabitants. It was a place of warmth and dignity. Of it he once wrote: "I shall never cease to thank God for a childhood home in which there was for one thing a family altar, for another thing music, and good books, and high standards, and the love of the beautiful."

He must have become acquainted with the great outdoors almost as soon as he was able to turn a doorknob. His first job was with a neighboring farmer—to fetch from the pasture every day his cow and bring it back to the barn. For this errand he was given twenty-five cents a month. Then one day when a heavy storm overtook him and he still brought the cow in, he was rewarded by having his stipend raised to fifty cents a month. To a curious small boy these trips must have been full of exciting things, a bumblebees' nest perhaps, or some baby bunnies in a covert of weeds, a scarlet tanager in flight, maybe a hummingbird hovering over a columbine, or a meadowlark in song. Out in the fields there was always color and life and music. All his life he remained sensitive to the beauties of nature, to the rainbow, the "snow-clad majesty of a mountain," the "creamy spray" along a beach, "the strength and symmetry of the oak and elm" on the campus.[1] Of what sort the music was in the home we do not know, probably singing. There was no organ; it is hardly likely that there was a piano, yet at least some of the children were musical. In his father's old United Presbyterian Church of that day, one may be pretty sure, the singing from the Psalter was without any accompaniment, save only as someone in the congregation with a tuning fork set the key. Even when very young, Charles Wishart must have listened often while they sang:

> The Lord's my shepherd, I'll not want;
> He makes me down to lie
> In pastures green; He leadeth me
> The quiet waters by.

It was a haunting melody; besides, he could see it all. He always loved music. Before he went to college he was already playing the piano. In Monmouth he became the director for a while of the church choir. Somehow, somewhere he familiarized himself with the best from Wagner to Beethoven, and in later days he was often caught arguing with his brother John over the merits or lack of merit of Beethoven's last quartets. "One of the supremely memorable days in my life," he once wrote,

was that in which I first heard a symphony orchestra. . . . I cannot now remember the program. I only know that when this balanced chorus of musical instruments began to speak in tones so sweet and noble, so sonorous and yet so delicate, so vivid and so balanced, something clutched at my heart until it seemed for a time physically impossible for me to remain quietly in my seat. . . . And the memory of it can never die.

He knew of course also the popular songs of his day. At home in Wooster, on request of his own children and to their delight, he would sometimes break out with "Thompson's Mule" or "Strawberry Shortcake."

All his life, too, he was surrounded with books. At four, his mother had taught him to read, pointing out the letters on the big pot-bellied stove in the kitchen. In his father's little library there were many theological works, most of them in Latin, some in Greek, Scottish history, and some of the great poets, books he bought by mail, out of his meager savings, from a bookseller in Edinburgh. To one who reviews Mr. Wishart's sermons it seems as if at some time he must have read everything from Homer to Nietzsche to Mark Twain, so full are they of quotations and illustrations from many sources, from historians, philosophers, psychologists, biographers, poets, dramatists, novelists, essayists, theologians, scientists. He read much in Civil War history and for relaxation enjoyed detective stories. And he scanned with care all the current news. Even more remarkable, however, than the range of his reading was his memory for what he had read and his ability to summon to his use the right illustration or quotation. In "a message to the ministry" published in 1921 under the title of *The Range Finders,* he said:

But he [the minister] must not only be in constant touch with the practical lives of men, he must also be a reader and digester of the great books. The best preacher and the best new book are to be wedded together until death do them part. And some of the best new books are several hundred years old. . . .

On both sides of his house Mr. Wishart came of a family of ministers. All his years he had been surrounded and sustained by these close "sons of the spirit." In the dedication of the slim volume mentioned above he listed nine in his clan, his father, two brothers, a grandfather, three cousins, an uncle, and a nephew, "all ministers of God here or beyond the veil." Not only did he thank God for the family altar, but he cherished through life another memory, that of the

Communion service in my father's church,—the table spread with snowy linen, the silver vessels, the atmosphere of gravity, a certain fine dignity that seemed to sit on the rugged, gnarled faces of the simple-hearted farmers who served as elders, and, above all, the solemn tones of my father's voice as he led us in prayer that entered into the secret places of God.

There had indeed been standards set in that home. In one of his sermons he tells how when he "left home as a boy," his parents had had "absolutely no worldly goods to give" him; "nothing, that is, except their love and benediction, and a few great words, words like honor and truth and justice and loyalty and kindness and love." He might well have added a sense of the dignity of labor well done. At Hayesville (Vermillion) Academy, twenty-five miles or so away, the boy made his way by tending fires, sweeping out the building, doing whatever janitorial chores presented themselves. For three years he worked to earn enough to take him to college, at Monmouth—his family had moved meanwhile to Illinois. There he made a notable record, and incidentally won various prizes, which slightly bolstered his limited funds. In summer he took a job in a bookstore. Life had so many facets. He was young, and nothing was common.

Until middle life he enjoyed a game of tennis. In college he had played on the varsity doubles team. He could sit for hours watching the Cleveland Indians or his own Wooster college team. He had almost as much enthusiasm for sports as Coach Boles himself. He believed in them even as the ancient Greeks—and he believed in keeping them clean.

This zest extended into all aspects of life, into his parish work in Chicago, into his relationships with students, faculty and alumni at Wooster, and into his contact with many types and varieties of men as he moved about telling the story of Wooster or doing the work of the church, talking with business men, professional men, or politicians. He counted the happiest part of his life at Wooster the range of his friendships.

In his earliest years at Wooster, he was speaking, but not necessarily preaching, out of town two or three or four times a week. Ordinarily at the college, he preached at the beginning of the terms, at Homecoming, at Commencement, and now and then on other special occasions. And of course he was often a chapel speaker in the mornings:

What is Christian Education? Put briefly, it is civilization perpetuating itself. It is the process of handing down the best things of yesterday to those who come after. It is placing the results of human experience at the disposal of the next generation. It is not blind traditionalism. It is not unwillingness to accept new light. . . . Civilization ought to be a relay race, where one generation carries the torch and puts it in the hands of the next. If we are to meet the deadly menace of the future, we must hand down the torch to our children and our children's children, and we must begin in the home.

Or again:

The tragedy of our modern world is not its lack of enjoyments but its lack of enjoyment. . . . The tragedy of the world is not the absence of beauty, of joy, of humor, but the absence of zest to realize them and to respond to them. If we have no living inner joy, then we are compelled to increase the outer stimulus. If we have that spontaneous wellspring within, little stimulus is needed. . . . There never were more varied forms of entertainment than we have today. But these are not evidences of inner enjoyment. They are rather evidences of inner monotony.

Preaching on the Sons of Mary and the Sons of Martha, he stressed:

I have tried to make you feel how this stern practical age is calling upon you and me for the best possible equipment of brain and hand, and how it impels us to keep our feet upon the ground, to meet this world as we find it, and to put the best we have into our work.

Yet he goes on:

No matter how practical a life you intend to lead, unless you have some of this power of imagination and spiritual vision you will become a mere routine plodder, a one-sided man or woman. The more practical your life-work is to be, the more careful you ought to be in balancing the daily routine with that which will lift the soul out of itself and keep you from withering into a narrow machine-made existence.

. . . what many people in the busy routine of daily life need is the far view, to lift their eyes to the great eternal mountains of truth and beauty which will endure when all the results of our practical activities have crumbled to dust. . . . Ideals *are* the realest things in the world.

Mr. Wishart conceived of the vocation of the Christian ministry as that of both prophet and priest, for in a sense the minister is "the range finder of civilization's great battle. He looks backward through history . . . sees the sweep of events, the broad outlines of the battle, as the man on the street can never see them." After World War I he took a definite stand in favor of the League of Nations, lined himself

up against our national (and particularly middle western) isolation-
ism, our self-centeredness and the excesses of the after-war period:

We even rejected so mild a gesture as joining with other forward-
looking nations in a World Court which might lay down some principles
of international law. . . . We raised the outer walls of our national
isolation a little higher than they had ever been before. We demanded
that our allies, who had paid their part of the common cost of war and
blood, should pay our part in gold. And then we raised our tariff barriers
so that it was impossible for these countries to pay the debts which we
demanded of them. What cared we?

So the nation went the way of isolation in that dreadful period of
flapper girls and jazz music and stock gambling and Hollywood orgies,
when political gangsters looted the treasury, and fat politicians held
million dollar banquets in the Mayflower Hotel in Washington. . . .

Then after Pearl Harbor when we were already embroiled in the
Second World War, he spoke again with vehemence:

Probably fifty per cent of the American people do not yet know what
the war is all about. It is our business to try to understand that and to
help other people to understand it. A solemn responsibility rests on the
Christian pulpit. "For if the trumpet give an uncertain voice, who shall
prepare himself for war?"

.   .   .   .   .

I judge no man's duty. But here is the issue, . . . Shall the common
man have his right on this globe of ours as a child of God . . . to live
decently, protecting and loving his family; to go to the church of his
choice; to speak his mind about the issues of the day; to vote as he
pleases, the right to trial by a jury of his peers, and exemption from cruel
and unusual punishment? That, I think, is what it is all about. It is not a
war between nations. It is the culmination of 2000 years of struggle
between paganism and the Cross of Christ.

His social conscience was strong. Speaking one day of Paul's
eagerness to go on to Rome, he put it this way:

Paul wanted to go to Rome because he was stirred by the complex
problems of the social order in that Imperial City. . . . We dare not plant
our churches or preach our messages two and one half miles from the

crossroads of modern life. . . . When a man becomes a Christian that faith of his must soak through every layer of his life. . . . The Bible begins in a garden but it ends in a city. . . . Every phase of life is represented in it. . . . We go on to Rome so that, by and by, it may be Rome no longer, but the City of God.

In his final baccalaureate address in 1944 he spoke of how the modern world was obsessed with things, the telephone, the telegraph, radio and the airplane—he might well have added then the motor car and, today, television—

The motive power is to be found in ideas. For one thing, ideas precede things . . . outlast things . . . outfight things. . . . Back of all the gadgets we use are the minds that thought out, perfected, and adapted them. . . . Generation after generation, men die and are forgotten, but the solemn music of the Ninetieth Psalm . . . is, itself, immortal. . . . The Allied Powers . . . were practically unarmed . . . except in the possession of . . . ideas of decency and freedom and honor. . . . We were stirred to arm ourselves by great words which lifted us to the plane of sacrifice on the wings of deathless ideals. . . .

. . . Mr. Reinhold Niebuhr . . . has recently said, "Man lives in two worlds, and when he tries to make his home in one alone, something goes wrong with him. . . ." . . . It is my profound conviction that you cannot have a better world here unless you view men "under the species of eternity," with an eternal Word back of them; and, if there is an eternal Word back of them, there must be an eternal destiny ahead of them.

Mr. Wishart was indeed a luminous spirit on the campus, an excellent preacher and one with vision. Yet this is not to say that he did not have his faults as any man. Sometimes, perhaps, his eyes, too, were blinded; sometimes he was tired with the world and his part in it; sometimes perhaps his critical faculty was in abeyance, and his emotions got the better of him, and sometimes in his later years he was impatient of opposition within his faculty. Nevertheless he was an inspiring leader for young men and women of college age, growing to maturity, questioning everything they saw and read and heard. Sometimes in his sermons one felt that there was almost too much richness of illustration. Yet when listening to him one always knew where he stood on any subject, always felt his sense of "divine things in everything"—"If I take the wings of the morning and dwell in the uttermost parts of the sea, even there does thy hand lead me and thy right hand shall hold me"—and always realized that for him "life" was "the unrolling of an intelligent and definite purpose."

His reputation as a speaker had gone far afield. The summer of 1925 he spent mostly vacationing in the British Isles. While there, however, he preached in London, Bath, and Ipswich, and one day addressed a group of American and English clergy at St. Martin's in the Fields, London, defending the 18th Amendment (Volstead Act). His reception in that instance he reported as "cool, courteous, and critical." The same summer he went as one of several delegates from the Presbyterian Church, U.S.A., to the Conference on Faith and Order at Stockholm, "a world-wide ecumenical Protestant" assembly. There, too, he was asked to speak. Before ever he had come to Wooster he had been well known in the councils of the church at home.

Yet it was after he became president of Wooster, in the early twenties, that it fell to him to play a major role in the rising tide of dissension within the church. Dr. Mateer, professor of biology at that time and for many years before, had been teaching the theory of evolution without having encountered any serious objection. Wooster had been one of the first, if not the first, of the denominational colleges to do so. Before taking such a position Dr. Mateer had studied the subject carefully and had reached the conclusion that the theory was logical and in no way in conflict with the first chapter of Genesis. As Mr. Wishart put it, "Wooster had long held that the Genesis story was a divinely inspired, poetic picture of the creative process." In an infinite plan developed through millions of years there was implicit an even greater wonder than in creation by direct and immediate fiat. At Wooster very few differed with this point of view, yet there were still those within the church who thought this rank heresy.

One of these was William Jennings Bryan. For some years he had been lecturing far and wide on this subject, and in 1922 on his own volition and at his own expense he came to Wooster to explain the facts of creation to faculty and students. Mr. Wishart, who had met him on various occasions and knew his position, entertained him in his home and found him a delightful guest, amiable and full of stories. By this time Bryan had been three times defeated as Democratic candidate for President, had been Secretary of State under Wilson but had fallen out with him and had resigned in a huff. Everyone was eager to hear this "silver-tongued orator." That night Memorial Chapel was packed. Unfortunately at one point a freshman laughed when he should have been keeping his tongue in his cheek. Mr. Bryan was incensed, drew a deep breath and was off for another hour of his own creative activity. Ten o'clock passed, then ten-thirty. The students were amused; the deans fidgeted with their watches. But at last he reached the seventh day of rest. The next morning he was off to other worlds, and the students were left to fight it all out among themselves. It is said that Mr. Bryan went forthwith to the Presbyterian Board of General Education demanding the cutting off of all contributions to Wooster College until or unless it desisted from the teaching of evolution. Dr. Mateer made no change in his course.

In May of 1923 Mr. Wishart and Mr. Bryan met again at Indianapolis on the occasion of the Presbyterian General Assembly. Both had been named along with three other men as candidates for the moderatorship. It was to be supposed, at least by his backers, that as a national figure Mr. Bryan could easily win this election. There were several ballots, but on the third round after two of the candidates had withdrawn, Mr. Wishart won by a plurality of some twenty. At once the election was made unanimous.[2] Mr. Bryan did not extend the usual courtesy of coming over to congratulate him. When later Mr. Wishart sought him out in the Claypool Hotel and asked, "Why did you not offer me the hand of fellowship?" Mr. Bryan flung out, "When I lectured in Wooster, you rose in chapel the next morning and repudiated my address."

"I give you my word of honor," replied Mr. Wishart, "that that statement is not true." There was no response from Mr. Bryan. It was customary for a new moderator of the Assembly to appoint a vice-moderator, usually one of the defeated candidates, and the chairmen of the various committees. Mr. Wishart asked Mr. Bryan which appointment he would prefer. "None," was the curt response. Mr. Wishart proceeded with his appointments in his own way, assigning to Mr. Bryan the committee on national missions; whereupon Mr. Bryan came to him, refusing to serve but adding that he would have accepted the vice-moderatorship, implying that Mr. Wishart should even now make the change. But Mr. Wishart protested that the vice-moderator had already been inducted; he could no longer make a change. "Sure you can," retorted Mr. Bryan, "it's done in the Democratic Convention right along." But there was no change.

At a later session of this Assembly Mr. Bryan moved that no Presbyterian funds be allotted to any institution, academy, college, theological seminary or training school at which the doctrine of evolution was taught as a "proven fact." A long and heated argument ensued. For a while it looked as if Mr. Bryan and his cohorts might win. Then John Willis Baer, chairman of the committee on education, skilled in ecclesiastical politics, offered a compromise resolution in which there was no mention of money but which denied approval to any institution "which sought to establish a materialistic evolutionary philosophy of life." [3] This finally passed. The squabble was reported variously in the newspapers. The New York *Times,* in a slightly humorous vein, remarked: "College presidents have a reputation of knowing something about the arts of management, and doctors of divinity, children of light though they are, not always are deficient in the wisdom of the world." Wooster had pulled through, but the news of the fight at the Assembly had spread out across the country. There were repercussions.

The year of the moderatorship was in Mr. Wishart's own words "a nightmare." He shuttled back and forth across the country, sleeping in strange beds night after night, speaking in churches on Sundays, at other meetings often several times a week. To be sure, he met many friends, but enemies as well. One man refused to speak from the same platform with him. Certain of the ultra-conservatives among Wooster's alumni, too, began to write in not only to inquire as to the soundness of Wooster's Christian faith and teaching but to make charges, obviously inspired from outside.

Some weeks before the May, 1924, meeting of the General Assembly Mr. Wishart, completely fagged out, entered a Pittsburgh hospital. When the meeting opened, however, in Grand Rapids, he was back in the arena. Mr. Clarence McCartney of Philadelphia, one of the most vituperative of the fundamentalist leaders, was elected moderator, and Mr. Bryan appointed his vice-moderator. For two years now the fundamentalists across the country had been marshalling their forces. The church was being split wide open. Several pamphlets had been got out and circulated under the title of "The Fundamentals," namely the tenets of the extreme conservative position on matters theological. *The Presbyterian,* a weekly, published in Philadelphia, championed their cause, and a professor in Princeton Theological Seminary, J. Gresham Machen, was one of the leaders in the movement. The situation was further complicated by the fact that Mr. Harry Emerson Fosdick, a Baptist minister occupying the pulpit of one of the large New York Presbyterian churches, and teaching in Union Seminary, had come out as early as 1922 with a withering attack on the fundamentalists, and had been denounced far and wide as a heretic. For two years already the storm had been raging around him and those who were in even moderate sympathy with him. Bitter accusations distorting the truth one way or another were a commonplace. At a dinner meeting at this Assembly of 1924, therefore, Mr. Wishart made a ringing plea for church unity:

All of us are agreed, that there ought to be loyalty to essentials, and liberty in non-essentials. Just what are essentials and non-essentials? . . . when we ask ourselves just how much of doctrinal holdings or credal belief is involved in loyalty to Christ, differences of opinion will emerge. . . . Personally I am hopeful that present controversies may tend somewhat to clear the air as regards this vexed matter of definitions. . . . But I am pleading that even in controversy a passion for unity should have its place along with passion for purity of doctrine.

· · · · ·

Above all . . . scrupulous care should be taken to clarify the atmosphere through which we may the better understand each other. Fragmentary or garbled sayings should not be wrested out of their contexts and made the basis of broad and reckless generalizations; incidental or careless utterances should not be made the criteria of final judgments. Where speakers are quoted they should be given the opportunity of verification or correction before controversial use is made of their utterances. And where obvious injustice had been done through misquotation, prompt and full reparation should be made. These are the simple rules of elementary good faith and chivalry. . . . It is hard enough at the best to know what is going on in another man's mind. . . . All bitterness and wrath and clamor are in the end vanity of vanities. It has been charged that those whose voices are raised for tolerance and conciliation are timid souls who dread the clash of arms. . . . The charge is misplaced. . . . There are men in this group who, if they indulged natural instincts, might snuff the battle from afar, with great joy. But they are men who have studied history and therein learned the utter futility of the spirit of controversy in settling the deep and delicate questions of our holy faith.

. . . . .

Loyalty to this great Christian fundamental should stimulate us to the fellowship of prayer. Here is the great fusing factor which burns out many barriers.

. . . . .

The great Christian fundamental is to be approached also in the fellowship of service. Here is the corrective of many dangers. . . . Men lose their frigid, analytical rationalism when they confront the great problems of human need and sorrow, and are stimulated thereby to practical service.

At the end, it is said Wishart was cheered to the rafters; though, worn out, he had gone back to his hotel to rest. Mr. Bryan was also scheduled to speak, rose and talked only briefly. When they met on a parlor car after the Assembly was over they chatted amicably.

"Once more," Mr. Wishart reminisces, "we were to meet." It was at the General Assembly of 1925 at Columbus, Ohio. Both were members of the General Council and had remained on the platform for a conference with two or three of the others after most of the delegates had already taken off for home. "We talked briefly, and then Mr. Bryan put his arm over my shoulder and said, 'Wishart, will you pray.' So we knelt together. Somehow I have always liked to think about that last meeting."

In July of that same year the Scopes trial took place in Dayton, Tennessee. The prosecution of the young school teacher won despite the efforts of the famous defense lawyer, Clarence Darrow. But the conviction carried with it only a fine for $100. Five days later the news came of the death of Mr. Bryan.

Yet the controversy was not over. Here and there in random spots it broke out again. A small group of Wooster's alumni took up the cudgels. Their leader, a man from Maryland, who was apparently the bitterest of all, was invited to come and air his grievances before the Board of Trustees. He refused. Instead he, with others, prepared and distributed a pamphlet which was a veritable museum of such distortions of the truth as Mr. Wishart had decried in his plea in

1924 for unity within the church. A complete textbook was condemned solely because of one or two statements within. A professor was accused of heresy because of a statement or two taken out of context. The college was held to blame for certain lecturers that had spoken from its platform, with no mention of all the lecturers who would have passed muster with any of the most strait-laced audience. The deficit and a drop in attendance [4] were attributed to disaffection with Wooster on the part of its constituents, whereas they could clearly be explained otherwise, by an increase in routine college expenses on the one hand, by a general drop-off among colleges of Ohio on the other hand. It was a diatribe put out with obvious intent to harm the college, and was so recognized by most persons. The editor of *The Presbyterian Banner* of Pittsburgh asked Mr. Wishart to write a refutation. This he did. Gradually the tumult died down, as it had within the church itself.

Mr. Wishart's presidency was indeed no sinecure. He said once that in all his twenty-five years at Wooster there was hardly a year without some crisis, a boom or a depression, a crisis within the faculty or some serious disciplinary action among the students, war or war's aftermath. Yet when it was all settled he could sit back and smile and once more thank God for his goodness, for good books and music, for high standards, and for the beauty of the world.

XIX

At the End of the Line

Let your hook be always cast in the pool; when you least expect it, there will be a fish. (Ovid, *Ars Amatoria* Book III, 425)

IN 1931, in his Wooster Day address to the college students, Mr. William E. Henderson, '91, professor of chemistry at Ohio State University, and trustee of Wooster, impressed upon his hearers that:

The college is an environment. It is an intellectual, spiritual, and moral environment. It is the place above all other places where a young man can prepare himself for what lies ahead in life. It is not what he gets there but it is what he achieves for himself. . . . self control. . . . self mastery. . . . ways and means to get knowledge of whatever kind he wants at whatever time he wants it. College does not give him knowledge. It gives him a command of ways to get knowledge. It can give him a chance to develop his own personality and above all, it gives him the opportunity to develop ideals—ideals of life. . . . It needs to be a time of quiet reflection, a time of self searching, a time of creation of ideals, of points of view, of facing the world into which he is going. . . . [College] is simply a favorable, inspiring, helpful environment in which the man must create those things for himself. . . .

It was this environment that Mr. Wishart was trying throughout his administration to provide, first, to be sure, through trained and inspiring personalities on his faculty, then through adequate and inviting physical facilities in which both students and faculty might work at their creative best.

Wooster had fast been growing beyond its physical plant and equipment. In the fall of 1919 when Mr. Wishart came to Wooster there was an enrollment of 576. By the late fall of 1925 there were 873 students, over three hundred of whom were freshmen, a total increase of almost eight per cent over the preceding year. By September of 1926 attendance had reached 901, exclusive of the 158 of the conservatory of music. Kenarden was the only dormitory for men.

Hoover and Holden, even with the newly built Annex, were spilling over; 153 girls were living in homes in town (some below Bowman Street) or in other off-campus houses. The twenty-five girls in Long Hall [1] (the old Carey Kauke residence on East Bowman Street), as well as the others had to come traipsing up the hill in all kinds of weather not only for their classes but for their meals. By December of that year Miss Florence Root, the competent and forward-looking dean of women, who had come in 1922, was writing:

. . . I think we are in duty bound to house satisfactorily those whom we do admit. . . . There are 125 Sophomore women in college and none of them are in dormitories. . . . We have less than half our Freshmen in dormitories.

. . . . .

We have lists of approved houses accommodating from two to twenty. The fact that these houses are on the approved list does not mean that they are in all ways satisfactory. . . . Since the college has no financial control of these houses, we cannot always obtain the conditions we most desire. . . . The fact that Freshmen and Sophomores are so scattered makes it exceedingly difficult to have an effective self-government organization. It is hard for them to get acquainted with each other or feel themselves a part of the college as they should.

She then goes on to describe the set-up she would like:

. . . Close your eyes and imagine dormitories sufficient to house all the girls except those whose homes are in Wooster. And such dormitories! Plenty of single rooms; plenty of bathrooms; a nice guest suite in each dormitory for you when you come back; plenty of space for entertaining; residence units of not more than seventy so that the dining room and living rooms will have a homelike atmosphere; kitchens fitted to serve two units to save expense; one person at the head of all the buying and planning of meals for all the dormitories and that person one who is skilled in dietetics and who knows what good meals are; as a social head of each dormitory, a woman whose culture, refinement, good common sense, kindness and human sympathy would exert an influence beyond all calculation.

. . . . .

This isn't a mere matter of housing; it is a matter of education, of social training, of the development of those qualities of ease of manner, poise, courtesy, and consideration of others, which are potent factors in success after college for every girl, be she business woman, teacher, spinster or matron.

The girls had no proper gymnasium facilities of their own. They had the use of the big gymnasium at certain hours on certain days only. On Saturday afternoons they were allowed the use of the pool.

There was no social building whatsoever. The joint Y.M. and Y.W.C.A. receptions in the fall, the Gum Shoe Hop in February, and other all-college occasions were relegated to the main floor of the gymnasium. The lounges of the dormitories were inadequate for anything but occasional small parties, and the basement of Kauke was at best a gloomy setting. For some time there had been a candy kitchen in Holden Hall, with an entrance on University Street, that could serve as many as sixteen for a snack at lunch. This had been primarily for the girls from downtown. This, too, proved inadequate, and in the fall of 1923 the old observatory had been put to use as a Y.W.C.A. tea house with a resident in charge. There were two small living rooms and a dining room where breakfasts could be had from eight to eleven. Gradually it came to be used more and more, for small and select evening parties, as on the occasion of the installation of Theta Delta Chi, December 3, 1924, when a "gorgeous banquet" was served there.

There were no proper facilities for looking after the health of the students, no hospital, no official college physician; this had become alarmingly apparent in 1918 at the time of the influenza epidemic. At the instigation of the Women's Advisory Board some years before there had been set up on the top floor of Hoover a two-room suite as a make-shift infirmary where a girl could be isolated from the others and a nurse called in if necessary. Ordinarily the matron did whatever nursing was done. Not till 1922 was a full-time nurse installed. In 1923 similar arrangements were made for the men in Kenarden, in the guest suite of the fifth section. In an emergency students were taken to one of the local hospitals.

In the stadium the concrete bleachers overlooking the football field were now entirely inadequate for the crowds that came to watch Wooster's games. Townspeople flocked up the hill, alumni came from towns nearby, and often the competing team was accompanied by a sizable crowd of rooters from their home base. Mr. Boles estimated that the college should now provide seating in the grand-

stands for 6000–7000 persons. In the library where they were adding books at about 2000 volumes a year, they were running short of
shelf space and seating in the reading rooms. On special occasions
even Memorial Chapel was overcrowded. In Kauke Hall the president and treasurer were cramped in their quarters; and another
faculty member had been recently dispossessed of his classroom to
provide office space for the dean of women, the dean of men, and
their secretaries.

So far Mr. Wishart had been wisely spending his efforts mostly in
seeking endowment for professors' salaries. Yet when the campaign
of 1920–1922 [2] had been completed and all the money paid in (as
of 1925), the time had come when he must go out to find money
also for buildings and equipment. Mr. Wishart did not, one suspects,
enjoy begging for money. He once said of himself that he had neither
the flair for this nor the courage that President Holden had had; that
he was inclined "to wilt at the first rebuff." Yet to judge from his
own reminiscences, he approached this inevitable chore with a kind
of boyish humor, and in the end many of these tasks proved to be
adventures in friendship.

Of course there were rebuffs and disappointments. Once he went
to see a well-known and apparently cordial Presbyterian in Illinois,
yet when he had finished telling his story, he was met with "a cold
glint" in the man's eye. "I have plenty of stocks and bonds," he said,
"and other collateral. I am not going to give you a cent." [3] Once he
went to see a wealthy prospect in an eastern city who until the very
end gave every evidence of being interested; then she turned and
asked, "Is ——(naming a trustee) still on your Board . . . ?" and
finding that he was, said, "I will give you no money so long as he is a
trustee." On another occasion, accompanied by one of his trustees,
A. C. Ernst, he went to see Mrs. J. Livingstone Taylor, [4] who was a figure in Cleveland, austere, demanding of those around her, missionary-
minded, and in many instances very generous, a fundamentalist
Presbyterian. The appointment had been made ahead. Her secretary
met them at the door with Mrs. Taylor's request that Mr. Ernst leave
his cigar outside. Once greetings were over and they were seated, the
fireworks began. Mr. Wishart found himself deep in a "theological
argument" based on Wooster's reputed heresies. In the end she

relented, however, and gave the college $25,000 "in spite of our heresies."

Mr. Wishart's record in building in his twenty-five years was by no means meager: Holden Annex, the new bleachers at the stadium, Hygeia, Galpin and Galpin park, Douglass, Babcock, the Westinghouse heating and lighting plant, the Netta Strain Scott auditorium (an addition to Taylor Hall, for a little theater), the revamping of and the addition to the old observatory to make it serve as a student union, the acquiring of Merz Hall, partly by gift, partly by purchase, and the president's residence. Three of these came from Wooster men who were already or were to become trustees. One, Elisha P. Douglass, '77, had been a long-time friend of Mr. Notestein, who in turn had helped through those years to hold and nurture his interest in Wooster; another, John Franklin Miller, '81 [5] was a classmate and equally devoted friend of Mr. Compton. And Birt E. Babcock, '94, Mr. Wishart inherited in a sense from President Holden, though only in a sense, for Wishart was to make his own deep impression.

Hardly had the campaign been completed till Mr. Wishart settled to the problem of enlarging the grandstand of Severance stadium. With this idea in mind Mr. Boles had all the while been saving up the gate receipts and had $15,000 safely stowed away. The students were all enthusiasm. The seven sections of Kenarden vied with one another in an effort to average $10 per person. Hoover and Holden vied in turn with Kenarden. Mr. Walter D. Foss, a trustee from 1902 to 1917, took on the job of raising money in town, offering himself to give the final $5000 to make the campaign a success. The college took $5000 also from its treasury. Alumni and faculty contributed. In June of 1924 the contract was let, and in October of that year at the Akron-Wooster game (unfortunately a defeat) the new stand was formally dedicated. It was thirty rows high and accommodated 5045 persons. Each seat was numbered and reserved. All across the front were boxes, the two in the center for the president of the college and for Mr. Foss. Now with temporary bleachers at the north behind the baseball diamond at least 6000 persons could watch the games with relative comfort.

John Franklin Miller was an excessively quiet and modest soul. All he wanted was to do a good job, and this he did. Needs stood out in his mind like billboards along a country road; they spelled for

him opportunity. He had worked up in the Westinghouse Air Brake
Company till in 1916 he became its president. He had set up the
village of Wilmerding, near Pittsburgh, where they had a main plant
and he had his office. He had planned the pension system for their
employees, so generous a system that it is said to have shielded the
company from strikes. He wasn't a philosopher but he had been a
friend of one since Wooster days and in June, 1911, had established
at Wooster the first departmental prize, given at graduation to that
student "who has evinced the highest scholarly excellence in philosophy." He had observed at close range the devotion of Wooster's
professors to their profession, had noted also with what extreme
simplicity they had to live; and so in 1925 he had taken out an
annuity of $50,000 with the college, to become at his death endow-
ment for professors' salaries. For the two years preceding his election
to the Board of Trustees, he admitted, he had been "sizing up"
Wooster's president, and he liked him. There followed in 1926 a gift
for the building of a college hospital, and later $50,000 as endow-
ment for its maintenance. The gift was announced, but with no
donor's name. Later when the excavation was about to begin in the
early fall of 1926, Mr. Miller allowed himself to be introduced to the
students from the chapel rostrum. Between that time and the fall of
1928, the hospital took final form, thought to be the finest small
college hospital in the state.[6] It had twenty-five beds, a wing for men
and one for women, and a top floor as an isolation ward. On the
ground floor were offices, examination and treatment rooms, including an eye, ear, nose, and throat room, a dispensary, an X-ray room
(the X-ray for which had been given by Herman Westinghouse),
and a small surgery. There were nurses' quarters, kitchen, elevator,
and on the flat tiled roof provision for a future roof garden for
ambulatory or wheel chair patients. Though the building was specifically in memory of the donor's father, George Torrence Miller, Mr.
Miller insisted that it be named Hygeia Hall—Hygeia, the reader
will recall, was the daughter of Aesculapius, and her special province
was to watch over the health of mankind.

The dedication took place on October 2, 1928, with Dr. Hugh
Cabot, dean of the Medical School of the University of Michigan, the
principal speaker. At Mr. Miller's request Mr. William R. Farmer of
Western Theological Seminary spoke of the donor's father, of his

"honest, solid, human worth," his "kindly spirit," his "strong personal conviction of truth," his "broad and manly tolerance of others' convictions."

Even before the building was fully opened, it had been staffed by a medical director, a nurse, and an assistant nurse. Dr. Herbert Wildman was a graduate of Chicago University and of Rush Medical College with two additional years at Ford Hospital in Detroit. He had at Wooster the rank of an assistant professor in physical education and taught a course in hygiene. He was on hand at the first of the year to give each student a physical examination, to be on call at all times, and available at the hospital for the treatment of minor ailments. He attended all major athletic events ready with his first-aid kit.

Ten years later Mr. Miller was again to throw himself into the breach. The problem of supplying heat and light to Wooster's growing campus was becoming critical. Buildings were multiplying and the capacity of the power plant, built in 1902, was being pushed to its limit. What would happen if in a zero spell a breakdown should occur? He talked it over with his friend and business associate, Herman Westinghouse, and the latter agreed to give a major portion of the money for the building and its equipment though at the time anonymously. Mr. Miller during the spring of 1938 added some $66,000. The building thus became a reality at the corner of Gasche and University Streets just outside the stadium fence. At commencement time of 1939 it was dedicated at a simple service of Scripture reading and prayer in the dynamo room. "May the light and warmth we receive from it," said Mr. Wishart, "be only the physical symbols of the light and warmth which we this day receive from the kindly generous hearts whose motives prompted and the clear brains whose thinking guided the erection of this beautiful and useful building." [7] In the fall when finally it was fully equipped and in use, Mr. McLaughlin sent a telegram to Mr. Miller announcing the fact and expressing the gratitude of the college. It arrived too late; Mr. Miller had just died.

In the spring of 1926 the trustees decided that the time had come to build a new house for Wooster's president. The existing president's home (now Centennial Hall) [8] at the corner of Beall and Stibbs was old and run-down. It was still a handsome house of its kind and period, with high ceilings, deep windows to the floor, beautiful woodwork, especially that of the long curving stairway. Yet it was cut up into many compartmentalized rooms, strung along almost as if on a chain, providing no easy, gracious circulation for guests. Moreover it was hard to heat. Trustees had often stayed there and knew its disadvantages. To be sure, a president with personality could make of almost any house a home of warmth and gentility— President and Mrs. Wishart were doing just this. But it was at best an awkward house in which to live and work. Mr. Ernst was particularly urgent in this matter. The trustees sent for Mr. Daniel Everett Waid of New York City, a distinguished architect, and a Presbyterian as well, to come and look the situation over. He did so. He thought the president's home, in a small residential college, should be on the campus, somewhat screened to be sure from curious passers-by, with a lawn large enough for garden parties on occasion. The site chosen was that large plot of open ground across from the Frick library, facing into University Street and back of Severance Hall. The house when built was in the Collegiate Gothic style, but to give it individuality as a residence Mr. Waid chose not the white Kittaning brick of Wooster's public buildings but a brick of variegated shades of rose and tan, with the usual limestone trim. So it stands today, one of the more attractive buildings on Wooster's campus.

Mr. Waid was architect also for Wooster's second dormitory for men, the gift of Mr. Elisha P. Douglass. Unhappily Mr. Douglass did not live to see the fruition of his dreams. He had already been a trustee for almost five years when one day he asked Mr. Wishart to come down to see him in Florida where he was spending the winter. Mr. Douglass had not been well but was able to be up and around and to play a little golf. He proposed a game. Mr. Wishart did not play but offered to go along and carry the clubs while Mr. Douglass made the round of nine holes. Wooster was obviously much on Mr. Douglass' mind; he wanted to do something substantial for the college. He had two boys of his own and would prefer to do something that would benefit boys; besides he remembered so vividly his own early struggles in college. When they came in that sunny afternoon, the story goes, he told Mrs. Douglass: "I bet I am the only man in the United States who ever had a college president for a caddy and paid him a fee of $250,000." For that was what it was. He left in his will stock to that amount of the McKeesport (Pennsylvania) Tinplate Company for the building of a men's dormitory at The College of Wooster. The trustees were instructed to let the stock accumulate dividends for at least two years before selling so that the total would be somewhat augmented.[9] Mr. Wishart knew that Mr. Douglass wanted the finest dormitory that this money could buy, and he went to work to see that his wishes were carried out. The site— against an old oak grove—was chosen and the plans carefully studied. It was to house 105 boys, to be built of white Kittaning brick similar to those used in other Wooster buildings, with an Indiana limestone trim. Ground was broken on February 6, 1929. On that cold, snowy, icy day, Mr. Earl L. Douglass, son of the donor, and now a trustee, sent a warming telegram:

We are glad beyond our power to express that the memorial dormitory to be known as Douglass Hall is to be started today. It would have been the crowning joy of my father's life had he been spared to see it built. . . . It will always represent to us, and I hope in some measure to the students also, the devotion of one who faced life with no equipment but a stout heart and undying faith, and who looked to Wooster with the gratitude of one who had made good use of the chances she gave, and who after his own family, loved his Alma Mater above everything in life. . . .

The building was completed in September in time for the opening of college, and appropriately on Dads' Day, November 2, 1929, was dedicated. After telling something of his father's early life, the son, Earl L., on this occasion went on to talk of the reasons behind his father's gift:

He gave this dormitory to Wooster in the first place, because he believed in education. . . . It was here that he learned how to think. . . .

But he believed not only in education, he believed supremely in character. He used often to make the statement that a man did not deserve any credit for being honest; he should be sent to jail if he were otherwise. . . . I recall on one occasion how he discovered that a number of years before he had unintentionally transposed figures in writing a check and had sent a check for $217 to a client instead of $271. Then with a real satisfaction he sat down, compounded the interest semi-annually at six per cent for all the years that had passed, and mailed the check to what no doubt was a very surprised and pleased client. . . .

. . . I can say with a great deal of confidence that my father was led into the consideration of this gift because he believed in men. . . . Men like Dr. Taylor and Dr. Gregory were a real inspiration in his life. I think it will never be possible to estimate the effect of Dr. Jonas O. Notestein upon him. There was not much difference in their ages . . . but he looked up to Dr. Notestein as if he had been his senior by forty years, and the effect of that man's life upon my father is, I believe, the most striking example I know of the service that consecrated Christian personality can render. . . . one of the greatest joys of his later years was the contacts that he had with Dr. Wishart and the members of the Board. . . .

. . . If there is one impression that I wish might remain today it is that he believed in young men and their future. . . . As they gather here for their social hour we will often think of them back in our homes and feel that their laughter and their happiness is constituting an ever living memorial to a man who believed in life. . . .

. . . this dormitory was given because the donor believed in God. . . . To educate a man's mind without educating the conscience is to create a potential menace to society. . . . We rejoice that this college operates under the supervision of the Christian church. . . .

Douglass Hall, everyone thought that day, was the most beautiful building on the campus; and so it still remains, at least in the thought of many of us, beautiful in its architectural mass, its proportions, its color, its roof lines, its fenestration. It would have delighted the heart of the donor.

Then there was the man with a suitcase, elderly, white-haired, handsome, who was seen every once in a while on campus, usually in the company of Mr. McLaughlin. The denizens of Kauke Hall wondered about him but were told nothing, not even his name, his business, nor where he came from. In 1925, however, he bought eight acres of rough or rolling ground north of the campus, including what was known as Knight's Hollow, and gave it to the college for a park. Much of it, he hoped, could be planted to trees "with a view to the long future"; the rest he wished to have made into a wildflower sanctuary and a place for picnics. All this came out in Mr. Wishart's Wooster Day letter to alumni in December of that year. Almost at once college workmen began to clean up the place, carting away the brush and rubbish in an initial effort to make it look presentable. Even the cows that used to munch quietly in the pasture land above were whisked off somewhere and the fences removed. An open fireplace was built on a level spot at the top of a bank. Long since the small boys of the neighborhood had given up rounding up the garter snakes in the loose shale of the banks and draping them across the barbed wire fence along Bever Street; and the old well in the bottom of the gulley had been washed full of stones and gravel and general debris. The wildflower sanctuary did not materialize, however, save as spring beauties seeded themselves of their own accord—as they did also on the campus proper—and the black locust trees that had taken over the banks perfumed all the region in late May or June. Some years later the possibilities of this park for amateur outdoor theatricals were discovered, and in 1932 and again in 1934 Greek plays were staged there—Euripides' *Alcestis* was one of these. Such was the genesis of Galpin park.

In 1927 and in 1930 William A. Galpin of Buffalo established two $50 and two $30 prizes for graduating seniors "for general excellence in college life and work." The next year, 1931, Mr. Wishart announced an anonymous gift for an administrative building to be begun in the spring. The site chosen was that facing Bever Street, just east of the old power house and to the north of the unsightly old gymnasium, which for some time had housed all the service facilities.[10] It had been an exceptionally mild winter, and on April 2 work began in earnest with the cutting away of six oaks and elms. The building of white brick with Amherst sandstone trim rose gradually. It followed the traditional Collegiate Gothic lines. Just after the holidays, in January, 1932, the administrative offices were moved in, but not until Color Day, May 13, at the chapel hour, was the dedication held. Mr. Galpin [11] could not be present because of the illness of his wife. A letter from him, read by Mr. Galpin that day, told of his long-time admiration for the College of Wooster, for the quality of its instructors, for the record of usefulness of its alumni, for the guiding hand of its president, Mr. Wishart. Some eight years before, he had consequently taken out an annuity to which each year he had been adding capital with the thought that with this at his death some building for the college might be erected. But having later come to realize the urgent need for an administrative building, he had decided to build it now as a memorial to his father, Leman Galpin, for thirty-five years a dedicated and much loved physician of

Milan, Ohio. In February, 1933, Mr. Galpin once more made a trip to Wooster. On this occasion the tablet to the memory of his father was unveiled in Galpin. This was in a sense the warmer, more official dedication. Mr. Galpin expressed himself that he had always thought that a college should put on a "good administrative front." He was pleased with what he saw. Later, in his will, he left an endowment for the building.

There is yet another story, that of Birt E. Babcock. He had once come back for commencement in President Holden's time, had gone to the president's reception. Mr. Holden, he remarked afterwards, "treated me like I had a million dollars and I don't have a cent." In June of 1920, Mr. Wishart's first commencement, he came back again.

It was thirty years since he had been a freshman here, a poor boy, earning his way for the most part, taking the full classical course, his heart set on becoming eventually a minister. Now he was a business man, owner and president of The Empire State Pickling Company of Phelps, New York. Just the year before he had bought out the partner with whom he had started in 1901. He had come a long way, and that way had not been easy. After Wooster, Mr. Babcock had had two years at Lane Theological Seminary in Cincinnati, until he had been sent home an invalid, given by the doctor but two months to live. For a year he had stayed at a farm nearby. Then feeling stronger, he took a job in a pickling works, the only job he could get. He didn't like it but it was a job. Gradually he began to feel that sauerkraut was not only a good business but that it had something healing and beneficial to the human system. Eating it, he had become comparatively rugged. With $1200 and a partner in 1901 he started his own pickling business in Ontario County, New York State. Before many years they had six plants, all in that county. It was a cool country, good country in which to grow cabbages.

At Wooster he had been entertained in the president's home, and had been impressed with the college girl who was helping Mrs. Wishart about the house in return for her room and board. He asked questions with the result that he offered to pay her way through college. She was the first of a procession of young men and women whom he so helped. In June of 1923 Mr. Wishart announced Mr. Babcock's gift of $50,000 toward an eventual student social building.

He hoped in time to build up the fund to $200,000. Before, however, it reached this point, the boom of the 1920's had broken into the panic of 1929 and the succeeding depression. In 1933, consequently, he set up a trust fund for the college of $135,000 in short-term government bonds which could be used by the college as collateral for loans. The building was delayed for two years. A social building which would bring in no money to the college seemed to the trustees at this time far less suitable than a women's dormitory, also badly needed, from which rentals would provide income. Mr. Babcock concurred.

On February 8, of 1935, ground was finally broken. The building was planned for eighty-four girls, with both single (32) and double rooms, an attractive dining room, and a lounge with windows looking out to a long greensward to the east. Mr. Babcock from the beginning was interested in everything, even in all the details of the furnishing, the money for which he was providing. He wanted it to be beautiful and also practical. When it was suggested that there be set up in the basement a bakeshop and a refrigerating unit for fresh fruits, meats, and vegetables for all college dining rooms, this too, Mr. Babcock agreed to pay for. In January of 1936, immediately after the holidays, the girls moved in, freshman girls, though the dormitory was later to be allotted to seniors. Inside near the entrance one may read the plaque which was unveiled on the day of dedication: "This dormitory is the gift of Birt E. Babcock, class of 1894, in grateful recognition of a debt to the College of Wooster which cannot be measured by material standards." Wooster in turn had reason to be grateful to Mr. Babcock not just for this building but for much else, for his long and useful service as a trustee (1923–1941), his help to many students, his gift of a Steinway Grand to Memorial Chapel, of the great oak table in the trustee room of Galpin,[12] for the Scottish kilts and a bagpipe for the college band.[13] The story is told that whenever Mr. Babcock was asked how he had been able to outstrip all his competitors in business, he always answered, "Because I studied Greek." As Mr. Wishart recounts the story, Mr. Babcock was not just trying to shut off eager questioners, he meant what he said; "the breadth, the imagination, the flexibility, and adaptability of the cultural training [had] made him a great business man." [14]

In 1930 the small auditorium in Taylor Hall, which until 1918 had been primarily used for the daily chapel services of the preparatory department, and for the Sunday School of Westminster Church, was first used as a little theater. The door receipts from the plays put on by students of the speech department went toward the buying of stage accessories of various sorts. In 1936, however, another angel appeared, and presently an addition to the back of Taylor Hall began to take shape. In February of 1937 the Netta Strain Scott Auditorium was opened with the presentation, for three evenings in succession, of Sir James Barrie's *Dear Brutus.* So great was the student eagerness to have a part in this that Mr. Lean acceded to training two casts for the occasion. On the second night a few minutes before the curtain rose, Mr. Wishart dedicated this new addition. The new auditorium seated comfortably 490 persons on tiered red leather folding seats. Exit doors at either side and steel stairways led to the ground. The stage had been greatly enlarged, special lighting put in, and a theatrical curtain installed. Beneath in the basement were the facilities of a green room. Even the old lobby had been freshened up with a Chinese hanging and a glass exhibit case.

Mrs. Scott [15] had been a new name to Wooster's list of benefactors. She was an Ohioan, had married a superintendent of schools in Steubenville, and then had herself taken to teaching. Later she and her husband moved to Hawaii, each to the principalship of a school. After some years Mr. Scott had resigned to go into business. She, however, had continued to teach until she was fifty-four. When she finally left Hawaii, she made her home in Washington, D.C. There at her church she met various Wooster persons through whom she became interested in the college; her brother Elmer Strain had graduated at Wooster in 1885 but had died three years later. Besides the $22,000 she gave for the Scott Auditorium, she added to Wooster's assets in several other ways, $1000 once to general endowment, $2500 for scholarships, and in her will well on to $23,000 "to provide lectures, in literature, religion, or science, or for the purchase of books." There was another small but valued gift, a portrait of Miss Isabel Bevier, '85, for many years the distinguished head of the department of domestic science at the University of Illinois.

In the spring of 1941 the need for a student social building became so imperative that the trustees decided to do something about it. Mr. Arthur O. Angilly, successor to Mr. Waid, was employed to make plans for the transforming of the old observatory by a considerable addition to the back. A large room with wall booths and tables was added to the north. Snacks or light meals or soft drinks from the fountain were served across the counter, and students carried their own plates to the booths. For special occasions one or two long tables could be set up in the center of the room. Usually, however, the center space was allotted to dancing. To the east of the main room was the campus bookstore, to the west another large well-insulated room designated as listening room. In it was a piano, a Capehart phonograph with automatic record changer, 824 records[16] in albums; 250 scores, and 128 books on musical subjects, historical, biographical, and technical; cabinets, and a descriptive catalogue of everything. All of this special equipment had been a gift of the Carnegie Corporation. The room itself when not in other use could be signed up for special small meetings, and for band practices as well. A small octagonal room under one of the old observatory domes was redecorated and refurnished for use as a lobby. To the east of this were the kitchen, office, and storeroom. Miss Mabel Little, director of dormitories, was put in charge. In the basement there was storage space for the overflow from the library. The building was well situated, close to the two women's dormitories, the library, and the recitation halls. It was an answer to student clamor and would be their only union building for twenty-seven more years.[17]

While this remodeling was going on, another project was in the works, that of taking over and converting to use as a conservatory of music the fine Overholt white brick residence immediately to the south of the president's home. Its many rooms on three floors were readily adaptable for use as studios. John D. Overholt, '07, son of the original owner, had offered it to the college for $30,000.[18] In it he was leaving carpets, some draperies, a few pieces of furniture, and, for the present at least, several oil paintings.[19] The offer included the large two-storey frame barn that in the early days of the century had housed horses and carriages, that the college transformed into a rookery of practice rooms. The old Kauke Conservatory at the corner of Beall and Bowman was too far from the center of activity; besides, the cost of its maintenance was becoming almost prohibitive. It seemed best after some years to sell it, despite its memories of Captain Kauke and of old Wooster.

On Wooster's twenty-fourth Homecoming, and Dads' Day the building was officially dedicated and named Karl Merz Hall in honor of Wooster's first director of music.[20] On Friday afternoon there was open house at the new conservatory, and in the evening a dedicatory concert in the chapel. All the musical organizations of the college had a part in this, but the main feature was the rendition of one of Karl Merz's own compositions, the middle movement of a piano concerto, which Mr. Parmelee had specially arranged for the Wooster Symphony Orchestra. On Saturday morning there followed the official dedication. James Francis Cooke, president of the Presser Foundation and editor of *Etude* gave the address, sketching Merz's life and stressing the impact the man had had on musical education in his period. In his dedicatory remarks Mr. Wishart spoke in appreciation of the Overholt family whose home the college was this day making its own. Letters were read also from the son of Karl Merz, of the class of 1883, and from his grandson, of the New York *Times*.

In the afternoon Wooster won a signal victory over Muskingum (27–6), and in the evening a bonfire fed by the packing boxes from the Kauke Conservatory flamed high on Scovel field. Later there was the play in Scott Auditorium, *Pure as the Driven Snow,* between the acts of which Eve Richmond and a faculty quartet sang old-fashioned songs. Later there was a Homecoming dance in the gymnasium. The next morning Mr. Wishart was again at his best, in a war sermon— "with the trumpets of the United Nations sounding not 'Taps' but 'Reveille.' "

One could go on listing changes or additions to the plant, such as the opening of a dining room downstairs in Holden Hall, the complete refurbishing of Kenarden, the cost of which the boys themselves undertook to raise from among their alumni, or the addition to the swimming pool of a filtering system whereby the water was changed every twenty-four hours. Yet one or two of these deserve special mention. The college had acquired the old Willaman farm (165 acres) with its rolling fields and swales, and views, its woods and tangle of wild undergrowth leading down to the valley of the Little Applecreek. It was the ideal spot for what Mr. Boles had always dreamed of, a college golf course. He gradually laid out nine holes there (three at first), hoping that someday the course could be extended to a full eighteen. With more care than any truck farmer would give even to a field of prize strawberries he set up the greens, planting grass, watering, and tending them. On the same day that the new power plant was dedicated, this golf course, too, was dedicated, the pride of Mr. Boles' life.[21] In 1941 the DeWitt property, three acres between Kenarden and Douglass, came up for sale. This the college bought, and graded it and seeded it, and laid it out for a supplementary playing field. And in 1942 it bought also the home on Beall Avenue of Mrs. Robert Taylor, to the south of Babcock Hall. This became the French house where girls majoring in French could be housed together and speak only that language. As head resident of this house there was always either a native French woman or a French-speaking instructor. This was the first of Wooster's language houses.

In 1938–1939 the Henderson Apartments were built at the corner of Beall and Bloomington, for retired or furloughed missionaries. The $90,000 given by Mrs. Mary Henderson of Washington, D.C. for this purpose to the Presbyterian Board of Foreign Missions had been allocated to Wooster as the logical place where it should be expended.

Then in May of 1944, the spring of Mr. Wishart's final year as president, the large room at the top of Galpin Hall was dedicated as the Josephine Long Wishart Art Museum. Both Mr. and Mrs. Wishart loved beauty in all forms, yet Mr. Wishart found it more in nature, in literature, music, and personality, Mrs. Wishart more in painting and sculpture, and architecture, and all the little things that go into the adornment of a home; she was sensitive to color and shape, to proportion, texture, light and shade. In appreciation of this sensitivity the room was named for her. Now there was a place to exhibit those few precious things the college had been fortunate enough to acquire; now it could make a bid for occasional traveling exhibits to be rented from various galleries; it could even have a showing now and then of the work of some of Wooster's own students. The room had been designed and made over by the new visiting professor in art, Theodore Brenson.[22] It was a beautiful room, high, long, and narrow, running from east to west, getting its light from the high Gothic windows at either end, light that had already been filtered through trees. With small lights recessed in its blue and gold coffered ceiling, it was perfect for its purpose. For the dedication

Mr. Franklin Biebel, '30, assistant to the director of the Frick Museum, gave the address. On this happy occasion there was unveiled by two of his grandchildren a portrait of Mr. Wishart. This was given by Mrs. Alva Bailey, trustee, and foster daughter of Mr. Birt E. Babcock.

Mr. Kelso in his day (he resigned in 1932) had given a real fillip to the appreciation of art in Wooster. Summer after summer he piloted parties through various European art galleries, lecturing as he went. From time to time several students took advantage of these tours. For some years, too, he had given at the college a course in the appreciation of art.[23] Yet there had been no real art department and since the days of Claribel Durstine no practical instruction. As a beginning, in 1928, he brought in Mrs. Florence Kennard, with her B.S. from Michigan State Normal College and advanced study at the Chicago Institute of Art. She had had considerable experience in teaching, and in Wooster, where she was living, she had classes for both adults and children. Her house was full of her own paintings. She quickly established herself in the tower room of Kauke Hall, which offered space for both classroom and studio work. In 1935 the administration added another instructor, Edward S. Peck, who had his M.A. in art from Oberlin. The department began to form. Three years later another instructor, Wendall N. Gates, was brought in. When both of these men went to the armed services, Mr. Brenson came as head of the department.

Many minor gifts had come to Wooster in these years, some of them treasures, two Beauvais tapestries, for instance, a rich Persian rug suitable for hanging, a succession of portraits of Wooster's presidents, Holden and White as well as Wishart, and of the old guard of the professors, Notestein, Bennett, Compton, Mateer, as well as T. K. Davis.[24] Classes, sometimes two or three together, had also added small endowments for lectures, concerts, or special books for the library. The classes of 1925 and 1926 had given the cast bronze lanterns for the chapel, the classes of 1914, 1915, and 1916 had built the white brick entrance gates at the stadium. The Student Senate had employed Pitkin and Mott of Cleveland to landscape the north banks of the stadium. They had put in various plantings, flowering crabapples and evergreens especially, honeysuckles and creeping phlox to cover up the banks, had constructed a graceful stairway through the trees and down the bank with suitable approaches from the top. The college itself had employed these landscape architects to put in the planting around the president's house, later around Galpin and Douglass, and in 1924 had asked them to make an overall campus plan. This called for an east-west axis running from Galpin to the stadium. It was in this general period that the old lane from Bever to Beall Avenue, that had serviced the back of Kauke, was relocated. Beyond Kauke it had followed the contour of the land winding through the grove to the south of the swale, to the back of the observatory and thence to Beall Avenue. Now it was straight as a poker. It was about time for the old oaks on the campus to begin to murmur to the dogwoods that this world was no longer what it used to be.

Ledgers and Men

Y ET nothing comes for nothing, and the best and most welcome gifts in the end beget expense. As Wooster grew in attendance, in faculty, and in the physical plant, there was new urgency for money, for salaries, pensions, and scholarships, for books, equipment, and maintenance, and for additions to the plant. By 1925 the million dollars of the 1920–1922 campaign had been paid in and much of it stowed away in bonds and first-class mortgages. Even the then existing deficit had been paid off according to the terms of the Rockefeller challenge grant. Yet now again Wooster's garments were showing thin; the college must go once more a-begging. To be sure, the Alumni Association set up in 1927 an annual giving plan, but at first the return from this was almost negligible.[1]

The time, 1928, seemed right. The boom was at its height. Everyone was on top of the world, in a mood to spend and sometimes to give. The trustees had anticipated this moment and had set up an advisory committee of business men familiar with current trends and with persons who might be approachable in behalf of the college. They were A. C. Ernst, chairman, Oscar Hagen, Harris Creech, W. M. Clapp, Walter Chrysler, Cecil Gamble, John F. Miller, Samuel G. McClure, '86, and David Ross Boys, '79, who as president of the University of Oklahoma had known the hazards of being a college president. A. C. Ernst became the chairman of the national campaign, and was to devote much of his time and his brains to its organization. Marts and Lundy were put in charge of the actual fund-raising. The total was set for a million and a half. Quotas were announced. Wooster and Wayne County were again to lead off by raising $150,000 (November 30–December 10, 1928). By June, 1929, the alumni were to have completed their quota of $300,000. An equal amount was allotted to the Presbyterian Synod of Ohio. There was every expectation that individuals of large wealth could be touched for the remaining three quarters of a million.

The local drive was successful. The year before, Wayne County had ranked first in Ohio in wheat production (60,000 acres). It was estimated that the college and the students spent in Wooster and the county annually close to $750,000. Actually in 1929 the town did a retail business of nearly ten million dollars.[2] Walter Foss, former trustee, once more showed his loyalty by guaranteeing the last $16,000 of the local quota.

In June of 1929, the alumni also met their quota. Headquarters meanwhile had been set up in Cleveland, in the Hippodrome Building, and regular bulletins under the title of *The Standard Bearer* were going out stating the purpose and progress of the campaign, detailing facts and comments as to Wooster's needs and place in the world. The campaign in the presbyteries was set for the fall of 1929.

Wooster had much about which to be proud. It was a good small college. It was seeking money that it might maintain this position and go on to better things. In September of 1929 it opened with 834 students,[3] from twenty-two states and twelve foreign countries. It had won a chapter of Phi Beta Kappa. It had other departmental national honor societies. It had a faculty of seventy, one fourth of them with Ph.D.'s. Twenty-eight others had M.A.'s, and of these a good many were planning to continue their graduate work as soon as they could accumulate the funds. In the sciences Wooster was particularly strong. The arrangement made with accredited medical schools back in 1919 still stood. For graduation all Wooster students were required to take two full years of science. In the interval since the last campaign German had been restored to the curriculum. Departments in economics, sociology, and political science had been set up. Courses in Italian, World War history, and accounting had been added. English and history as always were popular. However, 194 students were registered in biology, 99 in trigonometry, 30 in calculus. In 1927–1928 nearly 600 of the 800 students were taking modern languages, 277 Latin and or Greek (204 of these Latin).

Wooster was proud of the alumni and their records. Thirty-two of them had become college presidents; 175 others had gone into college teaching. In secondary or primary schools, or as superintendents or principals there were nearly 900 others. Four hundred ministers and 112 missionaries were on the alumni rolls. Many others were distinguished in business, law, medicine, or other fields. In 1927 Arthur Compton had been awarded the Nobel prize in physics, and thereby Wooster felt itself, incidentally, greatly honored, and had celebrated the occasion one morning in chapel.

After the 1920–1922 campaign the college had raised salaries; it now needed to raise them again. It had just put in a full-time health service for the students. It had attempted to streamline its business by a budget system. It did not yet feel justified in putting in a full-time business manager. Since 1927 it had, however, employed a director of admissions who served also as director of vocational guidance and placement.

On February 1, 1927, a contributory pension plan (T.I.A.A.) was inaugurated for the college teaching staff, and on October 28, 1938, this was extended to include the non-teaching staff. Members became eligible after three years of service. They paid in a small percentage of their salaries, and the college contributed an equal amount.

In the fall of 1929 the third phase of the campaign was to begin. At a Wooster meeting on October 15 in Cleveland Mr. Ernst said:

We are fighting to maintain Wooster's position. . . . They [the faculty] mean more than any building on the campus. We pay our professors $1000 per year less than the average. *Is that fair to them? Is it wise in the face of competition?* Then take our material equipment. We have outgrown our library. Is it any credit to us to have twelve or thirteen thousand volumes for which we have absolutely no shelf room?

To back up what he was saying he announced that he was pledging $100,000. Columbus Presbytery was launching its campaign for Wooster on October 21, the first of the presbyteries. W. O. Thompson, retired president of Ohio State University and now, since 1927, chairman of Wooster's Board of Trustees, was quoted in *The Standard Bearer* as saying: "There are three Christian colleges in Ohio, Wooster, Oberlin, and Ohio Wesleyan University, which are doing more for the betterment of mankind than any six of our state universities." Then at the end of October the stock market broke wide open. Nevertheless on December 31, 1929, the total stood at $689,586.58. Nearly two years later, the outstanding pledges still came to $247,721.31. In the end the amount actually paid in in the 1928–1929 campaign was well on to a million. In the years just ahead when interest rates were dwindling, this was a useful backlog, even though it was far from what they needed.

The next few years culminating in the bank crashes of 1932 and 1933 were ones of worry if not of actual hardship for nearly everyone. Many persons across the country had been wiped out of their savings of years; many lost their jobs and had to sell whatever they still had, to support their families. The plight of students was just as bad in its way; they could not get jobs; and many of them did not have the money to come to college. Even before 1929 nearly half of the students at Wooster were earning at least part of their college expenses. The situation in the fall of 1930 was worse. Colleges must have students, yet if they were to have them, they must do something to ease the financial plight of these students. Wooster decided to give financial aid to those who must have it or leave college. In 1930 this meant 306 persons and a debt on this account alone of $34,000 plus. This action was in line with President Hoover's Commission on Unemployment and had the approval of Governor White of Ohio. (Tuition at this time was $125 a year, not including incidentals or fees for operation and maintenance.) It seemed an act of desperation, but it held the college together.[4] At the end of the year friends of the college contributed enough to bring the deficit on this account down to $12,000 plus. Deficits were nevertheless mounting. In 1932–1933 the college cut $64,000 from its current budget, $36,000 of this from the instructional column. Salaries of those in the upper echelons of the teaching staff and administration were reduced by thirty per cent. Other ranks suffered lesser cuts. Happily in April of 1932 the Carnegie Foundation for the Advancement of Teaching made the Wooster library a grant of $3000 a year for five years.

In some respects indeed Wooster had been fortunate in all this period. In 1930 and 1931 $65,000 in endowment for scholarships had come in two wills.[5] Later there were others. There had been various small gifts of books. In the bank-closing of 1933 only $20,000 of endowment had been completely tied up in banks "in charge of conservators and drawing no interest." Two hundred thousand of other endowment was "frozen in mortgages either under foreclosure, or in such condition the borrower cannot meet his interest obligations." Wooster had endowment funds in the trust departments of both The Union Trust Company and The Guardian Trust Company of Cleveland. In both instances these funds were not involved when the banks closed their doors. Those in The Union Trust were turned over to The Central United Bank of Cleveland, those in The Guardian to The Cleveland Trust Company. Of course one of the unfortunate things in this whole period was that the deficit was mounting not only in cash but in deferred maintenance. Everything that could be postponed had been postponed.[6]

In 1933–1934 the budget was once more balanced temporarily, and the trustees restored ten per cent to the faculty with the heaviest cuts in their salaries. The budget for 1934–1935 was, however, once more seriously out of balance. Interest rates on endowment were down from 5.7 per cent to 4. An emergency appeal went out to alumni, and by June of 1935 they had contributed $7500 toward this. So the story went on from year to year, up and down, usually down. Yet by June of 1936 the trustees were able to make an additional move toward the restoration of salaries.[7] Income on investments had risen, and the prospect was that full restoration could be made before long. It was in 1936, too, that John D. McKee was asked to take over as business manager. This position did not at all concern itself with finances but rather with the overseeing and maintenance of all buildings and grounds. The treasurer was thus relieved of this extra responsibility.

As the decade drew to a close the trustees decided that the time had come for another financial campaign, along the lines of the previous campaigns. The beginning, in 1939, was to mark the twenty years of President Wishart's administration, the end was to coincide with the seventy-fifth anniversary of the granting of Wooster's charter in December 1941. When they outlined to themselves Wooster's needs they recognized that two million were needed, yet under existing circumstances they thought it best to set the immediate goal for $500,000 only. They hoped of course for more than that. The alumni themselves, they felt, could give this much if so minded, the town and county $50,000 more. Wooster now had 1000 students,[8] the number Mr. Wishart had mentioned as the desirable maximum in his inaugural. Nearly eighty were on the faculty. Wooster was one of nine colleges with a working agreement with the Massachusetts Institute of Technology similar to that made in 1919 with medical schools. Among Presbyterian colleges its faculty ranked second in the number of books and articles published in the last five years. Every student had a faculty adviser, and fifty-two per cent of all entering freshmen went on to graduation. On the other hand a new building was urgently needed for the library, and an endowment for the library of $500,000.[9] Besides, endowments were needed for several chairs. The Compton Chair still lacked $60,000 of reaching its goal.[10] One hundred thousand each were needed for chemistry, biology, the social sciences, for fine arts, for music, to bring them up to what comparable colleges had. And there were still buildings needed, notably a dormitory for women.

The campaign of course started with the usual flourish, the faculty and students oversubscribing their quota. The great event was the dinner in January, 1940, to open the drive in town and county. Some three hundred persons were present to hear the address by Wendell Willkie, who was at that time a potential candidate for nomination to the Presidency on the Republican ticket and who would be the real candidate before too many months. Willkie was at his best and made a "great appeal for colleges like Wooster." [11] With such a beginning all should have gone well. Instead the campaign never really got going. It dragged on through 1940, and with less and less vigor through 1941. It had been unhappily timed. The second World War began in Europe in August of 1939 and though the United States was not directly involved till December, 1941, its shadow darkened the world. The total raised after expenses was only a fraction of what had been the expectation. In the meantime faculty and trustee committees had been set up to study possible economies. It had been a dismal end.

Yet even in disappointment Wooster had every reason to hold its head high. Though December 18, 1941, was the official anniversary, in October of that year on Homecoming weekend, the 75th anniversary of Charter Day was celebrated on the campus.[12] It was a time when alumni would be returning anyhow, and the plan was to make this day one especially honoring alumni. At noon of Thursday all classes were dismissed for the rest of the week. On Thursday afternoon and Friday there was a succession of lectures by alumni on subjects pertaining to their special fields or interests. John Mateer, Robert Wilson, Arthur Compton, Wallace Notestein, William Taeusch, Robert Caldwell, and Carl Weygandt all spoke. The premier of Fred Eastman's play *The Old School* [13] was presented in the Little Theater. Genevieve Rowe and Robert Hill gave a joint recital on Sunday evening. A tablet to the memory of James A. Reed was affixed to a rock in front of Galpin and dedicated. At the banquet on

Friday night Governor Raymond E. Baldwin of Connecticut gave the address. President Wishart preached on Sunday, and on Saturday there was the Case-Wooster game, the ensuing bonfire, and the dance in the gymnasium.

During the remaining years of Mr. Wishart's administration there were deficits every year ranging from $20,000 to $40,000. Committees of trustees and faculty cooperated in suggesting economies. In the summer of 1942 the faculty taught in the summer school without salary, thereby cutting $10,000 from the estimated deficit for the year. The alumni annual giving program seemed to be taking hold. In 1941–1942 alumni gave some $16,000, in 1942–1943 nearly $22,000. That same year the Presbyterian churches of Ohio contributed a wizened $7000.[14] It was in 1943 that the trustees finally began buying some preferred and some common stocks, blue chips only, such as American Telephone and Telegraph, General Electric, Union Carbide, and Chase National Bank.

The strain of these years was considerably alleviated by the president's having loyal and able assistants.[15] Yet in 1940 both the treasurer, James R. McLaughlin, and the assistant treasurer, Walter E. Painter, retired. Mr. McLaughlin had been in the service of the college for twenty-nine years,[16] Mr. Painter in the treasurer's office for eighteen, and also for the nine years from 1909–1918 he had served as instructor and then as assistant principal of the preparatory department. Mr. Painter had been quiet and efficient, a gentle soul who went his way, did his job, and sought no applause.[17] Mr. McLaughlin was a crusty Scotsman, able, and willing, and dependable, to whom the college owed much for his long service under many trying circumstances. He had been a loyal and watchful guardian of every penny, and had served also for part of the time as business manager as well. The college could well say to him, "Well done, good and faithful servant," for that he had been; yet there were those who couldn't remember ever having seen him smile.

In his place the trustees chose Bruce Knox of the accounting firm of Ernst and Ernst in Cleveland.[18] He was another Scotsman, penny-wise and pound-prudent, not so dour as his predecessor, though some found him difficult and liked to refer to him as "Mr. Noxious." He engaged indeed in many battles over the budget. He was tall and thin, always well-dressed, and he felt a certain dignity of office. He bought himself a house ensconced in a grove of old oaks within walking distance of the campus, and there in his off hours he tended his roses and grew fine pansies from seed. His clumps of Christmas roses were probably as fine as any in town. His pride and joy was his little dog, and when Terry strolled away on an errand of his own there was panic in the household. But he worried, too, about the college and its monies to the point of developing ulcers, and he was a careful guardian at all times. His regular reports to the trustees were always clear, businesslike, adequate, and informative. A college, however, was a new environment for him, and he soon discovered that he was in for a bit of educating. He wanted, for instance, to cut the budget for books; after all the library housed thousands of books; were they not enough for a thousand students? But he learned in time that knowledge knows no limits. The library, he found at last, was at the heart of any college.

In 1927 Mr. Wishart acquired a new secretary, who became a college institution. He was Curt N. Taylor from Kansas, a graduate of Emporia College. For some time he had been working in the offices of The Presbyterian Board of Christian Education. In the first World War he had served for sixteen months in Army headquarters at Chaumont, France. He was a quiet man, yet not too quiet, for he could smile and he could laugh, was gracious to every one, and was efficient and loyal, with that rare ability of knowing how and when not to talk. A secret was as safe with him as if it had been shut in an oyster. Presently he became not only Mr. Wishart's secretary but that of the college as well. He attended all meetings of the Board of Trustees, took the minutes, sent them out, and took minutes also of the administrative (formerly executive) committee. He became a storehouse of information. When all else failed, one asked Curt Taylor, and usually he could come up with the date, the place, the time, and the person. But he never told a word too much. He just did not know what he should not know. As he stored secrets in his head, like a squirrel he stored everything else. The filing cases were all in order, yet the top of every one of them and of everything else level in his office was piled high with precious papers, magazines, pamphlets. Strangers looking in gasped at what they thought disorder; they were wrong. In five minutes, or less, Curt Taylor could pull out anything one might ask for from those piles. He knew, instinctively, just as a new-born kitten knows where to look for its breakfast. He had other idiosyncracies, if one chooses to call them such. His two telephones were always perched on a small table by a windowsill, not on his desk. Persons were always dropping into his office to use the telephone; he did not want them leaning over his desk and perhaps inspecting confidential papers. He was canny, and he was also very human. He had plants on one windowsill. On the ledge of another he used to feed the gray squirrels who made a habit of stopping by. Beyond was an old dogwood tree that was always a joy to him as he looked out. He used to walk back and forth to lunch, often all the way to town. He didn't have a car and yet he could tell you on which road an especially fine red rhododendron in bloom was to be seen. He attended lectures and concerts, yet the lights burned many an evening in his office when all other lights in Galpin were out. He was just Curt Taylor, none other, and generations of students and faculty revered him for what he was. The president (Mr. Wishart, and later Mr. Lowry) could not have functioned without him.

XXI

A New Generation

Have you ever asked yourselves what quality best expresses
the American character . . . ? It is the spirit of expectancy.
. . . The whistle of the locomotive or of the steamboat . . . are
symbols of expectancy,—they carry our eyes, and then our
hearts, and wills, beyond the bend. . . . If there is anything this
nation has to give the world beyond its technological and
organizing genius, it is surely this sense of expectancy. . . .
There are individual human beings like that, for whom the
door to the future is always open. . . . It is the nearest thing
we know to perpetual youth.[1]

AS Wooster had marched into the twenties it was seeing the
last of the so-called Old Guard of the faculty whose memories stretched to the days before the fire. J. G. Black (Jacky
Black) though retired continued to live at his home on
Burbank Road for nearly sixteen more years.[2] Bennett had left in
1924 to pass the days of his retirement in California.[3] Behoteguy had
died in February, 1925, at the home of his son in Phoenix, Arizona.[4]
Mateer gave up teaching in 1926,[5] to remain, however, in Wooster
among his friends. Compton was struck down by illness, yet never
daunted, in 1927–1928, he went, with Mrs. Compton, to India to see
his daughter in the land of his youthful dreams, and on around the
world.[6] In June of 1928, he retired, laden with tributes from Wooster men and women as they gathered for the Compton Commencement.[7] Four days later, on a cold June morning in his tree-surrounded
home among his family and his books, J. O. Notestein was to say
farewell to this earth.[8] Miss Gingrich only was left. In 1924 she had
come back to reestablish her German department, which with some
assistance she carried on until 1935, when she, too, retired.

Now the old-timers were Martin, Vance, Dunn, Lean, Kelso,
Olthouse, Yanney, Knight, Remp, Boles, both of the Rowes, and the
Parmelees. On these one must rely. Yet as always there was a
younger generation of faculty, some of them still going and coming as
they took off for a year or two at a time to finish graduate studies.
Others had already found their place and had settled in. Some were

researchers by instinct and were to make names for themselves; some were teachers first of all.

Of the older generation Mr. Yanney was still advocating the reform of the calendar.[9] Mr. Martin was still singing, still playing golf, still happily interpreting the minor prophets.[10] Vance was still the punctilious dean of men though often with a twinkle in his eye, and so would remain until 1930 when he would turn over the deanship to the young James Anderson, and thereafter continue only as the Mercer Professor of Religion. In his spare time he had made a hobby of photography and kept a photographic record of his classes. He as well as his wife loved music, but his taste ran rather toward the heavier Wagner themes as in art he delighted in the depth and brilliancy of Rembrandt. Mr. Dunn was still striding across the campus, his eyes fixed on the pavement, his mind on something probably far away. On his personal agenda he always had some research project,[11] but that did not interfere with his usefulness as a member of the faculty; in 1924–1925 while Mr. Kelso was studying at Harvard and in California, he acted as temporary dean. Mr. Olthouse since 1919 had been professor of French and of French alone and so would continue throughout a long and useful career.[12] To his colleagues, in committee meetings he sometimes seemed inflexible, laboring a point unnecessarily, yet he was genuine and good-natured and never held a grudge. One of his delights was to sing in the oratorio chorus, in his church choir, and to lead off in singing French songs at the Epiphany dinner of the Cercle Français. He was after all a jovial soul. Since 1925 Martin Remp had been devoting all his energy to teaching psychology—he had become head of his department—and others had taken over the work in education.[13] He remained the friend and trusted counselor of many young men not too sure of where they were tending, and he took an active part not only in faculty but in community life. Boles was to spend his sabbatical year of 1926–1927 at Stanford and the University of Southern California studying the tactics of other distinguished athletic coaches.

Mr. Lean was still the droll person he always had been, much in demand as a speaker and as a judge of intercollegiate debates, going as far as Michigan and Evanston (Illinois) on such chores. In his regular courses he had sometimes a total of 100 students. He and his able assistant, Emerson W. Miller, who came as professor of speech in 1925, were advising many Ohio high schools not only in their methods of training debaters but in the rounding up of suitable material for debate. With all his various activities he still found time for his annual reading in December of Dickens' *Christmas Carol* and for another pre-Christmas activity in which he found great joy. Two days before Christmas, made up as a realistic Santa Claus, he called on all his little friends in the neighborhood, children, many of them, of colleagues on the faculty, asking of each of them Christmas orders and recording these in a little black book, a book he treasures to this day. He was as if to the chimney-born. He had a special technique [14] which never seemed to fail; and often he took along with him as clerk, an assistant Santa, Howard Lowry of the English department. He in turn was usually decked out in a discarded Santa costume turned inside out. It was not exactly in the academic tradition, yet it was a heart-warming experience for all who witnessed or had a part in it.

Mrs. Rowe since 1915 had along with her husband been teaching in the music department, instructing in piano, and from time to time also in harmony, or the history or appreciation of music. Besides this work she was hostess for the conservatory, entertaining the staff, going out of her way to make each one feel at home in Wooster and with one another. Her husband meanwhile had become one of Wooster's old dependables. The Parmelees, too, were always active within the conservatory and outside. Dan Parmelee had come back to Wooster in 1924 after seven years of absence. He had been to war. In 1919 he married Clarice Paul,[15] also a graduate in music of Oberlin, who for five years had been teaching piano in Cleveland. Together they set up a studio with others in Lakewood. With that as a base he taught for some time at Baldwin Wallace, and played as well in the Cleveland Orchestra. In 1923–1924 they both went to France to study, in Paris and at Fontainebleau. He still had connections in Wooster, however, and in 1924 he was brought back as an assistant professor in the conservatory, and once more took over the direction of the Wooster Orchestra.[16]

Wooster had never approved assembly-line education; it was a small college by choice. Except in special instances, classrooms rarely accommodated more than fifty, if so many. Its dormitories had been built in small units, usually for fewer than 100 persons, where a head resident could really know the students under his or her supervision. It believed in "cottage dining," where student could become acquainted with student, where manners were important. Though growing steadily it still hoped to keep untarnished the values of a small institution. The faculty were geared to this plan of working. They knew the individual students in their classes, their abilities, usually also their background, and some of their special problems. A few of them held open house at their homes on Friday evenings after literary society meetings. Some of them were honorary or sponsoring members of the various student clubs and organizations. Some of them had evening seminars in their homes, and this custom was encouraged by the new dean, Mr. Westhafer, when he took over in 1930.

One of these faculty members, though one of the least conspicuous, was Lyman Coleman Knight, assistant professor of mathematics since 1915, instructor even before that. He had been a teacher nearly all his life, a country school teacher first of all, before he had had a chance to go ahead with his own education. His background was different from that of most of Wooster's faculty. He had come up the hard way, on a farm. There he had learned to love the land and all it brought forth. He had learned also patience and a way of homely explanation that served him well in teaching. He had studied much, and had much experience to add to his native ability. Students used to say of him that he could arrive at the answer to a problem faster than they could read it. He still had a farm in Congress township which was for him both solace and delight. There was a 100–year old flowing spring, barns full of hay and fodder in their season, banks thick with hemlocks where underneath trailing arbutus bloomed in early spring, and hills where he could plant pines and practice reforestation. To this farm from time to time he took many college men, sometimes only to have a chance to talk with them or to give them a taste of country life, sometimes to give an afternoon's job to some who needed jobs—perhaps to cut and shock corn in the fall. He was always patient with their lack of know-how on these occasions, and with their awkwardness with unfamiliar tools. Howard Lowry, '23, was one of these; and once in later years he talked of these trips back and forth with Mr. Knight in his car and of the man he had then come to know: of his "love of earth, . . . his humor and human understanding . . . the homely grandeur of his soul. . . . these little roads he traveled, seeing with eyes of wonder each human and natural thing as divine—these obscure Wayne County roads," he said, "have led him [Mr. Knight] everywhere in the world." Yet of all the college boys those on the athletic teams were those to whom he was closest. He was faculty manager of athletics until the coming of Coach Boles. In an article in *The Daily Record* (December 26, 1950) Arthur Murray says of Mr. Knight: "More than any other single individual he was responsible for keeping football alive in the days before the era of Coach L. C. Boles. . . ." And after Boles' coming he was still on the job helping as he could. He was long a familiar figure in the Ohio Intercollegiate Athletic Association, once served as its president, for years thereafter on its executive committee. Lame though he was because of an accident, he was almost idolized by these boys.

Wooster faculty indeed were encouraged to be human beings in relation to their students, yet most of them were human beings naturally or they never would have taken to teaching as a profession. They played roque in Galpin Park, volleyball in the gymnasium. There was a group of faculty Thespians who from time to time provided dramatic entertainment for their colleagues, sometimes for a larger audience. In this Fred Moore was a leader.[17] Vocational conferences, too, were becoming the order of the day. When the director of vocational guidance asked them to put on their own conference for the students, they did: Westhafer talking of opportunities in science, Arthur Murray and John D. McKee on publicity and journalism, Tostlebe on business, Emerson Miller on law as a profession, A. A. Johnston on the social sciences as a life opportunity, Williamson[18] on both engineering and architecture. The faculty were indeed kept on the go in extra-curricular activity, until they needed to work out a point system of their own. They had to take their turn in speaking at daily chapel, and for some years they provided five o'clock lectures for the students on Monday afternoons in Taylor Hall on subjects related to their research, their hobbies, or their travels.

Through the twenties, and to a lesser degree, perhaps, in the thirties Wooster, so far as the faculty was concerned, was in an expanding period, a circumstance which one must probably attribute to the dean, though undoubtedly the president, too, deserves a share of the credit. Mr. Kelso with all his teaching, with all his summer traveling, had always clearly before him the goal of academic excellence. He knew where he was going. He was getting himself around in academic circles. He was all the time comparing Wooster with other like institutions, analyzing to see wherein lay its weakness and its strength. He was encouraging his faculty to better their work and their scholarly preparation for it.

In 1925 he had made a study of Wooster in comparison with Denison, Oberlin, Marietta, Ohio Wesleyan, Beloit, Knox, Carleton, Grinnell, and Swarthmore. The results had been enlightening, and these he laid before his faculty. He found Wooster below the median in endowment and in college income per student, yet slightly above the median, though still low, in salaries paid to professors and assistant professors, and definitely above the median for instructors. The standard rating for graduate study set by the North Central Association of Colleges and Secondary Schools at this time was two years for all teachers, and the possession of a Ph.D. or its equivalent for all heads of departments. In both these categories Wooster rated sixth among the ten colleges chosen, her rating being sixty-five and sixty-six per cent respectively in the two categories. Wooster's tally for the number of students per teacher was thirteen, the ideal eight, while the median for the ten colleges stood at a little less than twelve. In the number of students, however, entering as freshmen and remaining through graduation, Wooster ranked third. Where Wooster failed lamentably was in the number of books in its library and in the annual expenditure per student for library books. In that respect Wooster was then nearly at the foot of the class with only 60,000 volumes and only $4.10 spent per student. Over against this record Mr. Kelso listed Wooster's other physical equipment, the spirit of sound scholarship, the acceptance and promulgation of the scientific method, and Christian idealism. "These," he said, "are here, and the torch of high purpose, sincerity, and democracy has not fallen, it has been passed on to the younger men in leadership by the Old Guard.[19] If Wooster is to attain an academic program of high distinction, she must remain 'in the tradition.' But the impelling torch of the tradition must be a steady and increasing quest of the best."

Through the twenties Kelso had been working toward this goal, bringing in or promoting a younger generation who were not only in the tradition but measuring up or on the way to measuring up to the standards set. Some of them were Wooster graduates of unusual promise whom Wooster had kept for a year or two to test that promise in actual teaching, and to whom was then given leave for the pursuing of their graduate studies.

One of these, of course, was Warren Spencer, a teacher and a researcher born, who in time became a nationally and internationally recognized geneticist. His particular interest was fruit flies. Breeding generation after generation of these in the laboratory, under the microscope he watched each for possible mutations, then bred again those in which he found these, and so again and again. The lights shone late in his laboratory. When he finally went home to bed at midnight or often at two or three, he could hardly wait till morning to begin again the search, to see whether "the facts of today" would bear out the "hypothesis of yesterday." His was the search for pure truth, and of this search, he once said: "Maybe what he [the scientist] discovers will help mankind right away; maybe it won't help the race for hundreds or even thousands of years to come; maybe it won't help at all." He exchanged fruit flies with the zoological department of the Kyoto Imperial Institute of Japan, and he went to Edinburgh in the summer of 1939 to give a paper at the International Congress of Genetics. In World War II the government had him working in Rochester on the effects of radiation on fruit flies. In 1938 he was given a grant by the Rockefeller Foundation to assist in the selection of data for a book on the general biology of the fruit fly, and he spent a year at another time at the California Institute of Technology.[20] A researcher primarily, he could also teach with such enthusiasm that one after another of his students went off to graduate work, and he had more than one chance to go elsewhere. He preferred, however, a small college and a small town. Absent-minded and oblivious of time when his research was involved, he was in off hours a welcome companion, humorous and appreciative of many small delights. He loved to explore for himself the back roads of Wayne County and where they led, whether to "Mud College" [21] or elsewhere, and he was always alert to amusing bits in the local newspaper.

Ralph Bangham, who came to the biology department in 1923 from Texas, was a very different sort, yet a researcher too. His field was the parasites of fish, and he pursued these in summers at various laboratories throughout the country, at Woods Hole, at the Rocky Mountain Biological Laboratory, at the University of British Columbia, in Tennessee and elsewhere. His papers appeared in scientific journals and occasionally in those slightly more popular. In 1925 he published a life cycle of the fish tapeworm, and in 1926 he became the zoology editor of the *Journal of Science*. He gave one course in parasitology. Several of the fish parasites were honored in being named for him, "——banghami." He was a Quaker with the characteristics often associated with Quakers, serenity, dependability, reticence, and kindliness. An Ohioan he had gone to Haverford where he had taken both his B.S. and his M.A., where he also had been a graduate assistant and instructor in biology, and then to Ohio State University for his doctorate. He had come to Wooster after three years of teaching at Texas Agricultural and Mechanics Junior College and at Baylor University. At the latter a dispute had arisen over the teaching of evolution. This fact made the offer of an assistant professorship at Wooster attractive, where he knew he would be free to teach the theory without hindrance or complaint. To look at him one might pick him out as possible candidate for a track team; he had in fact gone out for track in college, and even while teaching at Wooster he was sometimes called to judge track meets. Quiet as he was, he was interested in his students, and made a point of seeing much of them and entertaining those in his courses. His wife, Margaret, shared this interest, and before Christmas every year they gave a party for the junior and senior biology majors. Again after commencement they gave the senior majors a buffet supper. For years Margaret Bangham was collecting the appropriate accessories for these occasions, a fishnet tablecloth, starfish candelabras, and whelk shells in which she arranged flowers. As head of the department later, he entertained his biology colleagues; on a Saturday afternoon they could often be found playing ping pong on the Bangham sun terrace.

In the same fall of 1923 another scientist joined the faculty as assistant professor of geology, Karl Ver Steeg.[22] He was explosive and, often, even irascible, and sometimes the girls in his classes were frightened by his big, booming voice; yet he turned out good geologists and helped them to get jobs. He took his students out on field trips to learn to interpret the landscape hereabouts in terms of geology, and to see whatever offered itself of special interest in the vicinity, such as a coal mine in New Philadelphia, the Blue Hole at Castalia, and the mines of the American Gypsum Company. He thus made geology a living science with practical applications, not just a chapter in the history of the earth. His own enthusiasm was so infectious that many of his students went on to advanced study in this field. His colleagues were consequently inclined to overlook his eccentricities. With time off in which to complete his doctorate at Columbia, he remained as head of his department until his death.

In Wooster's graduating class of 1923 there had been a boy who from the beginning had singularly attracted the president, the dean, the head of the English department, and others. He was discerning, insatiable in his zest for learning, sensitive to beauty of whatever sort; he was brilliant in analysis and in expression, humorous and human. He could come up with questions that made even his professors sit up. He had been a debater and college orator, he was a member of Delta Sigma Rho and Pi Kappa Lambda as well as the local general honor society (later to be chartered by Phi Beta Kappa). He played tennis, was an ardent rooter at baseball and football games, particularly baseball; and like the good Lord he loved everybody, even when his intelligence may sometimes have told him better. The college offered him an instructorship in English. He loved Wooster, he needed money, and he took the position. For two years he remained at this post, then he went off to Yale to begin the trek toward a doctorate in English. At the end of two years, when he had chosen the nature of his thesis, he went to England for some preliminary investigation, then returned to Yale to teach there for a year. In the meantime Wooster had offered him an assistant professorship. In the fall of 1929 he once again began work at Wooster, though he could have stayed at Yale, but in 1930–1931 he was once more in England and France as Sterling Fellow of Yale and on leave from Wooster. His special field was Matthew Arnold, with particular reference to Arnold's influence on French literature and culture. He had, however, been entrusted by the Arnold family with Arnold's unpublished diaries and notebooks and this had constituted a haul. He had also been so fortunate as to make the acquaintance of the son of Arthur Hugh Clough, who gave him first the Emerson-Clough letters to edit for publication, and then all of Clough's letters. In 1931 he completed his doctorate, and in the fall he was back in Wooster, this time as professor and acting head of the English department in the absence of Mr. Dunn. The latter had gone to Scripps College in California as visiting professor. Mr. Dunn, however, was to return to Wooster for only one year [23] and then Mr. Lowry became the actual head of the department.

George Bradford had left Wooster in 1923 as instructor of French; in 1928 he came back as assistant professor of English to begin a long career.[24] In the meantime he had taught for three years at Case, and then had gone to the University of Wisconsin for graduate work in English. When he began in Wooster he had as yet only his Master's degree but with some work in advance of that. His special joy was his course in Chaucer. Not only the personages of *The Canterbury Tales* but their way of living at that time, their manners, dress, food, their amusements, and language, all became matters of importance. It was 14th century England to which his class was being introduced. One night each spring, beginning with 1931, the basement of Kauke Hall became the scene of a Chaucer banquet. It was turned into a great hall, with tapestries, or banners,—when they could find them—on the walls, a giant fireplace, the floor sometimes "strewn with flowers." The guests all came in appropriate apparel; [25] and many was the trip to the library made by members of the class as they planned their costumes and verified details. When all was ready and the guests were waiting outside, a trumpeter sounded the summons and they entered and seated themselves on the far side of a U-shaped table made of rough planks on stretchers. Two roasted pigs were carried in and placed before them. There was a benediction in Latin, and after that they all set to, eating from trenchers of bread while they were entertained sometimes by wrestlers and tumblers, sometimes by the recitation of a hunting tale or the singing of ballads by a group of minstrels. Afterwards a puppet show might possibly be put on, the puppets having been costumed and strung by the students themselves. It was an occasion which no student who had the privilege of attending would have missed.

Another professor, who came in 1926, had a gift for bringing a by-gone civilization to life for his students, Frank Hewitt Cowles, '07. He, too, occasionally had superintended the presentation of a scene out of the past on the quadrangle, as we have noted, the costumes Roman. He had come as professor of Latin and two years later, in 1928, had succeeded to the Aylesworth Professorship. On him Mr. Notestein had in a sense cast his mantle, for Mr. Cowles had been not only his one-time student but his choice as successor. He had been watching him ever since he left Wooster, at Huron College in South Dakota, at Cornell where he had taken his doctorate, at Wabash College where he had succeeded Hugh Kingery, '84, as professor of Latin, and where after two years he had been asked to take over also the deanship. The year before he came to Wooster he had been teaching at Princeton. Mr. Cowles offered many of the same courses as Mr. Notestein, notably a literary study of the *Aeneid* for advanced students. He, too, taught Latin *con amore*. He is said to have had much the same genuine interest in individual students as his predecessor. Though he had never seen Rome, he had so steeped himself in its literature and history, and had so familiarized himself with its poets, orators, and statesmen, with its art and architecture and way of life, that he could conjure up for his students the background of almost any situation or occasion and make it real. He could lecture on the various buildings of ancient Rome, as if he had seen the temples, palaces, and streets themselves. He was in the tradition. Yet he kept his nose to the grindstone, never taking a vacation, but teaching nearly every summer somewhere, for years at Columbia, where he gave one or two graduate courses.

He was popular with students and with faculty and had their respect. At faculty meetings he spoke rarely but cogently. His was a considered judgment; he thought of all the angles. It was the same when he took part in discussion as an elder of Westminster Church. In an emergency he could and did step into Wooster's deanship. He was invaluable on the teaching staff committee. Years later Mr. Lowry was to speak of Mr. Cowles' insight and common sense, of "the spaciousness of his mind. . . . He went far out of his way, to bring to our attention some human need in some member of the faculty or community. . . . I have known few men who so completely caught the nuances of every idea and situation." The girls of the college looked on him as something of a Beau Brummel. He was tall, dark and handsome, always well dressed, dignified yet friendly. He was musical as well (as was his wife), and had been a director of the men's Glee Club at Wabash College.

Many persons have found it hard to understand Vergilius Ferm, who came to Wooster in 1927, fresh from graduate work and one year of teaching at a small college in Pennsylvania and who ten years later was occupying the Compton Chair of philosophy. A slight man physically, he could for years be seen early and late walking across the campus, heavy book bag in hand, his shock of auburn hair blowing in the wind. He was a simple man essentially, with a craving for friendship, a desire to be helpful, and an urge to scholarship that drove him relentlessly to the writing and compiling of many books. With all of this, it seemed, especially in his later years at Wooster, as if somehow he was standing in his own light, a disillusioned and somewhat bitter man, trying to create an image—as the current phrase goes. This was rather more apparent in his chapel talks than anywhere else. He had a following nonetheless among his students, and spent much time on many of them individually; and they weren't afraid even in the classroom at times to put on an act, as one morning when at a predetermined signal they all started rolling apples across the floor.[26]

Mr. Ferm was the son of a Lutheran minister, and was ordained to the Lutheran ministry, but during his first pastorate in Iowa he took courses in philosophy at the state university, and found that philosophy after all was his calling. He then took his Ph.D. at Yale. He had married early, a calm, well-poised, and loyal wife. Their first two children, a son and a daughter, they lost, and this was a heart-breaking blow.—One of his books was later dedicated to Verginia [*sic*]. —Three sons, however, grew up to make their father proud. When one of these was ordained to the Presbyterian ministry, the father was asked to give the charge:

. . . And be not tempted too much to be other than yourself: for the world has a way of trying to flatten us into moulds and extinguish the spark that is by birthright our very own.

· · · · ·

. . . The common folk are the stuff of mankind, those who fix chimneys or drive trucks or mend boots. Make friends of them. . . .

· · · · ·

. . . The Christian religion is not anti-this or that; it is a religion of fulfillment of all that is good found anywhere in any culture or clime. . . . You are not to defend something, any more than you defend the light of sunshine. You are only to help transmit it where the light is less powerful so that men to whom you minister may better find their way.

Here was the real Vergilius Ture Anselm Ferm, simple and straightforward, father to son.

Wooster had from the beginning been a coeducational college. The trustees had determined that "the young women may here pursue the same course of intellectual training with the young men." President Lord had rejoiced in this decision for, he said, "The essential test of citizenship in the commonwealth of science and letters should be character, mental and moral quality, and attainment, not condition, race, color, or sex." The college had lived up to this principle in its willingness to accept and to graduate a host of young women, many of them with high honors; it had gone no further. On its Board of Trustees no woman was accorded a place until the election of Mrs. Ella Alexander Boole, '78, in 1918 by the alumni. Grace Smith, '08, was the next, elected by the alumni in 1922. There followed in 1924 the election of Helen Harrington Compton, '12, and in 1934 of Marguerite White Talbot, '11. (The term of an alumni trustee is three to six years unless the person is re-elected by the Board itself to a further term.) Until quite recently there have rarely been more than two women at a time, if so many, on the Board. In 1967, out of thirty-six members, six are women, a record.

Until President Wishart's administration and the coming of Mr. Kelso as dean, few women had been granted any real academic status on the faculty. There had been the rare exceptions: Annie B. Irish (1880–1886), who after a few months as lecturer in German literature, became professor of German; Eva Correll (1886–1893) followed her, and after them Professor Gertrude Gingrich (1893–1920 and again from 1924–1935). Mary Rebecca Thayer had come in 1918 as assistant professor of English and stayed to become a full professor in 1928. Emeline McSweeney, after years of teaching in the preparatory department, began all over again in the college in 1918, and eventually rose to being a professor of French. Then there was Miss Elizabeth Pendleton, who, even in those years when teaching only in the preparatory department, had been a welcome, highly respected, and sprightly personage in the Wooster faculty family. Later she had taught for some years in a minor capacity in the college, both English and history. The deans of women were expected as part of their normal assignment to teach a course in whatever was their field, yet until Miss Florence Root came in 1922, only one of them had at any time attained a rank above that of instructor. Other women had occasionally, especially in the war emergency, been brought in for a year or two to teach French perhaps or history, or to substitute for some professor on leave. Then there were those young women who in earlier days had taught drawing, music, even elocution, the parsley of women's education of that day; they were occasionally listed as instructors, yet they had to take themselves and their jobs seriously, for no one else did. For a while the directors of physical education for women were in much the same category. In 1896 this director was called the instructor in Delsarte culture; in 1898 and 1899, the "director of the Ladies Gymnasium." The terms were not only Victorian but tinged with a slight condescension. But all this had to change and did change. From the time of Ruth Conrow on, and especially after the coming of Kathleen Lowrie, a real department of physical education for women was in the making, with courses that were not only required but given credit.[27]

From these rather unimpressive beginnings Wooster was to see a whole succession of women take their places on the faculty. Beginning usually as instructors, several of them were in time to attain professorships and the chairmanship of their departments. Aileen Dunham, as we have already noted, was one of these. In her later years she could count around fifty of her former students who had taken their Ph.D.'s and were teaching history in colleges across the country. Mary Z. Johnson (Mary Z. to nearly everyone) was another. She came as an instructor in political science in 1926 and in time became head of her department. "Miss Dunham and Miss Johnson," to quote a lawyer who is one of Wooster's outstanding trustees, "were the two best teachers I ever had." Miss Johnson had all the makings of a zealot; her whole experience had tended to make her one. She decided as a young girl that she wanted to teach. At sixteen she was riding horseback eight miles a day in order to teach in a country school. In Idaho with three other women she homesteaded and staked out a quarter section of land while she was teaching. Much of her work for her B.A. from the University of Chicago had been by correspondence and when she finally won it, she was already well along in her thirties. Two years later she came to Wooster.[28] She threw herself into her teaching with her whole soul not caring how much it took out of her. She did everything that way. She was an ardent Democrat, a working member of the AAUW and of the League of Women Voters, an organizer of a chapter of Phi Sigma Alpha at Wooster, the national political science honor fraternity (she was also a Phi Beta Kappa), and a woman who spoke far and wide across the state urging women to take their stand in matters political. Yet she was first of all a teacher, careful of her facts, reading widely and keeping abreast of her field. Even after taking her Ph.D. in 1931, and becoming a full professor and chairman of the department in 1932, she never felt that she could turn aside from her main course to do research. Her business was the teaching of students in constitutional theory and processes so that they would be informed and responsible citizens of this land and this world, understanding their laws, and working always toward the betterment of the government wherever and however they came in contact with it. Firm, even demanding in her classes, she was quick to discern the student honestly groping his way and in need of special help and with him she was infinitely patient. She had known struggle herself; and she had known the joy of attainment. "Mary Z" set little store by appearances; her hats covered her head, as her clothes her body; sometimes one felt that she had just stepped out of a Victorian painting. Such things didn't matter much to her. But she cared mightily for government and for people, for fairness, high-mindedness, for clarity of thinking, purposeful work, and integrity in all.

Eva Mae Newnan came as a young woman to Wooster, tall, straight, lithe, dark, and comely, a person one looked at twice. There was something about her that enticed one yet kept one also at a distance. She wasn't shy. Her smile was enigmatic. There was a light deep in her eyes, a light that made one wonder. Perhaps her face in some rare moment had been brushed by the winds of heaven and she had never again been quite the same. That was her secret, hers alone. Her field was Greek and Latin, and the field became her, though it was in Greek that she found her special joy. She was equally at home talking of Homeric legends or of a tenth century nun, but her favorite course was the one that she gave in the Greek New Testament for young men planning to enter theological seminaries. Summers she sometimes took off to Greece or the Greek islands, to Egypt, Turkey, Palestine, or Italy, and once at least to England to trace the Roman remains there. Once she spent a sabbatical year in Greece studying at the Classical School in Athens, and was richer by far for the experience. She joined with several of her colleagues in reading together in the classics on occasional evenings. She herself collected over the years an excellent library, both in the classics and in general literature. Along with Frank Cowles she was instrumental in the winning for Wooster of a chapter of Eta Sigma Phi, the national honor fraternity of the classics. She was a Californian, trained at Stanford, with a Master's degree and several years of college teaching experience before she came to Wooster in 1927 as an assistant professor. Later she was to take her doctorate at the University of Chicago.[29] Eventually, she was promoted to a professorship, and for a brief while (1948–1950) she was the only professor of classics on the campus.

She had deep family loyalties and, when she could, in the summer she went back for a while to California. Though she may have been hard to know, she had close friends both among the faculty and on the outside; and she could be gay. Those in the AAUW, of which she was the president more than once, remember how at one of their party-sales she modelled clothes with the zest of a school-girl. One of her colleagues has been quoted as saying that Eva Newnan had one of the finest natures he had ever known. Therein were beauty and serenity, and strength.

There were other women beginning their service on Wooster's faculty during these early years of Mr. Wishart's administration, women who were to put down roots and stay for many years, and two at least of them were eventually to succeed to the headship of their respective departments: Pauline Ihrig, precise and capable, whose field was 19th century French prose and drama, and Elizabeth Coyle who taught in her time all the botany the college offered and bacteriology as well. There were others, not to be slighted, who came for a shorter while. One of Mr. Kelso's first appointments (1922) was that of Florence Kellogg Root, a young woman already with five years of experience as a dean of women at Pennsylvania College for Women in Pittsburgh. She came also with her Master's degree in Latin from Smith College (from which institution she had also her B.A. and a Phi Beta Kappa key), an additional year of graduate study at Columbia, and teaching experience both at Smith and at Pennsylvania College for Women. In her eight years at Wooster she gave the deanship of women a dignity and importance it had never had before. She had stature both physical and mental; she had ideals for the college woman, executive ability, and social quality; she knew where to put the emphasis and when to stand up and be firm. She had lived in the East and in the West, had had her own freshman year in a small coeducational western college. In 1923 she served for a term as secretary of the National Association of Deans of Women. She established her home outside the dormitories. To this she brought her mother, and there she entertained informally. Though teaching a course in Latin, she had time to think up activities among the girls that would widen their horizons; among these was the organizing of a college branch of the League of Women Voters. Her whole influence was on the side of maturity.

Then there was Ruth Richardson,[30] who gave twenty years of her life to Wooster, first as an instructor in Spanish, then as an assistant professor before going on to Oberlin, and then to Adelphi. She was an excellent teacher, stiff in her requirements. In faculty she was equally firm and fearless, even when she was in the minority. Yet she never held a grudge and was generous in her personal life almost to a fault.

In music there were others, Mrs. Parmelee of course, and Eve Roine Richmond, who came in the fall of 1926 as instructor in vocal music in the conservatory. She had studied for four years in New York with Yeatman Griffith and had then been his assistant for a year. She immediately made for herself a place as a teacher and as a singer. One heard her nearly every Sunday at church in a solo or a solo-part in an anthem. She sang at weddings and at funerals. She directed the Girls' Glee Club, and in the years ahead she was to take the club on many trips. The programs on these occasions, as is almost always true of college glee clubs, tended toward the popular in music rather than the classical, but she had trained the girls with skill, and they were repeatedly booked for a return in the following year. Many Presbyterian churchmen and churchwomen came to know Wooster better through Eve Richmond and her chorus. Through this activity as well as through her normal teaching, generations of Wooster college girls came to love her. She instructed them, too, in much else, in how to dress and how to behave, and especially in platform manners. She herself seemed always cheerful and she had a dramatic flair of which she made the most. Her moment at Wooster of greatest triumph was probably when Genevieve Rowe won the Atwater Kent award.

Women indeed came into their own in this period. Though they did not receive salaries comparable with those of the men, they were recognized and valued. In the library the only person to have faculty status was the head librarian, Elizabeth Bechtel. For some years she had assistants at the desk or helping her in some minor capacity, recent graduates and even some students. Yet with the increase of enrollment, the constantly greater requirements in reference reading, and in the number of books being purchased, she found it necessary to enlarge her permanent staff. Though Gretchen White, *ex* '11, and Fern Kieffer had, for some years before, been assisting her, in 1927 Miss White became head of the reference department and Miss Kieffer head of the reserve department. In 1928 Ruth McClelland, fresh out of college, was added to the staff as an assistant, to serve in that capacity for a year before going off to take her B.S. in library science and to return as head cataloguer.

Yet in all this there is no hint that the period marked only the ascendancy of women. Nearly all departments were growing and in need of more faculty, and women were merely being given their chance along with men. Mr. Samuel Dodds, for instance, who had been a familiar figure on the campus since 1918, substituting during the absences of Mr. Vance and Mr. Martin, and then doing extension work under the auspices of the college in the Synods of Ohio and Pennsylvania. He now came in 1923 as an assistant professor of missions, and in 1924 became professor of Biblical doctrine, to remain in that position for seven years.

It was in the twenties that the departments of economics, political science, and sociology finally began to take firm shape. In 1924 with the coming of Earl E. Cummins as assistant professor with an M.A.

and his work toward a Ph.D. from Yale well on the way,[31] with a year of teaching experience at Princeton also, economics began to find its place in Wooster's curriculum. His classes were full. By 1927 there was need for a second professor, Alvin S. Tostlebe, whose special interest was in money, banking, and public finance. A middlewesterner, he had his B.A. from Iowa State Teachers' College. He had lived much in the East, however, while taking his doctor's degree at Columbia, studying also at the New School of Social Research and at the Wharton School of Finance. He was for a brief period an instructor also at the Wharton School and at Columbia University, and an assistant professor at the University of Vermont. When he came to Wooster he was content to settle down until his retirement, save for special leaves of absence. In 1931 he became chairman of his department, which flourished under his leadership. He was also a useful member of the faculty, a gentleman always, humorous, cooperative, thoughtful, impartial, and of great service on the committees. He became the author of several books and of various pamphlets issued by the U.S. Department of Agriculture. These, of course, came later, as did his work in Washington, while he was on leave from the college, as head of the farm mortgage and credit section of the Bureau of Agricultural Economics.

Sociology was for years a somewhat vaguely defined subject passed around from one instructor to another. Scovel had taught it in his day. Chancellor made somewhat more of it in his. Finally in 1927, it fell to A. A. Johnston, who had come to Wooster in 1923 as an assistant professor of history, had been moved the next year to economics, and then to sociology. From that time on, the department was recognized and grew, and Mr. Johnston also grew in the twenty-three years as professor of sociology. He went off almost at once to the University of Wisconsin for further study in this field. Years later one of his students was to write: "His is not a sociology of facts and figures but of living people. Always he attempted to broaden our viewpoints and to reveal how prejudice and narrow-mindedness limit and cripple a democratic society."[32]

All through Holden's administration and earlier there had been a course in political economy, a kind of hydra-headed course. From 1911 to 1914 Robert G. Caldwell had served as Hoge Professor of political science and later W. E. Chancellor made much of it. It was

Mary Z. Johnson who in the late twenties gave real impetus to the department and developed it, gradually filling in the gaps in courses and adding personnel.

One of the first of these, in the early thirties, was Louis Ingram, who though an assistant professor of sociology was prepared to teach also political science. Though he was a Republican and she a Democrat she welcomed him to her department, and they became firm friends. He was indeed a man of humor and understanding, versatile, ready and willing always to take his part whether at the college or in the community. He played the violin in the Wooster Orchestra, had been around the world as a young man, and he added flavor in many ways.

Among the young men whom Wooster welcomed to its faculty in the twenties was Emerson Waldo Miller, a Wayne Countian by birth, who had taught for two years in the Wooster high school after his graduation from Heidelberg College in 1911. He and Mr. Lean were the same kind of friendly, outgoing persons; they liked each other at once and found cooperation in the speech department a happy experience. Mr. Miller had taken his law degree at Western Reserve University, had practiced his profession for a year and then was lured into teaching at Pennsylvania State College. It was from Ohio Wesleyan, however, seven years later that he returned to Wooster as professor. Once he came, he settled in to stay until his sudden death in 1943. Like Mr. Lean he was a generous-spirited man who drew to him both faculty and students. On his bulletin board he posted this invitation: "I am in my classroom often in the evening between 7:30 and 8:30 Monday, Tuesday, Wednesday, and Thursday. I shall be glad to talk with anyone there." The invitation was often accepted. He was a man who knew his own mind and spoke up when he thought it necessary. He never rode the fence, though he was always courteous and always able to laugh.

Another somewhat older man, who came in 1928 as a professor of history, and who on the death of Mr. Hays in 1930 succeeded to the chairmanship of the department was the Reverend Mr. William J. Hail. He had spent most of his life in the Orient, first as the son of missionaries in Japan. After his education in the United States, he went back to the Orient, this time to China as an educator. For years he was dean of Yale in China, and when in 1927 it became necessary to evacuate citizens of the United States, he was allowed to stay somewhat longer to put the affairs of the institution in order. Naturally at Wooster he was considered something of an expert in Oriental history and the Oriental mind. His teaching, however, was old-fashioned in that he was still using the textbook approach, and his horizon was somewhat limited perhaps by too long an association with the "unco guid." At least he was shocked to discover that Wooster students were being exposed through their assigned readings to the life and theories of Machiavelli.

There was another man, having first nicknamed the Wooster team "The Scots," who deserves more than casual mention in Wooster's history, Arthur Murray, '20. In college, before going off to war, he played end in football in two successive undefeated teams. In baseball he was a first baseman. In 1924 he came back to Wooster as instructor in physical education for men, coaching at times football, baseball, even basketball. When Mr. Boles went off for a year Arthur Murray served as coach, and the football team made a notable record. All this time he had been in charge also of the college news service. In 1928 he went off to the University of Wisconsin to study journalism; and he became an excellent photographer. Honest and outspoken, endowed with common sense, the young men on the field recognized in him a friend as well as coach and instructor. In 1936 the college chose him as director of student aid, and in the early forties he was to teach meteorology in the Naval Pre-Flight Preparatory School. He was one of those persons who drew little attention to himself, often unappreciated save by those who knew him best.

Little innovations had occurred on the campus and in the town in these years, garnishes that added zest to college and community life. Up near the campus a new street named Scovel had been opened up; the bricks of Liberty Street had been covered with asphalt. And in the fall of 1924 Phil Goembel, '22, was busy flying passengers over Wooster and its surroundings for $2.50 a trip. In the winter of 1925 the new high school building was opened, and in the spring of 1928 the Ohio Hotel, with its seventy rooms and seventy baths, down on Liberty Street near the Pennsylvania Station. By 1930 Wooster's population had grown to 10,737. Yet it was still a country town; of an early morning one could hear up on Beall Avenue A. K. Miller's roosters crowing. At the college Color Day was now observed in the stadium, which offered greater possibilities for pageantry and greater comfort for the crowds that came to watch. By 1926 Wooster Day was being observed by thirty alumni clubs and President Wishart was addressing them over Pittsburgh's KDKA. As of the same year commencement began on Friday and culminated with the graduation exercises on Monday. In 1927 these final exercises were first moved out under the elms. Homecoming weekend had become a well-established time for reunion,[33] when after the big game on Saturday afternoon everyone foregathered at one of the college dining rooms for coffee and doughnuts at the least. Dads' Day too was now a recognized feature of the fall program,[34] when Wooster tried to show itself off at its best. Now on Saturday nights junior and senior girls might stay out till eleven o'clock, and on the occasion of dramatic performances even till midnight. Horseback riding had once more found a few enthusiasts, and water polo had become a winter intramural sport in the gymnasium. There were still winters when January and February were times of much snow and temperatures near zero, when there was coasting and skating, but bobsleds and sleigh bells were fast disappearing. In the winter of 1929 the tennis courts were flooded for skating. Best of all, in 1927 in December a week before the students took off for home, the first all-college Christmas tree was set up in the quadrangle.[35]

Wooster still had the spirit and atmosphere of a small college, though in 1926 the enrollment had reached 901. It was in this year that Mr. Kelso again spoke up as dean advocating "the limitation of numbers to those who can be properly handled and housed." He believed in a constantly greater selectivity, in keeping the admittances to the freshman class down to 300. He went on to say that should Wooster ever reach an enrollment of 2000, it should be split into two colleges, each with its own faculty and 1000 students. A common library, chapel, and administrative building could serve them both. Thus there could be preserved the values of a small college.—It is interesting that President Howard Lowry in his time shared this view and often expressed it.

Through all this period Dean Kelso had a firm hand on the helm. He was perhaps occasionally misled in his appointees, yet not often, and those few were soon encouraged to go elsewhere. He kept ever before him the standards at which he was aiming. He believed with

Miss Root in dormitories housing no more than 100 persons, in cottage dining also. The only excuse for the small liberal arts college was its smallness, its cultivation of the individual, where personality counted, and thought was given to aesthetics as applicable to everyday life. In his relationships with students and faculty he exemplified these principles. He believed for one thing in developing so far as possible the aesthetic taste of the students. He brought in copies of famous paintings and displayed them where students could not fail to see them. He gave one time a course in Gothic architecture. In connection with the annual Migration Day to Cleveland (on the occasion of a game with Case or Western Reserve), he organized for the morning of that day tours to the Cleveland Public Library, to the Cleveland Museum of Art, or an architectural tour of the city. He takes his place in Wooster's annals as a memorable dean and person.

In the twenties Wooster was reaching toward the future. It was an era of expectancy. There were persons on its faculty whose imaginations were always traveling around the bend. Some of them were young, and some middle-aged, and some were tending toward the edge of the horizon, their eyes steadily fixed on what might lie beyond, yet happily aware of an ever-rising generation to whom many so-called mysteries of today might cease to be mysteries in the tomorrow of this ever-revolving world.

XXII

The Changing of the Guard

An accurate view of the world cannot be obtained from a
hilltop; but the memory of a hilltop has many times had power
to alter and transform conditions down in the valley.[1]

HOWARD F. LOWRY

S the twenties introduced a new generation of faculty, and was
an era of expansion and of a growing intellectual ferment,
the thirties began a period, though not of frustration, yet
one perhaps of marking time, and much shifting of administrative personnel. The attendance that had once reached 901 in the
twenties dropped during the early depression years and did not reach
1013 until in 1937–1938. In 1929 Mr. Kelso resigned as dean
though he remained two years longer as professor of Greek. In 1930
J. Milton Vance resigned as dean of men. In 1930 Miss Root, also,
gave up her position to accept one at the new booming Cleveland
College, the downtown branch of Western Reserve University.

Mr. Westhafer now took over as dean,[2] eminently fair in his
dealings yet without the dignity, the buoyant personality, or the
practiced hand of his predecessor, however keen his natural intelligence. At best it was a difficult time for him because of financial
stringencies, and new appointments were necessarily few, except as
vacancies occurred. He had a noticeable distrust of the intellectual
capacities of women, born probably of the fact that so few women
seek out the fields of mathematics and physics for specialization. The
result was that though he accepted those women already on the
faculty, a new woman appointee had, so to speak, to sneak in by the
backdoor.

Mrs. Jessie Willis Brockman came as dean of women in the fall of
1930 fresh from her M.A. in English at Columbia. She was a widow
with two teen-age daughters. Soon after her earlier graduate studies,
in psychology and education, she had gone to Korea to teach. There
she met and married Frank M. Brockman, a Y.M.C.A. foreign secretary. They lived in Seoul, and later in Japan. Two years after their
return to the United States in 1927, he died, and she was confronted

with the problem of raising her children singlehanded. She at once determined to invest in further graduate work, this time in English. She had personality and had been an apparent success in teaching in two girls' colleges, but teaching in the Orient is vastly different from being a dean of women in a coeducational college in the U.S.A. She found the going hard at Wooster. Nevertheless she continued through the college year of 1936–1937 before taking a leave of absence.

In the meantime Mr. Wishart had introduced to Wooster in 1936 a young instructor in English and had arranged to have her serve also as associate resident of Holden Hall, Miss Rachel MacKenzie. She was from upstate New York, a graduate of Wells College. In Mrs. Brockman's absence in 1937–1938 she was asked to be acting dean of women. She was attractive, quick on the uptake, young and gay, yet willing to take responsibility, and tactful in her approach. She was not much older than the girls themselves, often wore a scarf around her head, peasant-style, yet always held her own, and was present when she needed to be present. With her brilliance, however, came a strong satirical vein and a gift with words, and she satirized everything when she was safely out of hearing of those involved. By her young colleagues she was admired and thoroughly enjoyed; the older generation looked a bit askance at her. She gradually became a somewhat controversial figure. In 1938–1939, when Mrs. Brockman did not return, Miss MacKenzie became the dean of women and so remained during the rest of Mr. Wishart's administration.[3]

The young James Anderson, who took over the office of dean of men, had come to Wooster in 1928 straight from the Rio Grande valley as an instructor in religion, and had been advanced to an assistant professorship the following year. He had completed his theological course, had even taken his M.A. and was on the way already to his Ph.D.[4] He was a personable young man with wide-brimmed cowboy hat, a Texas drawl, and a pleasant, rather easy-going, disarming way. Fast, as a tennis player, before long he was helping to coach the college boys in this sport. He was one of seven children of Scottish pioneer stock that had settled long before in the great open stretches of Texas. He had in his blood a zest for education, a love of the good earth, and through his experience, an understanding of and sympathy with youth. He had earned his way through college (University of Texas) by working in the Y.M.C.A.

and during vacations in a bank in San Antonio. He had taught for a while out in the hill country of Texas, at Kerrville, the goat capital of the country. When he had come back from his theological training, he had taken the pastorate of a Southern Presbyterian church at Donna, down along the Rio Grande in the citrus belt, and there he had married a girl from Wooster formerly of the class of 1927. Some time after he came to Wooster to teach, he bought a place in the country; even when he was no longer a dean he used on occasion to bring a discouraged young man for a weekend there or for at least a home-cooked meal, to send him back with a happier slant on life. After five years he relinquished the deanship and gave his full time to teaching courses in the New and Old Testament, and in comparative religion. He used to say: "I tell my students that I will have a wholesome disregard of what they believe when they come into my classroom at the beginning of the school year. It is none of my business what they believe as individuals. My job is to teach all I can about all religions." Later he was to give a course also in marriage, and during World War II in the Naval Flight Preparatory School he was called on to teach both physics and navigation. He was a useful man, serving long on the discipline committee and on the student-faculty relations committee. He was not a person to turn the world upside down. His was rather the gentler course; he cultivated the field he knew, slowly and carefully.

D. Luther Evans, Compton professor of philosophy, who took the deanship Mr. Anderson laid down, was a more forceful character. He, too, first came to Wooster in 1928, from an associate professorship at Ohio Wesleyan but remained for only nine years before he went on to the University of Wisconsin for a year as a visiting professor and then to Ohio State University. His term as dean of men was consequently for only two years (1935–1937), but during that time his practical good sense, his unassuming manner, and his firm but sympathetic hand with students counted for much. It was during his incumbency that the Kenarden Council was organized as a way of improving standards of living and general behavior in the dormitory. It consisted of section heads and faculty representatives one for each section. As a professor of philosophy he was a marked success. He understood the meaning of liberal education and the place of philosophy in that education. For discussion he enjoyed meeting informally with students. One small class he held regularly evenings at his own house. A few years later (1942) a book, *Essentials of a Liberal Education,* came out under his name.[5]

When once more the deanship of men became vacant in 1937, John M. Bruere was asked to take it, a rather popular instructor in religion as of the year before. He was young, ambitious, and to the general public seemed to accept nearly everything in life with a kind of gay nonchalance. An easterner of considerable sophistication, he had topped off his study at Princeton by a year at Oxford University, and then had taught at The Georgia School of Technology and at the Asheville School for Boys. He came immediately from a pastorate at East Stroudsburg, Pennsylvania, and was instinctively a leader. He smoked a pipe, wore tweedy suits, had a crew haircut, and his point of view was far from stodgy. The young men approved of him. Perhaps he knew their impelling motives better than most. Anyhow he stayed until the end of Mr. Wishart's administration.[7]

Administratively there were other changes in this period. With five dormitories (as of 1935) and several minor housing units, whose residents dined in the dormitories, Wooster now needed an administrator to see to the housekeeping end of the college. For this Miss Mabel Little of Norwalk, Ohio, was called in. She was named director of dormitories. An experienced dietician she had supervisory charge of all the cooking, the purchasing of food, the making of menus, and the hiring of the necessary help. She had a B.S. from Columbia in this field, had been a dietician at Lakeside Hospital in Cleveland, Director of Dining Halls at Cornell University, and at the University of Wisconsin Director of Halls and Commons as well as an associate professor of institutional management. In addition she had general charge of the management of the various housekeepers for the dormitories.

In the thirties the outreach toward adult education was well on its way. John D. McKee, who had been following closely the trends in alumni magazines and at association meetings, felt that Wooster must get in line and furnish "an intellectual program to alumni in fields of contemporary thought." This resulted in his setting up of an "alumni college" in the three days following Wooster's commencement of 1933. It began on Monday evening in the basement of Galpin Hall: violin numbers by Mr. Parmelee and readings by Mr.

Lean. On Tuesday, however, there were three morning lectures of an hour each, and an evening lecture; on Wednesday again three morning lectures. Mr. Ver Steeg talked on the evolution of the earth, Miss Thayer gave a critical estimate of modern novels, Mr. Moore surveyed the drama of the day, Mr. Tostlebe banking developments, Mr. Hail conditions in China, and Mary Z. Johnson spoke on democracy and dictatorships. So it went on and on. Too many of the alumni, mildly interested in finding out what the faculty of that day were really like, were more eager to get home than to be educated. The next year the alumni college was changed to the Thursday and Friday preceding commencement, and there it remained. After a few years it was discontinued for a period, and then again revived. But John D. was not discouraged. He presently asked the alumni what more the college could do for their cultural development. They mentioned reading lists in various fields. These assignments John D. dealt to various professors. The lists of books they compiled on their special subjects were published monthly in the *Alumni Bulletin.* In the meantime John D. himself went to the University of Chicago (1934–1935) and took his Master's degree in education, thus preparing himself for the teaching of an occasional course and winning, as of 1937, the rank of an assistant professor. When he came back from Chicago, Mr. Wishart at once claimed him as his assistant for a year to take some of the more routine business off the president's calendar. When John D. had left in 1934 he had turned over the alumni work to his assistant, Harriet Painter, who for two years was the acting alumni secretary until John D. Miller took over the office. When in 1941 the latter relinquished his job, John D. McKee once more accepted full responsibility this time as director of alumni relations in all its multifarious aspects. These included as well as the other routine duties of the office the developing of the annual giving program. Of course for this he had to have a staff of several persons. In 1942 he became also the coordinator for the college of the War Training Service of the Civil Aeronautics Authority.

Between 1936 and 1945 John D. McKee served also as business manager. In this capacity he had for five years the assistance of Donald Dickason, '21, a young man of parts, with both the executive ability and the geniality of his father, J. H. Dickason. For some years he had run the campus bookstore. While John D. passed on all major problems, "Mr. Dick" now really had charge of the campus crews inside and out: the janitors, the painters, the carpenters, the trucker, the plumber, the electrician, and the men who tended the grounds, who dug up, when necessary, the water, the heating, and lighting mains, who mowed the lawns, shovelled the snow, laid and repaired walks. His was the job of "the man of the house," multiplied many times, yet with a bare minimum available for maintenance. It was a question of "make-do" for the time being rather than of expert or even careful workmanship until "make-do" around the college became the habit for years thereafter, and people on the outside remarked disconsolately that any residence the college took over for supplementary housing for its students would soon be rotting down. When a roof leaked, a patch here and there was inserted until the whole became a patchwork. So with everything. The cheapest wallpaper that was decent without regard to design, color, or proportion, was slapped on walls in dormitories, the least expensive local person was employed to reupholster a chair or divan when it showed holes in its fabric or when its springs were sagging. Cheap materials and slapstick workmanship were the vogue. The business management was trying to stretch the dollar to its utmost, and in the end the college paid the price of a false economy. Yet what does one do when there isn't any money?

There were others in these years who seemed almost indispensable to Wooster's operation and growth, of whom many persons outside Galpin were scarcely conscious. One of these was Arthur Southwick, '17, who at one time or another was director of admissions (1927–1930), director of vocational guidance and placement (1927–1945), and registrar for many years beginning in 1929. He had the rank of an assistant professor of education and occasionally also taught a course in this department. After many months in a machine gun battalion in World War I, he had come back, taken an M.A. in history and education, had taught in Pennsylvania and Tennessee, had managed several chautauquas, and had been an associate secretary of the Presbyterian Board of Temperance and Moral Welfare. In 1927 Wooster called him back. For thirty-two years he remained a member of Wooster's faculty. The mass of detail he handled or supervised during his tenure at Wooster might have staggered almost anyone, yet he went ahead quietly as if he found satisfaction in the almost infinite recording, in the making out of examination schedules, in administering many kinds of tests,[8] and in checking data for incoming students, and of College Board examinations. He had to know the college inside and out, had to be familiar with professors, with courses offered, with requirements for entrance, and with the general quality of student personnel. He had to arrange vocational conferences, bringing in leaders in business and the professions to talk of possible opportunities in their fields. He had to counsel students about to graduate, to steer them if possible toward the kind of job they had in mind, or to advise them against it. The work he liked best, he was to say in later years, was that of admissions officer. He had visited nearly every high school in Ohio talking of Wooster, seeking out promising students. He enjoyed public speaking, and he enjoyed talking with individual prospects, with their instructors and their parents. When they came to Wooster to look the college over, he accompanied them on their tours of the campus, seeing that Wooster showed its best face. Summer was one of his busiest seasons, yet he often managed to take a brief vacation in the northern peninsula of Michigan by Manistique Lake where he could really get away from it all.

In the work of advancing Wooster among the high schools, Roy Grady, since 1924 Brown Professor of Chemistry,[9] took also a significant part. It all began with his eagerness to show off the work of the chemistry department, of which he was justly proud, but he had the wisdom to draw in also the other sciences, biology, physics, and geology. He thus was instrumental in introducing hundreds of young persons from Ohio, Pennsylvania, and West Virginia to Wooster. In 1930 with these other departments he developed "an open house in science" on a Saturday in late winter or spring. This event grew in scope and importance as the years went on. High school students were invited to come, along with their teachers, and a general chaperone, and they arrived by the bus load. Continuous exhibits were set up to illustrate what Wooster was offering in these fields, and simple lectures and explanations went along with the exhibits. There would be a sampling of experiments performed in laboratories, and occasional industrial or merchandising exhibits. There might be a collection of fruit flies, or an experiment with rats showing what vitamins or the lack of them mean in a diet. Once a motor built by Arthur

Compton and operated by a student was shown. Students in the college were from the beginning drawn in to help set up the exhibits and experiments, and to act as hosts for the college. Afterwards there would be a tour of the campus, a luncheon provided by the college at the dormitories. There might be a track meet on that day, in the evening a basketball game or possibly a play to attend. The idea took hold. By 1935 some 500 high school students were on campus for the occasion. In the early forties the college began to offer competitive examinations also in various subjects to these high school visitors. The student making the highest mark in each subject was offered, if he enrolled at Wooster, a $100 scholarship for his freshman year. If consistently thereafter he made a B average, the scholarship was continued year by year. No doubt many young scientists and others were first attracted to Wooster through this annual "open house."

In all of this Mr. Grady had since 1929 the able assistance of John W. Chittum, who came to Wooster in that year from Iowa Wesleyan, the college from which he had been graduated some years previously. Mr. Chittum had in the meantime completed his doctorate in chemistry at the University of Chicago. He, too, was to continue at Wooster for many years, becoming a professor and eventually succeeding to the chairmanship of the department.

Wooster was strong in science, yet various other departments were strong, too, notably that of English, with Waldo Dunn (until he left in the early thirties), Mary Rebecca Thayer, Frederick Moore, George Bradford, and Howard Lowry. There was also a young instructor coming on, Lowell Coolidge. Whatever can be said, and has been said, of all the others, Howard Lowry was the most brilliant, with a mind that flashed like a lighthouse in the darkness yet with the difference that one couldn't predict just when or where it would suddenly illumine the mind's landscape with a phrase or an interpretation; one knew only that moment would come. His classes were an experience to be long remembered. His apprenticeship over, his doctorate at Yale completed in 1931, he was advanced at Wooster to a professorship. He had been given in 1930 by Yale a Sterling Fellowship, and again in 1933 he was to receive this award toward the pursuing of his research. In 1934 there followed a John Simon Guggenheim Fellowship. In 1932 the results of his research on

Clough and on Arnold began to issue from the press, first *The Letters of Matthew Arnold to Arthur Hugh Clough,* edited by Mr. Lowry; then in 1934 the editing, with Ralph L. Rusk of Columbia, of the *Emerson-Clough Letters,* published by the Rowfant Club of Cleveland. In November, 1935, there followed *An Oxford Anthology of English Poetry* (with Willard Thorp of Princeton) for college classroom use. From that time on the books did not emerge from the press so fast, for in 1935 while he continued teaching at Wooster he became general editor and educational manager for the American branch of the Oxford University Press. This took him to New York one week out of every month, commuting by the Pennsylvania Railroad. As for the college, it thought him so valuable as professor and chairman of the department, thought his experience at the Oxford Press would be so advantageous that it willingly consented to the compromise in time. In 1936 he was elected also a director of The Oxford Press. Yet, however inspiring his life in New York, Wooster was after all the home of his heart. Here were his haunts, the old campus with its trees, the familiar buildings, his mother, many of his friends, Mr. and Mrs. Wishart to whom he had become almost like a son, and even the Wishart dog who had accepted him as if one of the family.—To be sure, this dog had been named Matthew Arnold.[10]—And so he remained in Wooster until the summer of 1940.

> Here cam'st thou in thy jocund youthful time,
> Here was thine height of strength, thy golden prime!
> And still the haunt beloved a virtue yields.[11]

He had made many friends meanwhile in New York and in the academic world. Princeton consequently invited him to come as professor of English. Wooster he still loved, but the lure of a great university where there were many persons whose minds he could explore was too great, and he went. That year, too, his *Poetry of Matthew Arnold* (with Professor Chauncey B. Tinker of Yale) was published. His inaugural lecture there, presented in 1941, was on "Matthew Arnold and the Modern Spirit." At Wooster Frederick Moore became chairman of the department.

Mr. Kelso, when he was dean, had been determined to make

Wooster's history department outstanding. He had gone a long way in this direction when he brought in Aileen Dunham. She had been teaching courses not only in general European history, but in the Renaissance and Reformation, in the French Revolution, in World War I, and later in Nineteenth Century Europe, from 1815 to 1914 including the industrial revolution, the growth of democracy and of nationalism, and the backgrounds of World War I, as well as the seminar to which reference has already been made, in international relations from week to week.

With the death of Mr. Hays, however, in 1930 the department lost a main prop, and they needed a man full time in American history. In 1931, therefore, Mr. Westhafer brought in Clayton Ellsworth, an Iowan by birth, who had taken his undergraduate work, with honors, at Oberlin, and his Ph.D. at Cornell in 1930. He had taught one year at Oberlin in 1930–1931. His field was American cultural and intellectual history, commonly known as social history. This was readily divisible into several courses, which together included nearly everything: education and religion, art and architecture, immigration, population movements, health, recreation, the exploitation of natural resources, women's rights, temperance, exploration, political conditions, the changes wrought by industry and labor, farm life and farmers' organizations. He was not only a substantial young man but one bristling with ideas and almost effervescent in his manner. He liked his subject, he liked to teach. A frontiersman at heart he loved also to explore new aspects of his field and to present his findings. From time to time these appeared as articles in *The American Historical Review* or elsewhere: "The American Churches and the Mexican War," for instance, or "Theodore Roosevelt's Country Life Commission." He enjoyed the editing and writing process, just as he enjoyed talking in the classroom or outside. The students liked and respected him; those who casually met him found his conversation enlightening especially when they drew him out on his own field. In four years he was advanced to an assistant professorship, and sometime later to a professorship. In the war emergency of the early forties he taught communications also in the U.S. Naval Flight Preparatory School. In time, too, he became a stalwart on various important faculty committees and had a part in the planning of significant changes in the curriculum. Eventually he built a house, half a mile or so away from the college, not early American in style as one might have expected but one in the early contemporary style, with a split-level roof. It was a kind of fortress or block house against the world, and behind it he planted a young forest of trees. There, however, he was very much at home to his students and to his friends.

Ennis Kingman Eberhart, who came to Wooster in the fall of 1938, after nine years of teaching economics at the University of Pittsburgh, was not a man to whom one warmed immediately; one tested him out with a degree of caution. He was relatively quiet, a man of generally good judgment but with unyielding convictions about a variety of things. His students invariably respected the breadth of his knowledge and his gift for the colorful phrase but found him lacking in the responsiveness of many of the faculty. His particular interest was labor problems, with special reference to methods of arbitration.[12] He was interested, too, in comparing varying economic systems. Tall and thin he was a good volleyball player. He was also a good bridge player. He had an urge to see distant places, and felt "the call of the running tide." Toward this he carefully was saving money, aiming one day to own a large well-stocked cabin cruiser onto which he and his wife could retire to sail coastwise from port to port in tropical waters.

After the retirement of Gertrude Gingrich in 1935, the German department was allowed to languish for several years. To be sure, Mr. Lister agreed to add its chairmanship to his responsibilities and Mr. Olthouse was borrowed for a course or two from the French department. Temporary instructors helped with the beginning and second year courses and with a course in conversation and composition. After all, with the rise of Hitler in Europe, German was once more under a cloud. Even in the last years of Miss Gingrich's tenure, the catalogue listed the more advanced courses to be given only if there were at least six (sometimes ten) students. Yet there were those going on to graduate studies in science, in music, even in the humanities, to whom at least a reading knowledge of German was a necessity. It could not be dropped from the curriculum. In 1937, therefore, there was added to the faculty an assistant professor of German who was to stay at Wooster. He was William I. Schreiber, who had come to this country a boy of seventeen and had become a naturalized citizen in 1931. He was married and had taught for four years already at Parsons College in Iowa. A graduate of a German gymnasium, of a small college in Missouri, also, with two years of additional study at Dubuque, he had gone on to the University of Wisconsin and then to the University of Illinois where he took his doctorate. From the beginning he sought to popularize German as a spoken language. Yet people lifted their eyebrows slightly when they heard German singing in his classroom. His teaching, however, was not just in conversation and composition; he taught classes in Goethe, in 19th-century German literature, and later a survey course leading up to the 19th century. It was natural, too, that he should have a large curiosity about the community to which he had been transplanted. He soon discovered that Wayne County had many families of German extraction and he began to delve into dusty local histories. He soon came upon the story of Wooster's first Christmas tree, of which he made much, and he pursued the subject until he found the stories of many other Christmas trees in the eastern states and Middle West set up according to the German tradition. He was interested in what brought German settlers to this region and the human story of what habits and traditions they had brought along with them, and how these might have been changed through the years and modified. Gradually this search took him all over this and neighboring counties. It took him to schools and churches and country stores, to farm meetings and auctions, to farmhouses, to funerals and weddings, and finally into accounts of similar settlers and settlements in other parts of the United States. It was local social history. So little by little he found his own place in both college and town. By 1940 after Mr. Lister's retirement, he was acting head of the department, and some years later he became the actual chairman and the Gingrich professor of German.[13]

There were others of course, whose work may have begun in the latter part of Mr. Wishart's administration but whose major service was to fall in Mr. Lowry's: Paul Bushnell from Minnesota, and E. W. Stoneburner in education, and Winford Sharp whose major interests were in experimental and applied psychology, in testing and measurements. There were several young instructors, William Kieffer in chemistry, Melcher Fobes in mathematics, and Charles B. Moke in geology who began their careers at Wooster in this era (and who were to become outstanding professors); and there were two young women, mentioned before, who had started early in Mr. Wishart's administration, and were to spend their lifetimes at Wooster. Besides in this period there was an instructor in French who was in time to become a distinguished member of the faculty, both for her research and her teaching, Frances Guille, petite and charming and gay, whose forebears had come not many generations back from the Island of Guernsey.

During these years, busy as he was with administrative duties, President Wishart craved a chance also to teach.[14] He was close to many students anyhow, especially as his own children came of college age. For some years he gave for one semester the course in apologetics, listed usually in the annual catalogue as "Christianity and the Modern World." He was still happier teaching "Literary and Aesthetic Values of the Bible," or more tersely, "Biblical Literature."

In all this period Coach Boles and his teams had continued to win laurels for Wooster. In 1935 after twenty years as football coach at Wooster he could chalk up on the scoreboard 115 victories, fourteen ties, and thirty-two defeats. In June of 1940, when he finally turned over the coaching of football to "Johnny" Swigart, some eighty former Wooster athletes came back to do him honor. He had been making Wooster known also by his personal triumphs in golf. Not only was it not unusual for him to win the local Country Club championship but in 1930 for the third season in four years he was the winner of the Cleveland District Association (Caravan) tournament, with twenty-nine strokes fewer than those of anyone else. On four different courses totaling seventy-two holes, his score was 302. Though he relinquished the coaching, he remained at Wooster several more years as professor of physical education and did a distinctive service during the war training emergency.

There were charges everywhere during these years that college athletics were being debased by a semi-professionalism, that by one devious way or another inducements were being offered to high school boys of athletic promise to come to one college in preference to another. Finally the Carnegie Foundation for the Advancement of Teaching undertook an investigation in more than 100 universities and colleges, Wooster among them.[15] They advocated that "American amateurism must be revived as the very keystone of college athletics in a democracy. The two fundamental causes and defects in American college athletics," they said, "are (1) commercialism, and (2) a negligent attitude toward the educational opportunities for which the American college exists." It was with pride that Wooster found no blot on either count on her scoreboard.

In 1930–1931 for the first time a minor was offered in physical education for those who wished to teach or to coach athletics. Courses in health, and the theory and practice of physical education were given to allow for the necessary sixteen credit hours. The physical education staff now included five men and three women. Golf had become a recognized sport on the campus.

In 1935–1936 a major in art, also, was listed for the first time in the catalogue. In addition to studio art (two courses), eighteen hours were offered in the history of architecture, of sculpture, a survey of painting, and a general survey of art and art-forms, with twenty-two additional hours required in allied subjects. The innovation, long needed, was popular; more than ninety students registered for at least some of the courses. The interest in art, after Mr. Kelso's resignation, until the coming of Mr. Edward Peck had been kept alive by Mrs. Kennard, and by the art exhibits provided periodically by the class of 1923. In November of 1935, for instance, an exhibit had been arranged through the American Federation of Arts. There were two groups, one of twenty-three contemporary oil paintings of European and American artists, the other from the Corcoran Gallery of twelve paintings by American artists. Mrs. Kennard and Mr. Peck both lectured during the exhibit. In 1939, at the instigation of Mr. Peck and some of the alumni, a lending library of framed reproductions of famous paintings was made available to students for their rooms, on a rental basis during the college year. After Wendell N. Gates was added to the department and during his short tenure, separate studio courses were offered in oil and water color painting, in life drawing, in plastic art, lettering and poster design.

In 1942–1943 one of the first of the orientation courses was given, Classical Humanities in English, the first semester of which was a study of Greek, the second of Roman civilization and their respective contributions to present day culture. It was a three-hour course planned and conducted in cooperation by Mr. Cowles, Miss Newnan, and Mr. Vergil Hiatt, assistant professor of Latin. Two of these hours were lectures, the third consisted of reports on outside reading, and of discussion. Art, archaeology, architecture, public and private life, education, religion, and philosophy were all "viewed in their historical setting." The course counted toward a major in Latin or Greek, and toward a minor in art or in English.

Other rather slight changes were made in the later days of Mr. Wishart's administration. In 1930 the catalogue announced that hereafter the B.S. would be discontinued and only the B.A. given for all students completing the requirements for graduation.[16] In 1932 there came another change in that the honors signalized by *cum laude, magna cum laude, summa cum laude* were dropped in favor of the simpler "with distinction." There were by 1944 eleven chapters of eleven national honorary fraternities on campus.

The library had been slowly growing. In 1942 it accessioned its 100,000th volume. In that same year it received a Lincoln collection, from Homer McMaster, '11, of 350 books, scrapbooks, pamphlets, and pictures. In addition during the years various classes (1903, 1914, 1916, 1925, 1929, 1931, 1941) had set up small funds for books usually in a limited field. The budgetary annual appropriations ran from $2000–$3000 a year for library books; and in 1943 the Board of Trustees expressed themselves that the figure should never be allowed to drop below that higher figure. Even that was less than the minimum set by the National Library Association. The annual expenditure for current periodicals at this time was $1200 a year. In June, 1937, at a breakfast meeting in Hoover Cottage, The Friends of the Library had been organized by a little group of eighteen which soon grew to fifty-four. Clarence Allis, *ex*'06, became its first president. Its purpose was to encourage interest in the library expressed by gifts of money or of books. At the annual June meeting a speaker usually talked on some phase of his or her research.

In 1935 Norine Flack, '27, and in 1931, Maudie L. Nesbitt, '25, both with their degrees in library science joined the library staff, the former as assistant cataloguer, the latter as head of the circulation department. Miss Nesbitt was drawn in also in the early forties by the Department of Education to give a course in some of the fundamentals of library work—in reference work, bibliography, cataloguing, a course "designed to meet the minimum state requirements for the teacher-librarian in the smaller schools."

In 1944 Miss Elizabeth Bechtel retired after forty-four years. Since 1915 she had carried the responsibility as librarian, always stretching the budget as far as it would go, always looking ahead, always considerate of the various faculty—and how well she knew them and their eccentricities—always expecting and getting the best from her growing staff of assistants, always there when somebody needed her, always cheerful. In her day she had hand-lettered thousands of library cards, she had shown eager students how to use a card catalogue and the various periodical indexes, and she had studied book catalogues, sent off orders, listened to faculty requests and complaints, and made out reports. She had begun in Old Main, had seen the library moved to the new Frick building, had seen that pushed out to the east to double its capacity, and had seen stack rise upon stack inside till there was no place left and the old and battered and little-used books were crowded into basement rooms to gather dust there and in the basement of the student union. Her own little cubby-hole of an office in the northeast corner of the old Frick library was her home. She never missed a day there. Outside her window was an old and rather sprawling elm and farther off some of the venerable oaks of the old campus. These and the books around her were her world.[17]

In 1934–1935 for the first time in years the number of Wooster's men students exceeded that of women. It was an encouraging sign. Nor had the women students been behindhand in their initiative in these earlier years. By the spring of 1931 they had raised $500 toward a building in the country, which they proposed to use for the women's physical education activities over weekends, camping especially, though it would be a base also for hiking in the neighborhood. For this since the fall they had been raising money by selling candy, sandwiches, peanuts, and coffee at the football games, and in the winter by giving benefit bridge parties. They found their way gradually into what had earlier been considered men's activities; women's debating teams challenged similar ones elsewhere. By 1943 there were women trying out in oratorical contests. The Y.W.C.A. still existed, and for this Mrs. Wishart was often consulted and was most helpful. The Women's Self Government Association went through an annual ceremony at which the head of the Association presented to a freshman woman a scroll indicating that it was the freshman's duty to carry on the tradition. Many, both men and women, were involved in college dramatics. Mr. Lean was continuing to put on outstanding plays, *Our Town,* for instance. The students were interested, too, in trips to Cleveland to see plays there. Pembroke started almost an epidemic when they went there to see *Richard II,* for over the Thanksgiving weekend five bus loads of students and faculty went up to see Helen Hayes in *Victoria Regina.* (The interurban electric line had discontinued its service in March of 1931.) The students patronized also the local movies, saw Greta Garbo in *Single Standard,* Rudolph Valentino in *The Desert Song,* George Arliss in *Disraeli,* Lawrence Tibbett in *The New Moon,* John Barrymore in *Moby Dick.* The faculty gave *Arms and the Man;* the Ben Greet Players presented *Hamlet.* Dame Sybil Thorndike was to be seen at the Opera House, and Albert Spalding played in the chapel. Besides there were the Wooster Symphonic Orchestra concerts and the recitals by the Parmelees—"such charming friendly people"—and the others of the music faculty.

Coeducation was in full swing, especially since dancing had been allowed on campus. "Bob" Hill and Henry Heyl were often the whole orchestra. Bob Hill played many other times. At the first of the year at the Y.M. and Y.W.C.A. receptions the big sisters and the big brothers helped the little sisters and the little brothers get their first Wooster dates. Christian Endeavor meetings on Sunday evenings were occasions, too, where dates could easily be picked up and were —though girls on Sunday nights had to be in by nine o'clock. There was tobogganing and skiing on the Wooster golf course in winter, skating and swimming at Miller's Lake. In the spring some of the girls of Hoover were sure to be announcing their engagements by passing out lollipops. There was a Gum Shoe Hop, now with a play written and produced by students at the Opera House, and Color Day in the spring with all the excitement attendant on the election of the Queen. There was a time when among the candidates was a mysterious Eureka, who had obviously a group of backers; her posters were all over the campus boosting her election. Yet no one knew who she might be. On the fateful morning she polled a considerable vote. When, however, the duly elected Queen walked out of the chapel there beside the Rock stood Eureka, with a sign on her back, a fine and very gentle cow. It is said that the Queen of that year still regrets not having had Eureka in her procession on that May Day morning in the stadium. Then there were those other occasions when some of the students made no slightest pretense of being grown-up.[18] There was the time, for instance, when the boys of Kenarden's section VII staged a funeral for a pup, one of seven born to a pet they had been coddling. Arrayed as bearers, trumpeters, clergymen, and mourners they processed to the quadrangle at the rear of Holden Hall and there conducted the final obsequies. There was "a eulogy, and a shotgun volley over the grave to the accompaniment of muffled drums and flying colors."

In the background of all this student gaiety loomed World War II.[19] Already students and faculty had been contributing "Bundles for Britain," had sent $750 toward X-ray equipment for a London hospital and $200 toward an ambulance unit in France. Wooster was offering Civilian Pilot Training, four hours a week either semester, under the direction of the Civil Aeronautics Authority (later called Administration in the catalogue). The ground-school courses in navigation, meteorology, civil air regulations, and general service of aircraft were given by Mr. Williamson (mathematics), Mr. Moke (geology), and Mr. Ford (physics). Actual flying was at the Wooster airport. During the year up to October, 1941, twenty-six persons received their flying licenses under this program, of whom seven were already in the Air Service. By March of 1942 forty-five had won their licenses, one a woman. The following year when the Navy also was cooperating, several courses were added in mathematics, physics,[20] code, military and physical training, aircraft identification, military science and discipline, and the faculty (all from the college) enlarged correspondingly. There were eight-week sessions, 240 hours of ground-school instruction and "a minimum of 35 hours of flight instruction." In 1941 the college completed an arrangement with the Frances Bolton School of Nursing in Cleveland whereby a woman desirous of becoming a registered nurse could after three years at the college (provided she had at least a "B" record) and one year of satisfactory work in the School of Nursing receive from Wooster her B.A. degree.

Soon after Pearl Harbor President Wishart offered the facilities of the college to the government, a little later, in the light of its experience in training pilots under the Civil Aeronautics Administration, making specific application for a Naval Flight Preparatory School. It was not until December 1942, however, that notice came of the granting of the application and of the date of arrival of the first contingent of 200 men on January 7, 1943. Others were to follow at intervals until by March fourth the full complement of 600 trainees was to be on campus. Wooster was one of twenty institutions over the country to be chosen for this branch of the Navy service. The only other in Ohio was Wesleyan at Delaware.

In the meantime much had been going on at Wooster. In the summer of 1942, in an effort to help the student eager to complete as much of his formal education as possible before going to war, the college introduced an accelerated program. This consisted of an annual summer session of fifteen (later twelve) weeks, divided into two terms. In each of these terms the student could accumulate eight credits. Thus if he chose to attend two or three of the full sessions in addition to the usual college program, he could win a diploma in three and one half or even in three years. This plan had been adopted by many colleges. In the fall of 1942 the 300 freshmen arrived to begin work on August 31, two weeks earlier than usual. There was a Christmas vacation but no spring vacation, and holidays only on Washington's Birthday and Good Friday. Commencement came in early May (on the tenth in 1943) so that the summer session could begin at the end of that month.

Of course liberal arts attendance during these years dropped. By the opening day of college in 1942, sixty-five men had already enlisted. There had been a blood donor service set up on the campus, and a rifle range, superintended by Coach Boles underneath the stadium. This practice shooting counted only as an extracurricular activity. In early November of that year (1942) a representative of the Joint Board of the Armed Services presented to the students the opportunities for both men and women in the various services. Later in the month a Joint Recruiting Board came and received 124 applications. There was of course a drive in the dormitories, as everywhere, to sell War Savings Bonds and Stamps. Some of the girls are said to have made corsages of these stamps to wear at formal dances.

The Naval Flight Preparatory School created other problems in adjustment. The cadets were assigned to Kenarden, Douglass, and

Hoover. The men of the liberal arts college were moved many into private homes, some to Livingstone Lodge, to what had been the old Kauke Conservatory, and elsewhere. The young women of Hoover were lodged in the various small college houses. Miss Little now had around 1200 persons every day for whom to prepare three meals. Cafeteria service for the Navy men was set up in Kenarden. The bakeshop in the basement of Babcock ran twenty-four hours a day. A Navy store was given space in the basement of Douglass as was the Navy barbershop in which three local barbers worked from five in the afternoon till nine P.M. Seven Naval officers had charge of the men, and twenty-eight classrooms were set apart for the use of the Navy. The cadets marched to their classes in column formation. In the evening they had supervised study in Taylor, Kauke, Severance, and Scovel Halls. Curfew came at ten o'clock. Some twenty members of the regular faculty, two others retired and living in town, who were drawn in,[21] carried the work in mathematics, physics, communications, and navigation; there were one or two others in aerology and airplane engines, and at the airport several flying instructors, who had no relation to the college. Once a week at the local St. Mary's Roman Catholic Church there was a mass for those cadets who wished to attend; and downtown a Marine Room was opened on Saturday nights and Sundays as a U.S.O. canteen.

At the October, 1943, meeting of the Board of Trustees Mr. Wishart announced his resignation as of September first of 1944, at the end of his twenty-fifth year as president. He asked that a committee be appointed to look for a new president, and that this committee confer with an advisory committee from the faculty and one also from the Synod. This was done. As Mr. Wishart looked forward to his final year he was also looking backward to a long record of accomplishment: at the enlarged campus and the buildings added, at the teaching staff that had grown by one third, at the increase in salaries, in some instances nearly doubled, at the departments that had been strengthened, and the courses that had been added, at the installation of Phi Beta Kappa and the departmental honor fraternities, at Wooster's record in athletics, and at the new degrees in music and school music that were now being conferred. He had seen the Old Guard pass one by one. He had welcomed the new generation, and had been watching them come to their prime. He rejoiced that

Wooster had kept its "vital religious tradition," and its "freedom of scientific inquiry," and that Wooster had "more students in Greek than probably any other college of its size anywhere." As he came to the final meeting with his trustees on May 12, 1944, he pointed to the fact that in Wooster's budget educational spending, including that of the library, was now 53 per cent of the total, that during his administration there had been received nearly a million more for endowment than for buildings. He warned his Board, however, that there would be a heavy deficit in the coming year. Nevertheless, he said, "the most fatal thing would be to balance the ledger by letting good teachers go, or wrecking their morale by lowered salaries. In a time of storm and stress, I beseech you, do not lose your nerve. I recall Danton's slogan, 'Audacity, audacity, and always audacity.' "

It was a great commencement, that of 1944. It had been planned to honor Mr. Wishart. Because of the accelerated program Color Day festivities were combined with commencement and put on Saturday afternoon at three o'clock. He had seen in his time one of his daughters as May Queen. Today Betty Lou Dickens was Queen but her crown bearer was Mr. Wishart's tiny grandson, Charles Wishart Hayford. The ceremony on that afternoon began with a review of the Naval cadets by Mr. Wishart and the Naval Officer in charge, and with the hoisting of the national ensign by the color guard. After the crowning there followed a precision drill with a review of the Cadet Regiment by the May Queen. At the banquet that night there were tributes to retiring faculty, to Martin Remp who had taught at the college for twenty-nine years, by "Mose" Hole; and to Miss Elizabeth Bechtel and Miss Fern Kieffer of the library who had served for forty-four and twenty-three years respectively, by Frederick Moore. Then Arthur Compton, chairman of the Board of Trustees, spoke in high appreciation of Mr. Wishart as leader and administrator through twenty-five trying years. Mrs. Raymond Dix announced that a beginning had been made among alumni toward the raising of a fund for a Wishart building. Then Mr. Winfred Leutner, who had come from Western Reserve University to do honor to Mr. Wishart on this occasion, spoke of what it takes to be a college president, of the patience necessary, the broad outlook, the reverence for and understanding of true scholarship. When all that was over, Howard Foster Lowry was introduced as president-elect of Wooster.

Some of the Board had wanted him all along, from the very beginning of the search, many also of the faculty. They knew him, they liked him; he was a scholar, a great speaker; he had "academic imagination," and a genius for friendship as well. In the secret recesses of his heart Mr. Wishart had hoped—and doubtless prayed—that Howard Lowry might be his successor. When he had been brought into the Board meeting the day before and told of his election, Howard Lowry said that he must have time to consider. This he repeated at the banquet on Saturday night. Indeed he had much to consider. He was happy at Princeton; there was a future there for him. He was more scholar than administrator; that he knew. Yet he tingled with excitement at the thought of what might still be done at Wooster. He had often dreamed of programs of independent study for students, of frequent controlled research leaves for faculty and of much else, and these dreams would not let him alone. He loved that hilltop. In two weeks he had made his decision. He was to give the rest of his life to Wooster.

> Too rare, too rare, grow now my visits here!
> 'Mid City-noise, not, as with thee of yore,
>   Thyrsis! in reach of sheep bells is my home.
> —Then through the great town's harsh, heart-wearying
>   roar,
> Let in thy voice a whisper often come,
>   To chase fatigue and fear:
>
> Why faintest thou? I wander'd till I died.
>   Roam on! The light we sought is shining still.
>   Dost thou ask proof? Our tree yet crowns the hill,
> Our Scholar travels yet the loved hill-side.
>   (Matthew Arnold, "Thyrsis")

Afterword

Minute of the Board of Trustees, July 12, 1967, as stated by W. D. Hopkins, vice-chairman

[Since this book was authorized by the trustees at the instigation of Mr. Lowry, then president of The College of Wooster, it seems appropriate here at the end to record the Minute of the Trustees on the occasion of Mr. Lowry's sudden death. It is one of my deep personal regrets that he never lived to read the completed manuscript.—L. L. N.]

THE members of the Board of Trustees of The College of Wooster record with deep sorrow the death on July 4, 1967, of their friend and the College's leader, Howard Lowry. No man ever loved a college with more intensity, intelligence, and imagination than Howard Lowry loved Wooster.

He was a scholar recognized in the world of letters for research and creative writing, and his bond of understanding with scholars in all fields was one of Wooster's great assets. The College's distinctive programs of independent study and research leaves grew naturally from his scholarly leadership. He was a teacher who led his students to ask significant questions rather than to learn easy answers. Although not ordained, he was a preacher of unsurpassed eloquence. As President, he was an administrator of vision and persuasiveness, but he also remained a great teacher because he inspired young men and women to find delight in the discipline of learning. He was keenly sensitive to beauty in its many forms—language, music, art, architecture, and landscape; and Wooster students yet unborn will benefit from campus beauty that he helped to preserve and to develop.

Perhaps the highest tribute to him both as a college President and as a man is that thousands of former students around the world now have vivid memories of his inspiring chapel talks and of their personal encounters with him. Thornton Wilder suggests that memory is the servant of a man's interests. This may explain Howard Lowry's amazing memory of students, their names, their faces, their concerns, and their successes; he remembered because he had a genuine interest in the individual person. What he said in tribute to another was true of him—"He had a perfect power to enter the life of another person."

He always shared credit and withheld blame. He could never be the cynic, but had a transcendent faith in the ultimate decency and good sense of people, especially those who worked with him, but also the vast circle of those whose lives touched his. His capacity for friendship was in no way limited by his own brilliance, and he never lost the common touch, although he was touched with the fire of genius. His talents were great, but he acknowledged that his Christian faith gave him inner resources to use these talents beyond his own ability. He was a man of faith, he knew he was a man of faith, and he knew the Source of his faith. He stated it so well in one of those glorious baccalaureates, "A conviction that his life has eternal significance is bound to affect all a man is and does—his actions, his loyalties, his daily sense of himself and other men."

We express gratitude for Howard Lowry to whom gratitude was a cardinal virtue. One of the precious legacies he has left us is Wooster's tradition of excellence. We pray that a portion of his faith, vision, and wisdom be granted to us, and that we may, as we believe he would have us, accept that tradition not as a tether to the past but as a gateway to the future.

Reference Notes

CHAPTER I

1. A. A. E. Taylor's father was Edward Taylor, for whom the Edward Taylor prizes were established. He was a trustee of the University of Wooster in 1866–1877. It was the Reverend James Reed making his rounds on horseback on an autumn day who was the first to envision a Presbyterian college on the site of the present campus. *History of Wayne County, Ohio,* Volume I, Indianapolis, Indiana: B. F. Bowen & Co., 1910, p. 463. See *Wooster of the Middle West,* Volume I, p. 1.

2. Reminiscing about former Wooster presidents at the 75th anniversary in 1941, George N. Luccock, '78, referred to President Taylor as having been "equally at home in the parlor, or galloping up Market Street like a streamlined cowboy, or stirring a congregation with sermons of power."

3. Mr. Holden's grandfather had been a Yorkshire blacksmith. Holden himself was one of nine children.

4. When on a snowy day the boys were dismissed for recess, the headmaster banned snowballing. The boys were called in because of rough play, and young Holden, angry, threw a soft snowball at the headmaster hitting the back of his neck. He was suspended for insubordination.

5. Incidentally, Judge Martin Welker had given to the college library during his lifetime a complete set of *Congressional Records.*

6. The Reasin Beall home was built in 1815–1817, and is considered one of the oldest houses in Wooster. It became the Juliana Long home for furloughed missionaries. For many years it served as a dormitory for the overflow of freshman girls. Eventually, in 1955, it was given by the college to The Wayne County Historical Association for its museum and headquarters. Two swamp cypress trees on the grounds have as of now (1970) a diameter of approximately two feet. Though no one seems to know their history, they may well have been part of the original planting of the grounds. Reasin Beall was involved in the War of 1812. By the end of that war the first steamboat was on the Mississippi, and the baby trees may have been brought up in a tub on a steamer and then transported by smaller boat or wagon, or both, the rest of the way.

7. Formerly the Faculty Club, now the Alumni headquarters. Col. Curtis Volosco Hard had in 1864 enlisted in the 125th Ohio Volunteer Regiment, a part of Sheridan's army. As a Lt. Col. in the Ohio National Guard he saw active service also in Cuba. He was instrumental in organizing the Wooster Electric Co., was manager of the Cleveland and Wooster Electric Railway, and was a banker. (*History of Wayne County, Ohio,* Volume I, Indianapolis, Indiana: B. F. Bowen & Co., 1910, p. 800.)

8. This son graduated from the college with the class of 1903. He was to be a trustee years later (1927–1945).

9. Captain J. B. Taylor transferred his home in 1906 for use as a city hospital.

10. Lucas Flattery came to Wooster in 1840 and married a sister of Reasin Stibbs. They had nine children, several of whom attended the college, and one graduated in the class of 1877 and became a librarian at the University of Illinois. After his wife's death he married again a young woman who had been teaching in Mrs. Pope's school in Wooster. (By this second marriage he had two children, Thomas Flattery, '91, and Irene Flattery Scott, '00.) Most of this note from information in article in *The Wooster Daily Record,* August 25, 1960, "Tom Flattery Recalls Past."

11. Mr. Kirkwood's house was built on land "in a plat of lots laid out by Ephraim Quinby." In 1913 the house and lot were again sold, "to settle the Kirkwood estate," to Minnie E. and Mary Myers who occupied it until in 1950 it "passed into the hands of the college." For some years during the period before 1913 it was used as a chapter house by the Beta Theta Pi fraternity. (John D. McKee, *The Wooster Daily Record,* August 31, 1962.)

12. This house stood where Westminster church house now stands. The grave of Orange Stoddard is to be found in Wooster cemetery on the hill to the right of the lower entrance and well toward the north.

13. There are some discrepancies between Holden's own account of the conversation on this night of his election and the *Minutes* of the Board, which indicate that he accepted immediately. It seems probable that his own version of this detail is the more accurate, for the minutes were not taken by a stenographer but composed sometime later.

CHAPTER II

1. The early years, through 1910, were covered in Volume I, *Wooster of the Middle West* (New Haven: Yale University Press, 1937).

2. Among the contributors to the Wooster campaign that ended in December 1910 appear the names of several Thaws, of Helen Gould, of the James family (who endowed Wooster's presidency), of Mrs. Morris K. Jesup and others. Mrs. Jesup gave $1000; while she might well have given a cold shoulder to Wooster's plea, she didn't. Her husband was one of the Peary Club that backed financially Peary's Arctic explorations. Cape Morris K. Jesup at the extreme north end of Greenland is named for him.

3. At its meeting in February, 1911, at the suggestion of the Executive Committee the Board appointed also from its own number a committee "whose duties shall be the employment of all teachers and professors." The committee chosen was Holden, as chairman, Hills, and McClaran. The Board accepted as its own proper function "responsibility for the educational policy of the College," but noted also that it "needs the cooperation of the trained minds of the faculty whose business makes them masters of the academic

ideals." Mr. Holden reported later that he had "invited three members of his faculty, Notestein, Compton, and Martin, to look through the applications of candidates now before the committee and without conference with each other to write up their reports." The result of this was the election as professor of Greek of John B. Kelso and as instructor in history of Clarence Gould. From such beginnings came eventually a teaching staff committee.

4. Harvey Carson Grumbine died on December 24, 1941, at the age of 72 at his home at Lebanon, Pennsylvania. He left in his will $200,000 for a public library to be built in Lebanon and for the buying for it of books and magazines. To the last he clung to his eccentricities requesting that no newspapers be given a place within its walls.

5. George A. Mosel, *Through a Rear-View Mirror* (Amherst, Massachusetts, printed by Hamilton I. Nearell, Inc.), p. 63.

6. These chapter houses were not owned but rented. The Betas and Alpha Taus were on College Avenue, the Phi Gams and Sigma Chis on Beall Avenue.

7. The Melrose Orchard on Portage Road beyond Little Applecreek. Students referred to it as the faculty orchard because two of the faculty were among its owners.

8. "To the west, almost as far as eye can reach and only dominated by a tree-tipped horizon far in the distance, is the beautiful Killbuck Valley. It is a valley of fertile farms checked by the darker colors of new plowed ground in contrast with the land where the wheat has recently been cut; here and there the sun glints upon the roof of some prosperous farmer's silo, and it all blends and harmonizes into one master picture, a scene worth traveling many miles to behold. Such is the country around Wooster." (Letter dated October 1, 1917, to his mother from Earl Meadow Dunbar, '21.)

9. The Women's Advisory Board has had a long history of useful but little publicized activity. It was the logical successor to the Women's Educational Association initiated in 1883 and sponsored by Miss Annie Irish, Mrs. A. A. E. Taylor, and a small group of faculty wives and townswomen. At a time when there was no dean of women, nor any thought of one, they constituted themselves as a kind of corporate dean, to give the young women attending Wooster some sense that someone locally was interested in them as persons, in their activities, in their living conditions, in all the new world with which they were confronted when they came away from home to college. These women had much in mind the establishing at Wooster of a cottage system similar to that at Smith College. They had "resolved to lay before the Presbyterian women of Ohio the present facts as to the advantages offered to women in our well-beloved institution, and to ask from them substantial aid. We feel," they said, "that many women in our church will be glad to give at least one dollar each year."

In 1892 at the instigation of the faculty and President Scovel, the Board of Trustees proposed to and had approved by the Synod of Ohio the setting up of An Advisory Board of Women, chosen and confirmed by the Synod. There was to be one representative from each of the fourteen presbyteries. One third of the members were to be elected each year, on nomination of the Women's Advisory Board itself. It thus became effectively self-perpetuating. "It was meant," said President Scovel, "to bring together representative women from each presbytery who with womanly tact and intention would find ways to increase the efficiency of the institution in all matters pertaining to the young women who come into residence in the University."

Of the actual activities of this Board between 1892 and 1895 little is known. Their meetings were not held in Wooster. At the October 10th meeting of the Synod in 1895, at Chillicothe when the long-hoped-for first cottage was nearing completion, a local executive committee, consisting of four women from each of the Presbyterian churches of Wooster, was added to the Advisory Board. They were Mrs. J. Emerich, Mrs. W. W. Firestone, Mrs. James Mullins, Mrs. William Annat from the First Church, and from Westminster, Mrs. S. F. Scovel, Mrs. H. W. Brown soon to be replaced by Mrs. S. J. Kirkwood, Mrs. N. J. Platter, and Mrs. J. H. Packer.

There was work to be done. Hoover Cottage must be furnished, and the money found for the furnishing. Most of these women with daughters of their own, some of college or nearly-college age, would be alert to the needs of young women away from home. A meeting was consequently held in Wooster almost at once, at which the organization was effected and preliminary plans considered. Mrs. F. L. Achey of Dayton was named president, Mrs. Frederick Hoover of Sandusky, wife of the man who by his gift of $8000 had made the building seem possible, became first vice president. Three more vice presidents were named in order of priority, Mrs. J. R. Calder of Toledo, Mrs. H. G. O. Carey of Zanesville, and Mrs. Nellie West of Bellefontaine. (One would have thought that this was going to be a large corporation, but perhaps instead they were making sure that there would always be someone to chair a meeting!) Mrs. W. W. Firestone became secretary for both the larger Board and the local executive committee, and Mrs. S. J. Kirkwood, wife of the mathematics professor, appropriately enough, treasurer. Mrs. William Annat, '82, was made president of the local committee, a wise choice, for she knew first-hand the problems of the young women attending Wooster, and she was also the wife of the leading merchant in town.

There followed meeting after meeting in quick succession, for the "cottage" was to be opened for occupancy at the beginning of the second term in early January. The women had been empowered by the trustees not only to do the furnishing but to set prices for the rooms and the boarding. After a meeting with President Scovel to hear his thinking on the matter and on the number of rooms to be immediately furnished, they went to work. Boarding was set at $2.75 a week, rooms were to be for each occupant $1.00 a week save for those occupying the southeast and tower rooms. The charge for these was $1.50. The floors in the downstairs, they decided, must be stained to match the doors, mouldings must be installed for the hanging of pictures, curtain material must be bought and made up, material also for napkins and bedding, including counterpanes. Carpets must be chosen and installed, dishes, silver, glassware found. For the great fireplace in the reception hall they recommended coal rather than wood. In the midst of their deliberations they were rejoiced to hear that one of their number, Mrs. Jeremiah Packer, widow of a member of the class of 1871, had been chosen by the trustees as matron. They decided that they would like to furnish the parlor and reception hall as a memorial to Miss Annie B. Irish. At the following meeting Mrs. Kirkwood reported that there was enough money already in the treasury to do this. Presently Mrs. Firestone and Mrs. Platter were commissioned to go to Cleveland (presumably by Pennsylvania train to Orrville and the C.A.C. to Cleveland) and select there special pieces for the furnishing of these memorial rooms, rugs, tables, chairs including rockers, and "bric-a-brac." They spent two days there, and their purchases were approved. But there was still much else to be bought here at home. Much of this came from the William Annat store, for Mr. Annat had not only sent for samples of carpeting and other materials—including silverware—but was furnishing to them much of what they bought at cost or at a very liberal discount. Other local merchants of course furnished some other things; Messers. Bryson and Zimmerman, for instance, were told to send in to the trustees their bids for the window shades.

The next move was to contract with the Ladies Aid of the local Reformed Church to make twenty-four comforters for the beds at thirty-five cents each. The executive committee furnished the material. In the meantime there was the problem of the sheets and pillowcases to be solved. A meeting was called of all women interested, for Monday, December 30, 1895, at the First Presbyterian Church to make these up—They were to bring along basket picnic lunches. A seamstress had been employed to superintend the work; all others were volunteers. In a single day the work was completed and arrangements made for its proper laundering.

Gifts in the meantime were coming in. Friends in East Liverpool donated china, glass, and earthenware "for present use." The Christian Endeavor Society of Mansfield sent money for furnishing a bedroom ($50—the estimate set for a bedroom; a little later this was changed to $75). The Donaldson brothers furnished another in memory of their sister. Still others came from Mrs. Jacob Frick, Mrs. Carey Kauke, and Mrs. Kirkwood. Mrs. James Mullins gave $100 toward furnishing the dining room, adding more at various later dates. Mrs. Frick and Mrs. J. S. R. Overholt both gave memorial stained glass windows, Mrs. Frick in memory of her little daughter Helen, Mrs. Overholt for her daughter Grace (beside the grand stairway from the reception hall). So little by little through these last few weeks with help of many persons Hoover Cottage was made ready. At the last President Scovel himself came over, took off his coat, rolled up his sleeves and helped the workmen put the furniture in place. Even so, when college opened on the sixth of January, the beds and mattresses were not there. Borrowed mattresses were brought in, and thrown on the floor; and there the girls slept for several nights, making a slumber party of the occasion. Not until June 10 of 1896 was Hoover Cottage formally dedicated. At that time a portrait of Mr. Hoover was presented and a portrait also of Mrs. H. C. Scovel, the president's mother. There were speeches and music of course.

Yet when all this had become but a matter of record, the work of the Advisory Board, particularly of the local group, had but begun. They must be a guiding and supporting hand for the matron in her work. They appointed from their number small committees to watch over many things, to see, for instance, that the matron was planning adequate meals, well prepared, and pleasantly served, that she stayed within her budget, that she had the proper facilities, a well-equipped, if simple, well-ordered kitchen, a good cook, clean and dependable.—Later they were to insist on a housekeeper as well. Another committee made monthly inspections of the bathrooms and sanitary facilities, still another arranged for speakers, from a distance, women who could talk to the girls on manners, or health and health habits, on the problems that confronted the college girl or that might confront her, on the opportunities open to young women in the world of their day. Others saw that the library in the Cottage was equipped with a dictionary, and an encyclopedia, and magazines; sometime later the Board asked the trustees to have the college library open for an extra hour in the afternoon for girls who could not use it earlier in the day. Some years later they were to ask that a suite on the top floor of Hoover be isolated and equipped as an infirmary. They saw to the planning and the financing, asking the local alumnae to put on some kind of entertainment to raise the necessary money. The arrangements of course were simple, but the suite was scrubbed and freshly painted, walls and floor. They sought the advice of Dr. Mateer and of Dr. Kate Johnson, '91, a local physician, as to the necessary equipment. The Women's Board interviewed nurses in town to enlist their interest in college service as occasion might demand. Through the years as dormitories came, both men's and women's, they continued their active interest in furnishing and refurbishing these, always looking for quality yet always stretching pennies as far as they could go. Some of us can remember a day when they gathered up old carpets, sent them off to be shredded and cleaned and rewoven into parti-colored rugs, thick and durable, but not beautiful.

In those earlier days the trustees looked to the recommendations of the Advisory Board with interest, sometimes inviting the Board to meet with them for an hour to discuss their common problems as they related to the women of the college, suggesting to them extra projects such as the furnishing of a women's rest room in Kauke Hall. Regularly, at least once a year, a committee from the Advisory Board went to them to report in person. They once had recommended the use of Hoover Cottage for freshmen and preparatory girls only, and later recommended the finding of a dean of women.

There was a time in the thirties and early forties when the organization all but died. But on the coming of Mr. Lowry as president in 1944 it was, at his instigation, revitalized and a decorating committee appointed that has been exceedingly active in these later years.

With the appointment of a dean of women the activities of the Advisory Board became more limited. Yet in addition to the furnishing and decorating, they have continued to interest themselves in many things, in helping to find scholarships for girls who need money, in endowing the dean of women with a small fund for emergency use; in entertaining girls in their homes, individually or in groups, particularly foreign students. They have sought through drawing in members from neighboring cities and even occasionally from outside the state, to interest in Wooster women from a wider field and more varied background, feeling that their wisdom and experience elsewhere might prompt suggestions, in the intellectual, the social, the physical, and the aesthetic realms. They have acted on the principle that whatever tends toward the development of the woman of taste and background should be their interest and their responsibility in helping so far as possible to supply it. The Women's Educational Association in 1883 had as its goal a cottage system. The Advisory Board of today still believes in small dormitories, and small dining rooms where the amenities of life may be observed, and the individual, man or woman, may be exposed to the best, to good taste in its many and varying aspects. As the presence of a dean of women has greatly strengthened their hand, they feel the responsibility of standing behind her and strengthening her hand, by furnishing support both moral and financial.

CHAPTER III

1. The Kittaning brick #12 used in the building of Kenarden Lodge cost $22.50 per thousand (*Minutes* of the Board of Trustees, February 14, 1911, p. 285).

2. Mr. Kennedy was a New York banker of some prominence. He had been born in Scotland and had grown up there. Later he moved to New York and married an American woman, Emma Baker, who became the donor of Kenarden Lodge. Later she gave $10,000 for Livingstone and Westminster Homes. She died in July of 1930 at the age of 96 leaving to the college $25,000 for scholarships.

3. In Iowa, where he was before coming to Wooster, he had made himself very much a part of the local community. He loved to walk but he loved also sometimes to go exploring farther afield. He and two or three friends formed a science club and hiring horses would sometimes search the countryside for special mushrooms or unusual plants. He was one of three or four men to start the first golf club in Iowa. For a clubhouse they brought in an abandoned log cabin from the country, swept and garnished it to their liking, and there even sometimes in winter held parties. He had a sterner side, too. The story is told of a small mathematics class he had, six or seven boys from the more affluent of Parsons's constituency. For several months he had tried

in vain to interest them in the beauty of mathematical precision, in short to make them work. Finally he gave up and flunked the whole class. For several days, it is reported, town and gown were in a state of shock. Mr. Gable was a man with several strings to his bow. Earlier in his life he had taught Greek, French, and mathematics at an academy in New York state, mathematics and Latin for eight years at Lafayette College before going to Parsons, where, as at Wooster, he taught both mathematics and astronomy.

4. Ross Thomas, as student and teacher, had first been associated with Mr. Yanney at Mount Union.

5. Before coming to Wooster Lyman Knight had taught for several years at Savannah, Ohio, Academy. He began the year at Wooster under grim circumstances. His son, an only child, had accidentally shot himself while on vacation in Michigan. His wife had died several years before.

6. He had grown up speaking Dutch at home. When he went to preparatory school he studied Greek, Latin, German, and Dutch. He first studied French when he went to the University of Michigan.

7. At first they boarded at Kenarden. Soon, however, they were exploring other possibilities in town. Ross Thomas meanwhile had brought on a sister to keep house for him, and she was a good cook. Rather often consequently they foregathered at his apartment. Clarence Gould, hungry for the delicacies of the eastern shore, presently ordered a keg (in the story told to me it was represented as a barrel) of oysters fresh out of Chesapeake waters. On these he and the others dined sumptuously and with glee.

8. Mr. Daniel Burnham, Director General of the World's Fair of 1893, considered by many "as the most eminent living authority (at that time) on group arrangement of buildings," was consulted on the plans for the new Wooster. He stressed the importance of the adoption of one style of architecture for a harmonious effect. His advice, given without compensation, was the deciding factor in the final argument of the trustees. Further information about this came in a letter to Mr. Dunn from William H. McSurely, '86, trustee at the time:

When the trustees met to determine the building program, President Holden presented his plans and sketches in accordance with his ideas and wishes. This plan contemplated that each of the new buildings should be of a particular architectural style, different from the others. One building should be Gothic, one Spanish, one Tudor, one French, etc. His thought was that by having these samples of various architectural types on the campus, students would be educated as to the difference between them.

Some of the trustees thought this . . . a serious mistake as violating a fundamental principle of harmony and unity of design in group building. . . . A majority of the board, after a strenuous conference for an entire day, became convinced that his plan would produce an architectural hodge-podge which would be a permanent cause for the derision of everyone with any architectural or artistic culture. . . . the majority voted that one architectural type should be followed in all the buildings, and adopted the Collegiate Gothic for the group, which was the type Dr. Holden had proposed for Kauke Hall. Dr. Holden . . . fought strongly for his ideas, but I believe that when the buildings began to assume shape and their harmony became more apparent, he was convinced that the trustees, . . . prevented a very serious and irreparable architectural blunder. (The Wooster *Alumni Bulletin,* February 1924.)

9. One morning in the spring of 1906 Ralph Plummer, awakened early, and sitting up in bed, upon the inspiration of the moment, wrote the words of the Wooster "Love Song." Later in the morning he asked his friend and fraternity brother, Will H. Heindel, '06, what he thought of the words. Together they went into the Sigma Chi music room where Ralph tried several arrangements, each somewhat similar to the form he finally evolved. On the same day, presumably, he passed the original draft of the words back to Laura Anderson West, '06, during a class in Sociology or Apologetics. It remained in her possession from that time until the present, when she has kindly contributed it to the archives of the alumni office. . . . For some weeks the music was merely in his head and fingers, but he transcribed it in quartette form to be used at a college minstrel show on March 15, 1906, at which time it was first heard by the general public. Jim Kelly, *ex* '08, sang the verse in his fine voice and a girls' quartette, composed of Margaret Marquis, *ex* '09, Margaret Pomeroy Keet, '07, Edith Lawrence, *ex* '09, and Laura Anderson West, sang the chorus from the gallery of the old Opera House (Wooster *Alumni Bulletin,* March 1928).

10. The kitchen of Kenarden was in the northwest corner of the basement between two large dining rooms lighted by outside windows. One of these could double also as a recreation room, for at present there was no need for a second dining room.

11. This tablet was later placed in the south vestibule of Memorial Chapel. It read as follows:

In Memoriam

JOHN ROBINSON, D.D., L.L.D.

1814–1888

Early Advocate Of A Synodical University

AND

President Of Its Board of Trustees

From

Its Organization To His Death

———

A GODLY MAN, AN ABLE PREACHER

A WISE COUNSELLOR, A FAITHFUL FRIEND

"The things that thou has heard of me among many witnesses, the same commit thou to faithful men who shall be able to teach others also."   2nd Tim., 11:2

12. Mr. Lean on this occasion had read from Oliver Twist, Mr. Dunn had given a paper on Charles Dickens, Mr. Douglass another on the novelist as a humanitarian and reformer. Jean Stoner of the senior class had presented a sketch, "Why We Love Dickens." There were songs, also interspersed, by a member of the music faculty and two of the college girls.

13. The *Minutes* of the trustees show that as early as June 1, 1908, they had sent a cable to Clinton Tyler Wood electing him to a professorship of missions at $1500. He had obviously declined at that time.

14. "At the recommendation of President Holden it was ordered that the Chair of History be called the Michael O. Fisher Chair. He having contributed $25,000 toward the Endowment Fund, (he receiving an annuity until the death of self and wife)." On the college books today the amount reads $20,000. The treasurer's explanation of the discrepancy is that probably $5000 had been used up in paying the annuity (*Minutes* of the Board of Trustees, February 14, 1911).

CHAPTER IV

1. Later on the occasion of Wooster's 75th anniversary, J. Harry Cotton, '21, in speaking of the "International Wooster" said: "This college and its youth have recognized that there are no national boundaries to the truth of science or of art or of culture or of religion. There has breathed through this campus an air of freedom that comes from every land and every country, and it has deepened the life of every student consciously or unconsciously." In 1904 thirty-six children of missionaries were enrolled at Wooster either in the college or in the preparatory department; in 1905 there were forty-four (*Annual Reports* of the Board of Trustees).

2. The Julia Gleason furlough home was the gift of Mrs. Samuel Mather of Cleveland in honor of her mother. The Lucy Crouch Leaman home was given by Mr. L. H. Severance, in honor of the first missionary who had gone from the college. The Juliana Long home on Bowman Street was given also by him in memory of his grandparents. The Sarah Adams home on Beall Avenue was given also by him and named in honor of a friend of the Severances, "the first lady school teacher in Cleveland." The Mary Reynolds Schauffler home (old Platter home on the northwest corner of Beall and Bowman) was given by Mrs. A. F. Schauffler of New York in memory of her husband's mother. The Hunter Corbett home, a bungalow just east of Holden Hall, was given by John L. Severance. The Calvin Mateer home, next to the Corbett home was given by Mrs. Dudley P. Allen of New York City. Mrs. Allen was a daughter of Mr. L. H. Severance.

3. Gordon Enders and Edward Anthony; *Nowhere Else in the World*, published by Farrar and Rinehart, Inc., quoted by permission.

4. Wooster's first glee club, the Nonagons, was organized in 1887. Two years later they made their first trip, with concerts scheduled in Bucyrus, Defiance, Dover, Loudonville, New Philadelphia, Paulding, Toledo, Van

Wert, and Wellington. On May 4 of the same year they gave their first home concert. For these occasions they wore black velvet coats and knickerbockers, with gold vests.

Information from Wooster *Alumni Bulletin,* February, 1934.

5. A letter from Roberts Lowrie, '82, has this to say of dancing at Wooster in earlier days:

We had a fine large hall, second floor front, on the main street in the center of town. There we gave many entertainments—dances to which we invited our favorite coeds. There was no objection to this by the college authorities and no supervision whatever. We could have danced all night, though we never did. As much propriety was observed, as there would have been in the President's own house. Honor was the watchword in all the Fraternities; a Fraternity man had two honors at stake; his own, and the honor of the Fraternity. (From the file in the office of the editor of the *Alumni Bulletin.*)

6. In June, 1899, the trustees were still concerning themselves with certain internal business of the college. They had voted that a definite amount of literary and oratorical work be prescribed by the faculty for each student as a minimum requirement, the work actually done in the literary society to be counted as a fulfilment of this requirement. In 1901 the faculty required that students not members of a literary society "shall be required to prepare and hand in each term one thesis of not less than 2000 words upon an assigned topic."

7. It was considered such an honor that acceptance of an invitation to membership was almost obligatory. Only after a new member's initial address, however, was he formally inducted. Then he chose not only the state but the party he was to represent. The club was organized with standing committees and special committees. Bills presented on the floor of the house were usually passed or disapproved only after extended debate. In 1911 the Club was giving special attention to the drafting of bills and to the internal needs and resources of the United States. The organization, however, aimed to promote awareness of international as well as national affairs. Later in 1925 membership was increased to twenty, nine seniors, eight juniors, three sophomores. And by 1949 the Club had more than 400 alumni members. After Mr. Scovel's death Robert Caldwell became the faculty sponsor; he in turn was succeeded by Clarence Gould.

CHAPTER V

1. George A. Mosel, *Through a Rear-View Mirror,* p. 66. Quoted by permission.

2. The *Minutes* of the faculty under date of July 22, 1910, are strikingly similar in their listing of regulations governing life in the fraternity houses to the rules set down by the Interfraternity Council. These include:

(1) That each fraternity occupying a house be required, on or before September 24, 1910, to submit to the Faculty rules for the government of its house.

(2) That these rules be then endorsed by the Faculty or returned for revision.

(3) That when they have been endorsed by the Faculty and adopted by the fraternity, a copy be filed with the dean.

These rules in detail provided for the maintenance of quiet and non-interference with stated study hours, a reasonable retiring hour, "conditions favorable to study and to moral life," such as limitations on smoking, card-playing, singing, playing on instruments, etc.; and finally a method of enforcement of these rules.

3. December 14, 1948.

4. "You know," said Mr. Severance, "I have been a very strong advocate of these fraternities at Wooster. I have been in their fraternity houses and talked to the boys at various times when I have visited there. I have liked the spirit and their hearty cooperation with the administration. But since this has happened, I have invited several college graduates to lunch with me on various occasions, one day a couple of men who were fraternity men, another day a couple who were non-fraternity men, and do you know, that I have learned more about this business by these conferences than I ever knew before, and I am absolutely convinced that I am wrong in advocating a system within a college that can do the harm to the college that this system can do and unquestionably does.

. . . . .

"I have concluded, therefore, that from now on, I shall never give another dollar to any Christian college that tolerates fraternities."

(From *Memoirs* of Louis Edward Holden, as published in *The Wooster Daily Record,* December 14, 1948.)

5. I have been unable to find this letter to Dean Compton anywhere, but it is possible that it may still exist somewhere. L. L. N.

6. He was entirely accurate in this statement; he had not promised Wooster any money on condition that it ousted fraternities. All he had promised was that he would give nothing more to the college if fraternities were not abolished.

7. George A. Mosel, *Through a Rear-View Mirror,* p. 67.

CHAPTER VI

1. There is some question about this date. In one place Holden says that he met Severance during his own first year in Wooster, which would make it sometime in 1899–1900; in another he states that it was just six months after Severance's first visit to Wooster that the fire occurred. I have accepted the later date.

2. See Volume I, p. 244, where Holden says, "I was talking as a man in his sleep."

3. A bronze plaque on the west wall of the north transept bears this inscription:

THIS CHAPEL
OWES ITS ORIGIN TO
THE LIBERALITY OF
SARAH FRAME DAVIDSON
THE GIFT BEING MADE
IN MEMORY OF
HER HUSBAND
JOHN B. DAVIDSON
of
MORRIS, ILLINOIS
ERECTED 1901

4. He often advised as to the minutest detail, as when he ordered brick walks to be laid with a slight arch so that the water would run off (e.g., that walk still existing along the north side of the chapel). In an article ("The Builder of Wooster") in the *Alumni Bulletin* of January, 1924, Mr. Waldo H. Dunn relates that President Holden had insisted that the painters of the interior of the chapel match a shade of yellow in a ring he had. He recounts also, how years later, looking at the ivy on the chapel, President Holden exclaimed, "Doesn't the beauty of that sight do your soul good?"

CHAPTER VII

1. "Professor Dickason understood people, had an amazing memory. And he had personality. His contacts with students were personal and vital. He gave of himself freely and he was always willing to help a needy student with work or a loan.

. . . . .

"One school superintendent tells of his own early struggles. Like many another he came to Wooster ill-prepared for college. After Dean Compton had evaluated his credits, he realized how absurd it had been for him to dream of college. But Dr. Compton suggested that he stop at the preparatory building and see Professor Dickason. 'He may have some suggestion that will help you.' It seemed hopeless but the preparatory building was on the way to the car line, so he went up the steps and looked around. He saw an office on the right and a big man sitting at a desk. He stopped at the door and was just turning away when the man saw him. 'How do you do, sir,' he said, and 'what can I do for you today?' What Professor Dickason did was to change that boy's life." (The Wooster *Alumni Bulletin,* January, 1932, p. 78.)

2. At the time of the emergency drive for rebuilding after the fire, Mr. Walter Foss, chairman of the local committee, asked Mr. Dickason to help in soliciting money from Wayne County farmers. This he did gladly. President Holden himself tells the story:

With his usual tactfulness he [Mr. Dickason] approached a certain farmer. . . . The farmer listened most respectfully, . . . and then replied: "Professor Dickason, I have no money to give. I might spare you that mule" (that he was leading to water). "Thank you," said Professor Dickason, "I'll take the mule. A man down the road has just contributed a load of corn fodder which will feed him until I find a buyer." It was a serious moment when the farmer saw his mule being led off the farm. . . . Before the Professor got through the gate, the farmer hailed him and said, "Really, I don't know how I will get along without that mule. I will give you $50.00 for him. What do you say?" "Sold," said the professor, "to the highest bidder." (L. E. Holden, "The Epic of Our Institutional Life," Wooster *Alumni Bulletin,* January, 1934.)

3. In 1914 Dickason had run for Governor of Ohio on the Prohibition ticket.

4. About the work offered in the preparatory department, the college catalogue of 1908–1909 offers the following information:

Five courses are offered, at the completion of any of which a diploma is granted. Of these three are preparatory to the corresponding courses in the collegiate department; the fourth, the Normal, for teachers and those preparing to teach, is complete in itself; the fifth, the commercial, is likewise complete in itself.

5. William Jennings Bryan came to Wooster on another occasion, on a Saturday afternoon in October, 1915, to speak on the public square for the prohibition of intoxicating liquors (*The Wooster Voice,* November 4, 1915).

6. "The Summer School, which has become such a force in the educational work of the State, and has for a long time been the second largest Summer School in the United States, having connection with a University, again surprised us this year, by an enrollment of 447 students, almost all of whom were teachers in the public schools throughout the State. . . . It is indeed a great opportunity that our church has in thus moulding the thought and life of those who are teaching the thousands of children in our common schools. No Christian college, since the history of education began in this country, has ever had the opportunity of service, in the short space of 33 years, such as God has given to this institution." (From the *Report of the Board of Trustees to the Synod* for the year ending June 18, 1903, p. 4.)

7. In 1914 the Synod had formulated a plan for every church within its jurisdiction to contribute to the college annually from fifteen cents to fifty cents a member. It remained to be seen whether this could actually be put into the budgets of the churches.

8. A committee to plan this campaign had been appointed from among the trustees: Sheldon Parks, E. W. Allen, John West, W. H. Hudnut, W. H. Weir, David J. Meese, and President Holden.

9. Mr. Rowe was an Ohioan, and a graduate of Oberlin Conservatory. He had been professor and director of music first at Fargo College in North Dakota, then at Tabor College in Iowa.

10. As early as 1888 there had been appeal made by the college for the organizing of local alumni clubs.

11. The field had been laid out so that the sun would not shine in the eyes of the players. Underneath were 11,000 feet of tile drains put in by student labor under direction of Jay Bryan, the college engineer. The next year all of this was covered over with three or four feet more of dirt, and the running track was made over, also largely by student labor.

12. By 1914 the students were tiring of the traditional celebration of Washington's Birthday and asked for a holiday instead. The faculty said "No," but one of them suggested that instead they read Irving's *Life of George Washington*. This they did yet without any real enthusiasm. Fearing a general student strike the next year, the Student Senate arranged for the night of the twenty-second an all-college party in the gymnasium, requesting that, for the sake of the floor, everyone come in gum-soled shoes. This custom caught on and was continued for years, though eventually its freshness, too, wore off. In 1932 it became instead a student musical comedy, "Where Men Are Men." There was "an original overture with complete orchestration." Music and songs were by Ford Ross, '32, and John Hartzler, '33, and several others. The costumes as well were designed by students. Of it, Howard Lowry, then of the college faculty, wrote in *The Voice:* "Now apparently has come a renaissance of just and admirable folly, and it moves to music. . . . Let us keep it in our tradition. Charm, melody, beauty, and sublime nitwittedness are not common enough in this so sober and prosaic world that we can take them for granted. . . . Let us have another show next year." Such is the history of the Gum Shoe Hop. (Wooster *Alumni Bulletin,* April, 1932, and from *The Voice*.)

13. Not till 1917 were the commencement exercises scheduled on Wednesday, according to the catalogue.

CHAPTER VIII

1. Calliope was the muse of heroic poetry, and wore a laurel crown.

2. Though Mr. White was a layman while president of Wooster, he was ordained to the ministry of the United Presbyterian Church some years later.

3. Throughout all this conflict Dean Compton was in a delicate position: his sister-in-law, Mrs. Charles R. Compton, was a sister of J. Campbell White.

4. In the college catalogue of 1914–1915, the Rev. William F. Weir is

listed among the "Collegiate Faculty." It is little wonder that Mr. White made this mistake.

5. In conversation the next day, at which he was complimented by a colleague on his courageous stand, the dean replied merely: "You have to act with the light you've got."

6. However carefully they reported interviews, one still cannot be sure how much of hearsay was actually reported as fact by persons on both sides.

7. This trustee years later gave several hundred thousand dollars to Wooster.

CHAPTER IX

1. He had been for one year at London, Ohio, six years at Fostoria, and was in his second year at East High School, Cleveland, when Wooster sought him out.

2. The story is told that once Lawrence, while at Fostoria, asked his father to come up on a Saturday to see one of the games, and when it was all over the father had exclaimed: "Gosh, I wish they'd had a game like football when I was a boy."

3. Kinley McMillan, '86, is given credit for having introduced football to Wooster and for having trained its first team. He had learned the game while he was attending Princeton Theological Seminary. He was so enthusiastic that on returning to Wooster he made it his business to train its first team, which did him honor by winning from Denison 48–0 in the fall of 1889. The next year they won every game they played: from Denison 58–0, from Ohio State University 64–0, from Kenyon 30–0, from Adelbert (Western Reserve) 50–0, from Washington and Jefferson 6–4, and from Pittsburgh as well. The star players of that day were George Burns, '93, Robert L. Campbell, '91, J. Graham Chalfant, *ex* '93, Edward W. Forgy, '90, John R. Jameson, '90, M. R. Limb, *ex* '92, Charles C. Long, '91, George G. Long, '91, A. G. McGaw, '91, Charles Miller, '90, Robert H. Moore, *ex* '93, William W. Riddle, '90, Addison S. Rose, '91, Harry Scovel (prep.), John S. Speer, *ex* '91, Roy Yoder (prep.). Then in 1891 intercollegiate athletics were banned by Wooster's faculty.

4. It was a habit of life for Lyman Knight to make the most of whatever opportunities presented themselves for education. In his still earlier days he had roomed with Charles F. Kettering during one of Wooster's summer sessions, and the two had studied Greek together each night for five unbroken hours. He had been also a charter member of the first debating club of the college.

5. The honor courses offered at this time were in quantitative and organic chemistry, in Latin prose composition, and in the *Aeneid,* in the history of philosophy and metaphysics, in English Victorian poetry, and in Victorian prose, in the history of the American colonies, the American Revolution and

the Constitution, and in general American history, in a study of Goethe, in political science, in mechanics, in electricity and magnetism, in anatomy and physiology, in embryology, in the short story, in Greek drama, in Biblical Greek, in New Testament doctrines, in the philosophy of religion, in advanced calculus, and in differential equations.

6. Other courses were: the history of religion—"an outline of the great historic religions with special attention to their literature and to the social conditions formed under each of them"; the Hebrew prophets of the pre and of the post exilic periods; ancient church history of the early days of Christianity in Rome; the period between the Testaments, that is, the development of the Jews from 175 B.C. to 70 A.D.; the life of Christ; the various Epistles; the challenge of Islam, the awakening of the new China, the uplift of India; sunrise in Japan—and yet others.

7. Pliny the Younger, *Letters,* Book VI, Letter 2.

8. "Noty" once stopped a class deep in verbs and gerunds with a lifted finger. "Listen!" he said. Hushed, the class listened to a shivered roar and thud as a tall oak fell in the grove just outside the window. The death of the tree came strangely to those looking at blackboards and desks, remote from struggle and age and death.—"We have lost a friend," he said. ("Metius" Wooster *Alumni Bulletin,* November, 1930.) Also see Volume I, p. 281, note 17, and p. 291 at foot of page.

9. Because of the excellence of his work at the University of Chicago, Perry Strausbaugh was chosen to accompany the H. C. Cowles expedition as a collector of flora. The purpose was an ecological investigation of the coast range flora as far north as Mt. Ranier. (*The Wooster Voice,* September 20, 1917.)

10. Mr. Dunn's book had been published in England by J. M. Dent as one in the series, *Channels of English Literature,* and in the United States by E. P. Dutton. Its title was *English Biography.*

11. When in 1908 President Holden wrote to the Emerson College of Oratory, asking them to recommend a candidate for the teaching of oratory at Wooster, he is said to have specifically requested "someone who would not look well in skirts." They sent on Delbert Lean. (Told to me by Ralph Young.)

12. Jay Bryan's part in the history of Wooster goes back to the day of Old Main and of the well known "Gus" Eberly, to whom he was indeed a first assistant. When the power plant on Bever Street was built after the fire he was both electrician and plumber, an indispensable man, turning off the current at ten at night for economy's sake, turning on the fans again at four in the morning so that the classrooms would be warm when the students came swarming in at seven-thirty. Regulating the water supply, and hunting down leaks was another of his activities. This extended even to the putting in of drains under the athletic field, and making repairs when necessary. He was dependable and honest. By 1920 he had set up a workroom in the south end of the old gymnasium and had been allowed an assistant.

13. When Memorial Chapel had been built in 1901, the northwest corner had been left in brick unfinished. It was here that it was confidently supposed that the wing toward the north would be added to house the Y.M.C.A., the Y.W.C.A., and the Sunday School of Westminster Church. People became used to this homely back door and nothing was ever done about it.

CHAPTER X

1. It had first been mounted on this high stone base and placed in front of the chapel between the rows of elms. By 1923 this position had come to seem not the most suitable. So placed, the statue stood in the way of the cherished view from Kauke Hall down College Avenue and to the hill across the valley. It was then set up south of Memorial Chapel, and attached by bolts to an underground base. This arrangement proved to be only a challenge to students, who worked the bolts loose and repeatedly absconded with the statue. Sometimes Mr. Lincoln was found in a section of Kenarden or reposing in an attic or under a porch. The statue appeared not to be an inspiration to students but rather an invitation to devilment. In 1956 consequently it was put in storage where it remained until 1963, when once more it was firmly established south of the chapel, still bearing the inscription, "With malice toward none. . . ."

2. The following is a letter from Mr. John G. Segesman, concerning his part in the making of the statue. This appeared in *The Wooster Daily Record* of March 25, 1948. He was then 83.

Mr. W. H. Mullins who owned the Art Metal Works in Salem induced me to take a job in his modeling room as a potential "artist." In 1896 I left Wooster and started work in Salem. Mr. Alfonse Pelzer was the sculptor then. In 1897 he modeled an oversize statue of Lincoln from photographs and other pictures. That figure went to New Jersey. I have no record of any duplicates that were made from that model. . . . In 1899 Alfonse Pelzer gave up his job on account of poor health and left Salem shortly after to return to Germany where he died in less than two years. The day he quit work I was "promoted" by Mr. Mullins, with Mr. Pelzer's approval, from ornament modeler to sculptor, by ordering me to make a 13-foot Statue of Liberty, which stands on the public square of Allentown, Pa. In 1915 I got orders to make a life-size model of Abraham Lincoln. I copied the face from a plaster mask sent from Washington, D.C. There was no beard, the eyes were blank spots. These "missing parts" I copied from an oil painting.

The Wooster Lincoln, the two in Detroit, and others strung out along the Lincoln Highway were all made from that model. At the dedication of the Wooster statue Mr. James Mullins in his presentation speech told the audience my name, "a celebrated artist, a former Wooster man," as being the one that made the model. . . . I did all the statue work for 24 years. . . .

The original plan was for Mr. Mullins to send me to some art school for an indefinite time. But I never got that far, as orders for statues came in so frequently that I would not have been able to be absent for even a short time without delaying the work.

3. Beginning with the year of 1916–1917 gold medals had been given each year "to the three most effective debaters in the College of Wooster," under regulations set up and approved by the dean of the college and the heads of the Departments of Oratory and English. These medals were the gift of John D. Fackler, '00, a Cleveland lawyer.

4. On one such occasion, in Mr. White's administration, after recounting the story of Wooster's early struggles to win a college, the Reverend T. K. Davis hesitated a moment and then said, "And now I am sure you will understand the desire of an old man to spend a few moments with you in giving my testimony to the Holy Scriptures." At this Elias Compton, stepping to the podium, put his hand on Mr. Davis's shoulder and said, "There will be another opportunity," and drew him back to his seat.

5. She had her Mus. B. from Oberlin, and had had a year of private vocal instruction in New York.

6. Self-government already existed in Hoover Cottage as early as 1901. There was a president and an executive committee. A constitution was in effect. This provided that offenders against rules were to be reprimanded by the Executive Committee, and that all extreme cases were to be reported to the matron "who shall report the same to the Committee on Dormitories." Study hours were stipulated: 8:00 to 11:00 A.M.; 1:00 to 4:00 P.M. and 7:00 to 10:00 P.M. during which times halls and rooms were to be quiet. Study hours were relaxed for Friday evening. Callers were permitted on Tuesday evening from 7:30 to 9:00 and on Saturday from 7:00 to 8:30, also on Saturday afternoon after 2:00. "Young ladies," it went on to say, "shall not drive in company with young gentlemen in parties of less than four and all driving parties shall be in by 9:00 P.M."

7. In 1917–1918 a club plan was put in at Kenarden which brought down the cost of boarding to the student to just under four dollars.

8. During the administration of President Holden, O. A. Hills, chairman of the Board of Trustees, and Horace N. Mateer often worked till midnight or later auditing the books of the college. (John D. McKee, *The Wooster Daily Record*, December 1, 1962.)

9. This was a well-established tradition.

10. The one course was for children under eleven, in the rudiments of music, scale formations, keys, signatures, position of the fingers, hands and arms, ear training and simple harmony; the other was for those no older than fifteen and was slightly more advanced.

11. This breakfast was prepared by Mrs. Lean and served by the children. The menu also was a part of the custom. The boys learned to expect grapefruit, creamed chicken on toast, jam, strawberry shortcake piled high with whipped cream, and coffee.

12. The charter members of the Toastmasters' Club, chosen by Mr. Lean

because of their leadership in various student activities, were: Ralph S. Alexander, J. W. Bowman, Clarence Eddy, Robert Hole, James V. McDowell, Roy C. Miller, Paul B. Patton, T. L. Richards, Herman Retzler, J. J. Albright, Harold Collins, Lawrence Freer, Daniel Funk, John D. McKee, John H. Millar, Cary A. Hudson, C. G. Johnson, Thomas E. Roderick, Wilbur M. Smith, Hubert White, Arthur F. Zosnick (Southwick).

13. See Volume I, pp. 300–301.

14. In the first three months of his first year at the Shack, Bill Syrios and his partner sold 5400 wedges of pie, 18,000 "dopes," 10,800 egg sandwiches, 6000 each of ham and cheese sandwiches, and half a ton of candy.

15. "Bill" had come to this country at fourteen from the village of Tropaia, in the Pelopenesus, Greece, first to Milwaukee, then after some years to Wooster. As soon as he could, he became an American citizen; and in World War I he fought in France in the United States forces. It was not until the summer of 1925 that he hied himself to his native village and brought back a wife, Anna. Then the building was again enlarged, faced with brick. A back part was added, an upstairs, and porches. It became a home. Syrios had a daughter Anna and three sons. Menelaus and Anna were graduated from college in 1950. Gus and Chris followed along in the class of 1952 but never graduated. When eventually "Bill" was incapacitated by a stroke, two of the sons took over; then one left and Gus carried on—and still does. In 1957 Bill died, and a memorial service was held for him in the college chapel, for he was truly a member of the college community. On the thirtieth anniversary of his taking over the Shack he had held open house and had passed out free Cokes to all who came. The students later in the day through a delegation presented him with a $50 war bond and a wallet, and his wife Anna with a huge bouquet. Greek and Latin had by some unhappy mischance by this time pretty much faded from the scene at The College of Wooster, but the simple inheritors of a tradition, Angelo and Syrios, had brought with them to the campus something of the blue skies and warmth of their native lands.

CHAPTER XI

1. One night in 1917 Mr. Edison telephoned Mr. Hibben of Princeton. A problem of submarine detection was before the inventor. He wanted the help of an expert physicist. President Hibben sent Karl Compton to him early the next morning. In due time the problem was solved. (*The Standard Bearer,* Vol. II, No. 3, 1929.)

2. "Beer Garden" was the name given by students to the home of a Mrs. Beer, who rented several rooms to students. It was at the northeast corner of Beall Avenue and Wayne.

3. In February, 1918, Mr. Chancellor talked to the students in chapel on Economic Phases of the War. In this address he said: "The economic world is in ruins. Government ownership and operation have come to stay, and increase. Whether we can ever return to the liberty of the economic life of

the first decade of this century is exceedingly doubtful. Let the war continue two years and there will be active starvation in America."

4. In Palestine Mr. Vance was for fifteen months captain of a Red Cross Commission in the administration of relief to civilians. In Aleppo later he was looking after the arrangements for 800 Armenian refugees. Later, in 1932 he, with Mrs. Vance, took a year off to go to India and teach at Ewing Christian College at Allahabad, then to go on around the world.

J. Milton Vance and Elizabeth Wood had first met at Lake Forest College as students. Then she went to teach music in South Africa. Several years elapsed before they met again, this time in Germany. They were married soon after he came to Wooster in 1906. (Wooster *Alumni Bulletin,* May, 1943.)

5. Miss Field was a graduate of Smith College of the class of 1903. She had received her Master's degree and her Ph.D. from the University of Colorado in 1909 and 1913 respectively.

6. The 2200-pound bell in the south tower of the Memorial Chapel bears this inscription:

This Bell was Presented to the University of Wooster in Memory of President William McKinley By A Staunch Friend, Senator Marcus A. Hanna
November 1, 1901

President Holden had, however, not made the announcement of this gift until November 7, lest such announcement might be interpreted as campaign publicity. This was a Senatorial election year.

CHAPTER XII

1. The family of Reasin Beall had come originally from Scotland, from a little town on the Clyde.

2. Of Frank Hays, "Metius," a columnist in the Wooster *Alumni Bulletin* (November, 1930), wrote: "Whoever learned of him learned more than history, and Wooster has inherited both the wisdom of his historical values and the memory of a gentle man." "Metius" was actually Martha L. White Frost '20, later a trustee of the college.

3. As late as 1920, though there was a commencement speaker, the audience still had to suffer through listening to a valedictory oration by a member of the class being graduated.

CHAPTER XIII

1. Mr. Wishart was considering also a call to a church in Portland, Oregon.

2. This boy was Howard Lowry.

3. Her father, the Rev. I. N. Kieffer, was a highly respected and beloved

member of the Wooster community. He had served in the Civil War as a musician, having enlisted at nineteen, and again in the Spanish-American War as a chaplain. It happened once while he was living in Wooster that his house burned down. A citizens' mass meeting was at once called at the City Opera House and in an afternoon enough money raised for the rebuilding. The present Kieffer Street where his home stood was named for him.

4. "Howard Lowry, '23, proved the appropriateness of his title 'Can't Hold My Tongue.' In a burst of eloquence never before equalled on college hill he reviewed the records and high standing set by the juniors, and predicted the course of '23." (*The Wooster Voice*, November 13, 1919.)

5. Mr. Boles' custom of wearing a yellow chrysanthemum at football games began in 1919. The first chrysanthemum was given to him by Mary Arnold, '22. After her graduation, Mr. C. Weir Ellenwood of the Ohio Agricultural Experiment Station carried on the custom. (Wooster *Alumni Bulletin*, December, 1932.)

6. A football sweater.

7. John Baird had been flying a bombing plane in the Toul sector in September of 1918.

8. In a letter to the alumni in the first four or five months of his administration President Wishart explained his position thus:

A problem so far-reaching in its implications, and so intertwined with old differences should not find any final adjustment in the first or even the second year of a new administration. I would have been quite content to accept the fraternity system and to work with it in all good faith had it the *status quo* at the present time. But it does not now have the *status quo*, and I am compelled to face, not the abstract question of the advantage or disadvantage of any system, but rather the very concrete question as to whether any advantage would compensate us for breaking up a harmonious student body, faculty, and Board into hostile camps along the lines of the old cleavage. (*The Wooster Quarterly*, January, 1920.)

9. Mr. Boles was at this time chairman of the faculty committee on publicity and Mr. Murray would be working under his supervision.

CHAPTER XIV

1. In 1967 the site of the old Highland Park was taken over by a new four-way highway in the making, north and south. Enchantment has yielded to speed.

2. The little graveyard on the knoll to the left of Portage Road as one goes up the hill toward Cleveland Road is now run down; the gravestones, many of them, have fallen flat and are almost hidden in weeds. It was deeded on May 3, 1853, to President Franklin Pierce and his successors in perpetuity by John and Elizabeth Plank in the hope no doubt that the little plot would have perennial care. The plan has worked out quite otherwise. Though it is

probably one of the older burial plots in Wayne County, even the local populace hasn't cared.

3. The Cleveland Pike, once many years ago a plank road, is now the northern part of Cleveland Road within the Wooster city limits.

4. In the succeeding years of Mr. Wishart's administration Wooster had many distinguished commencement speakers—administrators, scholars, and clergymen, among them Newton D. Baker, Irving Babbitt, John H. Finley of the New York *Times,* S. Parkes Cadman, Samuel Eliot Morrison, Mary E. Woolley, Frederic Lauriston Bullard, '91, of the Boston *Herald,* Harold W. Dodds, Bishop Francis J. McConnell, the Honorable George W. Norris, William E. Wickenden, George A. Buttrick.

5. He had seen active service in France. In 1929–1930 he was to become president of the American Alumni Council.

6. When as preparation for the campaign of 1920–1922 Mr. Wishart had sought out the Rockefeller General Education Board in New York, he found its representative "critical" of Wooster "for spending more for maintenance and administration than for instruction."

7. It was understood by the cast of this play as they were chosen that they would be the charter members of a new dramatic club. Howard Lowry, '23, was among these.

8. As business manager it was his responsibility to supervise the actual construction of new college buildings. This work for him began with Kenarden Lodge in 1911, and ended only with the building of the Westinghouse Power Plant in 1939. In this connection one should note that W. H. Wilson, Wooster's professor of mathematics, 1900–1907, had supervised the construction of Holden Hall.

9. See "How Memories Crowd" by John D. McKee, Wooster *Alumni Bulletin,* March, 1966.

10. The Alumni Council set up a variety of committees: Finance, Class Records and Organization, Secondary Schools, Alumni Clubs, Undergraduate Activities (songbook, etc.), Commencement, Vocational Conferences, Class Memorials.

CHAPTER XV

1. In 1919 Mr. Chancellor had been appointed by Governor Cox as one of the representatives from Ohio to the Plymouth (Massachusetts) Ter-Centenary. (*The Wooster Voice,* May 15, 1919.)

2. He had had published in the spring of 1920 a textbook, *Educational Sociology* (The Century Company).

3. Mr. Chancellor as councilman was advocating more paved streets, storm sewers, and a bridge over the Pennsylvania Railroad tracks at Liberty Street.

4. In 1963 Joe Follis and his wife celebrated their fiftieth wedding anniversary at the Faculty Club. It was appropriate that they should hold it there, for since 1926 he had been storeroom keeper and custodian for the

Department of Chemistry, and many students, faculty, and townspeople knew them and their family. One daughter indeed had been graduated from the college, another from Heidelberg. He was a graduate of Wooster high school, where he had been a football player. He was well known in town for his excellent, if untrained, bass-baritone voice, and was soloist for the Wooster Male Chorus. At his work he was often chuckling as he talked with students, and, like Bill Shack, he had a remarkable memory for names and faces. He had also the integrity and dignity of a man with respect for himself and his own job. And when one asked a favor of him, he made one feel that the favor was rather to him.

5. Those present were John Timothy Stone, president of the Board, S. S. Palmer of Columbus, Charles Krichbaum of Canton, L. A. Woodard and Robert R. Woods of Wooster, Adelbert P. Higley of Cleveland, Richard L. Cameron of Maryville, Thomas M. Bigger of Columbus, and of course Mr. Wishart.

6. Exact words taken from President Howard Lowry's oral account to me. L.L.N.

CHAPTER XVI

1. According to *The Voice* he had scored well on to half of all the points made by the Wooster team during the season. At the Case game on the Case field he had "returned a Case punt 80 yards for a touchdown." The award committee had been Gov. James M. Cox, chairman, Henry P. Edwards, football expert of the Cleveland *Plain Dealer,* Joseph Williams, a football expert of *The Cleveland News-Leader,* Clyde Tuttle, sporting editor of *The Ohio State Journal,* and Bob Newhall, sporting editor of *The Cincinnati Commercial Tribune.* Their decision had been unanimous. When Snyder had driven back with his Templar after the award, students and faculty were gathered at the gymnasium to greet him.

2. In this list were the names of Earl Dunbar, '21, winner of the Edward Taylor prize scholarship as well as a Fackler medal, Marshall Knappen, '21, of course, and Howard Lowry, '23, the first freshman ever to be awarded a Fackler medal.

3. *Minute* of Faculty dated, May 6, 1921, as quoted in Alumni Round Table, *The Wooster Quarterly,* October, 1921.

The Faculty places on record the deep sense of obligation which the College of Wooster feels toward Dean Elias Compton, who for the last twenty-two years has served here, in a position of great difficulty with consummate ability and success. Steady, wise, just, and eminently human, he has steered safely through many threatening crises of discipline; and in the end his judgments have been vindicated by the test of time. Through these years of service, ripening experience in academic affairs, a broad intercollegiate acquaintance, and deep study of collegiate problems, have brought him to a position of influence throughout the intercollegiate world, as well as in his own institution. His recent election as president of the association of presidents and deans in the Ohio Conference is concrete testimony concerning his position in the respect and affection of his colleagues. We join in tendering him our grateful good wishes, and along with them our deep sense of loss in his retirement from official service in the capacity as dean. Our hope and expectation is, however, that thereby his years of teaching service may be greatly prolonged, and that for a long time to come we may have the benefit of his presence and counsel in the solution of all our problems.

4. Later he was to become in Korea the president of Keimyung Christian College.

5. "The man to whom the College will forever owe a debt for his early and continuing solicitude for the library is Professor Notestein. As chairman of the library committee he was constantly on the alert for ways of obtaining equipment as well as books. When he saw an advertisement or heard of an auction of old books he would attend it if he could, or if not, he would write to an alumnus or friend in the area, and ask him to bid up to a certain amount. . . . He also begged cases, which were converted into stacks, from Ohio churches."

(Elizabeth Bechtel, Librarian in Wooster *Alumni Bulletin,* May, 1963.)

6. On this occasion the Rev. W. E. Feeman spoke for the citizens inviting Dunbar to give his oration at the City Hall, and Herman Freedlander was on the platform to say how proud he always was when traveling to announce that he came from the town where the College of Wooster was located. This is just an early bit of evidence of his long friendship for the college.

7. Later she took her bachelor's degree at Northwestern University, her Ph.D. at the University of Iowa, and studied also at Teachers' College, Columbia.

8. During the summer of 1917 Mr. W. H. Dunn contributed six articles to the *Encyclopedia Americana* on Boswell's *Life of Johnson,* Johnson's *Lives of the Poets,* Lockhart's *Life of Scott,* Southey's *Life of Nelson,* Mrs. Gaskell's *Life of Charlotte Bronte,* and Trevelyan's *Life of Macaulay.* (*The Wooster Voice,* September 20, 1917.)

9. In 1909 Grace E. Smith, '08, went to Toledo as educational secretary of the Y.W.C.A. At the end of one year she became manager of their dining room, even converting a losing into a flourishing business. The result was the opening of Smith's Cafeteria in January, 1916. In 1921 it doubled its capacity. The Ottawa Hills Tea House opened in 1920 also. She was superintendent of the Sunday School of The Toledo United Presbyterian Church, only woman member of the executive committee of the Toledo Council of Churches, a member of the Y.W.C.A. board of directors, treasurer of the Woman's Club of Toledo, and chairman of the scholarship fund of the Association of Collegiate Alumnae of Toledo. (*The College of Wooster Bulletin,* October 1, 1922.)

10. This undoubtedly referred to the intercollegiate activities which brought honor to the college represented.

The Wooster undergraduate and alumni charter members were: Earl M. Dunbar, '21; Miles J. Martin, '21; Roy Sharrock, '21; James H. Spencer, '21; Willis B. Townsend, '21; David Allen, '22; John P. Cotton, '22; Herrick L. Johnston, '22; Theodore Cuyler Young, '22; Robert N. Wright, '22; Thomas Coyle, '23; Howard Lowry, '23; Craig McClelland, '23; John W. Miller, '23; Walter E. Rosenberger, '11; Robert Guinther, '11; Harry L. Post, '10; John D. McKee, '17; Irvin W. Stillinger, '18; Warren P. Spencer, '19; Walter C. Hart, '19.

11. By 1920 the date of the senior farewell communion service had already been changed to the Sunday preceding commencement week, and the Sunday morning service of commencement week was given over to a sermon by an alumnus. This custom persisted until in 1927, when the baccalaureate service was shifted from Sunday afternoon to the morning. An alumnus was then given a minor part in the morning service.

CHAPTER XVII

1. From "Wooster, 1919–1941: An Interpretation," an address on the occasion of the 75th anniversary of the granting of the charter to the college.

2. The song contest was won by Clinton Tyler Wood of the faculty. The music for this was written by his sister, Mrs. J. M. Vance. The second prize went to Howard Foster Lowry, '23, for his marching song.

3. The college band was first given "a superb set of instruments" by Henry Clay Frick. (Sylvester F. Scovel, "History of the University of Wooster," *History of Wayne County, Ohio*, Vol. I, Indianapolis, Indiana: B. T. Bowen & Co., 1910, p. 534.)

4. In 1924–1925 the men in college were all wearing balloon trousers.

5. Stanley Welty, now president of the Wooster Brush Company, was captain of the champion college football team of 1923.

6. In this game with Ohio State University, Howard J. Smith, '26, made a memorable 39-yard run to clinch a touchdown for Wooster.

7. No dates for walks on Sunday afternoon were allowed. Though doubtless this was an unpopular restriction, the students did have a code of their own that sometimes surprises. When in town, for instance, the subject of allowing Sunday movies came up, the student poll was against this. Roelif Loveland, writing a series of articles in *The Cleveland Plain Dealer* in the early thirties on the graduating classes of some Ohio colleges and universities, had interesting things to say about Wooster: ". . . the young folks in college these days are better behaved than their fathers were. They do not go around crowning each other on the head with beer bottles and dragging cows into chapel. They do not spend their days lighting one cigarette from another nor their evenings building up a Don Juan past. At least not at Wooster College." He added that the Wooster students he met were "pretty level-headed," that

they were "not belligerently religious but have a belief in a divine providence." Then he quoted a senior youth as saying, "Some of them lose their religion here at school, but not all of it, and what they retain they feel sure is correct, because they've thought the thing through." Mr. Loveland noted also that the Wooster students "studied hard" and had "a scrappy football team."

8. At the beginning of Mr. Wishart's administration the story was widely current that several sections of Kenarden Lodge were housing sub-rosa fraternities. Mr. Wishart called in the suspects and nothing more was heard of the organizations. It is of course possible that after the ousting of fraternities there may have been several groups that continued some kind of loose organization in the hope that fraternities would before long be reinstated and that they would be in a position to reapply at once for national charters, but that they had any sanction from the national fraternities I find quite unbelievable. No reputable fraternity would have carried on a sub-rosa organization.

9. By the end of 1926 Wooster teams had won thirty-five out of fifty-five debates. In the Civic Oratorical Contests (eight colleges from three states) Wooster had won four firsts in four years. In the Ohio Oratorical Association it had won three firsts in five years. (*College of Wooster Bulletin,* 19th Series, No. 9, January 1, 1926.)

The questions for debate chosen were on such subjects as: Resolved, That the power of the Federal Supreme Court to declare statutes unconstitutional be restricted; or Resolved, That the United States should ratify the Protocol for the pacific settlement of international disputes.

A Fackler medal was first awarded to a woman in 1928, Dorothy A. Critchfield of the class of 1929.

10. Marion Fitch's, '33, essay was entitled "Chemistry as an Aid to Cultural Enjoyment," C. Gerald Albert's (also of 1933) "Utilization of Chemical Wastes."

11. On May 9, 1925, Delta Sigma Rho held an all-college banquet in Kauke Hall at which the Fackler medals were presented. Mr. Wishart was toastmaster, Congressman John McSweeney spoke, Mr. Lean also and Howard Lowry. According to *The Voice* of the following week: "Howard Lowry gave a thrilling talk on everything in general."

12. Mrs. C. O. Williamson often helped to direct some of the college plays.

13. On that day the whole town turned out in the college colors of black and gold, and for the historical pageant in the afternoon complimentary tickets were passed out at the fair grounds to 5000 school children.

14. Mrs. Hoover's great-grandfather, on her mother's side, Joshua Weed, is buried in the Canaan Bend cemetery, northwest of Jackson. Her grandfather, Phineas Weed, had a stagecoach shop in Jackson on the northeast corner of the junction of Cleveland Road (Route 3) and the east-west road, directly across from the picturesque old house where there is now (1967) an antique

shop. His daughter, Florence Weed, became the wife of Charles Henry. For a while she attended the Grove's Female Seminary in Wooster of which Mrs. Pope was principal. (E. H. Hauenstein, *The Wooster Daily Record,* May 1, 1951.)

15. The judges were Giovanni Martinelli, Louise Homer, Marcella Sembrich, Yeatman Griffith, George Fergusson, T. Tertius Noble, Giuseppe Sturani. Genevieve Rowe was the unanimous first choice.

16. A full weekend had been arranged for them by the president of the Wooster Alumni Club. Before presenting a fifteen-minute program at the Women's Exhibition in the Public Auditorium, they had sung for the business men of the City Club.

17. By 1936 the Wooster Orchestra had eighty-five members. The Musical Arts Association of Wooster had by this time taken over the financing of the organization, and had just completed raising $1000 for it.

18. In 1942 there was organized also the Wooster Ensemble Society for the study of chamber music. To this students, alumni, and even high school students were eligible.

19. The discipline among the young women consisted chiefly of S. P. (special probation, which meant no dates for the time specified), for minor infractions of the rules, suspension for graver offenses. At the weekly women's chapel the names were announced of those who were summoned to appear before the women's discipline committee.

20. This was at a time when the financial going was hard for many students, when at least one fourth of them were earning a part of their way. They were waiting tables, reading papers for professors, helping downtown in restaurants, laundries, or at local hotels, ushering in theaters, doing odd jobs, earning a dollar wherever a dollar could be found.

21. At first this term in India was set for three years. Before long it was changed to two.

22. "One of the most interesting events of the year (1939) was the drive on behalf of refugee students from Germany. The initiative of this movement came wholly from the student body, and the matter was planned and carried out through them. The students, with some aid from the faculty, raised a fund of $1000.00 to care for two refugee students from Germany next year." (Annual Report of the Board of Trustees, to the Synod, 1939.)

23. Before our actual involvement in the war *The Voice* took an isolationist stand. The students who could not countenance this stand brought out *The Whisper.* Then came *The Whistler,* and finally *The Fence-Sitter,* "signed Mugwumps." (Wooster *Alumni Bulletin,* December, 1941.)

24. By the time he came to Wooster in the summer of 1921, Carl B. Munson, standing 6 feet 2 inches in his socks and weighing 195 pounds, had a considerable record behind him, Pony League baseball, semi-pro basketball; he had been a prizefighter also in the light heavyweight division. Of sturdy stock, the oldest of five boys, and a born athlete, he had been playing baseball,

basketball, football in his hometown of Jamestown, New York, since he was thirteen. He had attended Slippery Rock State Normal School, had married Ingeborg Carlson, and had been director of the Jamestown Y.M.C.A. athletic activities for some years, save when in World War I he served at Camp Lee, Virginia. At Wooster he had been employed as assistant coach in football, head coach in track. A year later he was organizing the first intercollegiate swimming meet in Ohio, with Case. At times he coached also soccer and wrestling. All in all in his forty-one years at Wooster he chalked up more than 300 victories in one field or another of athletics. After being at Wooster for some years he returned to the East to complete a B.S. degree and later an M.S. in physical education. He is reputed to have been a stern disciplinarian; very little escaped his eye. He could lose his temper on occasion, yet he earned the devotion of the men he trained. ("Mose" Hole's column in *The Wooster Daily Record.*)

25. The track and baseball teams of 1929, the football team of 1929, the basketball team of 1929–1930 lost but four contests and tied one with Ohio Conference colleges. Coach Boles said this was the best record for major sports since he had been in Wooster.

The baseball scores for 1929 had been as follows: Wooster 5–Baldwin-Wallace 2; Wooster 2–Oberlin 2 (16 innings); Wooster 19–Otterbein 6; Wooster 3–Mt. Union 2; Wooster 10–Ohio Northern 2; Wooster 11–Akron 6; Wooster 6–Kent 1; Wooster 3–Ohio State 9; Wooster 21–Baldwin-Wallace 6; Wooster 11–Akron 2; Wooster 5–Otterbein 1; Wooster 1–Cincinnati 2. (Wooster *Alumni Bulletins* for July, 1929, and July, 1930.)

26. In 1931 Wooster played the Navy at Annapolis, accompanied by a large crowd of Wooster students. Though defeated, they had a major satisfaction in seeing Harold Pryor, '34, score a touchdown. He was only a sophomore at that time.

CHAPTER XVIII

1. The fall of 1935 was particularly beautiful around Wooster. One morning President Wishart dismissed chapel because the outside world was too beautiful to admit of an inside program. (Wooster *Alumni Bulletin,* November, 1935.)

2. When President Wishart was elected Moderator of the General Assembly, "we rang the chapel bell and had a big celebration on the campus. You'd have thought Prexy had made a touchdown from kick-off." (Howard Lowry's column, *College of Wooster Bulletin,* July 1, 1923.)

When Mr. Wishart returned from Indianapolis, a celebration was held in the chapel. Representatives from the faculty, the students and Westminster Church spoke, Mr. E. C. Dix, also, from the Board of Trade, and the mayor. It had been in Indianapolis that in 1894 Mr. Wishart had won the interstate intercollegiate oratorical contest.

3. The resolution offered by Mr. Bryan was:

Resolved, that no part of the educational fund of the Presbyterian Church, U.S.A. shall be paid to any school, college, university, or theological seminary that teaches or permits to be taught as a proven fact either Darwinism or any other evolutionary hypothesis that links man in blood relationship with any other form of life.

The substitute motion, offered by Mr. John Willis Baer, chairman of the Assembly committee on education, was adopted:

Resolved, that the Synods and Presbyteries within whose bounds Presbyterian supported academies, colleges or training schools are located are herewith instructed to exercise careful oversight over the instruction given in such institutions, and that the Synods and Presbyteries withhold their official approval from such academies, colleges and training schools where any teaching or instruction is given which seeks to establish a materialistic evolutionary philosophy of life which disregards or attempts to discredit the Christian faith.

4. In 1928 the attendance had dropped to 862 from the 925 of the preceding year. Yet nineteen out of thirty-five neighboring colleges also had a decreased attendance. (As indicated in the *58th Annual Report of the Board of Trustees,* June 15, 1928.)

CHAPTER XIX

1. The Juliana Long missionary home on Bowman Street was bought in 1924 by Mrs. Alice C. Ebersbach of Ann Arbor, Michigan, as a memorial to her parents Samuel G. and Harriet Miller, long residents of Wooster. It thenceforth was given the name of Miller Manor and became a small dormitory for girls. It so remained until in 1958 the college gave it to house the Wayne County Historical Society and the local museum. She had been one of several persons who had made possible the building also of the annex to Holden Hall.

2. In 1922 Mr. Thomas A. Jacobs was appointed as assistant to President Wishart. He came with a background of forty years of experience in financial institutions in the Youngstown area.

3. By way of a parallel to some of his own experiences in hunting money for Wooster, Mr. Wishart records also one of President Scovel's. Mr. Scovel had one Sunday delivered an "eloquent" sermon in the New York church attended by Russell Sage. The next day he went to call on Mr. Sage in the interest of Wooster. "The latter listened, then wrote out a check. 'Here is $50 for your sermon. I don't give a damn for your college.' " (*The Wooster Daily Record,* December 1, 1951.)

4. Mrs. Livingstone Taylor was always especially interested in the two homes, Livingstone and Westminster, for the children of missionary children. She often had one of the young women in her home for a summer as a secretary or secretarial assistant of some kind. She was one of the substantial contributors in helping to build Memorial Chapel and later gave $5000 for

its pipe organ. In the financial campaign ending in March of 1908 she had given the college $25,000.

5. As a young man Mr. Miller had first entered what is now the University of Pittsburgh. After a year he transferred to Wooster. He did not go on to graduation, taking a position instead with the Baltimore & Ohio Railroad in 1880. Later he was employed by the Westinghouse interests in Philadelphia, then in Pittsburgh. During his long life he was identified also with many companies or banks: as vice chairman of the Board of Directors of the Pittsburgh Screw and Bolt Company, chairman of the Board of the First National Bank of Wilmerding, a director of the American Brake Company, of the Davison Coke and Iron Company, of the East Pittsburgh and Wilmerding Coal Company, the Fidelity Title & Trust Company, the Locomotive Stoker Company, the Massey Concrete Products Corporation, and others. He was decorated by the Japanese with the Order of the Rising Sun. Because of his outstanding record in business, Wooster voted him in 1921 the B.A. degree and enrolled him with the class of 1881. In 1931, on the occasion of their fiftieth reunion, Mr. Miller paid the expenses of all his classmates who could return for the occasion, took over a part of Hoover Cottage and entertained them all there for the commencement weekend. As a trustee of Wooster Mr. Miller is credited as having had much to do with shaping the administrative legislation and reorganizing the financial structure of the institution. He died at Goshen, New York, September 17, 1939.

6. The architects were Janssen & Cocken, of Pittsburgh, the contractor Long and Bogner of Wooster. Dr. John G. Wishard of the Board of Trustees, for many years a medical missionary in Persia, gave much attention to the planning of the building, and its facilities.

7. The architect for the new Herman Westinghouse Power Plant was Mr. W. Edgar Reed of Pittsburgh. The general contractor came also from Pittsburgh.

The old power house was not removed until the summer of 1940. The chimney had been struck by lightning at least once and, as the freezing and thawing of the winter loosened bricks at the top, the trustees finally faced the necessity of paying the bill to take it down.

8. In 1972 Centennial Hall, built by Lucas Flattery, will be 100 years old. Its bricks were burned in a local kiln; its foundation stones dug from the Coe quarries east of town, just beyond Little Applecreek. Its woodwork shows the master workmanship of a day when men were proud of what they did. It was on land that had been a part of the plat laid out and designated as "R. B. Stibbs second addition to Wooster." Lucas Flattery was himself a venerable character, one of the founding fathers of the college. Born in Lancaster, Ohio, he had moved to Wooster in 1840, a lawyer and a collector of federal revenue. Mr. Flattery, however, lived in the house for a comparatively short time, for in January of 1876 he sold it to John H. Kauke, who in turn sold it to the college for $6000 on March 31, 1900. All through Mr. Scovel's administration, the house, however, had been used as the president's home.

Lucas Flattery had moved to College Avenue, living for a while in the old McCuskey house (later that of Elias Compton) and then to his own house farther down the street. (Information largely from an article by John D. McKee.)

9. The actual cost of Douglass Hall was $262,000.

10. For many years the old gymnasium housed the workshop and tools of the college carpenters, plumber, electrician and grounds crew; the book shop, the sub-station post-office for outgoing mail, the garage for the college car with its gasoline pump just outside. It housed also the office of the maintenance director.

11. Mr. William A. Galpin was born in Milan, Ohio, on December 20, 1851. He had at one time been closely associated with L. H. Severance. A son taught in a New England college.

12. Other Board members contributed the chairs and other furnishings of the Board room in Galpin.

13. Mr. Babcock's interest in the band probably stemmed from his great love of music. In his home church in Phelps, New York, he was long director of the choir. The first shipment from Scotland of kilts for the band was in the early days of the war. The ship carrying them was sunk in the Atlantic by a German submarine. Replacements came through months later. The bagpipes, made by Argyll in Scotland, at first two only, were not added until after the war. Wooster Scots chose the MacLeod tartan because of its black and gold. They wear the Glengarry headdress. The band gradually grew till it included some fifty instruments. It annually gave a concert on the night of Color Day.

14. By 1941 The Empire State Pickling Company was furnishing one half of all the sauerkraut eaten in the United States, shipping out in a normal year a million cases.

In his plants Mr. Babcock is said to have "paid the highest wages in his industry and bonuses as well." He once remarked to President Wishart, "I am no communist or socialist, but I have made up my mind that labor is not getting its fair share of the profits of industry, and something will have to be done about it if our democracy is to be maintained."

15. Mrs. Scott had money in sugar stocks. In Washington she had proposed to the trustees of the New York Avenue Presbyterian Church to endow a memorial room to Lincoln. They were slow in committing themselves, and she, being a woman of action, withdrew the offer. It was shortly after this incident that Mr. Wishart heard of her and made a point of meeting her. (Information from Mr. Wishart's Reminiscences in *The Wooster Daily Record*.)

16. The records represent all nations, periods, styles of vocal, choral, and instrument combinations. There are songs, arias, miscellaneous vocal music, operas, Gregorian chants, masses, motets, madrigals, ballets, sonatas, fugues, choral preludes, and variations; miscellaneous pieces for piano solo, music for early keyboard instruments, miscellaneous pieces for violin and piano; chamber music for combinations of two, three, four, five, six and seven instru-

ments; symphonies, symphonic poems; orchestral suites, orchestral concertos, concert overtures, concertos for solo instruments with orchestra, and other orchestral works. These were valued at $2,500.

At the same time the Carnegie Corporation sent for the use of the art department a gift of photographs and prints, of a like valuation. (Wooster *Alumni Bulletin,* February, 1943.)

17. The cost of transforming this building into the student union, including equipment, was $54,737.97. (*Minutes* of the Board of Trustees, November 6, 1942.)

18. The expense of Karl Merz Hall including equipment, aside from the cost of the building was $19,420.96. (*Minutes* of the Board of Trustees, November 6, 1942.)

19. There were, of course, restrictions: the downstairs save for the kitchen was not to be altered; the paintings must remain on the walls; and no additions could anywhere be made to the house. Mr. Overholt, one assumes, wished it kept as something of a memorial to his family, though he wished it to be used to its capacity. The Overholt home was brimming with memories for many persons of the college community and of the town. Both John D. Overholt and Karl F. Overholt were graduates of the college. Grace Overholt, *ex* '94, their older sister, had died before graduation. Mr. J. S. R. Overholt, the father, was for many years president of The Wayne County National Bank. Mrs. J. S. R. Overholt was the sister of Henry Clay Frick.

20. See Volume I, pp. 110–112.

21. This new golf course, at that time one of three private college golf courses in the state, was fittingly named for Coach Boles. He had long felt that golf should be a "part of any well-rounded sports program" for it could be played by both sexes and all ages, and could be classified as both an intramural and intercollegiate activity. As head of the physical education department he sought to spread the emphasis about equally between these sports and physical education proper. Known widely as a coach and sportsman, he was also at one time elected president of the College Physical Education Association. He did, however, as we have seen, venture into other fields. At one time, indeed, he was baritone horn soloist at a concert of the Wooster Orchestra.

22. Theodore Brenson's background was European. Through friends he had come to this country via Spain. But his art training had been in north Europe, at the Academie des Beaux Arts in St. Petersburg, (1914–1916), the University of Moscow, (1917–1918), the University of Riga, (1918–1923). After that he was in Rome, London, and Paris, until he made his way to this country.

23. In 1925 the Carnegie Corporation for the Advancement of Teaching gave $50,000 toward the establishment of art courses in twelve American colleges, "in order to promote a general appreciation and knowledge of the fine arts." Wooster was one of the several beneficiaries.

24. The portraits of Wooster's first six presidents all hang in the Trustee Room of Galpin Hall. They were painted by the following artists:

That of President Lord and President Taylor by M. S. Nachtrieb of Wooster, obviously from photographs, in 1908 and 1903 respectively; that of President Scovel, given by the class of 1893, in all probability also by Mr. Nachtrieb though the painting is unsigned and has not been properly identified. It first hung in Hoover Cottage; that of President Holden was painted by Martin Grenhagen of Madison, Wisconsin, and presented by Mrs. F. F. Prentiss; that of President White by Alice Boscovitz, an Austrian refugee, and presented by his classmates of 1890; that of President Wishart by Sidney E. Dickinson of New York, and presented by Mrs. Alva Bailey.

In the Andrews Library there hang portraits of several of the professors of the earlier days of the college, as well as that of the first librarian, Thomas Kirby Davis, painted by W. H. Williams of Columbus, Ohio, and given by Mr. Davis's grandson, DeWitt Wallace.

The others are that of J. O. Notestein painted by Michael De Santis of New York from photographs, and presented in 1930 by a small group of alumni (W. E. Weld and Inez K. Gaylord, both of 1903, Thomas Ewing, *ex* '83, R. Reid Carpenter, '72, Charles W. Patterson, *ex* '77, Isabel Bevier, '85, and Earl L. Douglass, son of Elisha P. Douglass, '77; of William Z. Bennett by John Hubbard Rich, given by a small group of alumni and friends, headed by Dr. Lloyd Felton, '10; of Elias Compton by Walter H. Brough of Cleveland, Ohio, and presented by the Student Senate; of Horace N. Mateer by Martin Grenhagen of Madison, Wisconsin, given by alumni and friends.

Over the desk in the librarian's office hangs that of Elizabeth Bechtel, presented by the Friends of the Library and painted by B. H. Havill, niece of Mrs. Olthouse.

Long hanging in the mathematics room of Kauke Hall, and now over the fireplace of the Alumni Room in The Wooster Inn, is the portrait of William H. Wilson, professor of mathematics (1900–1907) and father of Robert E. Wilson, '14. It, too, was painted by M. S. Nachtrieb. It was presented by the class of 1906.

For the portrait of Annie B. Irish, Wooster's first professor of German, see Notes at back of book.

CHAPTER XX

1. The purpose of the alumni fund was "to establish a regular, permanent income for the college," on a voluntary annual basis, to serve also in promoting alumni loyalty and enthusiasm. There were at once transferred to it $8076.74 from class memorial funds still incomplete, and $5150.13 were given by individual alumni toward the general support of the college. Twenty-four per cent of the graduates contributed in that first year. The next year there were 762 donors and a total received from them of $7243.15. The

following year the plan was to devote the fund from alumni to the increasing of the endowment of the Compton professorship, the ultimate goal for which had been set at $75,000. Though in that year 472 persons contributed better than $3000 for this purpose, the general campaign for endowment got in its way. To this 1893 alumni contributed. In the first seven years $32,412 were given specifically to the alumni fund, of which $21,617 went to general uses and $10,794 to class memorials. When the fund had been first set up, all classes having failed to complete as yet their funds for class memorials were asked to transfer these to the alumni fund with the understanding that the treasurer of the college would keep these in trust and no disposition would be made of them without the consent of the class. All but two classes had complied. (*College of Wooster Bulletin,* Series 21, No. 3, October 1, 1927, and from later *Alumni Bulletins.*)

2. Wooster *Alumni Bulletin,* May, 1931.

3. Attendance for the year was 868.

4. In 1931 the college sent out an appeal to all who could afford to do so to help in the support of one or more students. Even $10 would help in buying some books for a student. Forty-five dollars would pay room rent for one student for a semester; $90 for a year. Sixty-two dollars and a half would cover the cost of tuition for a semester; $125 for a year not including "incidentals." One hundred and seventeen dollars was the cost of boarding for one student per semester. It was hoped that many persons could so be persuaded to adopt a student for some part of his expenses. Figures for permanent memorial scholarships ran from $1250 to $5000.

5. One of these, a trust fund of $40,000, came from John D. Steele, '77, in memory of his only son, John D., Jr., '15, who had died in 1922. The net income was to be used to help "worthy and ambitious poor boys" to go to college.

6. This unhappy situation continued through the remainder of the Wishart administration so that the accumulated maintenance deficit became a burden on the succeeding administration.

7. At the beginning of the year of 1935–1936, the deficit was $44,387.08. At the end of that year it had been reduced to $14,574.53.

8. Attendance was 1013 in 1937–1938 and 1001 in 1938–1939.

9. This was to include also endowment for the librarianship.

10. Necessary endowment for all professorships was now listed at $100,000.

11. When he left, Willkie refused all remuneration from Mr. Wishart for his speech or for his traveling expenses. Mr. Willkie was at that time head of the Commonwealth and Southern Company. The previous June Mr. Wishart had first met him at the Metropolitan Club in New York where Wishart was dining with Mr. O'Hara, another public utilities executive who "had helped various needy students" at Wooster. The three had dinner together. In ten minutes, Mr. Wishart reported later, Willkie had put him completely at ease, and in half an hour had "turned" him "inside out." He was tremendously

impressed with Willkie who "combined an extraordinary intellect with fine idealism." That day Willkie had "expanded and glowed as he talked about America," and he had predicted that "our pioneer days in chemistry, physics, and social development" had just begun. Later at Mr. O'Hara's suggestion Mr. Wishart had called on Willkie at his office and they had chatted for half an hour. Mr. Wishart was more than ever impressed with this man who "agreed that it was America's duty to stand by England," and he quoted Willkie as saying, "I don't care whether it's good politics or not, it's right, and I'm going to say so." (Willkie did in a speech shortly thereafter.)

After Willkie became a Presidential candidate, Mr. Wishart for the first time in his life was active in politics, becoming a member of the national citizens' committee. For this he was criticized by many persons, and received many anonymous letters. (Information from Mr. Wishart's account in *The Wooster Daily Record* in January, 1940, page 8.)

12. At the time of the seventy-fifth anniversary the quadrangle was officially named the Quinby Quadrangle in honor of Ephraim Quinby, one of the founders of the college, who gave the land of what is now the old campus with its grove of oaks.

13. This was essentially a plea for liberal arts education.

14. This was rather a low point. The Synod had sometimes done considerably better than this figure.

15. In 1937 President Wishart appointed Ralph Young, '29, as his promotional assistant. In 1938 Mr. Young became also director of admissions. Both positions he held until 1945. As he visited high schools over the state in seeking students for the college, he could also call on local ministers, possibly occupy local Presbyterian pulpits in presenting Wooster's financial needs. He had by this time his theological degree, and had held a pastorate. In college he had been a star athlete, a fact that made him especially acceptable in high school visitation. And he could tell a good story.

In the late thirties sometime after his return to Wooster to live, former president Holden was persuaded to help in seeking out money for Wooster. In 1940, however, he asked to be relieved. In mid April of 1948 he died and at the memorial service Mr. Wishart said of him in summing up his service to Wooster: ". . . the courage, the steadfast faith, the stubborn optimism, and the indefatigable industry of this one man was perhaps all that at one time [1901] stood between our beloved institution and utter collapse. He was President, as he said, 'of a hole in the ground.' But into that hole in the ground he planted the good seed of optimism and faith, and it sprang up a hundred fold."

16. At a College Circle tea in the spring of 1936, Mr. McLaughlin's twenty-five years of service to the college were appropriately celebrated. The administrative staff had had baked for the occasion by Grace Smith's cafeteria in Toledo a huge cake, signalling the anniversary, with the Wooster seal emblazoned on its top frosting. It was then "Mac's" time to start reminiscing.

17. Walter Painter was much interested in the Musical Arts Association,

of which he was treasurer, and he helped in the securing of money for the support of the Wooster Orchestra.

18. For fifteen years before coming to Wooster he had served various firms in various capacities, as printer, bill clerk, bookkeeper, cashier, office manager, first with Crowell Publishing Co. at Springfield, Ohio, later with the National Biscuit Company, then with Mitten Management, Inc., and finally with Ernst and Ernst. He was a baseball fan and loved the Scottish uniforms and bagpipes of Wooster's band.

CHAPTER XXI

1. Donald Adams in Wooster Commencement address, June, 1945.

2. He died on January 12, 1936, at the age of 88. At 80 he had one time walked the twelve miles from Creston to Wooster after church on a cold winter day. He had been many things in his day, a teacher in the public schools, president for several years of Franklin College, New Athens, Ohio, a missionary in Nova Scotia, pastor of various churches, and for many years a professor at Wooster. In 1920 he had retired.

3. "Professor Bennett is the living center from which the scientific departments have developed. He came to Wooster in 1880, . . . For three years,— 1883–1886—, he taught all the five natural sciences: Chemistry, Physics, Geology, Zoology, and Botany, and he taught them with such ability and skill as to command the admiration of all his students. . . . Not only so, but in emergencies and at sundry times, he taught French, first, second, and third year,—German on two occasions; Latin when Professor Notestein had scarlet fever in his home; Greek, Mathematics, including Calculus and Astronomy; Shakespeare for two years, and Elective English Literature for two years. That is a record that is hard to match. There are now eight men serving in the territory occupied for three years by Professor Bennett alone." (From Dean Compton's Wooster Day address to students in 1922 as recorded in *The College of Wooster Bulletin,* January, 1923.)

After writing about the joys of his long association with students, as an honorary member of various classes through the years, as sponsor of Stratford Club, as coach of student plays through many years, Mr. Bennett goes on to say:

But while I have enjoyed these wanderings in the by-ways of College life and love to recall them, . . . I realize that the sterner work is that which counts most in the valuation of past efforts and the question arises in my mind, what have I builded at Wooster. The designing of the present chemical laboratories, and their equipments I contemplate with some pride, . . . The planning of the present chemical curriculum with its constituent courses, is a higher work, but my successors will in time improve upon it. The highest work that I have done, the immortal part which none can destroy, survives in you, in your minds and souls and hearts. I have tried to help you to learn the facts of science and how to employ them as useful knowledge in life, but more important how to found thereon broad and important principles and thru (*sic*) the mental processes involved in the work to build minds capable of deeper and more accurate reasoning. . . . But higher yet I have sought to teach science as a means of culture, and to make you see and feel in the glories of this wonderful world and the heavens above it more of beauty than shines on a canvas of Raphael or in the rhymes and rhythms of the bards of all the ages.

Highest of all I have sought to point you out the way, by the logic of the immutable laws which we discover in the operation of the universe, to rise above the world and beyond the heavens to the throne of God. . . . (The Wooster *Alumni Bulletin,* July, 1924, pp. 2–3.)

4. At the memorial service in his honor in Wooster, Dean Compton had spoken of Mr. Behoteguy's courtesy, his unswerving principles, his humor. "It would be hard to find," he said, "a sweeter spirit."

5. Resolution of the Board of Trustees on the Retirement of Horace N. Mateer from the Faculty. Dated June 11, 1926.

Whereas Dr. Horace N. Mateer has been almost solely responsible for building up of the Department of Biology and maintaining it at a standard of excellence recognized throughout the country.

And, Whereas, he has throughout his teaching career exemplified the position of the College in searching for and fearlessly proclaiming the truths of science and, at the same time standing on the eternal verities of the Christian religion.

And, Whereas, after forty years of faithful and inspiring service he now finds it necessary to shift his load to younger shoulders.

Be it Resolved that the Board of Trustees of the College of Wooster hereby extends to Dr. Mateer its heartfelt thanks for his forty years of service as a teacher, administrator and leader in the community, and trusts that it will have the benefit of his advice and counsel for many years to come.

June 11, 1926
Minutes of the Board of Trustees

6.   "COMPY"
        "An institution"—so a wise man said—
        "Is but the lengthened shadow of a man,"
          Not one, but many, dreamed and wrought for Wooster—
          Many who sleep forgotten—but of all
          None served with longer patience,
                    keener sight
          and loyalty more blameless, than our Dean!

        So 'round the world his friendly shadow falls—
        Where Wooster memories waken, and for some,
        The old walls rise again untouched by flame,
        And wide halls echo to the steps we knew,
        And well-remembered voices—there walks "Compy,"
        Lean and erect with firm unhasting step,
        Straight as his logic, steadfast as his faith.

Burdens increasing, stark calamity,
Honors and strife and hydra-headed toil—
Through all, he held his steady selfless way;
Met the hour's need with shrewd and humorous gaze,
Wise with a love that books have not yet captured—
Kindly with years of looking on the young!

Doctor and Dean and sage of our "Old Guard,"
We of those lean and gallant years salute thee!
Some pour their wealth out for a cause they love,
Others, their time . . . but few and blest are they
Who build with life itself their high desire!
Builder of Wooster, thou! With life inwrought
Upon her walls, unseen yet ever rising. . .
Thy Wooster—that, God willing, shall endure
When these white walls are dust.

OLLA FERN KIEFFER, '95

7. At the alumni dinner honoring Mr. Compton four men spoke. Harry Cotton announced that during the year $8000 had been given toward the endowing of the Compton Professorship though they were still far short of the $75,000 sought. The president of the Student Senate presented from the students a portrait, still unfinished of "Compy." Mr. Luccock presented him with a $500 bond to be used "for nothing utilitarian," and Howard Lowry, who had spent so much time living in the Compton house that he was almost like a son, had the privilege of handing him the book of tributes written by hundreds of former Wooster students.

8.

AVE ATQUE VALE
by Olla Fern Kieffer, '95

Who can forget the chill of that June day,
    Even its light unreal!
The strangeness shadowing each familiar way
    Silently—till we feel
Our friendly campus change to alien ground,—
(*But on the other side—the trumpets sound!*)

Sadly his books, untouched, await the hand
    That loved each well-worn page;
They miss the keen and kindly eyes that scanned
    Each word with judgment sage;
They cannot think that eager mind could tire!
(*He has found Latium—Land of Heart's Desire!*)

Arching the paths where he was wont to go,
    Surely the trees do mourn!
As if their tallest oak were stricken low

They stand, his friends forlorn;
Deeprooted, many-branched and towering high—
(*So, too was he,—and born to seek the sky!*)

So needed here! When doubts perplex the mind,
    And faith grips with despair,
We turn for counsel, faithful, wise and kind—
    But to an empty chair.
Vanished that friendship never known to fail,—
(*Far off, the dear lost voices calling, "Hail!"*)

We wrong his life by mournful tone;
    The little band who laid
The walls of Wooster, stone on living stone,
    Met all fates undismayed.
Grim in disaster, stubborn in defeat,
The Old Guard trumpet never sounds retreat!

Even now it summons us with silver voice,
    Chiding our futile tears,
Calling us to remember and rejoice
    That long unswerving years
To us were given—for us he laid aside
The hope of written fame, the scholar's pride.

We are his books unwritten!—Ours to show
    He chose the nobler part,
Lighting our torches at the steadfast glow
    Of the wise scholar-heart
That knew a college is but stone and gold
If e'er its altar-fire burns low or cold.

Not us alone he served. His deepest lore
    Was wrung from pain and loss
He knew all earthly lights grow pale before
    The radiance of the Cross.
So through each lesson ran the scarlet line
Of deathless loyalty to Love Divine!

Last of the loved Old Guard! Our college hill
    Can never think thee gone!
Thy spirit stirs in hall and classroom still,—
    And in some fairer dawn,
Among the nobly wise—thy comrades all—
'Even these things thou shalt with joy recall!'

And as we lift the burden of our day,
    Following, not losing, thee,
We know that sometime, smiling, we shall say,
    When strangers ask to see
Wooster's memorial to our "Noty's" name,
"In Every Wooster heart—a living flame!"

9. Mr. Yanney was to live into his ninety-ninth year. At eighty he was still interested in pursuing research in his field, still interested enough in astronomy to write an annual article on the movement of the planets and on phenomena within the solar system. He was listed in *American Men of Science,* continued to read widely in professional journals but enjoyed reading also the works of Victor Hugo, of Thoreau, and Emerson. For amusement he played chess and bridge, and continued a long-standing interest in the world of birds.

10. Mr. Martin retired in June of 1929 after twenty-six years as a professor in the Department of Religion. He had served also for a time as chairman of the curriculum and of the religious life committees. For two years he was interim pastor of Westminster Church, preaching often also at College Hall. For ten years he was president of the oratorio society, and always an enthusiastic supporter of the Wooster Orchestra, and a member of the MacDowell Club. In town he was a member of the Century Club. Five times, at least, he won the Wooster golf championship. He was a welcome and useful member of the community until his sudden death in February of 1934. Of him Mr. Vance, a long-time colleague, said at the memorial service, "His life has added strength, character, and direction to the life of the whole." Incidentally Mr. Martin was responsible for securing for Wooster a collection of nearly fifty Babylonian and Assyrian cuneiform tablets, from Edgar J. Banks, archaeologist.

11. In these days he had already begun studies toward the later publication of his *Froude and Carlyle.*

12. In 1922 a faculty luncheon table on Fridays in the lounge room of Kenarden Lodge was started at the instigation of Mr. Olthouse. This was probably the great-great grandparent of the present Faculty Club.

13. By the beginning of 1923 the Ohio law governing teachers' certificates had reduced the number of hours required in education from thirty to twenty-four. Of these eighteen were in required courses, six were elective. These electives could be in the field of the student's major, including logic, ethics, economics, sociology. (*The College of Wooster Bulletin,* February 1, 1923.)

14. He made a point of knowing in advance the names of all the children he was visiting. When one of them asked for something that seemed unreasonable, too expensive perhaps, he puckered his lips and was thoughtful for a moment, then addressed the parents: "Do you think Johnny (or whoever) is old enough for that?" If the answer was yes, he took the order, if no, he found a good excuse; perhaps his stock of that item had already run out, but he had many other equally desirable things; he would see what he could do. He often told the youngsters what food or drink to leave out for Santa on the night of nights; he occasionally measured the chimney in width and depth to see whether he could make it down. Not only did he inquire into the behavior of the children in the past year but he instructed them in

their behavior in the year ahead. He had a very good time. So had the clerk and so the children.

15. She took special pleasure in teaching children. Her own musical education had begun when she was but a child, and her method book had been by Karl Merz. She was for years a member of the Cleveland Fortnightly Club, the youngest at that time ever to have been granted membership. (Information from Robert Hill's account in the Wooster *Alumni Bulletin*.)

16. The Parmelees were both dedicated musicians. Under Mr. Parmelee's leadership the Wooster Orchestra steadily developed. By 1936 it had a membership of eighty-five and was broadcasting occasionally over a hook-up of radio stations. In 1941, for its twenty-fifth anniversary concert, Rudolph Ringwall came to be its guest conductor. Though Mr. and Mrs. Parmelee often gave individual recitals, they also did much work as a team, as when in 1925 they gave a series of five sonata recitals, spaced a month apart, each with an explanatory talk. They were as always trying "to give to people a chance to become music lovers by knowing enough about [musical] forms to appreciate them." They were always sharing their abilities with those around them, the college and the larger community.

17. The two years of 1925–1927 Mr. Moore spent in England studying at Kings College, Cambridge University, from which he received his Litt. M. degree. At Wooster the most popular of his courses were those on The Drama and on Shakespearean Comedy. So great was his zest in teaching that his students caught it and went on from there. One of his students of a Shakespeare class records how every year in reading aloud the scene of Cleopatra's death, Mr. Moore wept. Another mentions his laugh, on occasion, that for him and other students would go on "booming down the years." He was a sensitive interpreter of literature whether as director of a play or as a professor in the classroom. In the fifties he remarked one day that he had read *Moby Dick* every year since 1919 and every year had found something new in it, and this something new he passed on to his students.

In 1934 the faculty players produced a play *Quare Medicine* by Paul Green based on lives and customs of the North Carolina mountaineers. Often on the night before Thanksgiving they had put on a play at the city Opera House for the students. And once a group of the younger faculty at the instigation of Mr. Moore presented Dunsany's *If Shakespeare Lived Today*.

18. Mr. Williamson received his Ph.D. in mathematics from the University of Chicago in 1928.

19. In 1923, on the occasion of the celebration of Mr. Notestein's fifty years of service to the college, Mr. Compton in presenting Mr. Notestein for the degree of L.L.D. told this story: "High testimony of Professor Notestein's power as a teacher was given years ago during President Scovel's administration. An expert from a European University, sent to study the teaching of Latin in America, came here incognito and saw Professor Notestein at work. The following week he told a company of college teachers in the East that

they must not think the East had all the best teachers of Latin, for a small college in the Middle West, Wooster, had the peer of any of them."

20. Mr. Spencer was one of seven authors of the *Biology of the Drosophila* (a fruit fly). The others were from Yale, Princeton, Stanford, Tulane, Rutgers, and the medical division of the Army Medical Center.

21. In *The Wooster Daily Record* there was a correspondent who detailed at intervals the news from Mud College. It turned out to be a community which had once centered around a schoolhouse of that name near Mohican-ville. The schoolhouse was, when finally discovered, in a state of disrepair, and used only by some farmer for storage, yet the community around it still held to the name.

22. Karl Ver Steeg had been born and grown up in Pella, Iowa. He had received his M.S. from the University of Chicago in 1920, had then gone to the University of Idaho for a year as instructor in geology and geography. From 1921–1923 he was professor of geology and head of the department at the Wisconsin School of Mines at Plattville. From there he came to Wooster. In 1930 he received his Ph.D. from Columbia. In 1918 he had served as a director of athletics at Camp Dodge.

23. At this point he accepted a permanent appointment at Scripps College and at the Claremont College Graduate School, and Wooster was to see him no more until after his retirement. The year of 1932–1933 he had spent in New Zealand gathering the material for a book he was later to publish on Sir Robert Stout.

24. At his death in 1960 the Ohio Poetry Society went on record in the following words: "We, the Ohio Poetry Society knew him well for many years. He was a close personal friend. We would like the literate people of Ohio to remember that George Bradford was a poet, a scholar, and a person of infinite goodness and understanding."

The last stanza of a poem, "Our Chapel" in his *Wayside Lyrics* may well be quoted here:

> Thou chapel, low and gray
> Remind us all to pray
> For power to win the battles of the night;
> With hearts made pure and strong,
> And faces lit with song,
> Point us the pathway to eternal light.

25. Of course as the years went on, there were variations in details. Yet the costumes alone would have made anyone come miles to see.—Reporters from neighboring cities indeed did come to see and write up the story.—As the "lords" and "ladies" gathered on the green quadrangle to await their summons, they were arrayed in all the colors of the rainbow, gold and green, pink and blue and lavender. There were "flowing gowns," "horned head-dresses," "belted jerkins and capes," "steeple hats," and "pointed shoes turned up at the

toes." To each student Mr. Bradford had assigned his part, the character or the kind of character he was to represent. This was that student's "independent study" of this period. (Much of the detail here taken from an account in the Cleveland *Plain Dealer* of May 24, 1947.)

26. This occurred in his advanced class in philosophy course in which some reference had previously been made to an old custom of fruit rolling. One day the students were all busy in a philosophical discussion when "to a man the class rose and began rolling apples, oranges, yes, and bananas toward the desk." (Information and quotation from Wooster *Alumni Bulletin,* December, 1937.)

27. Every girl was required to have for graduation two years of work in the physical education department. She must "qualify in swimming and in at least two outdoor sports." The result was that "the tennis courts were nearly always crowded with girls," and that "almost any day teams of girls in knickers" could be seen on the girls' athletic field. Miss Lowrie described her aim as "to teach them health habits . . . to teach them to build for health rather than to avoid disease, and to help them realize that their health is their own responsibility, and not the doctor's." (*College of Wooster Bulletin,* November 1, 1922.) *The Voice* of May 12, 1926, records also that 120 girls have enrolled for hiking and that thirty of them had already hiked fifty miles.

28. She had had six months also studying in Berlin.

29. One summer later she spent in studying history and archaeology at the Oriental Institute in Chicago.

30. She came to Wooster from Baker University where she had been an instructor in Spanish. While at Wooster she prepared a textbook for advanced students in Spanish, *An Outline History of Spanish American Literature.*

31. In 1925 a new system of budgeting for all college organizations was put in, and of this Mr. Cummins was in charge. This gave certain students some practical experience in economics. The literary societies, the small clubs, the various Christian societies, the classes, the Student Senate, *The Voice, The Index,* were all included.

32. Archibald Anderson Johnston came to Wooster from the presidency of Geneva College where he had been for three years. His familiarity with Geneva College, however, dated back much further. He had been graduated there, played three years on its baseball team, had been the tennis champion at one time of Beaver County. For several years he taught economics and history at Geneva. Yet he had much else in his background. Immediately after his graduation he worked in the engineering department of the Pennsylvania Railroad. Then the wanderlust struck him and he went to see what he could see in the British Isles, ending with a period of study at the University of Edinburgh. In the First World War he was educational secretary for the Y.M.C.A. at Camp Dix, then went overseas to the University of Beaune in France in the Educational Corps. He had some years before all this taken a theological course, received his B.D. and M.A. from Princeton and had been

in the ministry for six years. He had had an opportunity to meet many kinds of persons and see many aspects of life.

A. A. Johnston gave his classes in criminology a firsthand view of such institutions as the London, Ohio, Prison Farm, the Mansfield Reformatory, and the Ohio Penitentiary.

33. In the course of years one of the features of Homecoming came to be the decorating of the several dormitories. A plaque was given to the dormitory adjudged as having produced the best and most original decoration. In 1936, for instance, this was won by Livingstone Lodge. A large tank was shown with Coach Boles at the wheel "mowing down the Akron warriors [of that afternoon on the football field] behind a sandbag entrenchment."

34. Dads' Day was first instituted in the fall of 1927. The dads attended a football game in the afternoon and in the evening were guests at a special concert in Memorial Chapel. By 1936 those with sons on the team were seated on a special bench on the football field and wore numbers corresponding to those of their sons. Their wives, if they had come along, also wore numbers and were seated in the grandstand in a special section. Gradually Dads' Day was becoming Parents' Day. Then on Saturday morning the parents met with the faculty in a question and answer forum.

35. In the thirties it became the custom for the students after the conclusion of Mr. Lean's reading of the *Christmas Carol* to gather around the Christmas tree on the quad and sing Christmas songs. For several years, too, the senior girls went carolling in the community early on the Sunday morning preceding Christmas vacation.

CHAPTER XXII

1. From Wooster Day address, 1940, as quoted in the Wooster *Alumni Bulletin,* January, 1940, p. 69.

2. Dean Westhafer was elected by the Faculty Council (full professors and assistant professors of five years' standing) on June 12, 1929.

3. Rachel MacKenzie some time after she left Wooster joined the staff of *The New Yorker,* as fiction editor.

4. Mr. Anderson was a graduate of the Austin Theological Seminary, and had a theological degree also from the Union Seminary of Richmond, Virginia. He had an M.A. from Columbia, and had studied with Luther Weigle of Yale toward his Ph.D. degree. Later in life he was incidentally associated with the Department of Family Life of the National Council of Churches.

6. In 1928 D. Luther Evans had already had published jointly by the Oxford University Press and the Princeton Press, *New Realism and Old Reality,* and various papers of his had appeared in philosophical journals. In 1930 he had published, with W. S. Gamelsfelder of Ohio State University, *Fundamentals of Philosophy.* After leaving Wooster Mr. Evans was to go to Ohio State University.

7. Those who were inclined to think that Mr. Bruere took life as just a party must have been disabused of this idea in the years from 1944 to 1967 when he was pastor of Calvary Presbyterian Church in Cleveland, and a leader in the civic life of the city. Calvary had once been in the center of Cleveland's residential district, but gradually these people moved to the Heights, and the slums little by little moved in all around the church. In these surroundings Mr. Bruere's church stood its ground as a place to which all men of whatever race or station could look for inspiration and help. With courage and persistence he stood on a platform of human and racial justice to all, and his congregation stood with him.

8. In 1942 the vocational guidance program was extended to freshmen. Each incoming student was subject to testing to discover his vocational interests and aptitudes.

9. Mr. Grady was also author, with assistant professor John Chittum, of a book, *The Chemist at Work,* and of various articles in the *Journal of Chemical Education.*

10. In his boyhood Howard Lowry lost a dog under very unhappy circumstances, a blow from which he never quite recovered. He consequently made a great pet of "Matthew Arnold." The dog responded, and was jealous to the point of growling if down the street somewhere he had happened to see Mr. Lowry throwing a ball for another dog to retrieve.

11. Matthew Arnold, "Thyrsis."

12. Later Mr. Eberhart was to spend a year in Australia and New Zealand studying labor problems there and methods of arbitration.

13. At her death in 1941 Miss Gingrich left to the college $50,746. This was assigned by the trustees to the endowment of the Gingrich professorship of German.

14. In 1927 Mr. Wishart gave an orientation course in political science in the chapel on Wednesday evenings. This reflected his intense interest in national and world affairs.

15. Of the 112 colleges examined, eighty-four were found guilty, and twenty-eight were given a clean bill of health. These were Bates, Bowdoin, Carleton, Chicago, Cornell, Dalhousie, Emory, Illinois, Laval (Canada), Marquette, Massachusetts Agricultural College, Massachusetts Institute of Technology, McGill, Ottawa, Queen's, Reed, Rochester, Saskatchewan, Toronto, Trinity, Tufts, Tulane, U.S. Military Academy, Virginia, Wesleyan, Williams, Wooster, Yale. The study had taken three and one half years to complete.

16. This change was initiated by Dean Westhafer and took effect with the class entering in September 1931. The required work was at the same time reduced from 74 to 54 credit hours, and the number of credit hours for one's major was increased from 24 to 40. To effect this change the former requirement in English was reduced by one year, as also the requirement in modern language and in natural science.

17. "In the retirement of Miss Elizabeth Bechtel, Librarian, The College of Wooster loses one of the staunchest and most loyal of its faculty. Quiet,

unassuming, unflagging, she has been a fighter always for Wooster's library, to win for it its rightful place in Wooster's educational scheme. Seeing her budgets cut year after year, watching her plans for more adequate housing for her store of books fail to materialize, she was often discouraged but never downed. The next year she would always be back pleading the cause again, urging more money for books, calling attention to the special needs of specific departments, casting a careful eye around to see which of the faculty really used the books they ordered.

. . . . .

"A gentle soul, she has been an executive able to inspire her staff and to win their admiration and affection. The Board of Trustees takes pleasure in putting on record its appreciation of her outstanding service through forty-four years." (*Minutes* of the Board of Trustees, May 12, 1944.)

18. On Hallowe'en night of 1934 some of the boys from Kenarden went to the Public Square and gathering up the cannon balls around the Civil War Monument, rolled them down Liberty Street. Some of the others tried to crash the gate of one of the movies. A few who were caught spent the night in jail. In the same year in late November, on the occasion of Wooster's winning the Ohio Conference championship in football, the manager of Schine's movie theater gave a free show to all the college students.

19. In late 1942 the old safe that had been in use in the college treasurer's office down on the Public Square was taken out of storage and turned in as "Scrap for the Jap." (Information from the Wooster *Alumni Bulletin*, November, 1942, p. 30.)

20. "No description of the Navy program would be complete without an account of his [Warren Spencer's] uncovering a major cheating scandal. In many of the courses multiple choice questions were given on exams. An enterprising scoundrel among the cadets figured out that the five rungs of Kauke's stationary classroom chairs could very conveniently represent from left to right, choices A, B, C, D, and E. The cadet who knew the subject could arrange to signal the correct answers to less knowledgeable friends by tapping with his pencil the appropriate rungs of the chairback immediately in front of him. This was most effectively done with a languid manner, and was subtle enough to have escaped detection for quite a while. It remained for Warren [Spencer] to discover it while proctoring one of the examinations. He promptly reported it, and at least two cadets were removed from the program by the Naval authorities. One . . . was a nationally famous baseball player." (From a letter.)

21. Of the faculty and former faculty teaching in the USNFPS Anderson, Boles, Bruere, Eberhart, Fobes, Hiatt, Hildner, Parmelee, Stoneburner, Swigart, and Williamson were in navigation; Barris (music), Coolidge, Ford, Hutchison (philosophy), and Spencer in physics; DeVeny (music), Ellsworth, Ingram, Miller, Munson in communications; Hole and Sharp in the theory of flight; Hunter, Moke, Murray in aerology and aircraft engines;

Knight, Yanney, Mrs. Florence Fox, and the Misses Frances Guille, Josephine Heflin in mathematics.

Though they were undoubtedly glad to be making a contribution to the war effort, these men and women on the faculty who "were yanked out of their academic niches and set to teaching navy subjects in most cases very uncongenial," deserve special recognition. For some the experience may have been exciting; for others it was probably sheer drudgery while they saw colleagues pursuing their familiar ways.

General Notes

[These notes, by administration, are mostly throw-backs to Volume One that I came across after that volume was published. In fact some of them have actually been written since that time, as Edith Fitch's long story about the students campaigning for money for the rebuilding after the great fire. These notes do not have reference to any particular page or chapter.]

PRESIDENT LORD'S ADMINISTRATION

1. From the Board of Trustees *Minutes* in 1866, this subscription list toward the building is obviously incomplete.

E. Quinby	$25,000	Wooster Brewery	$ 25
R. B. Stibbs	3,000	J. Nachtrieb	25
Lucas Flattery	1,000	Henry Shreve	100
D. Robison	1,000	James Bruce	25
D. Robison, Jr.	1,000	Benjamin Wallace	125
John McSweeney	1,000	2nd Subscription	
Harry Howard	1,000	Robert Wallace	80
Thomas Stibbs	1,000	2nd Subscription	
J. H. Kauke	1,000	J. M. Wallace	25
Other Kaukes (5)	2,000	William Bruce	25
McDonald & Co.	1,000	John M. Wallace	5
D. Q. Liggett	1,000		

2. The Rev. Mr. Henry A. True, of Marion, Ohio, Wooster trustee from 1866–1869, was "a graduate of Bowdoin College, and a favorite pupil of Henry Wadsworth Longfellow. He was a very thorough Greek student and the story is told of him that he so interested the members of his Sunday-school group in Greek that they were willing to have him teach them the language and to use only Greek testaments in class." (Wooster *Alumni Bulletin*, February, 1929.)

3. "The plans for the old Main Building were decided on one cold January night in 1867. The next morning the members of the Board visited the hill to picture the edifice to be built there. Mrs. E. B. Raffensberger who had accompanied her husband to Wooster for the meeting, went with the men but sat in the sleigh as the men trudged the last part of the journey on foot. The little Raffensberger boy, a lad of about seven years old, floundered along in the snow after the men. Captain J. H. Kauke turned to the boy, picked him up and put him on his shoulder, and waving his arm toward the thickly wooded hilltop said: 'My boy, you will live to see one of the greatest

universities of the country among the trees on that hilltop.' " (Wooster *Alumni Bulletin,* February, 1929.)

Mrs. Raffensberger, who presumably was the source of this information, died in Marion, Ohio, December 25, 1925. Her husband, the Rev. Mr. E. B. Raffensberger was a trustee of Wooster from 1866–1870.

4. John McClellan, Wooster's first treasurer, was born in 1810 in Beaver County, Pennsylvania, and was brought to Wooster by his family in 1813.

5. "A touching expression of his [John Robinson's] love to Wooster University appears in the fact that, out of the scanty earnings of a long life, he had devoted one thousand dollars to establish a scholarship in memory of his beloved wife." (Sylvester F. Scovel, "History of the University of Wooster," in *History of Wayne County, Ohio,* Volume I, Indianapolis, Indiana: B. F. Bowen & Co., 1910, p. 514.)

6. "I remember his [O. N. Stoddard's] rapt enthusiasm one day as he finished two experiments in electricity and turned in a confident unfolding of what seemed to him wrapped up in the results obtained. His vision that day set before us great cities lighted in some coming time, by this strange force that seemed then at home only in the storm cloud; made us imagine their thronging multitudes carried along their streets on wheels driven by electricity." (Recollections of J. O. Notestein as recorded in Wooster *Alumni Bulletin,* April, 1926.)

7. The elms on the quadrangle were planted in the spring of 1873. (Recollections of J. O. Notestein of Wooster in the '70's, as reported in the Wooster *Alumni Bulletin,* January, 1926.)

PRESIDENT TAYLOR'S ADMINISTRATION

1. A. A. E. Taylor had been graduated from Princeton in 1854 at 19, and from Princeton Theological Seminary three years later. As a trustee of Wooster (1870–1873) from the Synod of Cincinnati, he had so impressed President Lord that he had been the latter's first choice as his successor.

2. When first organized in the early days the Y.W.C.A. met in an old fire engine house on Spink Street. The president of the college saw to paying the boy for opening the door and sweeping the room. At that time there were 14 members and a budget of $46. In 1916 there were 170 members and a budget of $650. (Information from *The Wooster Voice,* February 24, 1916.)

3. William D. Johnson of Clifton, Ohio, endowed the chair of mathematics in the amount of $25,000. "When the railroad bonds in which the endowment was transferred were repudiated by the county which authorized them, she [his widow] paid the interest [$1,500] for many years until finally by legal process the county was compelled to make good the principal." (Sylvester F. Scovel, "History of the University of Wooster," p. 512 ff.)

4. Miss Annie B. Irish may have been the first woman in this country to receive a doctor's degree in German, though this point has not been estab-

lished. When at sixteen she came back with her family from four years in Dresden, she is said to have had already an amazing facility in both French and German, and to have delved deeply also into German literature. Later she went back to Europe to further such study. When she was living with her family and working in Washington (as secretary to Secretary of Interior, Carl Schurz), she had occasion to do much translating of both German and French, letters, manuscripts, even books. One of the latter, *Landolin* by the German novelist Berthold Auerbach, was published by Henry Holt & Company. Although at seventeen, she found herself under the necessity, for two years, of supporting her family, father, mother, brother and sister, she also sometime later found a way during her life in Washington to go back and forth to Baltimore to work as a special student under scholars at Johns Hopkins, though as a woman denied status as a regular student. There she familiarized herself with Anglo-Saxon and Old English, and wrote a thesis as for a doctorate in German, though because of her sex she was ineligible for a diploma or degree. When she came to Wooster in 1881 and found that Wooster had just established a postgraduate department, she submitted her records and her thesis. These Wooster in turn submitted to authorities elsewhere and when they were approved as meeting the necessary requirements, Wooster granted her a Ph.D., the first such degree to be given by the college (1882). Even so the thesis was not immediately published but returned to her, and when finally in 1886, after her death, they sought to publish it in *The Post-Graduate and Wooster Quarterly,* it could nowhere be found. One assumes that along with the fumigation of the house (she and her sister had both died of scarlet fever within two weeks), many of her papers were destroyed, probably the thesis among them. It is true that there remained some other papers, clippings and a scanty diary. From these one gathers very little, however, about her personal life, save that she was a recognized figure in Washington's literary circles.

At her death almost an entire issue (nine pages) of *The Wooster Collegian* was given over to her memory, a very brief biographical sketch, tributes and resolutions, by the president of the college, the faculty, the trustees, the Women's Educational Association, individuals from both students and faculty, the students, the students of German, the Y.W.C.A. Some speak of her cheerfulness, of her reserve, her deep religious commitment, her industry, her executive ability, her interest in students, her intellectual interest and acumen; in fact she seemed a paragon of virtues. Of two letters from a distance included in *The Collegian,* one came from Mrs. Lucretia R. Garfield of Cleveland, the widow of President James A. Garfield, who speaks of having known Annie Irish in Washington, "a bright, intelligent young girl." Her portrait long hung in Hoover Cottage, is now in the vault of Galpin Hall, awaiting a decision as to where to place it. It seems to be unsigned. (For other information about Annie Irish see Volume I.)

5. At the backdoor of Old Main in the eighteen-eighties there was a pump

and a tin cup for drinking water. (Wooster *Alumni Bulletin,* February, 1926.)

PRESIDENT SCOVEL'S ADMINISTRATION

1. In his reminiscences of past presidents at the 75th anniversary, George N. Luccock told these two stories about President Scovel. During his own seminary days Mr. Luccock occasionally went to hear Mr. Scovel preach in his Pittsburgh church. Always, he said, when the clock struck twelve, Mr. Scovel would pause in his sermon and wait for the twelfth stroke. "Then in a most impressive manner he would say, 'Now after you have looked at your watches and replaced them in your pockets, we will proceed.'" The other story concerned his disciplining of students. Once Mr. Scovel caught and identified three students stealing his chickens. In due time these students were invited to dinner at his house. In front of each was placed a whole roasted chicken.

2. From letter of Samuel J. Kirkwood, dated January 19, 1891. He explains that because of his own illness, illness in his family and other things, it was necessary for him to economize "even in little things." He asked therefore that his name be dropped from membership in the New York Mathematical Society "as I do not feel justified in paying the annual dues."

3. At the instigation of J. Byron Oliver, director of the Conservatory of Music, the first small pipe organ was installed, in 1894–1895, in the old chapel. He also introduced to Wooster "The White Robed Choir," and the "Singers' Club." A memorial window in his honor was placed in the new Sarah Frame Davidson Chapel after his death. (Information from Sylvester F. Scovel, "History of the University of Wooster," p. 533.)

4. After the 1897 visit of 200 delegates to the General Assembly to Wooster, on their way back east Postmaster General John Wanamaker said: "Heretofore Wooster has only been a spot on the map where they didn't want the post office open on Sunday. None of us knew until today, what an important center for education and Christian influence is here."

The account of the incident says that when the delegates arrived, "The whole town met the train with everything that had wheels inside or out." (Wooster *Alumni Bulletin,* March, 1931.)

5. President Scovel used to say: "There must never be anything here that suggests a back door." President Holden said: "I'll build things so beautiful no one will ever want to deface them." (Both quoted by Gertrude Gingrich in *The Wooster Voice,* April 22, 1925.)

6. Of the 143 men who had served on Wooster's Board of Trustees during its first forty years, seven, including Willis Lord, were or had been college presidents: George C. Heckman, David A. Wallace, Thomas A. McCurdy, Willis Lord, David A. Tappan, J. B. Helwig, George P. Hays. Two others were presidents of theological seminaries. (Sylvester F. Scovel, "History of the University of Wooster," p. 518.)

PRESIDENT HOLDEN'S ADMINISTRATION

1. The total assets of the University of Wooster as of May 31, 1899, were $452,551.87 of which $181,737.42 was endowment. After the fire in 1901, including the $60,000 of insurance, the total assets were $328,377.87. On March 31, 1910, the total assets were $1,857,249.83 of which $755,368.52 were in general and special endowment, $229,911.11 in pledges and annuities, and $871,970.20 in buildings and equipment. (Sylvester F. Scovel, "History of the University of Wooster," p. 503.)

2. The foundation of $10,000 given in 1899 by the Rev. Robert Moore toward the endowing of a professorship of astronomy was a memorial to "his lifelong friend," Samuel Kirkwood, Wooster's first professor of mathematics and astronomy. (Sylvester F. Scovel, "History of the University of Wooster," p. 518.)

3. As early as June of 1900, President Holden "exhibited to the Board plans that he had had drawn by Nimmons and Fellows of Chicago of the proposed quadrangle and of the several buildings which he felt were already needed by the University." This was a year and a half before the fire. (Information from the *Minutes* of the Board, June 11, 1900.)

4. George C. Nimmons, '87, who designed Memorial Chapel, Taylor Hall, and the Frick Library, had studied in the Art Institute, Chicago, in the offices of Burnham and Root where he was a draftsman. Later he studied in Paris and Rome. After seven years of training and experience he set up for himself in Chicago. There he built the main plant of Sears-Roebuck, an addition to the American Furniture Mart with the high tower, the Commonwealth Edison Service Company building, the Olympian Fields Golf Clubhouse. He designed also the Philadelphia store of Sears-Roebuck. For a while he was also chairman of the Architects' Committee on Education. (From Wooster *Alumni Bulletin,* December, 1925.)

5. It was James Henry who painted 1901 in white figures three feet high on the face of the tower of the old Bitters' Bottle.

6. "And then came the fire! None of us will ever forget that cold winter's night when we gathered around the old building [Old Main] and watched it gradually disappear. The men helped to carry equipment from the laboratories as long as it was possible for them to work and the girls at Hoover Cottage brought their trunks from the attic without any assistance and packed them, picking out and choosing their choicest possessions. Some of them even moved them down to the front porch. It took the janitor a whole day to put them back where they belonged.

"A sorry group of young people gathered in the old gymnasium the next morning. Dr. Holden was out of town so Compy and Noty presided. Some of us had forgotten to lace our shoes and most of us looked as if we had been out all night. Class meetings were held after this to raise money for the building fund. Very few of us had any money but we dumped in all we possessed. Class banquets, the social event of the year at that time; new hats; any five or ten spot you had carefully saved up for some cherished luxury; Christmas presents, everything went into the melting pot to help swell the fund. In the evening there was a big Mass Meeting in the City Hall and everybody opened their hearts and their purses once again.

"One wonders how the profs ever had the courage to carry on. To those of us who rely on notes, card indexes and reference books it seems an almost superhuman task. . . . Everything went along just the same. We were positive examinations would be omitted, but not so.

"Many students spent their vacations soliciting funds for the University. One girl took a horse and buggy and made a systematic canvass of all the Presbyterians in her home town, returning with several hundred dollars in her pocket, notwithstanding the fact that she lived in the southern part of the state where there was little interest in Wooster.

"On our return after Christmas we found everything in readiness for us. The old gym had been converted into class-rooms, each heated by a big round stove of the district school variety. Few of the faculty were successful firemen; they just warmed up to their respective subjects while the rest of us were toasted on one side and frozen on the other. The board partitions were so thin that we had a conglomeration of French, Latin, German, Math., etc., at one and the same time. Classes were also held in the seminar rooms of the new library. Dr. Scovel's lectures were given in the basement of the new Memorial Chapel accompanied by the moans and groans of the new organ which was being set up. . . . Science, presided over by Dr. Mateer and Prof. Bennett, was housed in the old Music Hall on Bever Street. You either ran or slid down College Avenue, crawled over or under fences and arrived so out of breath that you had to refresh yourself at the watering trough nearby. No one ever seemed to mind these inconveniences; in fact, we quite enjoyed the novelty of them.

"One of the requirements of Mr. Carnegie's offer was that $40,000 should be raised in Wayne County within sixty days. During January and February the seniors and juniors gave entertainments in nearly all the towns and hamlets of the county. If neither a church nor a hall was available, a school-house was secured. The program consisted of recitations, solos, a quartette, a pantomine, and a marvellous chorus which could execute anything from "Men of Harlech" to "Solomon Levi". . . . After the entertainment a member of the faculty, usually Noty, Compy or Dicky, made a speech and then the job of raising money began. When everything else failed, we passed the hat several times lest a stray nickel elude us unawares.

"The Fredericksburg trip proved to be the most thrilling. It was a cold, raw winter's day with the thermometer hovering around zero. There were wild reports of bad roads and snow blockades but nothing daunted us in those days. We started out in the early afternoon in two big bobsleds accompanied by Noty. Everybody had a copy of the Wooster *Republican* on their chests, and many other things if the truth were known. Unfortunately Benny was only experimenting with the X-ray then. The trip was a great success and everybody arrived in great glee. The girls thawed out by a big stove in the little hotel while the men went out to explore the town for bits of local color to add to our show. At six o'clock about fifty sat down to the most comprehensive meal many of them have seen before or since. It included every vegetable that ever grew in a garden and nearly every animal that ever strutted in a barn-yard. Everything was there from apple-butter to cucumber pickles greened in a brass kettle. The entertainment was a great success, big hits being scored by the leader of the chorus and the hero of the pantomime. We returned to the hotel in the seventh heaven of ecstasy and proceeded to array ourselves in our Wooster *Republicans* and borrowed wraps. And then we waited and got sleepier as we waited, for our drivers refused to take us back until we gave them more money. About midnight we started for home. Just outside of Fredericksburg the larger sled tipped over, dumping everybody into a huge snow drift. If Carnegie medals had been in vogue then, one would have been awarded to Noty who dug us out and deposited us in the sled right side up once again. Fancy starting out on a twelve mile ride plastered with snow and half frozen. 'Washington crossing the Delaware' had nothing on us. The 'life of the party' saved the situation by diverting our attention with facetious remarks such as 'I am so cold that my floating ribs have stopped floating,' and when we passed a Catholic cemetery, 'Isn't that what you might call a cross patch?' " (From "Wooster at the Turn of the Century" by Edith Fitch, '03, Wooster *Alumni Bulletin,* March, 1927.)

7. Taylor Hall was so named because "Dr. Taylor founded the Academical Department during his presidency." (*Report of the Board of Trustees to the Synod* for the year ending June 18, 1903.)

8. The Y.W.C.A. had a committee "which arranged to teach six classes at the Children's Home each Sunday. It also arranged to visit the poor and the sick and to bring its cheer wherever possible. The committee also visited the old women at the County Infirmary and kept them supplied with papers and magazines." (From the *Report of the Board of Trustees to the Synod,* for the year ending June 15, 1905.)

9. The cost of Holden Hall was $110,000. Mr. Severance's contributions added up to more than half of this. It was his wish, stated in a letter to the Board from California, that the building should bear Mr. Holden's name, and with enthusiasm the Board so acted. (Information in part from Sylvester F. Scovel, "History of the University of Wooster," p. 502.)

10. Besides Mr. Severance some of the substantial givers toward the building of Holden Hall were Mrs. Mary Thaw, Flora Stone Mather, Mr. John Converse, Mrs. N. S. McCormick, Julia Turner, Miss Helen Gould, and E. O. Emerson. (From records in the office of the Treasurer of the college.)

11. The *Minutes* of the Board of Trustees for June 10, 1907, record that College Avenue is about to be paved.

12. Since the water supply had been unsatisfactory in price, quantity and quality, the Board of Trustees in 1908 had decided to drill two test wells.

These were about 250 feet apart and went to a depth of 275 feet. Water rose in the pipes to within 89 feet of the surface. When tested by pumping for 24 hours, each well showed 110 gallons per minute. Mr. Bennett pronounced the water exceptionally pure and satisfactory. The water will be pumped into a reservoir of 60,000 gallon capacity, which will be roofed. Over and above this there will be a gravity steel storage tank of 40,000 gallons, 60 feet above the grade line. The tank will be connected by a six inch pipe to a house-service pump and a fire pump. The reservoir and storage tank will be just north of the heating and lighting plant. The pumps will be in that plant. (From the 38th *Annual Report of the Board of Trustees to the Synod* for the year ending June 18, 1908.)

13. The Board of Trustees authorized the purchase of the first horse-drawn lawn mower for the college in the spring of 1908. The first typewriter for the use of the faculty was purchased and installed in the dean's office in April, 1910. The faculty first recommended a night watchman for the dormitories in the summer of 1910.

14. It was in 1908 that by faculty ruling chemistry, biology and physics became year courses. In the same year they abolished the requirement for the writing of senior orations. Instead the highest six of the senior class in scholastic rank spoke at commencement. There were two alternates.

15. Harry Lloyd, *ex* '08, who became director of athletics in 1911–1912 and then coach the following year was a star pitcher while in college in 1906 and in 1907, a year when Wooster defeated Ohio State University.

16. In the *Minutes* of the Board for February 2, 1909, mention is made of the death of Mrs. Samuel Mather of Cleveland and of "her many and generous sacrifices for this institution and her sincere and loving loyalty to everything it represented." In this her husband followed through, for at the end of the campaign in 1910, on December 30, he is listed as having given $10,000.

17. This slightly amusing sentence appears in the *Minutes* of the Executive Committee of the Board of Trustees for December 11, 1911: "Prof. Dickason presented a list of names selected for the Summer School faculty for 1912. Same approved, by motion, but we express our wish that the Professors in the University shall hereafter refrain from teaching in the Summer School."

18. William J. Seelye, Wooster's professor of Greek from 1891 to 1911, was born in Schenectady, New York, April 10, 1857, where his father, Julius Hawley Seelye, was pastor of the Dutch Reformed Church. A year later the father became professor of mental and moral science at Amherst College, and in 1876 became president of Amherst. William J. Seelye's mother was Elizabeth Tilman James, a cousin of William and Henry James. He was graduated from Amherst in 1879, continued there as a graduate student for a year and then went to Johns Hopkins for a second year of graduate study before going abroad for two years further study, seven months at the University of Edinburgh, and a semester each at the University of Halle and

the University of Leipzig. Later he was to spend the year of 1886–1887 at the American Archaeological Institute in Athens. Before coming to Wooster he had taught at Iowa College, Grinnell, Iowa, at Lawrenceville Academy in New Jersey, at Amherst, and at Parsons College. In September 1886 he had married Alice Clark of Iowa City, Iowa.

19. After a year of relaxation, most of it spent in Florida, in 1916 former President Holden moved to New York City to become associate director of the Presbyterian Board of Church Erection.

PRESIDENT WHITE'S ADMINISTRATION

1. The week of prayer beginning every year with the first Sunday of January had been instituted in 1846 by the newly organized Evangelical Alliance of London. The purpose of this Alliance had been the "manifesting and promoting of Christian union and religious liberty" among Protestant Christians of different denominations and countries. The American branch of this Alliance was organized in 1867. (Information from Webster's *International Dictionary*.)

PRESIDENT WISHART'S ADMINISTRATION

1. Reminiscing of the 1918 influenza epidemic, "Mose" Hole in his characteristic fashion once wrote in a column in the Wooster *Alumni Bulletin:*

But speaking of rapid recoveries, when the armistice was signed in the morning, there were some twenty serious [student] cases in the hospital, and at two in the afternoon the last case was seen three miles north on the Three C's highway with bared head, thumbing his way dexterously into the north.

2. During the cold bleak winter of 1920 Mr. John C. Boyd, '79, had died. His services to the college had begun the year after his graduation, had ended with the closing of the preparatory department in 1918. For many years he had taught there, Latin or German, or both and sometimes a course in civics as well. He was a conscientious, strict, and careful drillmaster to hundreds and hundreds of boys and girls. Twice he had taken himself off to Germany for further study and practice in the language. Through all the years he had eked out his meager salary by taking student roomers, and by booking passages to Europe on the North German Lloyd lines. For five years (1904–1909) he deserted teaching altogether for business, only to come back for nine final years, to round out thirty-three in all. His house on College Avenue was large, presided over by Mrs. Boyd, a loyal, gracious, and comely "hausfrau"—and by no means unintelligent—who balanced out her husband's quirks (over which students had been known to make merry) by an open-hearted hospitality.

3. Wooster has had a succession of loyal employees to whom students and faculty have paid tribute from time to time, persons serving in seemingly

minor capacities whose work was nevertheless significant through the years, Jay Bryan, for instance, Glenn Joliff, and Joe Follis. One of these memorable characters was Carlo Nolletti who served the college for thirty years as custodian and general factotum in Holden Hall, lifting trunks, moving furniture, and doing those thousand and one odd jobs where a man is suddenly needed to help in a women's dormitory. He lived across the road from old Highland Park, and was the father of sixteen children, a whole Nolletti clan that had come originally, as had Angelo Santoro, from Collepietro, the Abruzzo, Italy. One of these sons, Lewis Nolletti, has continued the tradition, and is now, in 1968, in his twenty-fifth year at the college, an expert chauffeur, and head as well of the college trucking department. His has been a record of doing many things well and loyally.

4. Glenn Joliff was one of Wooster's dependable employees, serving first as fireman in the old power house for a year when he was only eighteen. His real service began, however, when he became Jay Bryan's assistant in the south end of the old gymnasium. As years passed he assumed more and more responsibility, eventually becoming the senior employee of the maintenance staff. In the earlier days of his employment he had bought himself an automobile, and his pleasure was to serve as chauffeur often for Mr. McLaughlin and other college officers in a day when the college itself owned no car at all. He had grown up on East Wayne Avenue, one of the populous Joliff clan in and around Wooster. Later he established a home of his own, on a fifty-acre farm, within a mile and a half of the college, and there in his free time he grew cattle and hogs. (Information from article by John D. McKee in *The Wooster Daily Record,* February 16, 1963.)

5. Another whom Wooster should remember for her service is Flora Grosenbach, who came in 1912 as secretary to the registrar, then, Lester Wolfe. Her job was to record grades, make out schedules for examinations, transcripts for students leaving college, to write letters, of course, and eventually to supervise the detailed procedures of the office. The second secretary to be employed in Wooster's history, she was to remain until 1944. The first one was Pearl Zaugg in the office of Jesse McClellan, from 1907–1913.

6. After one of the various vocational conferences at which the boys of the college listened to speakers extolling the various professions, those of journalists, of community workers, of business men and so forth, the young Howard Lowry remarked characteristically in his column in the *Bulletin:* "By the end of the day we were so mixed up that we decided to start manufacturing designs for Persian rugs and settle the problem."

7. Three of the basketball stars of the early twenties were Homer Hess, Leroy Weir, and Joseph P. Van Nest, all of the class of 1922.

8. "The lawn between Kauke Hall and the Campus Book Store (old gymnasium) resembles a March weather chart. Last summer the authorities recognized several of the most important trunk lines by injecting brick and ash walks. . . . A traffic survey is being prepared by Custodian Schneider who

predicts that in five years the entire campus will be paved. We wonder where the students will walk then." ("Mose" Hole, in Wooster *Alumni Bulletin,* January, 1926.)

9. John M. Swigart was another all-round athlete to whom the college has owned much from the time when as a student he entered its doors until his retirement as member of the faculty of physical education. As an undergraduate he was, according to "Mose" Hole, "the best quarterback Wooster ever had," and the hero of a game (1922) with the University of Cincinnati when Wooster won 21–6. He was also a star on the track team. After his graduation in 1924, he coached for a year in the high school of Napoleon, Ohio, and for another year in the Wooster high school. Then in 1926 Coach Boles brought him back to the college as an instructor in physical education and backfield coach. In 1939 he became an assistant professor, and on Mr. Boles' retirement as coach in 1940, Swigart became head football coach. He had already been coaching baseball since 1937. At one time or another for a year or two or three he has had the responsibility of coaching swimming, track (1927), and golf. He has been one of Wooster's old dependables.

10. Jimmy Hall's old place (See Volume I) at the corner of Beall and Bowman, after various incarnations, became in the thirties, a popular eating place for students and others, "The Black and Gold."

11. It was the cool of the evening and a Chinese nobleman was walking in his garden, at the end of a day. It was a time "to enjoy the cool and serene atmosphere," to meditate "for the enrichment of his inner self in true Oriental pattern." He stopped to gaze at a magnificent porcelain vase decorated in a lotus-flower design, and lingered there, while the night birds just beginning to rouse themselves from the dark corners circled overhead.

That is a story of a different world and different era. In the early thirties another vase, modern, yet similar, equally magnificent and decorated with the lotus-flower design, stood among the treasures being exhibited by the Chinese at the World's Fair in Chicago. Mr. Wishart, escorted by Robert T. K. Kah, Chinese Consul-General in Chicago, stopped in front of it to admire and to ask its story. Delighted by his admiration, with true Oriental courtesy, Mr. Kah promised that after the closing of the Exposition he would send this vase to the College of Wooster as a gift.

So in time the magnificent porcelain vase came to Galpin Hall to find its place not in a private garden but at the head of the long stairs leading to the second floor. There it stands where many may admire as they pass by, a reminder of the long tradition of Oriental artistry and courtesy and an invitation to meditate on the close relations, through its many sons and daughters, that Wooster once had with the China of the past. Robert T. K. Kah, of the class of 1920, later was Consul General in Chungking, China. He died in 1945.

12. In October, 1937, the college hooked into the city water supply. It was happy to find that the pressure was almost double what it had been when

they were drawing from their own supply, and was better water. (Information from the Wooster *Alumni Bulletin,* January, 1938.)

13. In 1937 an exchange student from Lyon, France, Albene Farges, instituted a French table at Babcock, and at noon, three times a week in Holden Hall. The same year Wooster had an exchange student in France.

14. In the summer of 1939 University Street was first paved. The town had years before ceded that part of the Street between Bever and Beall Avenue to the college. (Information from *News from Wooster's Campus,* Vol. v, No. 8, August, 1939.)

15. Wooster has always had its share of great teachers. In the June 18, 1966, issue of *The Saturday Review,* P. W. (Paul Woodring) singled out one of these, Miss Aileen Dunham, as the basis of an article, "Who Are the Great Teachers?" In doing so, he quoted at some length from an article in the Wooster *Alumni Bulletin* (April, 1966) by Katharine Sommerlatte Van Eerde, '41, herself a professor of history, but formerly a student of Miss Dunham's. At the end Mr. Woodring says:

Students in small colleges often reveal their own status-seeking propensities by asking their favorite teachers why they stay in such a college—why they do not hie themselves off to famous universities. Miss Dunham heard the question often. Her answer was firm: "I am one that believes in small colleges. I do not like the anonymity of great universities—which I have experienced at first hand. Essentially, I love to teach, and the primary function of the Wooster faculty has always been teaching. Always a great reader (my normal consumption of volumes of history is about eighty a year) I much prefer what I like to call the 'Big View' to the minute research involved in writing monographs, and after all somebody must coordinate the monographs."

Almost every small college, however obscure, has one or more professors who do for their students what Miss Dunham did at Wooster. Some rarely publish but devote all their intellectual energies to teaching and preparing to teach. Some are unknown beyond their own campuses. But they are the truly great teachers for it is they who bring their students to intellectual maturity.

16. In the spring of 1944 on the recommendation of the dean of women and the director of admissions, the administrative committee of the Board of Trustees "voted to restore table service to both dining rooms of Holden Hall." Cafeteria service inaugurated during the war as "an emergency measure" when help was scarce, had proved, according to these staff officers of the college "detrimental to the best interests of the college." (From the *Minutes.*)

17. The Faculty Committee on Conference with the Faculty Relations Committee of the Board of Trustees was initiated and set up at the meeting of the Board of Trustees in May, 1944, at the suggestion of and on motion by Howard Lowry, then a member of that body.

Appendix

LEGAL BRIEF ON ACTION OF FEBRUARY 1, 1915

Judge John E. West, Bellefontaine, Ohio

[This argument was presented to the Board of Trustees of the
College of Wooster at the special meeting held May 18,
1915, and was by them deemed of such cogency
that the action of February 1, was rescinded
by an unanimous vote.]

By an Act of the General Assembly of Ohio, passed April 9, 1852, as
amended March 11, 1853, it was enacted, among other things, that any
number of persons, not less than five desiring to establish a college, university, or other institution for the purpose of promoting education, religion,
morality, agriculture, or the fine arts could, by complying with the provisions
of said Act, become a body corporate and politic with perpetual succession,
and might assume a corporate name by which they might sue and be sued in
all courts of law and equity, have a corporate seal, hold all kinds of estate,
which they might acquire by purchase, donation, devise, or otherwise, necessary to accomplish the objects of the corporation.

It was further provided by said act that the corporators of any college or
university, organized in accordance with the provisions of said act, might
elect five or more trustees, of whom not less than five should be resident
freeholders of the county where such college or university is located, who
should constitute a board of directors for such institution, who should have
power to fill all vacancies that might occur in their board, and hold their
offices until their successors were elected and qualified according to the rules
and by-laws that might be adopted by the board of trustees; that at all times
at least five of such board of trustees should be resident freeholders of the
county where such institution is located; * * * and said trustees shall have
power to appoint a president, professors, tutors, and teachers, and any other
necessary agents and officers, fix the compensation of each, and might enact
such by-laws, not inconsistent with the Laws of Ohio or of the United States,
for the government of the institution, and for conducting the affairs of the
corporation as they might deem necessary, and should have power to confer,
on the recommendation of the faculty, all such degrees and honors as are
conferred by colleges and universities of the United States, and such other,
having reference to the course of study and the accomplishments of the
student, as they may deem proper.

Said Act further provided that the president and professors shall constitute
the faculty of any literary college or university instituted under the provisions
of said Act, and that the faculty should have power to enforce the rules and

regulations enacted by the trustees for the government and discipline of the students, and to suspend and expel offenders, as might be deemed necessary.

Acting under the provisions of said Act, in the year 1866, eleven persons, eight of whom were residents of Wayne county, Ohio, applied for incorporation, by the name of The University of Wooster, stating therein that the object of such corporation shall be the promotion of sound learning and education under religious influences such as is usually contemplated in colleges and universities, and named nineteen persons as the first board of trustees thereof, of whom seven were resident freeholders of Wayne county, Ohio, and providing that at least five of their successors should be resident freeholders of said county.

In 1901 said charter was so amended as to provide that the number of trustees should be increased to thirty, in addition to the president, and of whom at least seven should be resident freeholders of Wayne county, Ohio.

Acting further under the powers of said Act, the board of trustees subsequently proceeded to enact such by-laws not inconsistent with the Laws of Ohio, or of the United States, for the government and conducting of the affairs of the corporation as they deemed necessary, and as a part of said by-laws provided:

ARTICLE I.

Section 8. No member of the Board of Trustees, other than the President of the University, shall be eligible to a position in the faculty, so long as he shall remain in his office as Trustee of the same.

ARTICLE II.

Section 1. The Officers of the University of Wooster shall consist of the following: * * * The Faculty, The Executive Committee * * * and such other necessary agents and officers as may be appointed or elected by the Board of Trustees.

ARTICLE IV. THE FACULTY

Section 1. No professor, or instructor, shall be a voting member of the faculty, unless personally designated by name as such by the Board of Trustees.

AMENDMENTS

Section 1. Amendments to these by-laws having been presented at any regular meeting in writing may be adopted at any regular meeting by receiving sixteen affirmative votes therefor.

Section 2. Amendments to these by-laws without previous notice may be made at any regular adjourned or called meeting by receiving twenty affirmative votes therefor.

At the February meeting, 1915, of the Board of Trustees, the following action was taken by a vote of fourteen affirmative votes to seven negative votes:

1. Resolved, That the two-year Normal Course be adopted.
2. Be it Resolved that this department be organized on a basis separate from the college proper; that a Committee of Control be responsible for its work, pass upon the merit of the credits to be given, and certify to the State Superintendent the work done.
3. In order to bring about a closer relation between the Summer School and The College of Wooster, be it RESOLVED, that a Committee of Control consisting of Dean Elias Compton, Dr. J. O. Notestein, Dr. J. M. Vance, representing the Faculty; and Dr. Heron, Dr. Weir, and Dr. Wishard, representing the Board of Trustees, be appointed to have charge of the selection of teachers, both of the Summer School and of the Normal Course, the giving of credits, the use of buildings, the apparatus, and any other questions of internal administration that may arise.
4. Be it Resolved that, for the present, the students of the Normal Course be assigned to college classes for such work as the Normal Courses may require.

This action, in so far as it undertook to place a member of this Board upon the Faculty, either of the College or of the two-year Normal Course, or of the Summer School, was a violation of the By-Laws of this Board.

This action, in so far as it undertook to authorize a special committee other than the Faculty of the College, or to create a Faculty other than the President and Professors of the College, to pass upon the merits of the credits to be given, was a violation of the Statutes of the State of Ohio, empowering this Board to confer such credits, and to confer on recommendation of the Faculty all such degrees and honors as are conferred by Colleges and Universities.

The action, in so far as it attempted to confer upon the Special Committee, or Committee of Control, the decision of all questions of internal administration of the Summer School and of the two-year Normal Course was a violation of the Statutes of the State empowering the Faculty to enforce the rules and regulations enacted by the Trustees for the government and discipline of the students.

The attempted inauguration of the two-year Normal Course, the creation of the Committee and the powers conferred upon it, if within the declared purpose and object of the corporation, as stated in its charter, to-wit: the promotion of sound learning and education under religious influences, such as is usually contemplated in colleges and universities, did not receive sufficient votes to authorize its adoption by way of amendment, as it did not receive at said meeting either twenty votes, or sixteen votes, and therefore was and is contrary to and against the provisions of the By-Laws or Constitution of the Board.

No authority exists in this Board to confer on any student in any course conducted under the supervision of the corporate body, known as the College of Wooster, or as the University of Wooster, any degree, honor, or credit otherwise than upon the recommendation of the Faculty of the College; and until the Summer School comes under the supervision of the College, and until the two-year Normal Course comes under the supervision of the College, to the extent that all credits to be given in either can be and are given by this Board on the recommendation of the Faculty of the College, this Board is without power or authority to certify or authorize the certificates of any such credits.

There is not, nor can there be, under the law as now in force, any other authority authorized to confer credits on behalf of the College than this Board, and this Board can only do so upon the recommendation of the Faculty.

Section 7807–3 of the General Code, the present School Code, which provides that a graduate from any Normal School, Teachers' College, College, or University who has completed a full two years academic and professional course in such institution shall upon application to the superintendent of Public Instruction and the payment of a fee of One Dollar be granted without further examination a provisional elementary certificate, valid for four years in any school district within the state; provided that such institution has been approved by the Superintendent of Public Instruction, does not mean that a certificate of credits signed by certain teachers or professors who have been temporarily engaged in teaching either in the Summer School or in the two-years Normal Course, independent of, and distinct from the college, will entitle the holder of such certificate to a provisional elementary certificate; but it means, and can only mean, that a graduate from this college, or university who has completed a full two years academic and professional course in this college, shall be granted an elementary certificate, provided that this college has been approved by the Superintendent of Public Instruction.

No one can be graduated from this college, except by authority and direction of the Board of Trustees upon the recommendation of the Faculty.

And all statements and expressions contained in letters of the State Superintendent or emanating from him as to the validity of the certificates necessary from the College of Wooster to entitle its graduates to the elementary certificate must be understood and construed in connection with the plain language and meaning of the Statute.

That the work of the Summer School, and the completion of the two years Normal Course may be effective so as to secure the graduates a certificate authorizing them to teach in any district of the state, the Summer School and the two-year Normal Course must be taken over under the control, direction, and supervision of the College, and must be administered by the College, that is, the Corporate Body through its Board of Trustees acting by and through the Faculty of the College.

If it is, therefore, the sense and judgment of this Board that it shall enter upon the work and labor of graduating from this College persons who have taken the two-year Normal Course, either through the Academy or the Summer School, or the College proper, or any two or more of them combined, it will become absolutely necessary to take such action as may be requisite thereto, either by amendment of its By-Laws, an enlargement of the scope and objects of the corporation as stated in its charter, or by additional legislation or change in laws relating to the incorporation of colleges and universities.

Index

man English department, 330; tribute to retiring faculty by, 342; personality, career of, 387n

Moore, J. E., 72

Moore, Robert H., 361n

Morris, Samuel, 28, 31, 114; left Wooster, 155, 187

Morris, Mrs. Samuel, 71

Mt Union: sports record with, 256, 257

Mullins, James, 3, 153; ordered Lincoln statue made, 363n

Mullins, Mrs. James: Member of Women's Advisory Board, 334n

Mullins, Walter, 4

Mullins, William H., 155, 363n

Munson, Carl; led in team swim meet, 256; successful coach, 257; record preceeding Wooster, 373–374n; personality of, 392n

Murray, Arthur, 303, 367n, 392n; successful football coach, 257; notable record of, 319

Music department: growth of, 36; courses, 146; funds needed for, 148; out-going faculty of, 159; new instructor in, 184; size of faculty, 193; concert fund established, 250; women instructors in, 315–316. *See also* Conservatory of, names of instructors, organizations

Musicals: biennial minstrel show, 28, 43, 132; "Where Men are Men," 360n

Muskingum, 72; sports record with, 256, 286

Myers, John A., 151

Myers, Mary and Minnie, 347n

Nachtrieb, M. S.: portraits by, 379n

Navy Flight Training Program: co-ed dining, 243; courses taught in, 339; application made for, 325; college participation in, 339–341

Nesbitt, Maudie L.: joined library staff, 336–337

Netta Strain Scott Auditorium (Little Theater): addition to Taylor Hall, 275; dedication of, 284. *See also* Dramatics

Newnan, Eva Mae: personality of, professorship, 313–314; added orientation courses, 335

New York *Times:* topic for seminar, 255; covered Bryan-Wishart controversy, 267

Nightshirt parades, 51, 67, 241

Nimmons, George C.: buildings designed by, 398gn

Nolletti, Carlo: service to college, 403gn

Nolletti, Lewis: tradition carried on by, 403gn

Nonagons: first glee club, 356n

North Market street: homes on, 4, 5; parade on, 234

Normal department. *See* Junior School of Education

Notestein, Jonas, 21, 33, 110, 244, 348n, 362n, 370n; chairman of library committee, 12; planted dogwood trees, 18–19; articles, 70, 197; minority group led by, 96; Latin language mastered by, 135–136; 1916 Charter Day speech by, 149; chapel talks by, 173; stand-by on faculty, 184; friendship with E. P. Douglas, 233–234, 275; portrait of, 288, 379n; death of, 299; fifty years with college, 387n; recollections of, 395gn

Notestein, Wallace, 295

"No Where on Earth": life at "the Inky" described in, 38–41

O. A. Hills Club: purpose of, 246. *See* Clericus Club

Oberlin, 72, 170, 292; sports record with, 27, 72, 165, 189, 201, 213, 224, 257; in debate with, 245; Kelso made study of, 304

Observatory, 6, 188, 197; inadequacy of, 66; became student union, 275; YWCA tea house in, 273; enlarged, 284–285

Ohio Agricultural Experiment Station: interest, 91, 174

Ohio Conference, 230; Wooster's record in, 166, 256; Wooster record with, 257. *See also* football

Ohio Hotel: opening of, 319

Ohio Intercollegiate Oratorical Association, 112, 372n. *See also* Speech department

Ohio Northern: sports record with, 189

Ohio State University, 72, 92, 271, 324; sports record with, 166, 241, 361n

Ohio Wesleyan, 292; sports record with, 113, 166, 189; "Back to the Farm" movement of, 170; loses oratorical contest, 238; debates with, 245; Kelso made study of, 304; Navy Flight Preparatory School at, 341

Old gymnasium, 188, 281, 377n; laundry plan for, 111–112, 154

Old Main (Bitter's Bottle), 5, 397gn; burning of, 27, 78, 107; anniversary of corner stone laying, 177; chapel in, 193; library in, 337; plans for, 394gn

Oliver, J. Byron, 397gn

Olthouse, John W., 31; French instructor, 25, 300; taught Spanish, 137; is stalwart on faculty, 184; studied

About the Author

Lucy Lilian Notestein comes from a dyed-in-the-wool academic family, her father and three uncles professors in small colleges, her grandfather principal of one of the early Ohio academies, her brother Wallace for many years Sterling Professor of English History at Yale. She grew up in Wooster and earned her B.A. at the College. Following an M.A. at Radcliffe, she taught English and short story writing at the University of Illinois and at Western Reserve University. An opportunity to work for the Presbyterian Board of National Missions took her to New York for five years where she handled a variety of publicity writing, and from there she moved to the editorial staff of *The Reader's Digest* where she remained for nearly twenty-five years, retiring as a department editor.

Miss Notestein wrote the first volume of *Wooster of the Middle West* from voluminous notes gathered by her father, Professor of Latin at Wooster. It was published in 1937 and is now reissued as a companion to Volume 2, which takes the history from World War I through World War II. She is also the author of *Hill Towns of Italy* (1963).